Southern Asia:
The Politics of
Poverty &
Peace

Southern Asia: The Politics of Poverty & Peace

Critical Choices for Americans

Volume XIII

Edited by

Donald C. Hellmann

Lexington Books
D.C. Heath and Company
Lexington, Massachusetts
Toronto

Library of Congress Cataloging in Publication Data

Main entry under title:

Southern Asia.

   (Critical choices for Americans; v. 13)
   Includes index.
   1. Asia, Southeastern—Politics and government. 2. Asia, Southeastern—
Economic conditions. 3. Asia, Southeastern—Foreign relations—United
States. 4. United States—Foreign relations—Asia, Southeastern. 5. South
Asia—Politics and government. 6. South Asia—Economic condition.
7. South Asia—Foreign relations—United States. 8. United States—Foreign
relations—South Asia. I. Hellmann, Donald C., 1933-   II. Series.
DS518.1.S63   309.1'54   75-44731
ISBN 0-669-00427-8

Published simultaneously in Canada.

Printed in the United States of America.

International Standard Book Number: 0-669-00427-8

Library of Congress Catalog Card Number: 75-44731

Foreword

The Commission on Critical Choices for Americans, a nationally representative, bipartisan group of forty-two prominent Americans, was brought together on a voluntary basis by Nelson A. Rockefeller. After assuming the Vice Presidency of the United States, Mr. Rockefeller, the chairman of the Commission, became an ex officio member. The Commission's assignment was to develop information and insights which would bring about a better understanding of the problems confronting America. The Commission sought to identify the critical choices that must be made if these problems are to be met.

The Commission on Critical Choices grew out of a New York State study of the Role of a Modern State in a Changing World. This was initiated by Mr. Rockefeller, who was then Governor of New York, to review the major changes taking place in federal-state relationships. It became evident, however, that the problems confronting New York State went beyond state boundaries and had national and international implications.

In bringing the Commission on Critical Choices together, Mr. Rockefeller said:

As we approach the 200th Anniversary of the founding of our Nation, it has become clear that institutions and values which have accounted for our astounding progress during the past two centuries are straining to cope with the massive problems of the current era. The increase in the tempo of change and the vastness and complexity of the wholly new situations which are evolving with accelerated change, create a widespread sense that our political and social system has serious inadequacies.

We can no longer continue to operate on the basis of reacting to crises, counting on crash programs and the expenditure of huge sums of money to solve our problems. We have got to understand and project present trends, to take command of the forces that are emerging, to extend our freedom and wellbeing as citizens and the future of other nations and peoples in the world.

Because of the complexity and interdependence of issues facing America and the world today, the Commission has organized its work into six panels, which emphasize the interrelationships of critical choices rather than treating each one in isolation.

The six panels are:

Panel I: Energy and its Relationship to Ecology, Economics and World Stability;

Panel II: Food, Health, World Population and Quality of Life;

Panel III: Raw Materials, Industrial Development, Capital Formation, Employment and World Trade;

Panel IV: International Trade and Monetary Systems, Inflation and the Relationships Among Differing Economic Systems;

Panel V: Change, National Security and Peace;

Panel VI: Quality of Life of Individuals and Communities in the U.S.A.

The Commission assigned, in these areas, more than 100 authorities to prepare expert studies in their fields of special competence. The Commission's work has been financed by The Third Century Corporation, a New York not-for-profit organization. The corporation has received contributions from individuals and foundations to advance the Commission's activities.

The Commission is determined to make available to the public these background studies and the reports of those panels which have completed their deliberations. The background studies are the work of the authors and do not necessarily represent the views of the Commission or its members.

This volume is one of the series of volumes the Commission will publish in the belief that it will contribute to the basic thought and foresight America will need in the future.

WILLIAM J. RONAN
Acting Chairman
Commission on Critical Choices
for Americans

Members of the Commission

LEO CHERNE
Executive Director, Research Institute
of America, Inc.

JOHN S. FOSTER, JR.
Vice President for Energy Research
and Development, TRW, Inc.

LUTHER H. FOSTER
President, Tuskegee Institute

NANCY HANKS
Chairman, National Endowment for the Arts

BELTON KLEBERG JOHNSON
Texas Rancher and Businessman

CLARENCE B. JONES
Former Editor and Publisher,
The New York Amsterdam News

JOSEPH LANE KIRKLAND
Secretary–Treasurer, AFL-CIO

JOHN H. KNOWLES, M.D.
President, Rockefeller Foundation

DAVID S. LANDES
Leroy B. Williams Professor of History
and Political Science, Harvard University

MARY WELLS LAWRENCE
Chairman and Chief Executive Officer,
Wells, Rich, Greene, Inc.

SOL M. LINOWITZ
Senior Partner of Coudert Brothers

EDWARD J. LOGUE
Former President and Chief Executive Officer,
New York State Urban Development Corporation

EDWARD TELLER
  Senior Research Fellow, Hoover Institution
  on War, Revolution and Peace,
  Stanford University

ARTHUR K. WATSON*
  Former Ambassador to France

MARINA VON NEUMANN WHITMAN
  Distinguished Public Service Professor
  of Economics, University of Pittsburgh

CARROLL L. WILSON
  Professor, Alfred P. Sloan
  School of Management,
  Massachusetts Institute of Technology

GEORGE D. WOODS
  Former President, World Bank

Members of the Commission served on the panels. In addition, others assisted
the panels.

BERNARD BERELSON
Senior Fellow
President Emeritus
The Population Council

C. FRED BERGSTEN
Senior Fellow
The Brookings Institution

ORVILLE G. BRIM, JR.
President
Foundation for Child Development

LESTER BROWN
President
Worldwatch Institute

LLOYD A. FREE
President
Institute for International Social Research

*Deceased

J. GEORGE HARRAR
Former President
Rockefeller Foundation

WALTER LEVY
Economic Consultant

PETER G. PETERSON
Chairman of the Board
Lehman Brothers

ELSPETH ROSTOW
Dean, Division of General and Comparative Studies
University of Texas

WALT W. ROSTOW
Professor of Economics and History
University of Texas

SYLVESTER L. WEAVER
Communications Consultant

JOHN G. WINGER
Vice President
Energy Economics Division
Chase Manhattan Bank

Preface

For many Americans, the critical choice in Southern Asia would probably be to ignore it. After one of the costliest and longest wars in our history, most Americans feel that the region is now peripheral to our national interests and that development of the poorest, most overpopulated countries in the world is simply beyond reach. Frustration, disappointment, and the scars of war are not easy to erase. Yet, the United States' commitment to world peace and the economic interdependence of the world today will demand that we face the challenges of Southern Asia in the years ahead.

Southern Asia: The Politics of Poverty & Peace is one of seven geographic studies prepared for the Commission on Critical Choices for Americans, under the coordination of Nancy Maginnes Kissinger. Companion volumes cover Western Europe, the Soviet Empire, the Middle East, China and Japan, Africa, and Latin America. Interdependence has long been a fact of the twentieth century—our neighbors to the north and south and across the oceans to the east and west are clearly involved with America's future. Our once seemingly domestic problems, solved with our own resources, can now be solved only in view of other nations' needs and priorities.

Donald C. Hellmann has directed a study of Southern Asia which offers fresh and varied views on shaping American policy in this region. To bring American ideals such as democracy and economic progress into line with the realities of South Asia will require first our understanding and secondly, the best that the American people have to offer.

— W.J.R.

Acknowledgments

Of the many people who contributed to this study, special acknowledgment must be made to those who were most directly involved in its successful completion. The contributors presented drafts of their essays to a meeting at the Commission offices in New York on February 7 and 8, 1975 and this spirited and stimulating interchange substantially shaped the overall direction of these two volumes. In addition to the paper writers, the participants included a number of distinguished scholars and government specialists on Asia who provided comprehensive and provocative commentaries; Professor Lucian Pye, Department of Political Science, Massachusetts Institute of Technology; Professor Edwin O. Reischauer, Harvard University; Dean Henry Rosovsky, Harvard University; Professor Paul R. Brass, Department of Political Science, University of Washington; Professor Klaus Mehnert, Professor Emeritus of the Institute of Technology, Aachen (West Germany); Winston Lord, Chairman, Policy Planning Staff, Department of State; Dr. Michael Armacost, Policy Planning Staff, Department of State; and W.R. Smyser, National Security Council Staff. The directors of the other area studies of the Commission, William E. Griffith (Soviet Union and Eastern Europe), Helen Kitchen (Africa), David Landes (Western Europe), and Avrom Udovitch (Middle East) and Nancy Maginnes Kissinger, the general coordinator of the Project, all took part in this meeting and offered valuable assistance in many other ways over the entire course of preparation. Charity Randall and Anne Boylan of the Commission staff provided exceptional help and counsel at all stages of the project. From my perspective, the critical ingredient was the forbearance, encouragement and felicitous editorial assistance of my wife, Margery.

Contents

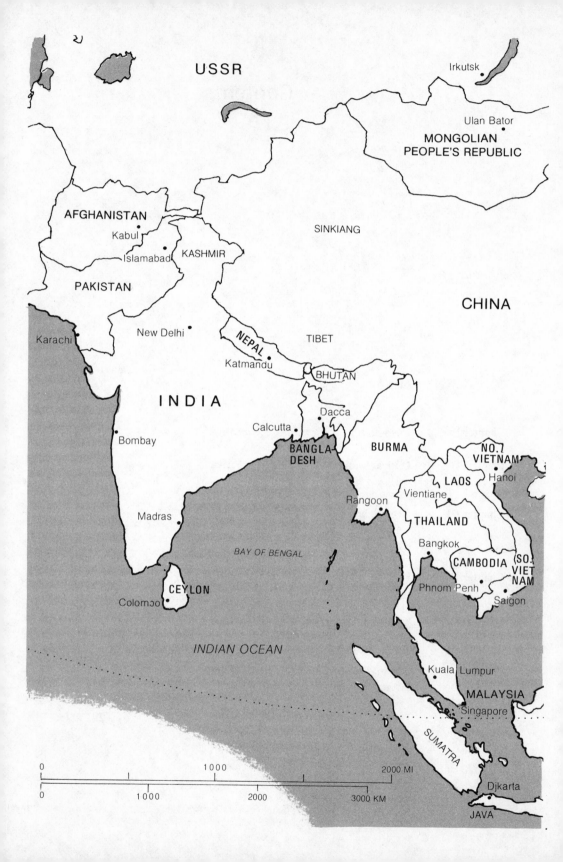

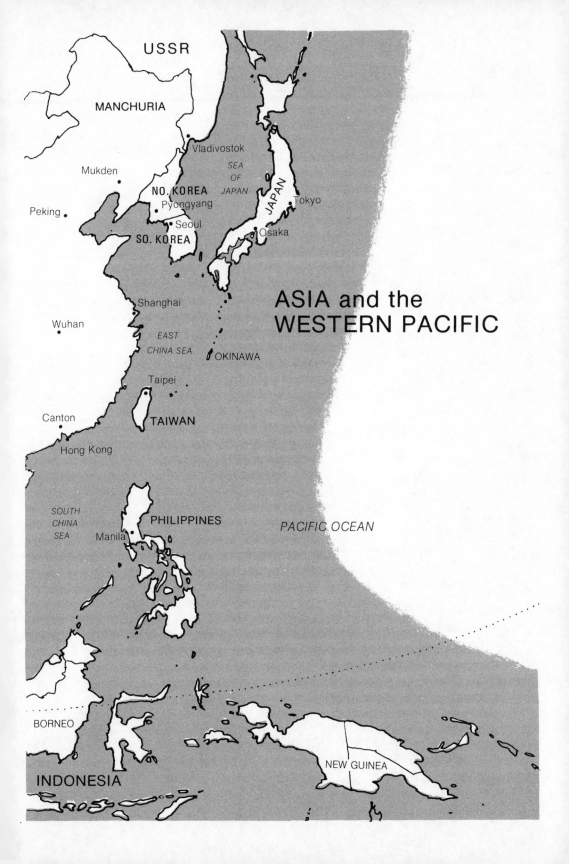

I Introduction

Donald C. Hellmann

In no area of the world has American foreign policy met with more frustration and disappointment than in South and Southeast Asia. The bitter legacies of defeat in Indochina, the seeming irrelevance of democratic ideals in culturally alien and physically remote societies, and the real prospect for Malthusian catastrophe in several nations create an understandable sense of futility among even the most informed and concerned sectors of American society. Indeed, in the wake of the longest war in our history and years of massive aid expenditures, for most Americans peace in the region now seems peripheral to our national interests and the promotion of development in some of the poorest, most overpopulated nations in the world simply beyond reach.

In a basic sense, the breakdown of American policy in Southeast Asia was the original impetus for the so-called neo-isolationist sentiment in this country. The sudden collapse of democracy in India, the development of nuclear weapons by New Delhi, and a growing belief that in a world of scarcity efforts to deal with overpopulation in this region are Sisyphean tasks have all added to the aura of disillusionment. For most Americans the critical questions are reduced to one, why bother? Yet to turn in despair or resignation from all concern for this portion of the world, however appealing in terms of the current mood and the press of other problems, would have disastrous long-term consequences. It is not an option that should be considered seriously. While it is essential for the United States to remain engaged in Southern Asia, it is inadequate merely to extend past policies which were built on strategic assumptions from the cold war era and a projection of our own pattern of economic and political development.

1

Economic interdependence and the related imperatives for a global diplomacy (including security requirements) compel the United States to face squarely the international problems of Southern Asia in the last quarter of the twentieth century. The critical choices relate to our own priorities, which must be built upon a clear perception of Asian realities and an equally realistic appraisal of our own capacities to influence events. If the United States is to remain engaged in the international politics of Southern Asia, there is an additional challenge: that of juxtaposing American ideals with Asian conditions in order to justify to ourselves and to the world the purposes of our engagement. A policy of "new realism" internationally can be viable only if it finds legitimacy in a set of values which are widely shared within the United States.

The essays in this volume address the most important international questions in the region from a long-term perspective with an eye toward establishing the parameters of choice for American policy. The size and complexities of the region, as well as unforeseen difficulties in organizing the project, prevented a truly comprehensive discussion of all international problems. Most regrettably, there is no detailed treatment of either Indonesia or the Philippines, nations which will play major roles in the future of Southern Asia and regarding which the United States has special interests. Nevertheless, some problems of Indonesian foreign policy are analyzed in Robert Scalapino's chapter and many of the questions which are raised in other contexts concerning matters such as American bases, foreign aid, demography, and regionalism are relevant to the Indonesian and Philippine cases with only minor qualifications. To assure that the fullest possible range of critical choices is presented, special effort was made to include divergent viewpoints. Moreover, the significant differences among the authors are not over specific short- to middle-range policy options (although such differences abound), but rather concern strategic and fundamental questions such as "why foreign aid?," the prospects for and nature of international conflicts, and the capacities of the United States (or any outside power) to affect decisively events in this part of the world. This introduction is designed simply to highlight selected critical points in the wide-ranging discussions that follow and to bring into the open some of the underlying assumptions of the essays in order to clarify the critical choices that our government must make in Southern Asia in the years ahead.

Among other things, the American experience in Vietnam provided two lessons regarding our future role in this region. First, the stumbling efforts to comprehend the most elemental contours of the local political landscape firmly established the necessity for understanding Asia on its own terms and in a broad historical context. Second, because of the ongoing radical and revolutionary changes throughout the region and the frail and/or transient governmental institutions in virtually all countries, there was and continues to be a particularly close and complex linkage between domestic and international politics. These lessons provide the basic guidelines for this study. All but one of the following essays explore in depth conditions within countries of Southern Asia and, in order to sharpen the distinction between regional and global concerns, emphasize the international politics of the area as perceived by Asians themselves.

The studies do provide authoritative and timely discussions of the contemporary problems of international politics in Southern Asia and simply by asking questions about policy from a long-term viewpoint, they also offer a fresh and more appropriate perspective for analyzing international problems in this part of the world. Indeed, it is the kind of undertaking that has been lamentably absent from or peripheral to the policy-making procedures in our government since the early cold war debates over isolationism, foreign aid, alliances, and containment. It is somewhat ironic that one of the best ways to address the essential requirements of a new American global strategic calculus is through consideration of that portion of the world in which our policies have met with the most acute frustration and failure.

Southern Asia and the Future: The Moral Dilemmas of American Policy

For the United States, the problem of future policy toward Southern Asia goes well beyond devising actions appropriate to the constantly changing balance of political and economic forces in the region. Involved are the fundamental ethical assumptions of the Western world in general and the American diplomatic tradition in particular. The pervasiveness of poverty and the persistence of conflict among and within states challenge the bedrock humanitarian values of our civilization and the aversion to power politics that is so central to our diplomatic heritage. Before turning to the specific essays, it is appropriate to sketch the moral dilemmas which our policies are destined to confront during the years ahead no matter what the peculiar twists and turns of international power may be.

A prefatory word is in order on the implicit approach taken in this study. Many contemporary efforts to examine the future of the world (futurology) avoid consideration of the structure and processes of history and make forecasts based on aspects of social life such as demography and production which can be most easily measured and projected as "scientific trends" (e.g., studies by the Club of Rome and Herman Kahn).[1] Social institutions, (the political, cultural, and economic organizations through which men adapt to their environment), are largely ignored or treated as dependent variables. Especially when applied to South Asia (India, Pakistan, and Bangladesh) with its relatively stagnant economic growth rates and high levels of population increase, the futurologist's approach yields startlingly pessimistic results. These conclusions are useful in pointing to a potentially Malthusian population problem, but they fail to answer the critical questions regarding the kind of political and economic institutions that will be fostered by these conditions and the sort of international and domestic crises which may be provoked. It is through the answers to these latter questions that American interests in the region will be defined and to deal with such issues all of the essays in this volume have stressed the modern history of the region and placed discussion of the future squarely in an historical context.

No matter how successful United States diplomacy may prove in the short run, Southern Asia will continue to challenge two basic ethical assumptions of the American diplomatic and political tradition: (1) the belief in progress, both ethical and material, and (2) the rejection of participation in power politics with nations with whom we share few common values of human rights and with which we have no direct, tangible security interests. The politics of poverty and peace in Asia during the last quarter of the century will provide the United States both with uniquely difficult international circumstances and unprecedented moral choices.

For two hundred years, the most important single idea underlying the American experience has been that of progress. Our nation was future oriented from the outset, touched by the philosophical optimism of the Enlightenment and propelled by the good fortune of having achieved nationhood at a moment when the industrial revolution made possible the conquest of the material world on behalf of human interest. In America, the liberating promise of technology found realization side by side with the belief in democracy, an ideal that saw all political conflicts capable of resolution within a framework of law and in which fulfillment of the potential of each individual was the end of society. The concept of progress, in both the economic and political senses, found direct expression in the policies devised by the United States regarding the emerging nations after the onset of the cold war—and it further tied to the liberal vision of a democratic and peaceful new world order most dramatically set forth in this century by Woodrow Wilson.

The belief in progress found fullest expression in policy in the justifications propounded for extending assistance to the poorer countries. In essence, it was argued that economic aid was conducive to development, that development created conditions conducive to democracy, and that nations built on democratic pluralism provided the conditions for world peace.[2] For some years now, this argument no longer has had wide currency as justification for foreign aid, partly because the United States (after years of aid) found itself allied with many authoritarian developing nations and partly because the prospects for eradicating poverty have dimmed substantially. What is involved is more than the abandonment of a flawed short-term policy. Rather there is an implicit repudiation of the American idea of progress as relevant to much of the world. Thus it is hardly surprising that the efforts to find justification for American internationalism have either drifted toward unvarnished power politics, fallen back on the shibboleths of the cold war or sought reassertion of the possibility of progress through the application of technology in terms of a "global humanism" (e.g., pronouncements by the World Bank and the essay by John Lewis in this volume).

The prospects for substantial improvement of the economic conditions in the overpopulated lands of Southern Asia in a world of scarcity during the years ahead are not promising, even with massive transfers of wealth and radical restructuring of the world political and economic order—no matter what the United States may do. To turn from this situation, over which we have no basic control, would carry high costs. Indifference to extensive misery abroad would damage our capacity for international leadership and ultimately could not but have a corrosive effect on our domestic politics as well. At the same time, to fashion a policy of realistic humanism juxtaposing our capacities for action with our ideals, involves, in effect, adding a new dimension to the American diplomatic tradition. The problems of poverty in Southern Asia present the United States with critical choices that concern not only policy, but the moral foundation on which the policy rests.

Active military intervention by America in South and Southeast Asia or even arrangements to exercise force under restricted circumstances would also raise moral as well as tactical problems for the United States. Suffocating restrictions on individual freedom in all but a couple of Asian nations (non-Communist as well as Communist), the recurrent examples of oppression that reach holocaust proportions (most recently illustrated by the forced evacuation of Phnom Penh), wide cultural differences, and the seemingly intractable conditions of poverty discussed above, make irrelevant most of the basic concerns for human rights that has underlain American intervention in world affairs. All of the emotions that shattered the internationalist foreign policy consensus in the latter half of the 1960s would be rekindled if the United States were to participate militarily in a conflict in this region in the wake of Vietnam and the attenuation of all American alliances throughout Asia. Nevertheless, conflict will persist in the region and the prospects are high that it will involve extraregional powers and/or global strategic implications (e.g., nuclear weapons) in the long run. Thus in a second important way, the capacity of the United States to participate in the international politics of Southern Asia is limited not only by the new structure of power, but by a basic moral premise of America's approach to international affairs.

South Asia: India, Pakistan, and Bangladesh

There is remarkable agreement regarding the current structure of power in South Asia and on the limited role that the United States is likely to play there in the immediate future. However, there is also substantial uncertainty and skepticism regarding the long-term economic and political prospects for the region and, accordingly, ambiguity regarding the kind of policies the United States should pursue in the future.

The low priority which India has received in American policy since the 1971 war which gave birth to Bangladesh (in which the United States supported Pakistan against India) is partly the product of a general shift in policy by the United States regarding aid to Third World countries.[a] It also rests on the new configuration of power in South Asia and the links between this new regional situation and the global power balance. The main factors underlying American disenchantment with India are readily identified: a general disillusionment in Washington regarding foreign aid to developing nations, of which India was the largest single recipient (over $10 billion); the failure of American policy to prevent the breakup of Pakistan in 1971 and the strong tilt by India toward the Soviet Union since the war; continuing anti-American rhetoric by the Indian government, which was given added and negative meaning first by the explosion of a "nuclear devise" in 1974 and then by the suspension of democracy and the establishment in mid-1975 of an "emergency" authoritarian political system of indefinite duration under Prime Minister Indira Gandhi. Moreover, victory in the Bangladesh War assured Indian dominance over the subcontinent to a degree that now offers far less incentive for the United States to become involved in seeking to share the regional power balance.

These considerations, together with the fact that we have extremely limited trade and investment ties with India, have led the United States to adopt a very low posture toward New Delhi. In view of the limited incentives to do more than maintain formal diplomatic contact with India, it is worth emphasizing the importance of assuring that our bridges to New Delhi are in good repair. If the policy of neglect or hostility evident in the early 1970s becomes what Weiner calls "the new American orthodoxy in South Asia," the possible long-term international costs to the United States will be substantial, both within the region and globally. This rather obvious point is worth making because there is likely to be an increase in anti-Indian sentiment over the full spectrum of American politics in the face of continued authoritarian government.

In the increasingly pluralist world order that is likely to prevail in the future, regional patterns of conflict and cooperation will take on added importance for individual countries and the superpowers will face a series of critical choices regarding the relevance of regional problems to the continuing global rivalry between Washington and Moscow. The strategic calculus in South Asia has been greatly complicated by the emergence of Iran as a major force in all areas adjacent to the Arabian Sea, by the interest of the Soviet Union in strengthening its position in the Indian Ocean and on the periphery of China, and by the continuing and unpredictable involvement of China in the region.

The critical choices for the United States concern criteria to establish the level and scope of our involvement in the regional power balance. On matters such as the decision to build a naval facility in Diego Gracia in response to a

---

[a]In 1961 the United States gave slightly more than 50 percent of the world's development aid, while in 1974 this figure was less than 20 percent.

mounting Soviet naval presence in the Indian Ocean and Persian Gulf, it is relatively easy to overlook the regional costs once the global strategic need is established. However, it is not necessary to accept Weiner's assertion that past American policy was dictated entirely by global strategic considerations to accept his contention that the foreign policies of South Asian nations have been shaped primarily by regional political and security concerns and that their relations with outside powers have been established with an eye to their usefulness in the region. The lesson is clear. The United States must pay scrupulous attention to the local political landscape and move with restraint, lest we allow other nations to determine what our critical choices are and the timing of our actions. The absence of entangling alliances should aid in policy restraint.

If the time frame for American security policy regarding South Asia is extended into the future, the situation becomes drastically different. India (and perhaps eventually Pakistan) has the potential to become a regional and global nuisance. In basic ways India is a prototype of what countries like South Korea and Taiwan may become: a relatively weak state with substantial aggregate wealth, a high level of scientific and technical capacities, and the political will to develop nuclear and other military capabilities to become an effective regional power. Moreover, these capabilities can be readily extended onto the global level.

The scenarios for mischief are limitless, but the capacity of New Delhi to export nuclear technology or to provoke others (i.e., Pakistan) to develop nuclear weapons, serves as a dramatic illustration of what might transpire. To be sure, there is no assurance that such behavior will occur, but unless there are major breakthroughs in economic productivity and in slowing population growth, the prospects for increased internal tension and domestic political instability in India are high. Whether this will lead to internal disruptions or revolution (rejected by Weiner)[b] or to radical and disruptive international policies is conjectural. However, the threat is real and the international behavior of a nuclear power propelled by the despair of poverty is *terra incognita* in world affairs. How the United States can deal with such an eventuality and in what ways we can deter its development is a long-term critical choice which is best addressed by considering the economics of India and Bangladesh.

The problems of the Indian economy center on the questions of population and productivity. There are certain inescapable consequences of past and present demographic trends that must be noted. By the mid-1980s, India's population will be 200 million larger than today and the government will be faced with larger numbers of illiterates, growing unemployment, increased urban congestion and mounting pressures from the countryside to produce (or import) the essential inputs (e.g., fertilizers, seeds) to maintain, if not expand, food production. Gaps in income will grow between India and the developed world

---

[b]It is unlikely that large-scale turmoil within India could persist for long without involvement of some of the great powers.

and between classes and regions within India. Weiner stresses that India has long had a stable political coalition which can govern the country, but can not accelerate economic growth or effectively distribute income. The question is how long can political order continue to be maintained in the face of economic stagnation, especially in light of the recent drift toward authoritarian rule.

The alternatives for American policy encompass issues both political (what can we do and how can it be done most effectively?) and moral (what ought we to do in the face of chronic misery?). John Lewis presents his case for continued and augmented aid as a liberal internationalist with extensive personal experience in America's aid program in South Asia. His argument is distinctive in three respects: (1) It starts with a vision of what the world ought to look like in the future and then addresses the political-economic means through which this goal may be reached. (2) Emphasis is placed on the ethical issues as they relate to the problems of scarcity not only in India and Bangladesh but in the poorest nations in general. (3) The truly formidable political obstacles to implementing his proposals (within the United States, in India, and internationally) suggest the limited parameters within which American policy can be made regarding two of the most potentially explosive global issues during the last quarter of this century—chronic poverty and truly enormous and widening inequalities between nations.

The essay asserts that there are, in particular, three forces operative in the world which will inexorably transform the structure and dynamics of the nation-centered international order. First, the condition of interdependence among all countries (including the rich and poor) is accelerating, to push international relations away from traditional "high policy" concerns toward issues such as environmental management, resources sharing, and the like. Second, an increasingly united Third World bloc is raising pressures of various sorts for a more equitable "new international order." Third, the policy elites in the rich countries will eventually yield to their consciences to adopt policies that transcend concerns of national welfare. In view of growing interdependence, the trend toward globalism will be reversed only by a worldwide disaster on the order of nuclear holocaust and, therefore, it is essential to make critical choices regarding the poorest countries (India and Bangladesh account for two-thirds of the "fourth world's" one billion people) in terms of criteria of global welfare.

After a lucid summary of the general problems of the poorest nations in terms of the above assumptions, Professor Lewis elaborates in detail the specific ways in which the Indian and Bengali development programs can be effectively implemented to bring about a major productive breakthrough. It is an exercise which graphically illustrates how sophisticated American aid specialists now are—at a time, alas, when the bloom has fallen from the aid enterprise.

The most serious objections to this approach relate to its political feasibility. Most basically, to implement the kind of massive aid program envisaged requires as a minimum precondition that the recipient nations get themselves organized to use it effectively. It is hard to see how this could be managed given the condition of the Indian and Bengali governments. To further monitor the program to insure that the aid reaches the poorest in these countries would be even more difficult. Even if these tasks could be handled, it is singularly unlikely that the South Asian governments would countenance this degree of interference in their domestic affairs—interference that would, in effect, constitute a massive rural reform program. Finally, even if these political obstacles could be overcome, it is as probable that the perpetuation of welfare dependency in the international arena would in the long run hurt, not aid, India's ability to develop itself. In addition, whether the oil rich countries will participate in a major way (as is recommended by Lewis) in an aid scheme of this magnitude is, of course, a matter over which the United States has minimal control. Furthermore, the likelihood is extremely remote that the Congress, the president, or even the silent majority of the foreign policy elite would in the forseeable future transcend their national predispositions and constituencies to undertake a vastly expanded foreign aid program in the name of global humanism.

Yet the seeming impracticality of the proposal should not dim its importance. Whatever the fate of democracy in India, there can be little doubt that a near Malthusian situation is quite probable in parts of South Asia during the next decades. If a program of aid to meet this situation is politically impractical, one often-mentioned alternative, the concept of "triage" (in a world of scarcity help only those who can be salvaged) repudiates the most elemental ethical tenets of Western civilization. The problem of poverty in South Asia presents the United States with a truly critical choice, but no visible policies from which to choose beyond continued support for the World Bank and other aid consortia.

In aggregate, American strategic and material interests in South Asia should remain modest during most of the next decade. Partly because of the Indian position of dominance, the prospects for war in the region are now the lowest since the end of the colonial era. Conflicts will center on ethnic not ideological differences, with only remote prospects for involvement by the United States. The "Balkanization" of Pakistan, a matter of concern to America and seen as a real possibility following the Bangladesh War, now seems an unlikely development, especially in view of the active concern of Iran in preventing the occurrence of such fragmentation. India's international influence outside of the region is likely to be limited to the role of "nuisance" in the nuclear field or as part of a Third World bloc. Barring extraordinary changes, the critical choices for American policy in this region lie in the more distant future, with the uncertain political prospects of societies in abject poverty in a world ever more sharply divided between the rich and the poor.

Southeast Asia

Future American policy toward Southeast Asia will be shaped, above all, by the traumatic experience of the Vietnam War. An entire generation of the elite (politicians, military leaders, diplomats, and intellectuals) as well as the public (especially the young and the families of veterans) have had both their careers and personal lives profoundly altered by this experience. Any effort to point to future policy options for the United States in this region must start with this clearly in view. Our concern here is with the future, and there will be no rehash of the debates over the war that dominated American Asian policy for more than a decade. Nevertheless, in attempting to reconstruct the past in order to understand the range of choice in the future, it is necessary to consider the war as a central feature of regional international affairs along side the broader historical picture of regional political, cultural, and economic developments.

The essay by Alexander Woodside provides a remarkably lucid synthesis of the recent history of mainland Southeast Asia, particularly regarding Vietnam. One of the most astonishing features of the debate over the war was how little attention was given to the cultural and political landscape of the region. People in and outside of government became experts through field trips and crash programs in the very limited literature on the area. Government deception notwithstanding, it is easy to see why the "debate" came to involve what the facts were. But it is appalling. Consequently, the place to begin consideration of our future role is with a broad sketch of the political and cultural history of the region.

What is especially instructive about Professor Woodside's essay is that the complexities of modern Southeast Asia are related in terms of five propositions about critical features of contemporary society with particular import for international relations. In explaining why authoritarian rather than democratic regimes are likely to prevail on mainland Southeast Asia, an intellectual excursion is made through the values of traditional cultures, the legacies of the colonial era (especially the bureaucratic structures), and the post-independence exigencies of maintaining order and fostering rapid socioeconomic changes in nations that are typically potpourris of feuding ethnic groups.

Southeast Asia resembles South Asia in the important respect that regional political conflicts (both intranational and international) center on ethnic disputes in the context of extreme ethnic heterogeneity. The colonial experience bequeathed the boundaries of the nations, the idea of nationalism, and a residue of anticolonial resentment. With regard to future relations with Western countries, Woodside sets forth the provocative proposition that fear of excessive domination by foreigners will be more important than ideology. The incongruities between political and ethnic realities and national boundaries plus the limited experience of all countries in nation-state diplomacy virtually assure that international conflict and instability will persist even without great power intervention. These features about mainland Southeast Asia convey a feeling for the broad historical forces still working to alter profoundly the fabric of all societies in this part of the world. The essay can be seen as a primer for understanding the critical choices the Southeast Asians will face in ordering future relations among themselves.

In considering the impact of the contemporary international system on the region and the future of American policy, the essay sets forth into stormy seas still turbulent from the Vietnam War—and provides a controversial proposal for the neutralization of the area. Simply stated, the case is built on three linked propositions. Conflict in the region will be exacerbated (as in the Vietnam War) if the superpowers continue to seek active political or military allies on the basis of ideological selectiveness. For the Southeast Asians, economic problems are now likely to take precedence over ideological confrontations for the foreseeable future, despite the intensification of nationalism in all countries. Therefore, the neutralization of the region from great power conflict would be to the advantage of all and the United States should take initiatives to remain aloof from all regional conflicts. In order to ascertain the utility of the suggested policy, each of these propositions requires careful scrutiny.

It is most improbable that Southeast Asia will be insulated from great power politics, no matter what institutional arrangements for neutralization are made. The area has been a cockpit for international conflict since the beginning of World War II, and it is singularly unlikely that this pattern will now abruptly end—especially in view of the uncertainties and inherent instabilities that persist in the region. However weak its position at the moment, the Soviet Union will continue to intrude into the region for multiple reasons; to "contain" China, to strengthen its position in the Indian Ocean, and simply to cultivate allies in order to expand influence in an important sector of the world. China is the major power on the Asiatic mainland and everyone in Southeast Asia perceives Peking in this light. Whether they will be "expansionist" or (as at the moment) largely passive and somewhat stalemated in relations with these countries will depend upon international conditions and China's own changing policies. Japan is now the leading trading partner, aid provider, and investor in the region by an overwhelming degree. Even if Japan does not undertake autonomous actions as a great power, its ties with Southeast Asia require that the other great powers take these relations into account in fashioning policy toward Tokyo. In short, Southeast Asia, unlike South Asia, is linked with patterns of power politics in East Asia and globally that make isolation or neutralization all but impossible, no matter what the countries of the region may desire.

It is also dubious that economic (developmental) problems rather than political and ideological issues will be the central basis of conflict among the countries of mainland Southeast Asia. A pattern of behavior, focused overwhelmingly on economic matters, however rational and desirable, would posit an historically discontinuous pattern of apolitical behavior, not only for the most explicitly ideological Communist governments but for others such as Burma and Indonesia which have had clearly political dimensions to their foreign policies. Moreover, if, as is clearly implied, nationalism is the most vibrant political force in the region, then it is hard to see how economic growth will be the dominant policy priority, especially in an international setting in which Third World nations are using political control over economic resources as instruments of policy and in which the prospects for sustained economic growth globally is seriously questioned.

Finally, the prospects for neutralizing of the region depend not upon American withdrawal, but upon the nature of our involvement in any neutralization plan. The strategic choices for the United States should perforce proceed along the general lines suggested in the Pacific Doctrine of President Ford; that is, recognition of the new Communist governments in Southeast Asia (favored by Woodside), placing the security of Southeast Asia in the broader context of East Asia, and broadening areas of economic cooperation. From the long-term perspective, what is lacking in this vision is the articulation of specific aims through international instrumentalities (e.g., agreements, treaties) to indicate how the United States would respond in the face of a specific challenge.

Because the Nixon Doctrine stated that "our interests will determine our commitments" and because there is basic doubt whether and in what way the United States would intervene with force in Southeast Asia, the mechanism for a "power balance" is left highly indeterminate. Given the fluidity of international conditions and the lack of a broadly based foreign policy consensus in this country, it is understandable that such a largely unstructured and flexible posture is taken. However, it is not a viable long-term arrangement,[c] and if the United States is to remain engaged in Southeast Asia, a more explicit set of operating procedures regarding our political and military commitments should be worked out either with Southeast Asian nations or in a broader great power context. If we do not embark on creative diplomacy, initiatives will fall either to Peking or Moscow, or find direction from the drift of events.

Indonesia is the single most important nation in Southeast Asia and will have a critical role in the future pattern of regional international relations. The country has played two dramatically different roles in Southeast Asian affairs. From the time of the nation's independence until 1965, Indonesia, under the leadership of President Sukarno played a highly activist and increasingly anti-Western role in regional affairs. Following an abortive Communist coup in 1965, the country switched from grandiose foreign policy to internal economic development. Adopting a nonaligned posture, the Indonesians have turned to industrial societies, notably the United States and Japan, for foreign assistance. Impressive strides have been made in raising production and strengthening the economy thanks to the rich natural resources in the country, shrewd economic management, and massive external aid. Nevertheless, the country continues to be beset by serious conditions of overpopulation on the main island of Java and the prospects for persisting severe socioeconomic problems insure that political instability will be a problem in the future. Indonesia will remain simply a regional power, but like India, has the material and political potential for

---

[c]That it is quite unsatisfactory in the short term as well, is evident from the repeated public urgings from the Chinese that the United States stay in Asia—fulfilling commitments initially devised to contain China!

becoming a "nuisance" if the international situation deteriorates or there is a domestic political crisis. At present, Jakarta is working hard to promote regional cooperation through the Association of South East Asian Nations (ASEAN)—an organization of non-Communist Southeast Asian states—and the United States has substantial latitude to promote a constructive and cooperative bilateral relationship. It should be one of the main tasks for American diplomacy in Asia in the next decade.

The United States and Asia

The final contributions to this volume are more directly concerned with the problems of United States foreign policy and focus on issues that encompass East as well as Southern Asia. One of the main criticisms that has been made of America's policy toward Asia since 1945 has been its failure to consider specific actions in terms of their meaning in the broader context of the region. Professor Robert Scalapino is one of the few people capable of dealing with the full range of Asian societies, and his chapter encompassing the policies of the great powers most engaged in the region (the United States, the Soviet Union, China, Japan, India, and Indonesia) provides an extraordinary overview which synthesizes and develops themes that run through these two volumes dealing with America's critical choices in Asia.[3] Dr. Robert Pranger's essay addresses two problems: (1) the unique role Asia has played historically in American foreign policy with particular stress on the way this has shaped our use of force in world affairs and (2) an elaboration of five possible future military strategies for the United States in Asia.

Asia has had a unique and important role in the modern history of American diplomacy and our future policies toward this region will grow out of this heritage. Despite the enormous heterogeneity and size of Asia, it does make sense to examine the role of the region in modern American diplomacy. There is indeed a "vagueness" about Asia's lands and peoples to educated Americans, even though our emergence as a world power has been peculiarly linked to the region.

The reasons for this vagueness are easy to find. First, there is a cultural distance between the Western civilization of the United States and the Eastern civilizations of Asia. Paradoxically, this cultural distance gave an idealistic dimension to American relations with Asia. It underlay both the extensive and largely abortive missionary efforts that were a major source of contact prior to World War II and the idealistic postwar attempts to create democracies (Japan, Korea, Vietnam) and then to defend them from communism. Second, unlike Europe and the Middle East, there are no powerful Asian ethnic groups to link domestic sentiment with foreign involvement. Yet, during World War II, the United States spent more time in Asia than in Europe and has since engaged in its only major military actions in the Far East. Indeed, America's rise to a global power, during the modern era in which the utilization of force was the critical instrument of foreign policy, was integrally and centrally tied to activities in Asia. As Pranger concludes, Asia proved to be "a *deus ex machina* in American foreign policy, a premise for idealism and a pretext for intervention." Suggesting that force ultimately came to be employed by the United States in Asia without "realistic" constraints (partly because of the peculiar juxtaposition of idealism and "vagueness" regarding the region), he also concludes that failure in Vietnam may finally have brought military intervention in the region into line with more mature and realistic goals and the limited capacities of our country.

The history of the roles of force and idealism in past American policies toward Asia serves as a prelude to a stimulating and provocative discussion of future American military strategies in Asia. The basic premise is that the United States is searching for a coherent global strategy to protect its national security interests, but presently lacks such a consistent defense posture in Asia (and beyond). Five possible future strategic alternatives (and corresponding forms of military force) in Asia are then elaborated: (1) revised containment; (2) neo-Mahanism; (3) selective engagement; (4) strategic disengagement; and (5) futuristic planning. The most impressive aspects of this part of the essay are not the concrete proposals but the framework that is devised to pose critical choices regarding defense planning. Pranger breaks out of the orthodox mold and moves the discussion beyond comparative force levels (the logic of the defense debate under the premises of containment) to consider the various purposes for which force can be used. Then the linkage between strategic goals and the composition of forces are established. The strategic alternatives, the brief synopses of the alternatives in the text and a table relating each option to Asia provide a highly original basis for a strategic debate that is long overdue.

At the moment, nothing has yet replaced the increasingly outmoded cold war containment doctrines (spelled out officially in NSC-68 of 1950) and defense planning has been bogged down in a morass of bureaucratic and congressional politics featuring sterile arguments over the semantics of slogans (e.g., détente), consideration of the latest innovations in military hardware without regard to the ends for which the weapons will be used, or interminable discussions about how U.S. forces compare with those of the Soviet Union. Future American security policy in Asia must go beyond shoring up old alliances, justifying the existing base structure and liquidating outdated commitments. What is required is devising a new set of strategic aims, encompassing political and economic as well as military interests, and then providing the appropriate support policies to achieve these goals.

The scheme set forth in this essay opens the door for initiating this kind of long-term planning endeavor. Without exploring in detail the substantive proposals, it can be said that, on balance, there is an implied need for (1) a reduction in forces in line with selective engagement, (2) a shift toward greater mix of political negotiations with the great powers rather than augmented force levels, and (3) an intensification of ongoing efforts to take into account the defense implications of radical shifts in international politics (e.g., the proliferation of nuclear weapons among smaller regional powers) which are clear possibilities in the future of Asia.

Professor Scalapino's chapter offers an inventory of critical choices and policy options for not only the United States but the Soviet Union and all major Asian powers. There are two themes in the essay which warrant particular mention. The first concerns the United States. America is seen as continuing to be the leading global power in international relations and adjustment to trends in our policy will remain, with but few exceptions, the critical element in Asian affairs. Accordingly, the credibility of United States policy is viewed as the *sine qua non* for establishing a viable order in Asia in the long term. Flexibility is the other requirement for American policy (and that of other powers) because international conditions globally and in Asia are so fluid. Therefore his prescriptions for American policy are predicated on continuing active involvement of this country in the region, but not in the form of the relatively rigid alliances built in the 1950s. The specific recommendations on the full range of issues from Taiwan and Korea, to aid to India, offer balanced options on policy reflecting the position of a "realistic" internationalist and display a sophisticated understanding of the complex international and domestic political forces that bear on all of these questions.

The second theme concerns the international landscape in Asia, which is seen as highly fluid, but still serving as a battleground for competing ideologies as well as national interests—with the revolutionary dimension of communism in Asia a continuing force. While the Soviet Union will move to expand its influence throughout Asia, the primary regional concern for Moscow will be on relations with Peking. Similarly, the touchstone for China's strategy in Asia will be Soviet relations, but the Chinese will have unique advantages in regional affairs that the Russians are not likely to match. Scalapino is particularly sensitive to intraregional international linkages and is emphatic in asserting the folly of American policy built around selective involvement with only the power centers of Tokyo and Peking.

The essay is predicated on the assumption that peace in Asia can be built only on a complex balance of power involving smaller nations as well as the great powers. The recommendations are made more compelling because of their continuity with current American policies toward the region. The ultimate goal is peace under American leadership, with priority given to Northeast Asia (strengthen ties with Japan, underwrite the security of Korea and Taiwan), selective "tilt" toward Russia or China as the circumstances require, negotiation with the great powers regarding peace in Southeast Asia (since American military involvement is most unlikely), and a low profile in South Asia.[d] This package, part of a global posture labeled "selective internationalism" in which East Asia

---

[d]The proposals regarding the Korean and Taiwan problems are particularly insightful and provocative.

and Western Europe are given special priority, is easily related to our present policies and provides guidelines for action which can profitably be applied in Washington.

While it is hard for me to criticize the substance of these even-handed recommendations, two caveats are in order, the first of which the essay itself discusses at length. The policy proposals presume an institutional capacity for action and a broad domestic political consensus within the United States which permits such action. The United States has the material capacities to act, but the strong institutional arrangement (essentially the presidential-bureaucratic-congressional establishment) and the basic consensus on long-term goals which prevailed in the decades after World War II, no longer exist. No bold initiatives can be forthcoming under these circumstances. Since Vietnam, leadership in Asia has consisted largely of preventing further unraveling of our current position (e.g., Korea), attempting to prove we really are credible, or cautiously probing toward new working relationships with China and Japan. In a word, the policy options suggested depend on a will to lead internationally in Asia and it is an open question whether leadership of that kind will be possible in the future.

This leads to the second caveat. Even if the United States re-establishes the institutional and consensual bases for leadership, there is no assurance that policies proceeding within the orthodox pattern of diplomacy will succeed. The approach taken by Professor Scalapino focuses on policy options within a nation-state system functioning along lines quite similar to those of the recent past. It down plays those elements of international affairs that lie beyond the direct control of the policymakers, the changes in the basic structure and dynamics of the system itself that establish the broad parameters within which policy is made. The potential for such systemic changes in Asia in the future is substantial: the proliferation of nuclear weapons among the smaller powers, a regional system so indeterminate and conflict prone that none of the great powers can act effectively, domestic political strife in a number of countries that leads to highly destabilizing international consequences, just plain miscalculations in policy so great as to alter the features of regional affairs (e.g., U.S. policy in Vietnam, the Sino-Soviet split) and the impending tensions between the rich and very poor nations. Asia has been the scene of more upheaval, war, and revolution than any portion of the globe in recent years and, with the perspective of hindsight, the efforts of the United States and the Soviet Union to manage conflict and to structure enduring alliances has, to put it modestly, not met with conspicuous success.

In considering the prospects for future developments in Asia, it is instructive to look at the extensive efforts made during the last years of World War II to forecast the postwar landscape. What was missing in those forecasts were fundamental changes such as the cold war and the decolonization process, which in turn led to new strategic doctrines (containment) and specific policies (aid, alliances, military intervention) that were without precedent. In considering the critical choices that the United States will make regarding Asia during the last quarter of the twentieth century, it is necessary to build on present policies in the manner of Professor Scalapino's essay. But it is also essential to consider the fundamental political, economic, and military forces sustaining the current system and the prospects they hold for radically changing the *modus operandi* of international affairs in ways beyond the control of statesmen. Discontinuities have been the rule in Asian affairs during the last four decades and their persistence should be the premise in any realistic long-term American policy toward the region.

Notes

1. This point is made in an interesting fashion in Robert W. Cox, "On Thinking about Future World Order," *World Politics* 28, 2 (January 1976): 174-177 and *passim.*

2. See, for example, the influential book by Max F. Millikan and W.W. Rustow, *A Proposal* (New York: Harper and Brothers, 1957).

3. See the companion volume which I have also prepared for this series, Volume XII, *China and Japan: A New Balance of Power.*

II Critical Choices for India and America

Myron Weiner

Prologue: A Political System in Transition

For nearly twenty-eight years, from 1947 to 1975, India was widely regarded as among the few newly independent countries that had successfully maintained both a stable and democratic form of government. In June 1975, the government of India declared a national emergency, arrested thousands of members of

For commenting on an earlier draft of this essay and for discussions of various points made here, I am grateful to Jagdish Bhagwati, Paul Brass, Pran Chopra, Donald Hellmann, Samuel Huntington, Mary Katzenstein, John Lewis, Joseph Nye, Lucian Pye, Kartikeya Sarabhai, George Verghese, and Nuri Yalman. Many of my ideas were further honed at a meeting of Asianists and Washington officials held under the auspices of the Commission on Critical Choices.

Since this is an essay and not a research monograph which draws from materials that are widely known, I have omitted the footnotes that customarily adorn works of scholarship. Demographic data, and projections based upon them, are drawn from the 1971 Census of India; economic statistics are drawn from reports from the Indian Planning Commission and from the World Bank; descriptions of recent political developments are taken from the pages of the *Times of India*, the *Overseas Hindustan Times, Economic and Political Weekly*, and *India News*; electoral observations are based upon data provided in four volumes edited by myself and John Field entitled *Studies in Electoral Politics in the Indian States* (South Asia Books, Columbia, Mo., 1975). I have also drawn heavily from the research of many American political scientists studying South Asia, including William Barnds, Paul Brass, David Bayley, Stephen Cohen, John Field, Francine Frankel, Marcus Franda, Lloyd and Suzanne Rudolph, Robert Hardgrave, Stanley Heginbotham, and others, who have shared with me an understanding of developments in South Asia and the role of the United States in the region that has so often been at variance with United States policymakers and journalists.

opposition parties, suspended the right of *habeas corpus*, imposed censorship on the press, banned twenty-six political organizations including militant groups on both the extreme right and the pro-Peking left, declared illegal the holding of public meetings, expelled numerous foreign journalists, and amended the constitution to limit the power of the courts.

The government justified the emergency by asserting that the opposition parties—barring the Communist party of India which supports the government—had been resorting to extra-parliamentary and extra-constitutional methods to force the governing Congress party out of office. The government accused Jayaprakash Narayan, a leading opponent of the prime minister, of seeking to "incite" the police and the armed forces to commit acts of "indiscipline." The government also blamed the opposition for seeking "to disrupt the economy" through a nationwide railway strike.

Mrs. Gandhi's domestic critics and most foreign observers concluded that the prime minister acted less to meet a national threat than to meet a challenge to her own power. In mid-June 1975, the Allahabad High Court found Mrs. Gandhi guilty of violating the Representation of the People Act in her 1971 election campaign—not, ironically, on the major abuses that are widely practiced (such as the illegal collection of "black" or untaxed money by political parties from companies and individuals), but on a series of relatively minor technical violations of the law. A few days later, the Supreme Court gave her a "conditional stay" until her appeal could be heard by the full court. The opposition parties, which had just defeated the Congress party in elections for the state assembly in Gujarat, announced that they would launch a campaign to have her resign. Five of the country's leading national newspapers also urged her to step down. On June 26, Mrs. Gandhi struck against the opposition, the press, and dissidents within her own party. Parliament was subsequently called into session to ratify the declaration of emergency and to amend the electoral law retroactively so that the offenses committed by Mrs. Gandhi would no longer be illegal.

Mrs. Gandhi declared that she was acting within the framework of the law since the Constitution of India permits the government to declare an emergency when the security of India "is threatened by internal disturbances." Moreover, within a few weeks parliament approved the emergency as required by the Constitution; hence the arrests, restrictions on public assembly, and the press censorship were within the law.

Mrs. Gandhi's critics retorted that she had broken the rules, for never in the twenty-eight years of Indian democracy, not even during the wars with China and Pakistan, had the government clamped down so hard on the opposition or the press or ever arrested dissidents within its own party. Moreover, the manner in which she had proceeded—her decision to request the president of India to sign the declaration of an emergency before discussing the matter with members of the cabinet—suggested that the prime minister intended to take a series of measures to create an authoritarian structure that might not win the support of senior officials within her own government.

Within a few months it became clear that Mrs. Gandhi had fundamentally changed the Indian political system. Through a series of parliamentary acts, restrictions on the press are now independent of the ordinances declared during the emergency. The proceedings of both parliament and the courts will be censored before appearing in the press, while the press is barred from publishing articles "likely to excite disaffection against the constitutionally established government," or to publish "defamatory" writings against the president, prime minister and other key officials. A number of newspapers published by the opposition were closed by the government, including the Socialist *Janata*, the leftist *Frontier*, the Gandhian *Everyman's Weekly*, and the Jan Sangh Delhi daily, *Motherland*. The government has consolidated the wire services, presumably to facilitate control over the collection and dissemination of both domestic and foreign news.

The government issued a series of ordinances empowering officials to arrest individuals without disclosing the grounds for detention or arrest—even before the judiciary. These ordinances were subsequently confirmed by a parliamentary act amending the Maintenance of Internal Security Act (MISA) so that the government will continue to possess the power to detain political prisoners without charges even when the emergency ends.

The expansion of two institutions during the past few years substantially facilitated the movement toward an authoritarian regime: the strengthening of central intelligence, and the expansion of centrally-controlled paramilitary forces.

An intelligence gathering unit was created within the prime minister's secretariat—the Research and Analysis Wing (RAW), which provides the prime minister with her own independent source of political information. The expansion and consolidation of intelligence gathering facilitated the nationwide arrest of thousands of members of the opposition on the morning of June 26, and has helped to keep control over the underground press that has emerged since the declaration of the emergency.

With the expansion of the Border Security Forces and the Central Reserve Police, the central government has acquired paramilitary forces that are independent of the defense ministry and the state governments. The government was thus able to impose the emergency without the deployment of the armed forces.

The prime minister has also made considerable use of India's limited television facilities. The Satellite Instructional Television Experiment (SITE) has made possible the spread of television to thousands of villages and there are presently television centers in Amritsar, Bombay, Calcutta, Delhi, Lucknow, and Madras. The prime minister has appeared on television frequently since the emergency and there is reason to believe that she is eager to see the dissemination of television receiving units throughout the country. The expansion of television would presumably enhance the government's capacity to influence the cities and countryside without depending on the local units of a weakening Congress party organization.

While it is clear that the emergency has meant an end to the open, competitive democratic system, it is less clear as to the effects of the emergency on India's long-term economic development. Were the economic improvements that accompanied the emergency the typical initial effects of establishing an atmosphere in which fear motivates more efficiency and there is less corruption, or are there indications that the government is now able to end the paralysis that has characterized the Indian political economy for the past decade?

India's fundamental political problem in recent years has been that the governing elite has been unable to move the country either in the direction of greater economic growth or toward greater equity in income. Each major force in the political system has been carefully poised to protect its own interests. While the cumulative effect of this well-established balance was to provide India with a degree of stability that few other countries in the developing world had experienced, there were also no significant political forces for change. By arresting members of the opposition and dissidents within the Congress, censoring the press, and establishing emergency rule, the government hoped to set into motion forces that would break the deadlock. But neither the opposition, the press, nor even the dissident members of Congress were responsible for the deadlock—in spite of the government's efforts to cast blame upon them. The opposition had been divided and its voice in both parliament and in the state governments has been limited, especially since the overwhelming Congress electoral victories of 1971 and 1972. And while it is true that the opposition parties had won considerable support from the urban middle-class and the organized working class, and had supported strikes among workers in the railways and in other public sector industries, the growth of urban dissidence was probably more the consequence of inflation, declining personal income, and governmental corruption than the organizing skill of the opposition. The press, too, had been vocal, but it reached only a small fraction of the country, and its influence on government was in any event minimal. And the arrested Congress dissidents were largely in the left wing of the party, critical not of Mrs. Gandhi's policies but of her failure to implement them.

The prime minister's declared objective was to generate change through imposing a new sense of discipline that would lead the bureaucracy to work more efficiently, stir workers to increase productivity, prod state governments into carrying out land reform policies, eliminate hoarders and black marketeers and thereby bring down the prices of essential commodities, and in general improve the country's self-confidence. Indeed, during the early months of the new political order there was a noticeable improvement in government efficiency as government workers came to office on time, the rate of inflation (which had been 30 percent per annum) droppped precipitously, food production rose, and industrial production and exports increased.

But how many of these changes could be attributed to the steps taken since the emergency, as opposed to developments independent of the emergency (such as the improved monsoon), or to policies that preceded the emergency (such as anti-inflationary monetary policies initiated in 1974)?

A twenty-point program, which included promises to implement land reform, abolish rural debt, provide assistance to college students, encourage industrial production, end bonded labor, and eliminate corruption in government, was, in the main, welcomed, but it hardly represented any bold new measures to accelerate the country's modernization. A variety of new economic policies did, however, appear to offer incentives to the private sector to expand their investment and make greater use of their underutilized industrial capacity: the ending of compulsory bonuses for industrial workers irrespective of the profits of firms; the decontrol of cement, steel, and other commodities; the simplification of regulations and licensing procedures; financial incentives to exporters and a loosening on import restrictions for spare parts and raw materials for industrial use; and reductions on both corporate and individual income taxes. But while these measures suggested that the Indian government was liberalizing its policies toward the business community (a paradoxical move for a government whose foreign policy was tilted toward the Soviet bloc and whose only support from the opposition is from the Communist party), the business community remained uneasy as to the government's long-term intentions. Did these policies represent a fundamental shift in direction, or are they simply a short-term governmental response to low demand, excessive inventories, and the industrial recession? Would the government again impose restrictions and controls on the private sector, once there is an increase in investment, a more rapid expansion of the private as against the public sector, and an increase in private profits? Moreover, even with these concessions, the pace of industrial recovery (as of early 1976) remained slow.

Authoritarianism also threatened to unleash new forces unwelcomed by the government. The overthrow of Mujib Rahman, the charismatic president of Bangladesh, by a right wing military group only months after he has suspended democratic rights in his country, should remind the Indian prime minister that a repressive regime stimulates illegal behavior among political dissidents and conspiracies within the government. With the decline of legitimacy implied by the suspension of democratic rights, the Indian military, its tradition of being above politics notwithstanding, must now be persuaded that the regime is more effective—a test that Mujib Rahman apparently did not pass and which Prime Minister Gandhi must now meet if her government is not to suffer a similar fate.

The prolongation of the emergency seems likely to create new forces. Some civilian critics have moved underground; the more militant and organized among these may grow as the emergency is prolonged. Conspiracies may develop within the governing Congress party, among members of the cabinet, within the Defense and Home Ministries, the military and the police. And if these underground movements and conspiracies grow, government is likely to tighten its exercise of power, convinced that it is even more justified in declaring and maintaining the emergency. Authoritarianism thus attracts—and creates—new personalities: those with a conspiratorial mentality, as well as those who believe in the necessity of employing coercion against their critics and enemies.

Even if Mrs. Gandhi continues, as she has in the past, to skillfully trod through the mine field that she has by her own actions created, and successfully outmaneuvers her opponents not only within political parties but within the civilian, paramilitary, and military bureaucracies, what kind of legacy will she leave for her successors? While she has demonstrated a capacity to dismantle institutions which appear to threaten her position in power (first the governing Congress party between 1969 and 1971, and most recently the opposition, the press, and the judicial system) it is unclear what political institutions, if any, will take their place.

In Mrs. Gandhi's view, these institutions—state Congress organizations with local leaders independent of the center, a hostile opposition, a critical press, and an independent judiciary—have impeded the movement toward a modern, Socialist, equalitarian social and economic order. Like so many Third World leaders she aspires to create a political order in which policies emanate from among her supporters in the national bureaucracy, are implemented by centrally appointed politicians and bureaucrats whose careers are dependent upon her support, and are backed by popular acclaim. The intermediate political institutions which process demands, stimulate dissent, and constrain government are to be dispensed with by intelligence and police surveillance. Should Mrs. Gandhi's policies unleash the forces of productivity that are latent within India, then India may come to resemble that handful of countries in the developing world that can be loosely described as authoritarian modernizing states; but if the government's policies do not unleash these productive forces, then India will have lost its democratic institutions but gained nothing in its place.

These internal political events in India are taking place at a time when uncertainties and changes in the internal affairs of other Asian powers open the possibilities of new international realignments that may affect the South Asia region. The Indian government is fearful of any rapprochement between Bangladesh and Pakistan, or of any expansion of Chinese influence that might appear to change the political and military balance of power within South Asia. A militarily insecure India that views alliances among its neighbors with concern is hardly likely to be relaxed about the role of the great powers in the region and in the Indian Ocean. Nor in fact should it be, for India's neighbors, themselves fearful of a militarily strong, nuclear India, may seek to increase the involvement of one or more of the great powers in the region. Nor can one exclude the possibility that in the not too distant future two of India's neighbors, Pakistan and Iran, may join India and China in becoming nuclear powers themselves.

In short, recent political developments within India, followed by military coups in Bangladesh, have created a new and fluid situation not only for the internal affairs of India, but for the regional power relations within South Asia, and hence for the great powers outside. While the United States presently views South Asia as an area of secondary importance, it is unthinkable to imagine that political and economic developments in a region of the world containing a fifth of mankind could leave the United States and its allies unaffected. What is needed is a clearer understanding of the critical problems which India as a nation is likely to face, the regional and international context within which India's development is taking place, and the kinds of issues likely to confront the United States, especially if, as seems increasingly probable, the India with which the United States must deal has an authoritarian government led by Prime Minister Gandhi or a praetorian successor.

South Asia: The Regional and Global Context

Introduction

A little more than a billion people, a quarter of mankind, live in industrial societies transformed by technologies that have made it possible for the vast majority of their populations to live long, if not happy, lives under conditions of relative affluence. The remaining nearly three billion people live in societies whose industrial (and agricultural) revolutions have only recently begun and, in some instances, have hardly begun at all. For more than a century, the industrial countries, directly or indirectly, dominated the politics and economics of the remaining pre-industrial world. That domination unraveled during and after the Second World War when the industrial powers lost their capacity, then their will and, ultimately, their need to dominate the pre-industrial countries.

The rearrangement of these relationships has been an unsettling element of international relations in the postwar era. What in any event would have been a difficult process of adaptation as peoples and nations once dominated by Western powers asserted their new found identity and independence, while once dominant states learned to accommodate themselves to more equal relations, was made even more difficult by conflicts between the two great powers.

Both Soviet and American policy in the Third World was primarily shaped by their relationship with each other rather than an assessment of what their relationship should be to the developing countries. American policymakers (and their counterparts in Moscow) looked at each political crisis within and between Third World countries in terms of how they might affect the long-term strategic balance between the great powers. In Asia, such considerations shaped American decisions to defend South Korea, create military alliances in South, Southeast and Western Asia, establish military bases and port facilities from the Philippines to the Persian Gulf, and led the United States to intervene in Vietnam and Cambodia. Concepts like "credibility" and "domino" effects were based upon the assumption that what happened in one small portion of the globe and what the United States did there affected American interests elsewhere in the world. Pentagon officials thus had to justify military aid programs and proposals for new bases abroad in terms of a global conception of security, while directors of AID missions to small and often obscure countries had to justify economic assistance by elaborate explanations of how a proposed program fitted into our global strategy and how Soviet (and later Chinese) influences might be reduced. Along with the willingness of a government to ally itself with the United States, the presence of a Communist party or an insurgency movement and evidence that a regime was endangered were themselves important arguments for assistance. Whether the question was one of helping the Thai or Philippine governments deal with a Communist insurgency, responding to Pakistan's request for military aid, meeting Nepal's desire for economic aid, or taking a position on the Indo-Pakistan conflict over Bangladesh, a central concern for American policymakers was how the Soviets or Chinese would interpret our actions.

The Chinese became part of this calculus, not only because they were a significant regional power in Asia, but because they were part of the global equation—first as an ally, and then as an adversary of the Soviet Union.

American policymakers emphasized two principles linking the Third World to the great powers. The first was that the nations of the Third World had the responsibility of settling their dispute peacefully, in order to avoid drawing in the great powers. The second principle was that the nuclear powers should not exploit differences among Third World countries to their own advantage, for unless they restrained themselves there would be a danger of military confrontation.

American policymakers were certainly aware of the importance of purely regional conflicts among developing countries, of the internal political fragility of many regimes, and even the broader issues of economic development and social change, but these invariably tended to be perceived in the context of, and secondary to, global security considerations.

The South Asia region mattered to the United States primarily in this global context. While South Asia is the most populous non-Communist region of the world—in 1975 with 838 million, the region was more populated than China with an estimated 823 million—the United States did not have any direct interests at stake. American private investment, though not an insignificant portion of India's total foreign industrial investment, is small in the context of American overseas investment. United States trade with India remains negligible, even though in recent years India has become one of the largest purchasers of food grains in the American market. Militarily, India is no threat to the United States or any of the major powers, notwithstanding its million man army and potential nuclear capabilities. India is expanding its navy, but she still hardly counts as a significant naval force in the Indian Ocean. As a regional power India can affect the economics, politics, and external relations of its nearby neighbors, but outside the region, in Western and in Southeast Asia, in the halls of the United Nations and in other international forums, India's influence over other nations remains small, especially as compared either to China or to the oil producing states. In an era when control over critical natural resources has given poor countries considerable international leverage, India stands as the largest country in what has been referred to as the Fourth World—a country which is dependent upon the oil resources of others, but which lacks the export capacity to afford to purchase oil at existing world prices.

Nonetheless, the United States has played a significant role in the region. It was not too long ago that India was the largest single recipient of United States economic assistance (a total of $10 billion); Pakistan was a major ally of the United States and a recipient of substantial quantities of arms; and the American presence was visibly felt through all of South Asia. But to most observers American policy in the region, as seen from the vantage point of the mid-70s, has not been successful. The United States government placed itself on the side of a losing military regime against a democracy in a secessionist struggle by the people of Bangladesh; the United States was unsuccessful in dissuading the Indian government from developing its nuclear capabilities; Soviet influence in India has substantially increased; and American relations with India—and indeed with a growing proportion of the countries of the Third World—has sharply deteriorated.

Many of the difficulties encountered by the United States in South Asia— indeed, in Southeast Asia as well—have been the result of an excessively global view of what were essentially regional and internal developments. Admittedly, it is not always easy to ascertain whether a particular internal conflict has been precipitated by the actions of one of America's global adversaries, or whether one of the nuclear powers has taken advantage of a regional conflict, but there is reason to believe that in recent years American policymakers have tended to err in the direction of exaggerating both the importance of great power intervention in local and regional developments in the Third World and the effect of these developments on the global strategic balance.

This chapter starts with a regional perspective. It focuses on India in the context of the South Asia region: the indigenous sources of conflict within the region, the role of India as a regional power, and the effect of India's internal economic and political developments on her capacity within the region. Only then shall we seek to place India into a global context and consider the critical issues which the United States may face in South Asia in the next decade.

Regional Conflict in South Asia

South Asia has been one of the most violent regions in the postwar world. There have been four international wars in the region: a conflict in Kashmir between

India and Pakistan (1947-48), an Indo-Chinese war in Ladakh and in the Northeastern Frontier Agency north of Assam (1962), a second Indo-Pakistan conflict over Kashmir with fighting in Rajasthan and the Punjab (1965), and a third Indo-Pakistan war over Bangladesh (in 1971). The most violent conflict in the region was not a war between states, but a war between peoples: the Hindu-Muslim-Sikh carnage that engulfed the Punjab and Bengal shortly after partition, resulting in massive movements of refugees from one country to another, and the death of hundreds of thousands, perhaps as many as a million, civilians. The dispute between India and Pakistan over Kashmir has rivaled the Israeli-Palestinian conflict and the Greek-Turkish-Cypriot dispute for its persistence, emotion, and impermeability to rational settlement.

In addition to these international conflicts, each country in the region has experienced internal turmoil that has had international repercussions. Civil conflict in Sri Lanka between the Sinhalese and Tamils in the mid-fifties created political tremors in the Tamil-speaking region of southern India, and the youth-peasant rebellion that struck Sri Lanka in 1971 was accompanied by a government request for assistance from Pakistan, India, the United States, the Soviet Union, and China.

Conflicts within Pakistan have had repercussions in neighboring Afghanistan and India: tribal revolts in Pakistan's northwest frontier province have affected the Pathan populations on the Afghanistan side of the border, while the civil war between East and West Pakistan precipitated the Indo-Pak War of 1971.

The use of force by the Indian government to deal with problems it considered internal has often been viewed as an international matter by others. The "police action" of the Indian government in Muslim-ruled Hyderabad in 1948 was denounced by the Pakistanis, and the "liberation" of Goa in 1961 from Portuguese rule was accompanied by both Portuguese and American denunciations of the use of force by India. In Nagaland and Mizoram in India's northeast, secessionists have sought external arms and political support. Recently, India's absorption of Sikkim, an historic protectorate of India, into the Indian political system has been denounced by the Chinese as Indian "imperialism."

Finally, in Nepal, the overthrow of the monarchy by Nepali nationalists received Indian support, while the subsequent overthrow of the parliamentary system by the monarchy has strained relations with India.

The Ethnic Dimension

Why has the region been the scene of such persistent violence? These international conflicts cannot be understood without reference to the complex overlapping of ethnic groups across international boundaries. Every country in the area shares a political or ethnic group with one of its neighbors, and in each case overlapping ethnicity has been a major source of conflict. Consider the following ethnic overlaps:

1. One-fourth of Sri Lanka is a Tamil-speaking population that originates from southern India.
2. The Bengali-speaking population of South Asia, numbering 120 million (greater than the combined population of France and West Germany) lives in two countries, Bangladesh with 75 million, and India with 45 million.
3. South Asia has 180 million Muslims, the largest number in Bangladesh (65 million), then India (60 million), and finally Pakistan (55 million).
4. The Punjab, an agriculturally prosperous region that provides military recruits for two armies, is divided between Muslim Punjabis in Pakistan and Hindu and Sikh Punjabi-speakers in India.
5. Baluchi tribesmen, all Muslims, can be found along the border regions of Afghanistan and Iran, with the largest number residing in the Baluchistan region of Pakistan.

The result of these overlaps is that ethnic conflict within each country affects at least one or more constituencies in a neighboring country. The clash between East Bengalis and West Pakistanis created a domestic problem for India, involving Bengali sentiment throughout northeastern India. Similarly, relations between India and Sri Lanka are affected by the way in which Sri Lanka treats its Tamilian minority, and how Sri Lanka treats its minority is influenced in turn by her relationship with India. Within Pakistan, the relationship between the Punjabis and Pathans influences Pakistan's relations with Afghanistan; moreover, given the special relationship that exists between Afghanistan and both the Soviet Union and India, how Pakistan handles its relationship with rebellious Pathans shapes its relationship with at least three other countries. Similarly, the status of Baluchis in Pakistan has repercussions in Afghanistan and especially Iran. Finally, every action taken by India in Kashmir, and every action taken by Pakistan in the portion of Kashmir under her control, has repercussions for the relationship between the two countries.

The overlapping of ethnic groups across international boundaries would not be such a critical element in interstate relations were it not for the fact that no state in the region can be wholly assured of the loyalty of all its ethnic groups. The government of each multi-ethnic state is anxiously aware of the way in which the behavior of external powers can affect the loyalty of its ethnic minorities and influence interethnic conflicts. Thus, communal tensions in either Pakistan or India have affected communal relations in the other, while Hindu-Muslim relations within Bangladesh would have repercussions in West Bengal and Assam in India.

Since every country of South Asia shares at least one important ethnic group with India—linguistic or religious—there is an understandable anxiety throughout the region about what India's response will be to any internal ethnic conflict. Nepal and Sri Lanka must take Indian sensibilities into account in dealing with the issues of Indian citizenship, while Bangladesh must consider Indian sentiment in its treatment of Bengali Hindus and even Bihari Muslims.

In turn, ethnic tensions in every country in the region are viewed with some anxiety by India, for linguistic or religious disturbances can have the following effects upon India:

1. Conflicts within neighboring states can be accompanied by the movement of refugees into India. Since 1947, there have been movements of Sikhs and Hindus from West Pakistan, Bengali Hindus (and in 1971 Bengali Muslims as well) from East Pakistan, Tamilians from Sri Lanka and Burma. Famine conditions within Bangladesh, even in the absence of ethnic conflict, can precipitate a flow of migrants into Assam, Tripura, and West Bengal.

2. There can be backlash retribution against minorities in India if an ethnic group of Indian origin is involved in violence in a neighboring state. Clashes between Hindus and Muslims in either West or East Pakistan often was followed by communal conflicts within India, especially in the states of Bihar, Madhya Pradesh, and Orissa.

3. There may be public sympathy in India for minorities clashing with a neighboring government, creating a political demand for intervention. The central government had to consider the impact of civil war in Pakistan on the internal politics of West Bengal, and the wave of sympathy for Bangladesh that swept the Bengali population within India. Similarly, conflicts between the Sinhalese and Tamils in Sri Lanka affect the state government of Tamil Nadu, and that, in turn, creates a political need to do something by the Ministry of External Affairs.

Finally, it is important to note that just as internal ethnic conflicts can generate interstate conflicts within South Asia, so too can interstate conflicts in the region influence ethnic relations within each of the states. Bangladesh-Pakistan relations will affect the well-being of Biharis in Bangladesh; Indo-Bangladesh relations will influence Hindu-Muslim relations on both sides of the border; Pakistan-Afghanistan relations will affect the position of the Pathans, and Pakistan-Iranian relations the position of Baluchis, again on both sides of the border; and India's relations with Nepal and Sri Lanka will affect Indian minorities in both countries.

The Great Powers in the Regional Conflicts of South Asia

These disputes within the South Asia area have assumed an importance outside the region because each of the countries has, at one time or another, sought the assistance of external powers.

When British India was partitioned in 1947 the two successor states, India and Pakistan, were in no way balanced. Pakistan was a geographically divided country, its administrative structure in shambles, its political institutions new and untried, its economy even more underdeveloped than that of India. India was overwhelmingly larger than Pakistan in both size and population. It was, and continued to be, politically stable. Its industrial growth in the 1950s was reasonably impressive. It had in Nehru a renowned international figure who had a vision of India's role as a regional leader and as a spokesman for the developing world in international politics.

Pakistan, hostile to India over Kashmir, and translating into regional terms the anxieties that Muslims had had within a united India, sought American military assistance at a time when British power had all but disappeared from the region, and it was apparent that the United States had emerged as a global power with a strategic interest in seeking allies on the rim of the Soviet Union. The result was a U.S. decision to bring the Pakistanis into SEATO and urge them to join the Baghdad Pact, and to create a military relationship that was to shape America's strategic policies in South Asia for the next twenty years. Pakistan had been incorporated into the American strategy for dealing with Soviet power.

It was a policy that also unintentionally undermined India's role in South Asia. From the Indian perspective, American support for Pakistan prevented India from playing her "natural" role in the region. India's regional status was still further diminished in the 1962 war with China over the northern borders. At that time it was India that sought American as well as Soviet military assistance. The United States, then in conflict with China, provided India with limited military aid, limited because America was concerned with not jeopardizing its relationship with Pakistan.

As India's relationship with China deteriorated, Pakistan sought to build a cordial relationship with China following the old adage that the adversary of one's enemy is one's potential ally. That relationship has remained intimate since 1962.

In both 1965 and 1971 when India and Pakistan clashed, Pakistan sought Chinese political support. In both instances the Indian government was anxious about the possibility of Chinese military intervention, although in 1965 the Indians believed that the Chinese would be constrained by their concern over what the United States might do.

During the 1971 Bangladesh crisis, the rapprochement between the United States and China (initiated by the secret trip of Kissinger from Rawalpindi to Peking) led the Indian government to conclude that the United States was no longer a credible deterrent against Chinese intervention in a war between India and Pakistan. The Indian government concluded that in the light of Chinese and Soviet enmity, only a closer relationship between India and the Soviet Union would serve to deter the Chinese. And so, in the summer of 1971, India and the Soviet Union signed a Treaty of Mutual Friendship.

The smaller states in the region were also affected by the pattern of relations established by India and Pakistan to outside powers. As relations between India and China deteriorated in the 1960s, Sri Lanka took steps to improve its relations with both China and Pakistan as a means of reducing India's leverage. In the 1971 India-Pakistan-Bangladesh conflict, Sri Lanka supported Pakistan by providing the Pakistan air force with landing and refueling rights in Colombo.

Nepal, geographically caught between China and India, and eager to maintain good relations with both, sought and received assistance from both the Soviet Union and the United States as a means of avoiding too dependent a relationship on either or both of her near neighbors.

After the 1971 war, the new state of Bangladesh, even though her creation was opposed by the United States, turned to the United States for economic assistance, partly because the United States had resources that the new nation desperately needed, but also because the Bangladesh government wanted to avoid too heavy a dependence either upon India or the Soviet Union. The recent military coups accelerated this shift by opening the possibilities of closer ties between Bangladesh and both Pakistan and the oil producing Muslim states.

Clearly the regional security concerns of each of the countries of South Asia have been decisive in shaping their relationships with the great powers; indeed, these security concerns have clearly had priority over ideological affinities. The conservative, land-based military elite of Pakistan sought (and received!) Chinese support, while a democratically inclined India has worked closely with the Soviet Union. Moreover, regional security concerns have also had priority over economic development goals. In 1962, India sharply increased its military expenditures as a consequence of the conflict with China—a conflict which increased New Delhi's anxieties not only about China, but about Pakistan's military intentions in Kashmir. After the 1962 war, the Indian government concluded that Pakistan, with American arms and Chinese support, might make a major military effort to regain Kashmir, an assessment which proved demonstrably true only three years later.

America's *political* relations with Pakistan ultimately proved to be far more important in the United States relationship with India than American *economic* assistance to India. In the 1960s India was the largest single recipient of nonmilitary economic assistance, and in the famine years of 1965-66, the United States provided ten million tons of food. But many Indians came to see this assistance not as an effort to strengthen the Indian economy, but as a policy to increase Indian dependence upon the United States and to prevent India from becoming the politically dominant force in Southern Asia. This viewpoint, held initially only by members of the left-radical parties, became more widely shared after the United States supported Pakistan in the Bangladesh War. This policy, one of the two or three most disastrous policy decisions the United States has made in Asia in the postwar era, made Indians so distrustful of American power that what might otherwise have been a minor question of enlarging a base in Diego Garcia became a major thorn in United States-Indian relations.

America's long-term commitment to Pakistan, in retrospect another major error in postwar United States policy in Asia, more than counterbalanced whatever influence the United States might have exercised in India as a consequence of its aid program, but neither on the Bangladesh crisis nor on the nuclear proliferation treaty did American views prevail. When security issues, from India's point of view, were at stake, aid proved to be a less effective instrument for American influence than American policymakers anticipated— one reason, no doubt, for growing U.S. disillusionment with aid.

India as the Dominant Regional Power

The Indo-Pakistan War of 1971 and the events that followed have had a dramatic effect on these regional conflicts, on the role of India in the region, and on the position of external powers. The division of Pakistan into two states diminished Pakistan's role as a threat to India. The termination of American military aid to Pakistan and economic aid to India also sharply diminished the role of the United States in the region. India's military victory, along with the partition of Pakistan, assured India of a secure military position in the subcontinent. While Pakistan may continue to seek support from the United States, China, and Iran, it can no longer militarily challenge India as it did in the past. Every country in South Asia now recognizes that India is the overwhelmingly dominant military force.

India's military capabilities remain high even while its economic performance continues to be poor: India has one of the largest armies in the world, a substantial defense industry, an expanding air force and navy, and now nuclear capabilities for peacetime use that could, if India chose, be turned to military purposes. In building its own satellite, India further demonstrated the capacity to develop high level technology even while remaining an essentially poor country.

Since 1971, India has become increasingly interested in extending other types of power over countries in the subcontinent. It is the dominant trading partner of every one of the nations of South Asia, with the exception of Pakistan; India has a Trade and Transit Agreement with Nepal which places Nepal within the ambit of Indian trade policy; and India has sought to coordinate industrial development and trade policy with Bangladesh. India has private investment in each of these countries and has sought to expand bilateral investment relationships. India has been negotiating with Nepal for the development of hydroelectric power projects in Nepal which would provide irrigation and power for India, and there have been discussions of the possibility of developing the entire Gangetic River basin which would involve India, Bangladesh, and Nepal.

But India's capacity to be a "local Leviathan" like Iran, Brazil, South Africa, and Nigeria is substantially limited by its poor economic performance and by a variety of internal developments. For one thing, India is not an export-oriented country. It can provide its neighbors with some consumer goods, but it cannot supply oil, steel or heavy industrial machinery, nor are its neighbors wealthy enough to import India's limited production of cars, air conditioners, and other high cost consumer durables. India has no petrodollars for investment, and neither the Indian government nor businessmen are financially capable of large-scale investments in Nepal, Bangladesh, or Sri Lanka. Nor does New Delhi have the resources to develop the Ganges-Brahmaputra river system which flows through Nepal, Bangladesh, and India.

If we are to properly understand India's role as a regional power, it is essential that we take a closer look at its internal economic and political developments. In so doing, we shall also consider why it is that India maintained a stable and democratic regime in spite of its poor economic performance, why there has been a movement toward authoritarianism since mid-1975, and what effects such political changes may have on subsequent political developments and economic performance.

India's Internal Development

Stalemated Modernization: India in the Seventies

Since 1966, in all fields other than agriculture, India's attempts to modernize have been stalemated. Even the dramatic strides that India made in the late 1960s in agriculture have been halted, the casualty of drought and rising fertilizer and petroleum prices. Food production declined from a high of 108 million tons in 1970-71 to about a hundred million tons in 1974. Per capita foodgrain production in 1975, following an excellent monsoon, was still below 1970 level. Stagnation in industrial development set in around 1965-66, notably in the public sector. And since the country is dependent on public industries to generate funds for other development projects, stagnation in the public sector has affected the rest of the economy as well. Industrial growth during the Fourth Five-Year-Plan was only 4 percent annually. There have been shortages of steel, power, coal, fertilizers, and food. Real per capita income has been declining since 1971, and in 1974 it was approximately at the same level as 1969-70. In 1974, inflation was running at 30 percent annually. Meanwhile, the population continues to grow at 2.2 percent a year, or more than a million persons per month.

Throughout 1974 and early 1975, there were reports from all over India reflecting the disarray in the economy: six and a half-million tribals in Bihar were said to be near starvation in late 1974—many were trekking to nearby towns in search of food and employment; in West Bengal the relief minister estimated that fifteen million rural people, especially landless laborers, were "either starving or living on one meal a day"; in northern India an estimated fifteen thousand persons were reported as having died in a smallpox epidemic in late 1974; in Goalpara district, in Assam, several hundred-thousand people were subsisting on wild roots and leaves.

Political and social tensions were mounting. In the city of Madras, local Tamilians launched demonstrations against migrants from the neighboring state of Kerala who had taken "their" jobs. In Delhi, ten companies of Border Security Forces were sent to disturbed areas of the old city where shops and houses were burned and dozens injured in communal clashes between Hindus and Muslims. In Patna, capital city of Bihar, a demonstration of a half-million persons marched on the state assembly to protest corruption, high prices, and food shortages. In Gujarat, student-led demonstrations against the state government led to the resignation of the chief minister, the establishment of central government rule over the entire state, then new elections which brought a non-Congress coalition to power. A national protest movement against the government, led by Jayaprakash Narayan, an aged and ailing Gandhian, became the rallying point for much of the opposition to the government.

In the months prior to Mrs. Gandhi's declaration of a national emergency, journalists described a political order that seemed incapable of arresting the economic decline. Ved Mehta, an Indian correspondent writing from New Delhi, described the country as a place in which "fear, corruption and violence" have become a way of life. B.G. Verghese, noted editor of the *Hindustan Times*, wrote that the country was experiencing a "moral rot," that "rising prices, shortages, corruption, adulteration, untaxed 'black' money, economic stagnation, empty sloganizing, indecision, and mismanagement have bred cynicism, frustration, indiscipline, anger and violence."

Few believed that the country was on the brink of revolution. "Revolution is not round the corner," wrote Verghese, for "that too connotes a larger purpose, a central effort, direction. The alternative is riots, a slide to anarchy, the weakening of central authority, a petty warlordism, and external pressures." And to those who said that things could not go on as they were, Ved Mehta approvingly quoted Galbraith as saying that India is a "functioning anarchy." Among both Indian and Western observers there was (and continues to be) a sense of foreboding: India could either move in the direction of a major political transformation—a political revolution, praetorian takeover, an authoritarian leadership—or, alternatively, slide steadily into greater corruption, disorder, and some form of "warlordism" or decentralized units of authority that resist central control. Few observers saw the political structure as in a state of equilibrium.

While the crisis led some to conclude that "something must be done" to break out of the stalemate, others, notably Philip Handler, president of the National Academy of Sciences, expressing a view widely shared by many in the West, concluded that the situation in South Asia was so hopeless that unless the West was prepared to take massive steps it would be more merciful to do nothing while using resources to assist other countries more likely to succeed. Thus, he argued, the humanitarian concept of aiding the neediest should give way to the more hard-headed goal of aiding those who have the best chance of survival and growth.

It was in this psychological environment that Mrs. Gandhi chose to arrest the opposition and suspend democratic rights. She blamed the opposition for politically exploiting the rising prices and food shortages (which she attributed to external events beyond the control of the government and to the venality of hoarders and blackmarketeers), while the opposition parties naturally blamed the government for the mismanagement of the economy, corruption, and administrative ineffectiveness.

In the months before the declaration of an emergency, vocal and organized opposition to the government came from the most modern (some might say the most privileged) sector of the country, the very groups which provided Mrs. Gandhi political support in her battle for political power within the Congress party in 1969 and 1970. The Congress Working Committee, in a resolution supporting the decision of the prime minister to establish emergency rule, pointed to the growth of "organized strikes, go slow movements by Government employees, Railway employees and industrial employees . . . student agitations and indiscipline," all urban-centered protest movements.

The establishment of an emergency brought to an end—for how long it is not certain—strikes, student demonstrations, and protest movements, while there was an immediate improvement in the performance both of the economy and the administration. But the country's long-term problems remain.

The Demographic Multiplier: India in the Eighties

In assessing India's prospects and the critical problems its government is likely to face in the near future, we shall first consider the country's demographic trends. Then there is an analysis of some of the key factors that have affected economic performance, and finally, the government's political response and the problems it is likely to face in the next decade are reviewed.

While predicting political events for India in the next ten years is highly hazardous, certain kinds of economic and social changes can be predicted with a reasonably high level of probability. Indeed, some kinds of changes, particularly those involving demographic events, can be estimated within a close range of error since there is very little likelihood that the changes that could take place within the next decade are likely to affect the outcome by 1985. We know, for example, how many children there will be of school age, how many young people will be entering the labor force, and how many women will be in the reproductive age group. To the extent that these demographic changes are virtually assured, there are a number of likely corollaries.

Other kinds of social and economic changes—such as the size of India's urban areas, the extent of rural density, levels of agricultural and industrial productivity, the rate of unemployment, the number of children attending school, the size of the literate and illiterate populations—are more difficult to predict, but even some of these developments are closely related to demographic trends, and some predictions seem fairly likely, given current tendencies.

What these changes will mean for the stability of the Indian political system, for the kind of leadership likely to emerge, for the kind of regime India is likely to have, for the kinds of policies likely to be chosen, are all problematic. But on two points we can be reasonably firm. The first is that many of the demographic, social, and economic trends now at work seem unlikely, and in some instances almost impossible, to be substantially affected by governmental policies in the next few years. They will take place almost irrespective of what government does, although in some instances governmental action could make things a little better or a little worse. Conceivably, a change in regime or some major changes in government policy might set a new course, but even then some of the processes at work could not be substantially affected within a decade.

Second, many of these changes will be the "givens" confronting any political system in the mid-eighties; whether India is governed by an authoritarian leadership of the Left or Right, a radical regime, the military, or returns to an openly competitive system of party government, these are some of the realities which will face whoever governs.

Population Growth. In 1971, India's population was 547 million. In 1986, it is unlikely to be less than 750 million, or more than two hundred million larger. What makes this outcome so likely is that the number of women in the childbearing ages, from fifteen to forty-five, has sharply increased from 115 million in 1971 to 129 million in 1976; their number will grow to 146 million by 1981, and 165 million by 1986. Since all the women who will be of childbearing age for 1986 have already been born, these figures could only be changed by some major catastrophe that would sharply increase mortality. It is this 42 percent increase in the number of women of the childbearing ages that will ensure India's high growth rate of the Indian population, even if there is an acceleration in the decline in the birthrate.

In 1986, India will have 43 million more children in the five to fourteen age group than it had in 1971, an increase of about 30 percent. It will take a very considerable increase in public expenditures simply to continue to provide primary and secondary school education for the same proportion as now attend school. To provide universal education for all in this age group—an unfulfilled objective of the Indian government since the goal was declared by the Indian constitution of 1950—will be exceedingly difficult.

Indeed, it seems likely that a larger number of Indians will be illiterate in 1986 than at present, not in terms of percentages, but in absolute numbers.

While the percentage of literates has continued to rise since independence, the annual increments in population have been greater than the annual additions to the number of literates; thus each year the number of illiterates has increased. In 1961, 335 million Indians were illiterate, and in 1971 390 million, although the number of literates rose substantially from 105 to 160 million. Compared to some developing countries, India spends disproportionately large sums on higher education and less on primary and secondary school education. Only a major campaign to expand primary and secondary schools (probably at the cost of investment in higher education) and massively to increase adult literacy, something comparable to the Cuban efforts of the 60s, could reverse the current trend.

Mortality Decline. It seems likely that India's mortality rate will continue to decline. In spite of the persistence of many endemic diseases, occasional epidemics, malnutrition, and periodic famines, India's death rate has been declining. Public health facilities continue to improve and per capita food consumption has, seen from the perspective of twenty-five years, increased. Since 1951, the per capita production of food grains (wheat, rice, corn, millet, sorghum, and legumes such as beans, peas, and peanuts) has increased by about 16 percent. The production of wheat, rice, and corn has increased from a little over 40 million tons in 1950 to past the 100 million mark in the early seventies. Some of the increases in food production, especially in the 1950s, have been attained by expanding the area of land under cultivation, but since the early sixties much of the increase has been the result of more intensive agriculture. Fertilizer consumption has risen sharply from less than 100 thousand tons in 1953 to 300 thousand tons in 1960, 784 thousand in 1965, 2 million tons in 1969-70, and 3 million tons in 1972-73, a thirtyfold increase in twenty years, with the sharpest increases after 1965-66. In 1972-73, 40 percent of India's fertilizers were imported, but internal fertilizer production continues to grow more rapidly than imports. Since an assured water supply is a condition for the intensive application of fertilizers, the expansion of irrigation facilities is likely to be accompanied by a growing demand for fertilizers. But, compared to the United States, fertilizer use in India is low.

While there may have been an increase in the number of deaths through malnutrition and starvation in 1974, the long-term decline in the death rate is likely to continue. For one thing, an improvement in the internal movement of food supplies, and India's ability to purchase food on the world market precludes the kind of death rate which India experienced in the past two hundred years. It has been estimated that a third of the population of Bengal (10 million persons) perished in the great famine of 1769-70; in Uttar Pradesh some 800,000 persons died in 1838, and in Bengal, Orissa and Rajputana an estimated 2.5 million persons died in the famines of 1866-69. In modern times some 1.5 million people died in the wartime famine in Bengal of 1943; but these famines occurred when the British imperial government was unwilling or unable to import vast quantities of food grains from the world market and distribution facilities were less developed.

Moreover, even a rise in mortality during a period of famine seems unlikely to affect the trend toward increased longevity, if only because the long-term tendency in food production continues to be upward, in spite of periodic droughts and floods.

The so-called Malthusian positive checks as a solution to India's problem of high population growth is hardly a solution at all; for one thing, it seems unlikely that any Indian government would stand by deliberately without taking steps to import food grains and improve distribution from more to less prosperous regions. (Droughts are usually confined to a few regions of the country and are almost never nationwide.) Moreover, even a death rate of historic magnitude would have a negligible impact on current rates of population growth, given the sheer size of India's population. A loss of a million lives is equal to the country's population increase of less than a single month. Death through famine is more likely to occur among the very young and the old, less among the fertile age groups. The death of a large number of infants in one year may be compensated for by an effort of couples to bear children the following year when food grain production has returned more nearly to normal.

India's population problems will be relieved not by an increase in mortality, but by a decline in fertility. Such a decline is already well under way. India's birthrate is about 38 per thousand, but there is evidence of a decline, especially in the more developed states like the Punjab and Tamil Nadu. The drop in infant mortality, the expansion of female education, the growing availability of contraceptives, the later age of nuptiality that accompanies an increase in education, and increased urbanization, all play a role in reducing fertility.

Urban Growth. Where will India's additional two hundred million people live? Between 1961 and 1971 India's urban population grew by 38 percent, compared to a rural increase of 22 percent, bringing India's urban population up to 109 million. About 70 million persons lived in towns exceeding 50,000, compared to 45 million a decade earlier. Population increases were greatest in cities containing more than a hundred thousand. In 1971, 10.4 percent lived in cities of this size, in comparison with 9 percent in 1961 and 6.5 percent in 1951. By 1981, if urban growth continues at the present rate, 103 million Indians will live in cities containing over 50,000 persons; by 1991 these urban settlements will contain 152 million Indians.

In short, urban growth is nearly twice the rural growth rate. In 1961, slightly less than one out of every nine Indians lived in a town of 50,000 persons; in 1971, it was one out of eight; by 1991, given the present rate of population growth and rural-urban migration, one out of every five-and-a-half Indians will live in a town or city larger than 50,000 persons. If there is no change in the present rate of rural to urban migration, about 62 million of India's 200 million additional population in 1986 will live in urban areas (of any size), while 138 million will live in the countryside.

Compared to many Third World countries, the rate of migration from the countryside to the cities is low in India. In many countries of South America and Africa, migration rates are double that of India. But even at India's present comparatively low rate of urbanization, by the mid-1980s India's urban population should increase from the 109 million of 1971 to over 170 million. More than half of this population—about 90 million—will live in settlements exceeding 100,000 persons.

The single most important political consequence of urban growth is that both the central and state governments will have to give more attention to the urban areas. For one thing, whatever problems India's cities now have—water and power shortages, overcrowded schools, unemployment, traffic congestion, pollution, etc.—are sure to be worse as a consequence of an urban growth rate in the 50-60 percent range over fifteen years.

Even with only 10 percent of India's electorate living in settlements larger than 100,000 persons, India's cities and towns have played a politically influential role that exceeded their numbers. The urban areas are important recruiting grounds for all the major political parties, particularly among the urban (and college-educated) youth. Moreover, urban constituencies tend to be more closely contested than rural constituencies, so that in a period when control over state governments by a party or coalition of parties is precarious these closely contested constituencies increase in importance. The massive defeat of Congress party candidates in urban constituencies in the 1967 elections—when Congress lost elections in half of the states and had a narrow majority in the national parliament—made Prime Minister Gandhi acutely aware of the need to offer a program and ideology that would bring the urban vote back to Congress. In the 1967 elections Congress won only eighteen out of the fifty-two urban parliamentary constituencies. After the Congress party split, the new Congress held only thirteen seats, including one each in Hyderabad, Bombay, and Calcutta. Many of Mrs. Gandhi's populist policies—the nationalization of the banks, the passage of the Monopolies Act, and fixed fair price food shops in the towns—were directed at winning support from urban voters. Mrs. Gandhi's strategy apparently succeeded, for in the 1971 elections Congress won thirty-three of the fifty-two urban constituencies.

Mrs. Gandhi succeeded in winning back the urban vote with a national program rather than with an urban development policy. If political parties pay little attention to urban problems as such, it is partly because municipal governments have few powers, and still fewer fiscal resources, so that municipal elections cannot readily be waged over questions of urban policy. India's urban problems are not easily handled within the existing governmental structures. Municipal governments are almost wholly dependent upon state and central authorities for funds for airport, bridges, roads, and for any forms of mass transportation, including bus lines and suburban trains. Urban real estate taxes are low, and there are almost no significant revenue sources that would make it possible for municipal governments to engage in any large-scale development and planning. Moreover, there are few metropolitan planning and development bodies capable of dealing with the range of problems confronting India's growing urban centers. As for the central government, it has thus far paid little attention to planning for India's urban growth.

Rural Growth. In the United States and in other developed countries, urban growth has been accompanied by a decline in rural population. No such development is taking place in India. In 1971, 438 million Indians lived in the countryside. In 1986, the number will increase to 576 million.

In many areas there has been an alarming increase in the number of landless agricultural laborers. Between 1961 and 1971 the proportion of the work force working as agricultural laborers increased from 16.7 percent to 25.7 percent in the country as a whole. Given the growth of the agricultural labor force this increase represents an *absolute*, not simply a relative increase in the number of rural people working as low income agricultural laborers.

The reasons for this growth need to be carefully examined; it appears to reflect a shift from tenant farming to wage-labor, the unintended consequence of land reform legislation that made it possible for landowners to dismiss tenants and "resume" cultivation themselves. The absolute growth also reflects the demographic trends of the early and mid-fifties when infant mortality dropped among the lowest economic groups.

During periods of declining food production, the agricultural laborers are the worst hit group, but politically they are the most difficult to organize, for they lack the economic power to disrupt the economy that gives the industrial working class, railway and communication workers, and government employees their political power.

With an increase in rural density, pressures will continue for more rather than less intensive agriculture, that is, for increasing the use of manpower in agriculture rather than for increasing the use of labor-saving machinery. Land holdings will be smaller. Legislation imposing ceilings on land holdings precludes the acquisition of additional land by larger landowners, while the system of equal inheritance to sons that prevail in most of India tends to increase land fragmentation during a period of rural population growth.

Since there is little remaining unused land in India suitable for cultivation, peasants will attempt to increase production on ever-*decreasing* acreage per person; the need to maintain *existing* levels of productivity *per person* on smaller holdings is now the single most important incentive for increasing productivity.

Peasants will respond in expected ways; they will want to increase irrigation on land in order to carry on double cropping, while to increase the productivity of each crop peasants will need to purchase more fertilizers, high yielding varieties of seeds, pesticides, pumps for irrigation, and fuel for the pumps. To purchase these inputs, cash is required—small farmers must obtain credit and they must produce some cash crops to repay loans. Thus, population growth in the countryside, by intensifying pressures for more inputs into agriculture, forces small land-holders to enter commercial markets. Increasingly, international prices of fertilizers, insecticides, pumps, and fuel affect more and more of India's peasants. Rural population growth thus contributes to linking the future well-being of India's peasants to developments in the international market.

Unemployment and Education. According to the Planning Commission, in 1971 India's labor force was 170 million people. In 1974 it was estimated at 183 million, and in 1986 it is expected to reach 248 million, an increase of 65 million in only twelve years. Estimates of unemployment are notoriously unreliable, since the lines between unemployment, underemployment, and employment with low productivity are not easily drawn. In 1969, the Planning Commission reported that 9 to 10 million persons were unemployed, though a special governmental committee on unemployment estimated that in 1972 some 18.7 million persons were in search of jobs. One prominent Indian economist, Raj Krishna, put the figure in 1971 at 21.5 million as those unemployed or severely underemployed and available for additional work.

The rate of population growth for the next fifteen years will have no effect on the size of the labor force, for everyone entering the labor force now, and until the year 1990, has already been born. In 1971, 28 million Indian males were in the 15-19 age group; in 1981, the number will be 38 million; in 1986, it will be 41.4 million; and in 1991, it will be 45.6 million. Each year the number of people entering the urban labor force exceeds the number of jobs available, and each year the number of graduates of secondary schools and universities far exceeds the employment opportunities. The result is a growing backlog of unemployed, in the urban as well as in the rural areas. More and more young men are dependent upon their families for support rather than becoming sources of family incomes.

Indian politics has thus far been less vulnerable to increases in the number of unemployed than the politics of advanced industrial societies largely because of the traditions of collectively shared family income. However, the political problem has become more acute in recent years, partly because of the magnitude of unemployment, but also because of the growing number of young men expecting to enter middle class life as a consequence of their education. The educational system provides opportunities for mobility while the employment market restricts those opportunities. The result has been an increasing demand on the part of the local urban middle classes to restrict the employment of migrants from other states, while giving preferences to local people. Similarly, there are demands for expanding public sector employment, demands that local firms (often owned by people from other states) hire locally or be nationalized, and that there be quotas for particular caste, linguistic, tribal or religious groups to ensure that each ethnic group has its share of whatever employment opportunities there are.

The growth in educated middle class unemployment has accelerated as a consequence of two factors: the low rate of investment growth (Raj Krishna estimates that the rate of investment has been declining or stagnating since its peak of 13.4 percent in 1965 to less than 10 percent per year between 1968 and 1972), and the rapid expansion of the educational system at the matriculation and college levels. Paradoxically, an important political incentive for expanding college enrollment has been the increasing unemployment of secondary school graduates. As unemployment increases, parents send their children to college with the hope that additional education will increase their chances of securing employment. The expansion of higher education has not actually increased unemployment, but it has tended to transfer unemployment from rural to urban areas, from unskilled to the skilled labor markets, from the laboring classes to the middle classes. The expansion of secondary school and higher education has meant that the unemployed are increasingly more educated, more urban and more middle class in aspirations.

Unemployment has been politically important in shaping the demands of states against the central government, less developed regions within states making demands upon state governments, and local political parties leading clashes against migrants. There is, in other words, a close relationship between higher education, unemployment, and regional political protest. Thus far, it has not taken the form of insurrectionary movements as it has in neighboring Sri Lanka, where the expansion of employment opportunities also failed to keep pace with the production of graduates. The openness of the Indian political system, the opportunities for political change at the state level through the electoral process, the political skill of governmental and party leadership in coopting dissenting leaders, the role played by the pro-Soviet Communist party in supporting Mrs. Gandhi's government and in opposing pro-Chinese insurrectionary elements, and the skill of the police and intelligence services in seizing weapons and in arresting insurgents have prevented a replication of Sri Lanka's experience, but there should be little doubt that the potentiality for regional insurrections or urban guerilla warfare remains high. To the extent that there is a decline in the opportunities for political change through the electoral process and a diminished need on the part of an authoritarian government to coopt dissidents, there may be a continued expansion of the intelligence services, greater use of the police, and a general rise in governmental coercion.

Critical Issues. To recapitulate: rapid population growth, a consequence of a more significant and rapid decline in the death than in the birthrate, will increase India's population by some 200 million in the mid-1980s over the last census of

1971. The result will be a rapid increase in the urban population, increased density in the countryside, a growth in the number of school age children, and an increase in the number of young people entering the labor force each year. India's government in the mid-1980s will be faced with larger numbers of illiterates, growing unemployment, increased urban congestion, and growing pressures from the countryside to produce (or import) more fertilizers, seeds, and petroleum, all essential inputs needed to maintain, if not expand, existing per capita food consumption.

These are the inescapable consequences of past and present demographic trends. No matter how successfully India reduces fertility in the next decade, there will be an unprecedented increase in the number of school age children, secondary school and college graduates, couples entering the fertile age groups, new urban dwellers, and peasants engaged in agriculture.

In the mid-80s, the gap in income between India and the developed world is likely to grow while the gap between Indians is likely to be even larger. For what gap can be greater than between those who are employed and those who are not, between those who are malnourished and those who are well fed, between those who are illiterate and those who are graduates of the universities?

The gap is likely to be particularly acute between regions. The country as a whole may progress slowly, and some urban centers and states seem likely to grow relatively rapidly, but other areas of the country will, at best, experience slow growth. This is particularly true of the Hindi-speaking region and the economically hard-hit urban centers of West Bengal, especially Calcutta.

Regional disparities within states are a source of acute political strain because the less developed regions demand a greater share of the state's expenditures on development as well as proportional representation in state employment. States with substantial exports complain that they are not given the foreign exchange earnings they deserve to accelerate their own industrial development, while the backward states demand a larger share of the central government's developmental funds. While these conflicts do not presage either the disintegration of states (though many Indians argue that the larger states like Uttar Pradesh would be more easily governable if they were broken into smaller units) or the dissolution of the Indian union, they make governance more difficult and hinder attempts to forge such interstate agreements of sharing of hydroelectric power and developing and sharing of irrigation facilities.

There is, however, one bright possibility in what may otherwise appear to be a picture of unrelieved gloom—the likelihood that millions of peasants, each faced with the prospect of declining income from his dwindling landholdings, will seek to increase their productivity. How successful that effort will be depends upon what government does to provide irrigation, fertilizers, seeds and other necessities, and the role played by international market forces and international politics in making such inputs available.

Economic Performance in Retrospect

The performance of the Indian economy for the last decade has been disappoint-
ing. True enough, the economic upturn which took place in India after
independence was a marked change from the preceding period of extended
stagnation, but India's long-term economic growth over a twenty-five-year
period has hovered around 3.5 percent per annum, little more than a 1 percent
per capita rise per year. Seen in historic terms, this is no mean accomplishment,
not only for India, but even from the perspective of Western industrialized
nations during their early years of growth. Nevertheless, it is far below the high
growth developing countries have achieved, far below what India is capable of
doing, given both the human and natural resources of the country, and far below
planned targets. Moreover, in recent years even this growth rate has not been
sustained.

Two broad factors account for the low rate of growth, those related to India's
external relations and a series of "external" developments which government did
not anticipate, and those that are internal, that is, are the consequences of
choices made by the government of India that have resulted in the misuse of
India's resources to the detriment of its economic growth.

External Constraints. India experienced a substantial economic upturn in the
1950s: there was a modest expansion in agricultural production after more than
fifty years of stagnation and a similar movement forward in industry and the
development of infrastructures—hydroelectric power, irrigation, and transport.
India's war with China in 1962 was a setback, not only because the war
temporarily dislocated the economy, but because India then diverted a considerable proportion of its resources to expanding its army, enlarging its defense
industries, and importing military equipment. The economy barely adjusted to
these changes when war broke out with Pakistan in 1965. Again, there might
have been an upturn had the country not experienced two years of drought that
brought down food production, depressed industry, and generated a foreign
exchange shortage and an overvalued currency.

In 1969-71, India's agricultural production increased as a consequence of the
widespread adoption of new agricultural practices, particularly in the use of
fertilizers and new high yielding varieties of grain. For the first time, India
established a substantial food reserve. But the Bangladesh crisis in early 1971,
the influx of millions of refugees into India, the war with Pakistan, all followed
by rising fertilizer and petroleum prices, and another two years of bad weather
in northern India arrested the growth of agriculture and forced India to use up
its limited food reserves. In 1974, 80 percent of India's annual export earnings
were spent on importing food, oil, and fertilizers. Nearly a half billion dollars
was spent on importing fertilizers. Again, India's economy spiraled downward

with food shortages, industrial stagnation, inflation, unemployment, and a dwindling foreign exchange reserve made worse by growing debt repayments and declining aid. Thus, the failures in the performance of the Indian economy can partially be attributed to events largely out of the control of India's policy-makers.

Internal Constraints. How much of India's slow and erratic growth can be attributed to poor economic policy and governmental mismanagement is a matter of some controversy. India's public sector firms have not done well, suffering from (a) shortages of equipment, spare parts, materials, and power, (b) labor problems, and (c) inadequate industrial management. There have been production shortfalls in the two industries which together utilized 45 percent of the public sector investment in the Fourth Five-Year-Plan—steel and fertilizers. There is a high demand for both and, it is argued, India should be able to produce both at competitive prices. India has a sufficiently abundant supply both of coal and iron ore to become an exporter of steel, but with severe labor difficulties, power shortages, underproduction in coal, and poor management, steel production continues to remain far short of meeting current demand. As for fertilizer production, existing plants are used at less than 70 percent of capacity; moreover, in spite of the rapid growth in demand, government has tended to move slowly in licensing new fertilizer plants. In 1972-73, India produced only 1.8 million tons, importing another 1.2 million tons to meet domestic demand.

Nor has the private sector performed well. A cumbersome system of industrial licensing has tended to delay private investments, and, since 1969, legislation intended to prevent the growth of monopolies and the concentration of economic power has hampered the expansion of larger firms, including firms that had proposed to expand fertilizer production.

The import substitution policy pursued by India created protected domestic markets so that private firms did not aggressively seek export markets. Nor were Indian prices competitive with similar manufactured goods produced elsewhere in the world. In recent years there have been some efforts to move from an import substitution policy to a more export oriented outlook—by providing export incentives, and by depreciating the rupee in relation to other currencies. In the past two years, India's export earnings have increased by 30 percent, but mostly as a consequence of higher world prices rather than an increase in export volume.

India's long-term growth rate in agriculture from independence to the early 70s has been at the rate of 3.5 percent per year; there have been substantial fluctuations—some declining years and a few spectacular years—but the long-term trend continues to be moving slightly ahead of population growth. From 1972 to 1974, water shortages plus shortages of inputs—fertilizers, power for irrigation and mechanization, and improved seeds—pushed production downward. The fertilizer shortage might not have been so great if the government had accepted proposals made by private firms to enlarge fertilizer capacity, if the existing public sector firms were more productive, or if India had purchased larger quantities of fertilizer in the world market in 1973 rather than postponed purchases in the hope that prices would decline.

India's energy crisis, which hampered efforts to expand production both in agriculture and industry, was made worse by falls in hydroelectric power generation, the result of drought, machinery breakdowns, shortages of spare parts, strikes by engineers, and other labor difficulties. According to one estimate, the supply of electric power during the Fourth Five-Year-Plan increased at 6 percent per annum, while the annual demand grew at 11 percent.

The story is much the same in coal production. India has one of the world's largest reserves of coal, but coal continues to remain in short supply. Production targets have not been met; again, there have been problems in management and organization, and a deteriorating labor situation. Moreover, as a consequence of problems in transporting coal by rail, supplies have not been delivered to industries when needed. Failures in coal production and distribution and in the supply of electric power have been major factors in the low level of productivity of India's industrial plants. If India were to make greater use of its *existing* industrial capacity, there would be a substantial increase in the availability of goods, a growth in savings, an expansion in government revenues, and an easing of India's domestic resource difficulties.

Domestic resource difficulties have intensified in recent years; again, both internal and external factors are responsible. The war with Pakistan, the need to care for Bengali refugees, and to provide famine-struck Bangladesh with assistance out of India's limited food reserves were all major setbacks in 1971 and 1972. Thereafter, two years of drought reduced the growth in tax revenues while increasing expenditures for drought relief. There were substantial pay increases to government employees, reflecting the greater capacity of government workers than other sectors of the labor force to present organized demands for raises to meet the rising inflation. One consequence is that an increasingly smaller proportion of government resources was available for development expenditures.

The revenue position of the state and central governments improved in 1975. This was partially the result of inflation and partially the consequence of a successful campaign to tax "black" money by promising taxpayers that they would be free of prosecution and could pay lower tax rates if they voluntarily disclosed their untaxed income. For the first time in several years an increased proportion of government resources were available for development expenditures.

The more successful agriculturalists whose income has risen remain largely undertaxed. The Indian constitution precludes central government taxation on agricultural income, a power left exclusively in the hands of state governments controlled by the more prosperous farmers; the result is that state governments neither tax agricultural income nor impose "betterment" levies, substantial irrigation and water use taxes, or other fiscal measures which would ensure that peasants whose incomes have risen pay a larger share of taxes.

Unlike some low income countries, India's potential for rapid economic growth is high. India has coal reserves of 80 billion tons, while annual production remains less than 80 million tons a year. Some 10 percent of the world's high-grade iron resources are located in India, along with substantial deposits of bauxite, copper, diamonds, manganese, and phosphate. Its hydroelectric potential, especially in northern India where there are assured runoffs from the Himalayan snows, is considerable and only marginally developed. While there have been substantial efforts to increase the installed capacity of power generating facilities, the achievements have been well below targeted objectives. (In the Fourth Five-Year-Plan only half of the planned additions to capacity were actually built.) India's offshore oil deposits also continue to remain largely unutilized, though recent explorations in the Gulf of Cambay, north of Bombay, are currently underway. Recent studies suggest that India may have a substantial offshore petroleum reserve.

Finally, India's greatest productive potential, its enormous agricultural industry, remains one of the largest underdeveloped agricultural landmasses in the world. In the few areas where irrigation has been extended, and seeds, fertilizers, pesticides, and other inputs made available, production has rapidly increased, but only 20 percent of India's agricultural land is presently assured of rainfall or irrigation, and India's fertilizer consumption in 1972-73 was, as we have noted, only 3 million tons—a more than sixfold increase in a decade (from 477,000 tons in 1962-63)—but no more than Americans consume for their lawns and golf courses. Per hectare application of fertilizers in India for 1970-71 was 13 kg, as against 749 for the Netherlands and 580 for New Zealand.

While India's failure to utilize effectively her own resources has been handicapped by external considerations—"external" including acts of nature, as well as wars with Pakistan and China, international price rises in fertilizers, petroleum, and food, and the unfavorable terms of trade for many of India's commodities—much of the responsibility lies with the kinds of policies adopted by the Indian government.

What weight one gives to "external" rather than "internal" factors shapes one's perspective as to India's long-term economic prospects and the role which might be played through international transfers in accelerating India's development. This controversy has also given rise to a growing interest in exploring the political economy of growth, that is, in examining both the structure of power in the Indian political system and the ideological underpinnings of policies. This also leads us to consider why it is that a country in which the growth rate has been so slow and erratic and income disparities have been increasing, succeeded in maintaining a stable and democratic political structure for so long and, in turn, in what ways that political system created constraints on economic development. Such an analysis will permit us to consider whether the shift toward a stronger center and an authoritarian government might offer the prospects of releasing new forces or generating new policies that could accelerate the country's economic development.

The Political Economy of Development

For many years India provided an extraordinary contrast between her economic failures and its political successes. While the leadership has not been skillful at coping with economic affairs, the tensions that elsewhere in the developing world led to unstable governments, praetorian regimes and civil war were, until 1975, effectively handled by India's political leadership within a democratic framework.

The Management of Ethnic Conflict. Consider, for example, India's success in the management of ethnic conflict for the past twenty-eight years. As is well known, India is a multi-ethnic society and, in common with most societies with divergent races, tribes, languages, and religions, her ethnic conflicts have tended to take precedence over class conflicts. India has a dozen major languages, a large Muslim population (it is the third largest Muslim country in the world, and has more Muslims than any country in the Middle East), 35 million tribals and numerous castes.

In the mid-50s India appeared to be threatened by movements for the creation of linguistically homogeneous states. These conflicts took a variety of political forms: demands for secession, demands for autonomous, culturally homogeneous states, and demands for control over education and employment. Hardly a year has passed since independence that one region or another has not been afflicted with ethnic conflicts, sometimes electorally, but more often in the streets, the bazaars, and in the fields. These conflicts are frequently perceived incorrectly outside of India as a sign of that country's impending disintegration. Can a society with such enormous internal differences long endure, or will India join the lengthy list of moribund multi-ethnic empires that litter the history books—such as the Ottoman and Hapsburg empires? And would an authoritarian regime have been better able to manage these ethnic conflicts?

Viewed from a comparative perspective, India has not done badly in the management of ethnic conflict; certainly better than Pakistan's military regime that proved so inept at coping with the claims of the Bengalis, and certainly better than the Nigerians and several other ethnically-torn African states. Indeed, over the past twenty-eight years India's national leaders have demonstrated an almost instinctive feeling for when to be responsive and when to use force, and how best to negotiate political settlements that will reduce the level of conflict.

Nehru successfully unraveled his way through the linguistic controversies of the 1950s, and while the creation of linguistic states has been accompanied by a new set of problems, it successfully dissipated what threatened to be a long drawn-out period of linguistic conflict within more than half the states. Similarly, Mrs. Gandhi managed to resolve some of the tribal conflicts in India's northeast, areas where the famous Nagas and Mizos were engaged in armed revolts against the government, while elsewhere in India other tribes, though less violent, also demanded greater political autonomy. The Indian government appears, in the main, to have had better success in coping with the tribes than the other states of southern Asia who have also had difficulties in dealing with the rebellious, militant, independent tribals that dwell in the hill zones extending from northern Afghanistan, through northern Pakistan, northern India, the hill tracts of Bangladesh, the northern regions of Burma, and further across Southeast Asia into Laos, Cambodia, and Vietnam.

Order-Maintaining Structures. At least three factors appear to have been particularly crucial in India's success thus far in the management of ethnic conflict. One is related to the peculiarities of its social structure, the other to her political structure, a third to the organization and use of political intelligence.

India is a highly segmented social system. Each state has its own peculiar ethnic configuration. Conflicts within a state—ethnic or otherwise—do not readily affect most of the other states. The demands of a linguistic or tribal group in one state—either for autonomy or for more services—ordinarily does not affect demand-making in other states, that is, not to the extent it would if the ethnic group resided in many states and the country had a highly developed system of mass communication. For this reason, government can handle one conflict at a time without having to face the kind of massive national problem that was experienced by both Nigeria and Pakistan. The government's handling of conflicts in Assam has had little impact on Kerala or Andhra, and while the government must take precedent into account, it is often free to choose a solution that seems to be politically appropriate in one region while opting for quite a different solution elsewhere. Thus, the government accepted the demands for statehood by some tribes but not by others, and acceded to the demand for a separate state by the Sikhs in the Punjab, but rejected a similar demand by the Telengana region of Andhra.

The democratic and federal system lent itself well to the management of ethnic conflict. The federal arrangement permitted the central government to provide political autonomy to groups that have territorial contiguity and political cohesion, without jeopardizing the powers of the central government. The democratic system, by making it necessary for party leaders to be responsive to groups with electoral power, tended to make political leadership sensitive to acutely felt concerns. National and state leaders also learned to dissipate demands by coopting the leaders of ethnic communities. By giving posts within the party or government to dissident tribal leaders, Muslims, scheduled castes, and minority leaders in each of the states, the Congress party was also able to attract leaders who were often able to ensure that their followers would continue in election after election to vote for the ruling party. Thus, by satisfying the desire for sharing power and wealth by the leaders of minority groups, the governing party at a relatively low cost has been able to maintain the political loyalty of low income communities.

In assessing the capacity of India's political leadership to cope with ethnic conflicts—or, for that matter, any kind of political conflicts including trade union-management conflicts, agrarian conflicts, and party and factional struggles—one should not underestimate the importance of intelligence gathering services or law enforcement institutions. Through the Home Ministry the central government has been able to keep remarkably well-informed as to what has been happening in any part of this large country. Some of India's most capable administrators have spent a substantial part of their career in the Home Ministry; the Ministry is itself in charge of personnel appointments and transfers for the entire central government, so that the Ministry has the first pick of talent within the senior administrative cadre. It is the Home Ministry—working with the prime minister—that had responsibility for the management of the states reorganization controversy, for the integration of the princely states into the Indian Union, for the management of the tribal areas, for central government policy toward Kashmir, for intelligence gathering on the frontiers, for decisions concerning the takeover by the central government of unstable states, and for the intelligence and police activities involved in counterinsurgency activities (from the Communist insurgency in Hyderabad in the late 40s to the pro-Chinese Naxalite movement in the late 60s and early 70s). Moreover, while the police services are under the control of the state governments, there are central reserve forces and a number of other special police units that are directly under the management of the Home Ministry of the central government. The Indian constitution provides that in the event a state is politically unstable or is unable to maintain law and order, the central government may take control over a state and establish "President's Rule," or, in effect, rule by the central administrative services. Since it is the Home Ministry that takes primary responsibility for state governance in the event of President's Rule, Home Ministry officials have a special authority in relationship to state governments not possessed by other central government ministries.

The skill with which the Indian political leadership balanced competing interests and claims, assessed the electoral power of those who made claims, coopted dissidents, and reached out into the countryside for political support has been quite extraordinary. No doubt the capacity—both through the Home Ministry and the Congress party—to acquire political intelligence, the coercive instruments at the government's disposal, and the many resources with which government can reward those who support it and deny to those who do not are all elements in this skill. Nonetheless, there is an added, not easily defined element of political acumen, a kind of sensitivity to the political market place that Nehru, Shastri and, until mid-1975, Prime Minister Gandhi displayed. Should India be governed by an authoritarian regime, its capacity to be responsive to competing claims and to cope *politically* with secessionist movements may well decline, thereby forcing government to rely more heavily than in the past upon its coercive powers.

Prime Minister Gandhi's Government. Mrs. Gandhi took office in 1966, a year of drought and famine, when India was dependent upon the United States for food imports. The devaluation of the rupee failed to arrest India's declining share of world trade while it further eroded the popularity of the governing Congress party. The Congress party failed to win a majority of seats in half of the state legislative assemblies and won only a precarious majority in parliament in the 1967 elections. There followed an intense conflict between the prime minister and the state and national Congress party leaders, a struggle that ended with a split in the Congress party and an electoral triumph for Mrs. Gandhi's Congress in the special national elections of early 1971. This victory was reconfirmed in the state assembly elections in 1972 when Mrs. Gandhi's Congress swept all the states, even West Bengal where the Communists had earlier undermined Congress dominance.

Mrs. Gandhi's emergence as a powerful national leader, in some respects even more powerful than her father, was accompanied by the pursuit of a populist set of policies: she abolished the special privileges of the former princes, nationalized the country's major banks, passed a Monopolies Act to regulate the activities of some 800 large firms, and nationalized the wholesale trade in wheat. Simultaneous to her attacks on the wealthier strata, Mrs. Gandhi promised to adopt measures to provide greater wealth and income to the lowest 40 percent through land redistribution, the extension of credit, irrigation and seeds to dry areas not thus far affected by the green revolution, and public works to increase rural employment to agricultural laborers. But little of this program has been adopted, partly because of the resource bind of the central government, and partly because the state governments have not supported many of her proposals.

At the risk of vastly oversimplifying India's complex politics, one can say that two groups within the states limited what Mrs. Gandhi's government could do: the land-owning peasant proprietors, and the middle class with its dominant position in the state bureaucracies. The peasant proprietors have been eager to prevent the passage of land reform legislation that would transfer land from the larger landowners to agricultural laborers and tenants, and when state governments imposed ceilings on land-holdings, landowners have been typically able to find ways to evade the implementation of the legislation. The peasantry has also been concerned with preventing state governments from imposing agricultural income taxes upon them and they have been able, through their influence on the state governments, to oppose proposals to transfer such taxes to the central government. Agriculture thus remains the least taxed sector of the Indian economy.

The middle classes want an expansion of the public sector because of the employment opportunities they believe such an expansion would provide, while members of the bureaucracy continue to press for higher wages, though it is accompanied by deficit financing and the growth of non-plan expenditures. At the insistence of the middle class, the government has invested heavily in higher education (to the proportionate neglect of primary and secondary school education), provided low rent, not taxed housing for government officers in urban areas, and kept urban taxes low.

A third group, the business community, has been much abused by government as a source of corruption and as an opponent of many of Mrs. Gandhi's policies (such as the nationalization of the grain trade), but it is, in fact, much more limited by government than it is a force imposing limits upon government. The business community has been forced to work closely with the bureaucracy in order to obtain contracts and licenses—to open or expand a plant, to import machinery or spare parts, even to purchase raw materials for production. The degree of dependence upon the government is illustrated by a study conducted by the Planning Commission which reported that on the average it takes 460 days to obtain a license to import capital goods. The study also estimated that it takes nearly four years for an Indian businessman to run the gamut of government regulations to start a business. The businessman may eventually earn a high profit—given India's protected market and protected prices—but the opportunity costs to the economy from delays are staggering.

In this highly regulated environment the businessman must work closely with both the local bureaucracy and the governing party, corrupting the one while also providing financial support for electoral campaigns for the other. The political leadership may be ideologically critical of the business class, but the party and the bureaucracy, especially at the state level, finds the relationship profitable. Between the business community and the government there is thus a symbiotic relationship.

Paradoxically, the strengthening of Mrs. Gandhi's authority in the center has been accompanied by declining stability in the states. Between 1965 and 1973, twenty-two state governments collapsed and were taken over by the central government through President's (i.e., central government) Rule, while in the previous sixteen years these emergency powers were utilized only ten times. In a substantial number of instances, presidential rule was established because of internal factional conflicts within the governing Congress party. In Uttar Pradesh, factional conflicts following a police mutiny against the state government in 1973 resulted in the resignation of the chief minister, while at the same time in Andhra regional conflicts within the state took such a violent turn that the central government sent in the military and suspended the state government.

In 1974, factional conflicts in Gujarat, combined with charges of corruption and governmental mismanagement, resulted in the resignation of the chief minister, the establishment of presidential rule, and new elections, which brought a non-Congress government to power.

Few of the states have political leaders powerful enough to keep party factionalism under control, as was the case when Nehru and Shastri were prime ministers. Mrs. Gandhi's assertion of national leadership was made possible, not through the consensus of state leaders, but through her success in eroding the political position of many of the state leaders. But by politically eliminating those who threatened her, she also removed from influence the very men who, for so many years, were able to maintain leadership in the states. The state leaders who replaced these men were largely chosen by, and are therefore beholden to, Mrs. Gandhi; this may have strengthened her national position, but these leaders have often been politically impotent in dealing with conflicts within their own areas.

Of the three major social groups at the state level, neither the peasants, nor the bureaucracy, nor the business community are necessarily damaged by the breakdown of state governments and the establishment of central government rule, for their interests are likely to be respected by the central government. Superficially, the instability of state governments would appear to be a political problem, but in fact there is a careful balancing of forces that continues even when the state government is unstable. It is, however, a balancing of forces that tends to impede rather than facilitate social change.

The business community has been able to make its profits, create untaxed wealth, and protect itself against stringent taxation, but it has not been free enough to play an expansive role in the economy. The bureaucracy has not demonstrated that it can run the public sector profitably or productively, but it can impose restrictions on the expansion of the private sector, limit the investment of the larger industrial houses and, with the support of the Left, threaten to nationalize industries. The peasant proprietors, at least those who live in areas with assured irrigation, have demonstrated their ability to raise substantially agricultural productivity, but they have been politically able to resist efforts to impose an agricultural income tax. It is this balance of forces that has created limits on India's capacity to tax, to raise the rate of savings, expand investment, and thereby substantially increase economic growth. And it is this same balance of forces that has limited the capacity of government to achieve a more equitable distribution of wealth and income.

Economic failure is not, in itself, likely to lead to a major restructuring of Indian economic policy. The government is committed, rhetorically at least, to a policy of economic growth, equity in income, self-reliance, and socialism. "Socialism"—by which is meant a large public sector and heavy state control and regulation of the private sector—is not viewed by the Indian leadership as the *means* for achieving the goals of growth, equity and self-reliance, but is itself a goal of policy. The country's intelligentsia (for ideological reasons), the political leadership (for reasons of patronage), and the bureaucracy (for reasons of self-interest) are committed to an extension of state power into the economy and tend to be critical of moves to expand opportunities for private investment.

Political Order with Economic Stagnation. While the non-Congress opposition parties pointed to their victory in the Gujarat state assembly elections of June 1975 as an indication that Congress had nationally lost its national mandate, and though there had been a substantial increase in political protest in India's urban areas throughout 1975, it is nonetheless striking how successful the regime had actually been in maintaining political support in the face of a declining economy, substantial unemployment, a high rate of inflation, food shortages, and corruption at high levels. But if the Indian political system has been stable in spite of the low growth rate, it can also be argued that the policies that have been conducive to maintaining stability have also contributed to the low growth rates and to the low levels of equity.

What precipitated Prime Minister Gandhi's decision to suspend the democratic process was her defeat, not by the electorate or her own party, but by the Allahabad High Court when it ruled that Mrs. Gandhi had violated the election law and had to relinquish her seat in parliament and hence her position as prime minister. Though her appeal was pending before the Supreme Court the opposition parties, led by Jayaprakash Narayan, declared that they would launch a national movement for her resignation. The agitation was evidently intended to build up popular support for the non-Congress parties and to strengthen their organization in preparation for the forthcoming national elections, but Mrs. Gandhi chose to interpret their actions as a move to bring her and her government down even before the elections. She pointed to statements by opposition leaders calling upon the army and the bureaucracy not to obey "illegal" acts of government as a call for subversion and rebellion. Whether the army or the bureaucracy would have actually disaffected is uncertain, but what is clear, however, is how successful India's national leadership has been in maintaining the support of the military and the bureaucracy, along with their own Congress party—and the importance of these three institutions in maintaining a durable central government.

The military has been well nurtured by the government, especially after the military defeat by the Chinese in 1962. Until then, India spent less on defense than almost any major country; but since 1962 there has been a massive expansion of the army and navy and the development of defense industries. Moreover, the government has readily deployed the military for internal security when neither the state government nor the central reserve police seemed adequate to meet threats of internal disorder. In recent years the central government has used the army to curb violence in the Brahmaputra valley of Assam, in the Naga and Mizo hills, and in the Telengana region of Andhra. The readiness of the regime to utilize the military has not, as elsewhere, politicized the military, but apparently ensured the regime of the military's support.

An important element in maintaining army support has been the government's policy toward the Punjab where a large part of the officer corp, as well as the common soldiers (*jawans*), originate. The decision of the government to permit the Sikhs to create their own Punjabi-speaking state was partially motivated by the belief that the country (and the army) could ill afford a restive Sikh population, nor could one envisage the use of the army to maintain law and order in the Punjab if there were violent clashes between Punjabi Sikhs and Hindus.

In spite of the efforts by the Indian government to recruit more broadly and from a wider range of castes, ethnic groups, and regions into the Indian army, the army still draws heavily from what were once characterized as the "martial" races, and many soldiers belong to military families whose fathers and grandfathers also served. As Stephen Cohen in his study of the Indian army points out, electoral politics has enabled representatives of these martial classes—the Sikhs, Jats, Rajputs, and Dogras—to resist broadening the recruitment into the army. But since 1965, there has been considerably wider recruitment into the officer corp, and there are now more multicaste, multiregional and multi-ethnic units.

While the Indian army, like the Pakistan army of the 1950s and early sixties, emphasizes its nonpolitical outlook, the military has remained out of politics largely because of its acceptance of Indian political authority as legitimate, and its recognition that the Indian government has by and large been successful in maintaining a strong center, deterring secessionist movements, and sustaining law and order. But the officer corp is imbued with a strong technocratic sense, and like a substantial part of India's educated classes, would like to see a stronger center, a corruption-free leadership, and a more efficient administration; each of these factors are likely to be weighed against their disposition not to intervene in political affairs, particularly if the legitimacy of civilian authority should be undermined by a governmental decision to suspend the electoral process.

The morale of the military, greatly weakened by its defeat by the Chinese in the 1962 war, was restored by the military accomplishments of the 1965 war with Pakistan, and again, with the overwhelming Indian military victory in the 1971 war over Bangladesh. With its national outlook, its professionalism and concern for efficiency, and its generally high self-regard, the military is a potent force behind the government—but is potentially dangerous should it turn against the government.

The expansion of paramilitary forces, especially the Border Security Force and the Central Reserve Police, was intended to reduce the dependence of the central government on the regular Indian army. But while expenditures on these police forces reportedly doubled between 1969 and 1971, the army has continued to play the major role in the maintenance of internal law and order, not only in Kashmir and in the states of northeastern India, but elsewhere in the country. On one occasion, army units were used to disarm a rebellious Provincial Armed Constabulary in the north Indian state of U.P. when police units sided with the students, then demanded pay increases. The clash, the first since independence, raised the spectre of future conflict between the army and paramilitary police forces. How the military is likely to respond to a decline in the legitimacy of the prime minister, to an expansion in the use of paramilitary forces, or to their own use in coping with domestic disturbances are questions of considerable importance for the present government.

While the prime minister justified the declaration of an emergency on the grounds that the opposition sought to instigate rebellion within the army and police, it is the improvement in the performance of the administration that is most often given by government to support its claim that the country has benefited from the emergency. According to the government, there has been a marked decline in administrative corruption, officers report to work on time and remain at their desks throughout the day, trains and airplanes depart and arrive on schedule, and there are no longer strikes in the public sector. Moreover, the government claims that many of its programs—e.g., land reform, the distribution of housing sites to the landless, antismuggling and antihoarding programs, improved tax collection—are all now being implemented by the administrative services.

The powers of the civil bureaucracy have markedly increased under the emergency; indeed, the decline in the power of members of Parliament, the state legislators, and local Congress officials has meant a corresponding increase in the powers of the civil service. The senior civil servants have now a freer hand in dealing with recalcitrant or inefficient junior officers, who in the past, were able to turn to elected officials or party leaders to protect themselves against senior officers. One result is that after the emergency was declared the government was able to dismiss thousands of civil servants, mostly through early retirement.

How far the government has been able to implement the twenty-point program is a matter of conjecture, but one point is noteworthy: the twenty-point program was itself the program of the bureaucracy, especially of members of the prime minister's own secretariat and selected officers within key ministries of the central government.

Probably no group in India is as supportive of the prime minister and of the emergency as the country's bureaucrats. For one thing, the civil service continues to be well nurtured by both central and state governments, which provide officers with low-rent housing, special low-interest loans, educational facilities for their children, cost of living allowances, and tenure of employment. For another, as we have noted, the emergency diminishes the power of those who are elected and increases the autonomy of government officials. Resentful of "too much politics" and "interference," senior bureaucrats are now free to carry out their favorite programs.

One such program has been a campaign, launched by officials of the Delhi Development Authority, to clear Delhi of its unauthorized dwellings. An estimated 43,000 dwellings were moved from the city, containing a quarter million residents. In the past slum clearance programs aimed at removing squatters were opposed by municipal councilors, who defended their voters against proposals by administrators to clear unsightly slums and improve the appearance of the city. With the suspension of the Delhi Municipal Corporation by the government, the officials were able to carry out their program. The government claimed that the uprooted residents were all adequately relocated on the outskirts of the city, but the critics remained skeptical, especially since the censor barred one newspaper from continuing its series of articles on the relocation program, and questions raised by opposition members of parliament on the subject were banned by press censors.

For nearly three decades the Congress party was the third part of this institutional triumvirate which formed the basis for the stability and authority of the Indian political system. To those who joined, the party offered a share of power, the status, and sometimes the financial gain that went with holding political office. An historian of eighteenth and early nineteenth century agrarian India once described India's land system as one based upon reciprocity and redistribution, a system in which those who had access to the wealth of the land shared portions of that wealth with others on the basis of services provided to them in turn. A similar pattern of exchange prevails in the contemporary political system. Those who wield power and wealth within government share that power and wealth with circles of supporters. It has been an open system which has permitted previously nonparticipant social classes, castes, tribes, and linguistic groups to demand and then receive a share of power. But in a system of severe scarcity, sharing has often been with the leadership of potentially dissident groups rather than with the rank and file. The cooptation of elites is a comparatively inexpensive way of sharing power.

What can be most readily shared is the resources of government—jobs, social programs, educational funds, etc. What is protected are those interests vital to each portion of the coalition. Hence, the absence of effective land reform and the low incidence of agrarian taxation can be understood by noting the political influence of the peasant proprietor classes; the inadequate managerial performance in the public sector can be understood by considering the way in which the administrative sectors have taken over the public sector and the desire of the bureaucratic management to preserve bureaucratic procedures (seniority in preference to merit, regularization of procedures rather than innovations and risk-taking, price fixing to avoid competition, and performance criteria that excludes profit-taking and market performance).

Thus, India has had a stable coalition which could govern the country but which could not accelerate economic growth or distribute income effectively. The coalition was not necessarily threatened by poor economic performance so long as its relative status and income remained secure. What has been important to India's dominant social-economic groups is the share of status and wealth which they acquire, not absolute growth. Moreover, during a period of economic stagnation and decline, the regime has been particularly careful to preserve the position of its supporters; hence during inflation, pay raises for the bureaucracy have been a high priority; during food shortages, special efforts were made to provide food at fixed prices to government employees; the wealthier peasants have had first claims on fertilizers and irrigation; educational targets for primary schools could not be met, but expenditures on higher education for the middle classes continued to rise; unemployment grew, but state governments gave employment preferences to "local" members of the middle classes (as opposed to migrants from other regions). The system by no means satisfied its supporters—the level of discontent and cynicism even among those social classes that supported the regime has been very high and growing—but thus far there has been no large-scale shift to more radical alternatives.

Moreover, those who govern and, to a large extent, even those in opposition to government, share many assumptions concerning the nature of the social, economic and political order. For one thing, there are few educated Indians who believe that India is likely to enter a period of accelerated growth. It is this acceptance of a steady state economy or slow growth that places a premium on finding ways to share more equitably what is available rather than on undertaking measures to accelerate the pace of economic change. Another shared viewpoint is a deep belief, almost religious in its dimensions, that a well-ordered society is one in which individuals perform their duties and avoid conflict. In a good society, so educated Indians believe, each social group is entitled to some "appropriate" proportionate share of both goods and status: equity, not equality, is the moral foundation of such a social order. While the concept of equality suggests that everyone is to have equal access to opportunities (implying thereby a competitive system) or equality of condition (implying the absence of hierarchy), equity suggests that each social group should have some socially-defined share. Thus, those who are currently downtrodden (scheduled castes, tribes, minorities) are entitled to a larger share of "seats" in colleges and universities, a larger share of appointments in government service, and reserved "tickets" for election to public office.

Another expression of this viewpoint is in the regulation of monopolies by the Indian government. While in the United States monopoly regulations are adopted by government with the intention of freeing the marketplace for greater competition, in India such legislation is intended to protect smaller businesses by ensuring them a share of the market. Similarly, government has preferred to license small firms to produce textiles, fertilizers and automobiles, rather than license large firms where economies of scale might prevail, and then fixed prices so that one firm does not drive out another.

Competition within the work situation is also discouraged. Merit promotions are not wholly absent within the administrative system, but, ordinarily, those who are employed are rarely dismissed, promotions are routinized, and there are few opportunities to move from one level of the administrative system (e.g., from non-gazetted to gazetted positions) to another since the education system certifies (in the way caste traditionally did) the place one can rightfully expect within the job market.

In the midst of India's turmoil and conflict, violent upheavals, and electoral struggles, one cannot but be struck by the extraordinary regularity of the Indian social order, the durability of India's institutions, the social conservatism of its leadership, and the consensual character of its belief systems.

Is India's Choice Authoritarianism or Political Disorder? India's persistent food shortages and inflation have increased the possibilities that the country will waiver between large-scale violence, ethnic and religious conflicts, and political disorder on the one hand, and a more authoritarian and repressive regime on the other. Events of the past few years tend to confirm this pattern. Less obvious, however, is whether it is food shortages or inflation that constitutes a political threat to India's government, for each has a different impact on India's social classes.

That food shortages result in large-scale suffering in India seems certain, for so many people live so close to the margin that shortfalls of production bring malnutrition and death. That there will be protests and violence under such conditions also seems likely, although in areas suffering from severe malnutrition it is uncertain that the sufferers will even have the physical energy necessary for protest. But that these disturbances will necessarily destabilize the government is less certain, for in the past there have been large-scale famines with remarkably little in the way of political breakdowns.

Under conditions of famine, the Indian political and administrative system often works remarkably well. During the Bihar famine of 1966-67 the state and central administrative services provided famine relief and medical assistance on a major scale. Twenty thousand fair-price shops were opened throughout the state, free grain was distributed to children, mothers, and the infirmed, high-protein foods were made widely available, thousands of weils were dug for drinking water and irrigation, an emergency immunization program was established, and farmers were provided with loans to purchase fertilizers, pesticides, seeds, and cattle. Without the administrative structure, storage, and transportation facilities that existed in Bihar, the international aid that came into the state from the United States government, the United Nations, CARE, and many other voluntary agencies would not have been effective. Millions could have died instead of a few thousand; this record exists in a state with a reputation for administrative incompetence and political factionalism!

However, while the government may be able to manage famine, it is less able to cope with the effects of inflation. The political effects of the latter are far greater, for while famine affects the poor peasantry, landless laborers, the unemployed and low-income urban dwellers (none of whom have much political power), inflation threatens the more politically influential middle classes, the organized industrial labor force, the bureaucracy, the police, and the families of the military. Inflation threatens the opportunities for mobility of the children of the lower middle classes who thus become available for urban protest movements; it provides an impetus for corruption on the part of bureaucrats, generates deficit state budgets that strain central-state relations as states attempt to meet the deficit by making new demands upon the central government, and worsens regional disparities between and within states as funds available for development dwindle.

It is this fear of rising prices that made the government reluctant, in 1974, to pay open market prices to farmers for the procurement of food grains, even though the effect of the policy was to reduce the amount of grain the government was able to purchase domestically. In the past such a policy would have worked if the government had been able to purchase food on the world market at concessional rates. But the worldwide rise in food prices, combined with the rise in petroleum and fertilizer prices, has made it impossible to separate the problem of managing regional food shortages from the problem of nationwide inflation. In the midst of a worldwide inflation, the importation of food at market prices is no longer an effective anti-inflationary measure.

While India has experienced famines in the past, far worse than the one that affected portions of northern India in 1974, it has not previously experienced the prolonged inflation that was running at 30 percent per year in 1974 and early 1975. For most of the past twenty-eight years, the Indian government has successfully maintained a foreign exchange reserve, avoided large-scale budget deficits, and pursued a conservative monetary policy, with the result that the annual inflation rate has been small, as compared with many other developing countries. The low inflation rate has been an important element in the stability of the regime. Only once was that stability jeopardized. In 1966, following two years of drought, a war, a foreign exchange crisis, and rising prices, the government of India decided (after some pressure from the Aid Consortium, the World Bank and the United States government) to devalue the rupee; the initial effect, on the eve of national and state elections, was a still more rapid rise in prices. The Congress party victory in early 1967 was the narrowest the party had ever experienced.

The inflation of 1974-75 proved to be even more threatening to the government. Had Prime Minister Gandhi not been so alarmed at the way in which the middle class and organized labor in the cities were rallying behind the opposition, perhaps she might not have declared a national emergency. The Congress electoral defeat in Gujarat a few weeks before the emergency not only revealed how seriously Congress had declined (a particularly bitter blow to Mrs. Gandhi who personally toured many of the constituencies of Gujarat), but also suggested that the opposition parties were capable of building a coalition for the forthcoming national parliamentary elections that were scheduled for early 1976.

Since the declaration of an emergency it is by no means clear that the Congress party will ever relinquish power to any national opposition party or coalition of parties. Many Congressmen, including the prime minister, have made it clear that they view the transfer of power to a motley collection of opposition parties that included the right-wing Jana Sangh, which, Congress believes, threatens the secular framework of the country, as unacceptable. Mrs. Gandhi said as much to a group of Yugoslav journalists when she

accused some extremist political parties, which together with "big money" and the "big press" were trying to subvert the Government: "We had to declare a state of emergency in order to deal with this situation and some of these people were arrested." She said that most of these parties were opposed to socialism and to our foreign policy, and some were backed by rich farmers. (*Overseas Hindustan Times*, August 14, 1975)

In another interview she noted that

As for the future of democracy in this country, Mrs. Gandhi thought it would be perilled only if a party of the extreme right or the extreme left came into power. These parties either were wedded to violence or were intolerant of the minority religions and communities: "It (Indian democracy) is being weakened by those who, claiming to be non-violent and democratic, give respectability to and ally themselves with fanatic religious organisations and with parties wedded to terrorism." (Ibid)

The popularity of the Congress party has been on the wane for the past few years. The Congress hold on the electorate declined in the 1960s, reaching its low point in the parliamentary elections of 1967 when Congress won only 40 percent of the vote—but a majority of parliamentary seats because of the divided opposition. In 1971, after the reorganization of the party, Congress won 53.5 percent of the vote, the highest it ever achieved. Congress did equally well in the state elections that followed India's military victory over Pakistan. In retrospect, these elections may prove to have been an interlude in the party's electoral decline unless Prime Minister Gandhi (or her successor) can find an enemy (the "old" Congress in 1971), or a triumph (victory against Pakistan in the elections of 1972) to pull back disillusioned voters. Some sections of the Congress party, and the Communist party of India, see the United States as an enemy against which the electorate can be rallied: by pointing to alleged CIA activities in India, the expansion of American naval facilities at Diego Garcia, United States support for Pakistan, assertions of United States interference in Bangladesh and among other neighbors of India, and real or imagined slights of Indian officials by Americans.

Nevertheless, while in its rhetoric the government may shift to the left and may even take an anti-American posture, within the government there are strong pressures for a more conservative economic policy. Many in the government recognize the dangerous parallels between the problems of the mid-seventies and those experienced by the government in 1967: both are periods of agricultural stagnation, industrial slowdown, high inflation, and a time of cyclical decline for the Congress party. Then, as now, the opposition parties were strongly motivated to build electoral coalitions to prevent Congress from winning seats with a plurality; in both periods the opposition sought to undermine the position of the Congress with the urban electorate, especially the middle class bureaucrats, the intelligentsia, and the labor unions.

Should Congress win a parliamentary election with a substantially reduced number of seats and become dependent upon the pro-Soviet Communist party of India for support, then the problem could again emerge of various dissident groups *within* the Congress party trying to undermine and alter the party's national structure, as in the post-1967 election. If so, then we might see a national political struggle similar to the 1967-70 period when factions within Congress allied themselves with one or more opposition groups. In that struggle one faction of the party, the one led by Mrs. Gandhi, emerged so triumphantly that it no longer needed the support of the opposition parties; neither the Communists nor the D.M.K., both of which supported Mrs. Gandhi's faction, were given a share of national power as they might have been had Mrs. Gandhi's subsequent electoral victory not been so overwhelming. In the next electoral round, assuming national elections are soon held, Congress may need the support of the pro-Soviet Communist party and be forced to share national power with them, but not all the members of the Congress high command are likely to willingly accept such a coalition.

In any event, the question of the electoral prospects for the Congress party may very well be moot. If Mrs. Gandhi ends the emergency and calls for national parliamentary elections in early 1977 the conditions under which these elections will be held will be different than those which characterized India's free elections in the past. With the press censored, and television controlled by the government, several political groups outlawed, the MISA regulations intact, and the business community reluctant to provide funds to opponents of Mrs. Gandhi, the elections would soon take on the character of a plebiscite intended to legitimize an authoritarian one-party state.

Keeping the lid on inflation, improving the food supply, increasing urban employment—in short, some marked improvement in the economy particularly as it affects urban India—are critical if the government is to avoid a recurrence of the turmoil of early 1975. For this reason many members of the government, especially within the prime minister's secretariat, have pressed for increased expenditures for agriculture (including irrigation), greater incentives for the private sectors, the nonenforcement of the Monopolies Act, loosening import restrictions, providing greater incentives to exporters, even encouraging foreign investment. This group, while accepting the existing Socialist rhetoric, would rely more heavily on the marketplace and would be less doctrinaire about the role of domestic or foreign private investors. While maintaining a low profile politically, they would seek increased World Bank and International Development Agency (IDA) support, noting that only an improvement in the economy could halt the drift toward the decline of the Congress party and the strengthening of the Communist party or greater authoritarian moves by the government in an effort to avoid both.

"Judging by all objective indicators," declared Finance Minister C. Subramiam in a speech to Parliament a few weeks after the emergency was declared, "the Indian economy is now poised for a major phase of rapid economic expansion." He went on to predict a doubling of the industrial growth rate to 5 or 6 percent per year, a rise in food production to 114 million tons, a 20 percent increase in power generation, a rise in coal production by ten million tons, a 40 percent growth in fertilizer production, and a growth of salable steel from 4.9 to 5.7 million tons within a year. In an equally optimistic statement, the petroleum and chemicals minister, K.D. Malaviya, reported that the country would be self-sufficient in oil in five years as a result of current offshore and onshore explorations and development (*Overseas Hindustan Times*, August 14, 1975).

Outsiders remained unimpressed, for such optimistic predictions have been made before. In a political economy marked by elaborate bureaucratic regulations, hostility to the business community, anxiety over foreign investment, an inefficient public sector, influential landlords, and corruption within both the administration and government, would the expansion of the powers of the prime minister be enough to change the country's direction?

India in a Changing World Order

Three developments since 1971 have changed the regional and global context within which India must operate. The first is the rapprochement between the United States and China; the second, India's defeat of Pakistan and the breakup of Pakistan into two states; the third, the emergence of Iran as a dominant military and economic power in Western Asia.

The United States-Chinese rapprochement provided the Soviets with an opportunity to strengthen their ties with India and has, in turn, led India to move more closely toward countries with Soviet leanings. India's regional domination has resulted in an extension of her influence into Bangladesh where for some time India was the new country's largest single aid donor; a new trade and transit agreement with Nepal tied that country more closely to Indian import-export policies; and in 1975 India absorbed Sikkim as her twenty-second state. Pakistan has remained an adversary, but geographically and militarily reduced to the point that it no longer constitutes a significant threat to India.

Iran, with its new found oil wealth, its security concerns in the Persian Gulf, and its imperial vision, established closer ties with Pakistan and sought to increase both Indian and Afghanistan dependence on Teheran through aid programs, long-term oil concessional arrangements, and a program of investment. Iran hopes thereby to reduce the possibilities of efforts by Afghanistan or India (alone or with Soviet support) to undermine Pakistan's precarious ethnic balance. Iran also hopes to win tacit Indian acceptance of its efforts to expand its naval power in the Arabian Sea and Indian Ocean.

Since 1971 the United States has virtually withdrawn from South Asia. Although the United States terminated its embargo on military supplies to Pakistan in early 1975, there has been no effort to resume the large-scale program of the 1960s; the United States has written off the bulk of the debts India accumulated under the Public Law 480 food program, but Washington has not reestablished (nor has India requested) the economic aid program that once made India the largest single recipient of American economic assistance.

The New American Orthodoxy in South Asia

A new orthodoxy has emerged in Washington's conception of the United States role in South Asia. According to this new orthodoxy, South Asia is an area of low priority for the United States. Unlike the Middle East, Indonesia or Nigeria, it has no resources vital to the American economy. Unlike Latin America it is not a region with substantial American private investment. Its geopolitical position raises no fundamental problems for American security, although the United States maintains an interest in the Indian Ocean as a sea lane connecting Western Asia with Japan and the Far East. Unlike China, India's influence is largely confined to the countries within the region—in that sense India is seen as a regional, not international power. South Asia has no deep cultural or historic ties with the United States, and unlike the countries of Western Europe, Israel, and Greece, no significant segment of the American population originates from nor has an enduring association with South Asia. In short, none of the elements exist that would attract the daily concerns of the president, Congress, the press or the foreign policy publics.

Moreover, many Americans see involvement in South Asia as costly and risky. As long as there is such a disparity in wealth and power between India and the developed countries, any great power involved in the region will find that major claims will be made upon it—for arms, assistance, or food. As the largest of the low income regions of the world outside of China, South Asia has an enormous capacity to absorb American resources with few if any tangible benefits to the donor.

The present view is a reversal of America's image of South Asia in the 1950s and 1960s when India received American economic aid and Pakistan was an important recipient of both economic and military assistance. The United States also had a substantial involvement in Nepal, and, if public reports on the CIA are accurate, in the entire Himalayan region including Chinese-controlled Tibet. As long as the United States had an adversary relationship with both China and the Soviet Union and there were strong fraternal bonds between the two major Communist powers, the United States was concerned with minimizing both Soviet and Chinese influence in South Asia.

The growing détente between the United States and the Soviet Union, the bipolar character of Communist power, the new relationship between China and the United States, the disillusionment of Americans over the role of aid in the Third World countries in general and in India in particular, and, finally, the breakup of the political coalition in the United States which underlay the liberal, prodevelopment policies of the Eisenhower and Kennedy presidencies—all these changes have diminished the role of India in America's view of the world.

Even the doomsday visions of India no longer arouse sentiment for action: neither large-scale famine, internal strife, anxiety over Soviet penetration, fear of a military takeover and the end of parliament government, nor the establishment of a one-party dictatorship seems to be sufficient to mobilize the State or Defense Departments, Congress, the White House, or American liberals. For none of these developments, sad as many of them would be for India, appear to threaten American interests; nor, some would argue, does it seem likely that American involvement could even prevent these occurrences from taking place.

Indeed, some Washington policymakers even see advantages to the persistence of anti-American sentiment within India. According to this view an anti-American India is likely to deepen Soviet involvement which, in turn, antagonizes the Chinese and reduces the prospects of a Soviet-Chinese rapprochement. Close Soviet-Indian relations makes Pakistan and Iran more pro-American and increases support or at least acquiescence by littoral states for the expansion of the American presence in the Indian Ocean to balance the Soviet role in India, East Africa, and the Persian Gulf. Finally, the Soviet Union, not the United States, will have to bear the burden of providing food and other economic assistance, while India purchases American grain on a cash and carry basis.

The United States government pays no domestic political price for its estranged relationship with India, since India has no substantial political constituency in the United States. Conservatives look with disfavor upon India's ineffectual planning and its Soviet ties; radicals are more sympathetic to China's revolutionary regime than to India's lack of equalitarianism; and liberals who might have been moved by former Ambassador Moynihan's India-is-a-democracy argument are turned off by India's anti-Israeli policy, its decision to develop a nuclear device, her poor economic performance, and now by the waning of its democratic institutions.

The United States can obviously no longer predicate its relationship to India on the assumption that New Delhi's government will be either democratically elected or durable. Even if Prime Minister Gandhi terminates the emergency, frees political prisoners, ends press censorship, permits public assembly, and calls national parliamentary elections, it is clear that a precedent has been set: that a central government controlling a majority of parliament can re-establish, even if temporarily, an authoritarian government, and that, at any stage, the military might choose to intervene, no longer constrained by the notion that it was suspending or abolishing the democratic system. If a conspiratorial atmosphere replaces the electoral process, predictions of India's political future will increasingly be based less upon an assessment of the changing mood of the electorate than on an insider's knowledge of sentiment within the military, paramilitary forces, sections of the bureaucracy, and the senior leadership of the governing party.

India's Strategic Perspective

There is considerable sentiment in India that the United States is committed to a policy of preventing India from becoming a major power, either in the region or globally, and that America's policies toward Pakistan as well as in the Indian Ocean are intended to curtail Indian influence; therefore it is believed that, under these circumstances, no genuine rapprochement with the United States is feasible at this time. India's experience with the United States as a supporter of Pakistan has made Indians leery of any role the United States plays in the region, for Indians fear that American power might again be used to limit India's role as a regional power. The result is an acute anxiety among Indians over any extension of American activities. Indians tend to see the United States' decision to expand base facilities at Diego Garcia, not as an American response to growing Soviet naval power in the Indian Ocean and Persian Gulf, but as a threatening extension of American military power in the region. Similarly, Iran's purchase of arms from the United States was initially seen, not in terms of Iran's desire to secure its position in the Persian Gulf or strengthen itself in relation to the Arab states, but rather in terms of possible Iranian support for Pakistan against India.

Moreover, many Indians see their ties with the Soviet Union as a means of strengthening India's relations with radical Arab governments whose oil and assistance is needed by India, and whose relationship India hopes to retain even in the event of an Arab-Israeli war and an oil embargo. Soviet support also provides India with some leverage in dealing with its neighbors, while anti-Americanism links India more firmly with the anti-American Third World countries that now make up such a large proportion, if not a majority, of the United Nations.

Domestically, an anti-American policy is useful to the Indian government to rally support against the opposition which can be accused of pro-Americanism and of trying to undermine the Soviet-Indian relationship. For many Indians view American aid, especially in food, as a dangerous renewal of Indian dependence upon a country that once used assistance to influence India's domestic and foreign policies.

Finally, some Indians argue that the Soviet Union has a long-term interest in strengthening India vis-à-vis China, while the United States has a contrary interest in keeping China strong. The Soviet Union can thus be relied upon, as in the recent past, to help India develop its defense capabilities, obtain food supplies and oil at concessional terms, assist in the development of the public sector, and provide technological aid in the development of a satellite capability and even possibly in nuclear development. In short, the global realignment that links the United States and China necessitates a similar alignment between the Soviet Union and India.

A few Indians have sought a more balanced relationship with the United States, arguing that continued tension between the two countries is not in India's interest. An improvement in relations with the United States, they have suggested, could be a key to a rapprochement between India and China, a policy that would ease tensions at the borders and diminish Chinese support for Pakistan. India might also thereby discourage the United States from resupplying the Pakistan military and make more difficult a United States decision to create a major naval base in Diego Garcia (both of which become politically easier for United States policymakers in the face of Soviet and Indian opposition). An improvement in United States-Indian relations, moreover, would also reduce Indian dependence upon the Soviet Union and provide alternative sources for economic assistance, technological aid, and expanded trade. Finally, to the extent that the Indian government seeks private foreign investment (made more acceptable by the readiness of both the Soviet and Chinese regimes to move in this direction), an improvement in relations with the United States is essential. None of these arguments, however, outweighs the prevailing sentiment in India that internal political uncertainties in China warrant continued close Soviet-Indian relations, and that India's interests in Western Asia are best served by a closer link with the Soviet Union than with the United States.

India as a Potential Regional and Global Nuisance

The American perception of India as a country of little strategic value has led American policymakers to overlook India's potential as a strategic nuisance. Among students of international affairs, it has been a commonplace observation that a country's international power and influence rests upon the strength of its economy, the stability of her regime, and the cohesiveness and loyalty of its population. International power, it is argued, rests on domestic power.

Events of the last few years demonstrate that this commonplace observation is false. The oil producing countries, most of which are otherwise poor, their populations illiterate and malnourished, their educational systems underdeveloped, and in some instances their regimes fragile, have demonstrated that by controlling a critical resource sought by Western nations they can exercise great power. Similarly, by exploding a nuclear device, India demonstrated (as China did earlier) that a poor country with a substantial GNP (by virtue of size, not per capita income), a commitment to higher education and research in technology and sciences, and a willingness to use scarce resources to invest in a high level technology, can extend its international power (how much and in what direction is less clear) while remaining, fundamentally, a weak state.

International power can rest on the capacity to do harm: China's power grew out of its capacity to engage American forces in Korea and to threaten Soviet borders; the power of the Palestinian Liberation Organization (PLO) rests on terrorism, and the power of Iran and Saudi Arabia on their capacity to deny oil to the developed nations. What harm can India inflict?

1. India can export nuclear technology. Countries that have not signed the nonproliferation treaty (and even those, like Iran, that have) may find that India is willing to provide assistance for nuclear development without the constraints of international supervision. India's declining foreign exchange reserves, its need to import petroleum and fertilizers at higher prices, and its limited capacity to expand foreign trade makes the export of nuclear technology an attractive possibility.

2. A regime that is economically weak but militarily strong may choose options in the 1980s that may seem unthinkable in the 1970s. A different regime and a different leadership in a world order that is viewed by an Indian prime minister as hostile to India's own interests may be willing and capable of considering military options that do not appear feasible now. Few in the 1940s envisaged an aggressive China in the 1950s; is it inconceivable that an Indian leadership armed with nuclear weapons and a sophisticated space technology might consider a variety of threats to obtain what it needs to feed its population, procure energy for its factories and farms, or respond to what it considers aggressive interventions in the region from outside? Indeed, is it conceivable that a desperate leadership would *not* entertain such thoughts?

3. India could attempt to undermine the stability of the Pakistan government by influencing political events in the northwest frontier region and in Baluchistan. By politically supporting elements opposed to the regime, by encouraging the Afghans to play a more aggressive role, by urging the Soviets to provide arms and supplies through Afghanistan, India could contribute to the destabilization of the Pakistan regime. For this reason, among others, the government of Iran has sought to placate India, provide oil at concessional prices, assure India that Iran would not become a major arms supplier to Pakistan, and that Iran's activities in the Indian Ocean are not hostile. A renewed effort by the United States to re-arm Pakistan might enhance Pakistan's military capacity, but at the

cost of an arms race in South Asia; it would also tempt India, Afghanistan, and the Soviet Union to encourage internal conflicts within Pakistan. It is not in India's interest to precipitate the disintegration of Pakistan—unless the alternative were an aggressive, armed Pakistan intent upon using military means to gain control of Kashmir.

Paradoxically, then, a weak, chronically declining India could continue to have the capacity to inflict damage upon other nations. Let us continue our catalogue of speculative horrors.

4. With the emergence of an international market in food, a substantial shortfall in food production in any one large populated region of the world has an impact on world prices. In 1973-74, India purchased 5.3 percent of America's wheat production; in addition, the Soviets provided India with two million tons of grain drawn from stocks replenished by purchases in the American market. United States decisions on long-term investment and production in food grains must take into account the food requirements of India, China and Japan, the three Asian countries that are now among the world's largest importers of food. (China alone imported 7.2 million tons of grain in 1974.)

To the extent that India is unable to meet the food requirements for its growing population and is forced to buy, borrow or beg food, world food prices will be affected. Even if the United States chose, as some have suggested, to "write-off" South Asia as hopeless, concluding that United States food should be made available to those countries with a better chance of meeting the food-population crisis (the notion of "triage"), it seems unlikely that the rest of the world's major food producers and suppliers (the Soviet Union, Canada, and Australia) would choose not to help India or that India would be totally unable to make some purchases in the world market; however and wherever India obtains her food in the world market would affect domestic food prices within the United States. Indian food imports are large enough to affect world markets, and their annual variability can have a notable impact on supplies and prices.

From the viewpoint of avoiding a continued upward spiral in world food prices, the United States has an interest in finding ways to increase India's agricultural self-sufficiency through expanding production. In the next decade India will need assistance to purchase fertilizers, obtain raw materials to expand fertilizer production, build more fertilizer plants, obtain the energy needed to operate these plants to full capacity, build concrete warehouses so that the substantial losses from rats, insects and mildew will be reduced, expand irrigation facilities, and improve agricultural research in order to develop new varieties of grain that are less susceptible to local diseases and insects and thrive best in local climates and soils. In the next decade India will need to substantially invest in agriculture to increase average yields on its land. India, as we have noted earlier, has little virgin land that could be more arable, but its low productivity on existing land offers the promise of large increases in production.

Each dollar of investment in Indian agriculture is likely to yield a higher return in increased food productivity than a similar investment in the United States. It has been estimated that a million tons of additional fertilizers in India will produce upwards of ten million additional tons of food, compared to half the amount in America's already productive lands. To the extent that the United States has an interest in increasing the world's productivity in food, it is as important to provide investment capital to India and other LDCs to increase their productivity as it is for the United States to increase its own investment in agriculture.

5. Still another way in which India's economic decline could prove damaging to America's interests would be if India's deteriorating foreign exchange reserve made it impossible for India to meet her international debts.

India's trade deficit of $750 million in 1968-69 sharply declined through 1972, and foreign aid was reduced from $700 million in 1968-69 to only $200 million in 1972-73, while her foreign exchange reserves increased. However, since 1973, India's trade deficit has sharply increased and its foreign exchange reserves have remained intact only because of an increase in international aid (some of which is in the form of rescheduled debt payments). India's import bill in 1974 was estimated at $1.5 billion dollars higher than in 1973 as a consequence of the rising costs of fertilizers, petroleum, and food imports. The trade deficit, including debt servicing, is expected to reach $2.4 billion—to be met through consortium aid and credit from the oil producing countries, especially Iran. The World Bank has estimated that India will need external financial assistance of $2.4 billion a year for the next five years. In the long run, however, India will need to make a transition from an import substitution policy to one which emphasizes expanding exports; as long as India's oil and fertilizer requirements so greatly exceed its own productive capabilities, India has no other choice but to expand both imports and exports.

Should India fail to substantially expand its exports, and should the oil producing nations and the developed nations fail to cover India's trade deficit, the Indian government will find it increasingly difficult to pay its international debts. Indeed, had there not been a significant increase in consortium aid in the past year, India could have become a net exporter of foreign exchange at a time when its import bill had sharply increased. Is it unlikely, then, that a regime, perhaps of a different political persuasion than the present government, finding itself unable to make payment on loans, might repudiate some or all of India's international debts? Simply to avoid a unilateral declaration by India to postpone or repudiate debts, the international aid givers will find it necessary to expand assistance unless India's trade deficit rapidly declines.

Debt repudiation by a country of India's size could have a substantial impact on the structure of international finance: on the World Bank, the International Monetary Fund, on international foreign investors, and on the entire financial and political relationship between the developed and the developing countries.

6. A deterioration of the Indian political system is as likely to have

international repercussions as a deterioration of its economy. An economically weak India could be militarily strong, ideologically strident, and politically centralist and authoritarian, but it could also be in a state of turmoil, with government using its military power to deal with internal disorder. The repercussions elsewhere in South Asia would not be trivial for, as we have noted earlier, ethnic overlaps between India and its neighbors suggest that Sri Lanka, Pakistan, Bangladesh, Nepal, even Afghanistan and Iran could be affected. And is it likely that large-scale political turmoil in India would leave the great powers unaffected any more than the disintegration and subsequent transformation of China in the late forties?

Let us turn from doomsday scenarios to consider developments within India that could have beneficial consequences for world order and development.

The disintegration of Pakistan in 1971 and the clear-cut military victory by India has established India as the undisputed power in the South Asia region, while the détente between the United States and its two major adversaries, China and the Soviet Union, has ended America's long-term hostility to nonalignment. As Kissinger said in his address in New Delhi on October 28, 1974, "The United States accepts nonalignment. In fact, America sees a world of free, independent, sovereign states as being decidedly in its own national interest. Support of national independence and of the diversity that goes with it has become a central theme of American foreign policy."

"The size and position of India," Kissinger went on to say, "give it a special role of leadership in South Asia and in world affairs." Kissinger indicated that the United States does not intend to re-arm Pakistan, that it welcomes India's efforts to exercise leadership in the region, and that it is eager to encourage India's economic independence. In 1973, the United States wrote off the largest foreign debt ever cancelled in its history, while Kissinger's visit itself was intended to persuade the Indian leadership that the United States was eager to undo the strains of the sixties and early seventies.

For the first time since 1947, the prospects for avoiding war within the region are excellent. The outcome of the 1971 war makes it highly unlikely that there will be a major international conflict within the region in the near future. A region that once nearly matched the Middle East in its potentiality for war now has the prospect of being one of the more peaceful regions of the world. In a region where economic and demographic prospects seem so discouraging, this is the most promising feature of the region's political future.

Whether the diminished prospect of war can be turned to advantage in the form of regional cooperation is less certain. Joint export marketing arrangements between India and Bangladesh, and India and Sri Lanka, greater efforts to emphasize the complementarity of development investments within each of the countries, and arrangements for the development and use of the region's resources are among the most promising forms of regional collaboration. Of these, the most exciting would be joint efforts on the part of Nepal, India, and Bangladesh to develop the Brahmaputra-Ganges river systems, the world's largest river system that still remains largely undeveloped; a source of flooding throughout the region, it could instead be a major source of irrigation and hydroelectric power.

Realistically, however, it seems unlikely that India will be able to play the economically influential role that the world's other major regional powers, Brazil, Iran, Nigeria, and South Africa can play. An economically prosperous regional power can influence its neighbors in a variety of ways: trade, investment by public or private capital, the flow of students, the diffusion of political ideologies and movements. An economically stagnant India is not likely to exercise much influence upon its neighbors, for the natural anxieties that accompany any collaborative relationships between unequals will not be balanced by any obvious economic gains. Bangladesh, finding India unable to meet its financial needs, is already turning toward Pakistan and the countries of the Middle East in the hope that resources for development can be found there. Moreover, an economically weak India will not be in a position to press for costly international joint development projects without the kind of external foreign assistance that India is likely to consider unacceptable.

The Structure of World Order and Development

Since 1966, the Indian government has seen the international order as either unhelpful or hostile to India's interests. The 1965-66 agricultural crisis in India was accompanied by what Indians saw as a period of international (mainly United States) arm twisting, when aid was used to influence India's domestic and international policies. During the Pakistani civil war in 1971, India concluded that the United States and other nations were prepared to see India take on the refugee burden and the risk of political instability in its own northeast rather than countenance Indian military intervention.

When India did intervene militarily, its policies were condemned by virtually all countries outside the Soviet bloc. The United States and China condemned India and supported Pakistan. The Muslim countries were hostile to what they perceived as India's efforts to dismember the largest Muslim country in the world. The countries of Africa and Southeast Asia, themselves committed to the integrity of existing boundaries against the claims of dissident ethnic groups, were sympathetic to Pakistan's effort to restore control over the Bengalis. In addition, India's neighbors, Sri Lanka and Nepal, both feared that Pakistan's disintegration would make India too dominant in the region.

Moreover, Indians have not seen themselves as the beneficiaries of generous international aid, even though the volume of assistance in the 1960s was high. Per capita aid has always been small, and much of the assistance has been in loans, not grants, and the terms have not always been favorable. A substantial portion of aid is now necessary simply for debt repayment, and the proportion of debt repayment to aid continues to rise. In general, the role of advanced industrial countries in accelerating Indian development either through public or private investment or through trade and aid has been and continues to be small.

The rising prices of oil and fertilizers and of the industrial goods that India imports for her development has still further slowed India's growth. The terms of trade, never favorable to India, have worsened. Though Iran and Iraq have both signed new agreements with India, in the main neither the oil producing countries nor the industrial world have provided enough assistance to compensate for the losses India has incurred by a change in the international terms of trade since 1973.

In short, Indians have little sense that the present structure of international order has been helpful either for the security or development of their country.

Long-Term Trends and Critical Issues

A central theme of this essay is that the major threat to India in the remainder of the 1970s and early 1980s may not be upheaval, political disorder and revolution, nor even more authoritarian government (all of which are possible dangers), but the continued stagnation of its modernization; indeed, many Indians and a large number of Western observers would see turmoil or a deepening of its present authoritarianism—if either is a preclude to change—as preferable to further stagnation, for the model of incrementalism that seemed so promising to observers in the 1950s and 1960s looks less and less promising for the 1970s and 1980s.

The demographic and food problems are particularly severe. While fertility rates are declining, the present age structure ensures a high level of population growth, a burden on the country's educational, health and food resources, and an unemployment problem that will create severe difficulties for whatever regime governs India in the mid-1980s.

Indian food production moved ahead of population growth, especially with the introduction of new technology in agriculture in the late 1960s, but India's ability to expand rapidly its agriculture in the future depends on the availability of both fertilizers and irrigation, both of which are dependent upon oil. In the absence of any reserves, the safety margin between food and population is now so precarious that another drought as well as floods, crop diseases or the failure to distribute adequately fertilizers could result in a devastating increase in malnutrition, epidemic diseases, and starvation. It is hardly consoling to know that India's food and demographic problems are shared in some degree by other low income countries, including populous China, Indonesia, Pakistan, and Bangladesh; indeed, to the extent that more than a billion other people are in need of either food, fertilizers or oil, the capacity of those who have these resources to help India is thereby diminished.

The ethnic situation in South Asia continues to remain unstable and will remain so until Pakistan is better able to win the loyalty of its Pathans and Baluchis, Sri Lanka finds a satisfactory place for its Tamils, Bangladesh integrates its Bihari population, and relations in India among diverse linguistic and religious groups markedly improve. However, ethnic conflicts, wherever in the world they occur, are often intractable, though new political-institutional arrangements can often make them more manageable. The peculiar feature of these conflicts in South Asia is that they almost invariably take on an international character.

The potential for regional insurgency is ever present, not only in India but throughout South Asia, given the problems of unemployment, regional disparities, urban inflation, and agrarian underdevelopment. There is little prospect that in the short run any of the regimes will be able to substantially change the conditions which give rise to such disturbances; realistically, the major question is the capacity of each of the governments in the region to manage these insurgencies.

In spite of the military dominance of India, regional tensions are likely to persist, though the probabilities of violent conflict are substantially less than in the past.

All of India's close neighbors are as anxious about India's intentions as China's neighbors are of that country's intentions. Should India's neighbors unite in their concern over Indian military power, they may seek, individually or collectively, to tighten their relations with the United States and China in an effort to balance what they perceive to be a Soviet-supported India. It will take considerable self-restraint on the part of United States policymakers not to succumb to the temptation of treating India as China was treated in the 1950s—particularly if India has an authoritarian regime that is linked to the Soviet Union and that is vocally critical of the United States in the Indian Ocean and in the Middle East.

While the United States will want to be supportive of those countries around India that seek its economic assistance and friendship, it would be counterproductive both for the United States and for the states around India if the United States acted in such a way as to provoke India into an aggressive, expansive posture. Clearly the difference between a position of supporting India's neighbors and one of stimulating them to assume an anti-Indian stance is a thin one, but it is the art of diplomacy to draw just such fine distinctions. For even if India were to have an authoritarian government—a one-person, one-party dictatorship, or a praetorian regime—India is still likely to be a pluralistic political system characterized by major internal differences both on domestic developmental strategy and on international affairs. An authoritarian prime minister will need the support of the army, the bureaucracy, the leadership of the Congress party, and perhaps one or more non-Congress organizations. Even the military could not effectively govern without the support of the bureaucracy and a substantial civilian political leadership, especially at the state level.

While it is not difficult to envisage some kind of authoritarian government in India's near future, it is more difficult to envisage a revolutionary government with a coherent ideology and organizational base comparable to the revolutionary regimes which have assumed power in mainland China, Vietnam or Cuba. If, in retrospect, it was a mistake for the United States to assume that China had a monolithic government, it would be even more foolhardy for the United States to formulate policies toward India without recognizing that within India there are likely to be, even within an authoritarian government, considerable differences of opinion.

No matter how much the United States may disapprove of India's government or its policies, domestic or foreign, the interests of the United States would hardly be served by a policy that explicitly exacerbates relations between the two countries; India may not be an American friend and ally, but it need not be an enemy either.

The countries of Western Asia will also continue to have a substantial interest in developments within South Asia; Iran, as we have noted, is a pivotal power, because of its concern over internal developments in both Afghanistan and Pakistan. Iraq is not to be dismissed as a force in South Asia, for it may continue to seek allies in its quest for influence in the Persian Gulf. Here, one should also note the fragility of many of the regimes surrounding or having an interest in India, and the effects that regime changes could have both on India's internal politics and its foreign policy. The death of the shah of Iran, a coup in Iraq, still another major change in Bangladesh, a civil conflict or military coup in Pakistan, the overthrow of the king of Nepal, a political upheaval in Sri Lanka—not to mention some fundamental transformation in China after the death of Mao—are all at least as probable as any major political changes in India.

The question of naval power in the Indian Ocean will continue to be a lively strategic issue for the next decade—for Iran, the Soviet Union, and the United States. A sea lane in such proximity to the Suez Canal and to the Persian Gulf and so close to the volatile Middle East is hardly likely to be removed from great power rivalries, or to be the nuclear free zone sought by India. The expansion of American naval power in the Indian Ocean is sure to be a source of tension between the United States and India.

These developments will tend to push American policymakers to think of India in strategic terms, and to consider the effects of conflicts within and between countries in terms of their global consequences, but the temptation to globalize issues excessively needs to be resisted. Many problems that ought to be resolved by countries (or ethnic groups) within the region can all too easily be internationalized because one or more local groups or governments seek external support. If external intervention in the region is to be minimized, then the

United States must know when *not* to respond to requests for assistance, even to overlook the intervention of others when they are on a modest scale, or in some instances to act in concert with other major powers. The support which India, Pakistan, the Soviet Union, China, and the United States provided Sri Lanka during its insurgency of 1971 provides some evidence that parallel, if not multilateral, assistance is sometimes a feasible alternative.

In the short run it is only natural that the great powers, including the United States, will view India and all of Southern Asia from a *strategic* rather than *developmental* viewpoint. Indeed, many policymakers in Washington see a focus on development issues as a soft-minded, unrealistic perspective on international politics at a time when world order, or to use the Kissinger-Nixon phraseology "the structure of world peace," rests upon strategic considerations.

Indeed, in the present political atmosphere in the United States, it is hardly possible to ask whether the United States has a long-term national commitment to reducing the vast disparities that now separate the Third World from the advanced industrial societies. Even to the extent that the United States is willing to commit some of its resources for development, there are few who assign high priority to India, on the grounds that its problems are so vast, its potentialities too small, its existing economic growth rates too low—forgetting that India's post-independence achievements have been impressive in the face of massive problems. Moreover, India's failures will have consequences for the world that can hardly be ignored.

The kind of international order which India requires to accelerate its development is, in its very broadest outlines, easily described. It is an international order which (a) improves the terms of trade for India's exports in relation to imports; (b) provides India assistance for the development of its energy sources, fertilizer plants, irrigation facilities and industries; and (c) facilitates the development and application of technology to meet its problems. The creation of such an international order is a complex matter; the question is whether its creation is an *objective* of American policymakers. While Americans see the central issue in international politics as one of how to create a "structure of world order," that is, how to reduce conflicts between states and to defuse the role of nuclear powers in local conflicts, for most Third World governments the singular issue differs. In the words of the prime minister of Jamaica at a recent Commonwealth conference, it is "how to manage the distribution of the world's wealth," that is, how to create a world order in which development can be accelerated in the low income countries.

Again, it is necessary to emphasize that an improvement in the international environment will in no way ensure India's development, for India's difficulties have been as much internal as they have been external. They lie less with her people than with the government, less with the social structure and the value framework of her population than with the structure of power and the ideological framework that guides her governing classes. Among many Indians there is a gnawing sense that government, rather than serving as the engine of development, is increasingly a hindrance and that many of India's most fundamental problems—the development of agriculture, the full utilization of the capacity of the public sector, the functioning of the family-planning program, the operations of the educational system—are largely related to ineffective management by government. There is also a growing awareness that, in spite of the rhetoric proclaiming a policy goal of self-sufficiency, some form of international aid is probably necessary for accelerating economic growth. Finally, Mrs. Gandhi's personal popularity and increased authoritarianism notwithstanding, there is a widespread sense in India that the country lacks effective cohesive leadership with a clear sense of where the country ought to go and how best to get there.

Indians alternate between an image of themselves as an ineffectual people barely able to cope with the horrendous problems which confront them, and a vision of their country as a major regional and global power on a par with China. The country and its leadership has fluctuated between manic moods—as when India ejected Portugal from Goa, Mrs. Gandhi triumphed over her political opponents, the Indian army defeated Pakistan over Bangladesh, and India's Atomic Energy Commission exploded a nuclear device—to periods of deep depression over the realities of the country's poor economic performance and the dismal poverty of the vast majority of its population.

It will make a great deal of difference to the region in which India is located and to the world at large if India, with its vast population, military power, advanced technology, and economic potential is an international nuisance, an aggressive or unstable force provoking instability and conflict in the region, or, alternatively, a force for regional order and development playing a constructive international role. While developments internal to India and events throughout the region will largely shape the role India will play, the influence of the United States is by no means trivial. Since 1971, the United States has played a significant role in finding for the Chinese leadership a more secure international position that has substantially reduced their anxieties. It remains to be seen whether the United States develops an adversary relationship with India driving it still further into the Soviet arena, or is responsive to India's quest for a larger role in regional and world politics.

Growth and Equity in Two of the Poorest Countries: India and Bangladesh

John P. Lewis

Introduction: Why Bother with South Asia?

For a decade there has been growing discontent with the results of postwar developmental strategy. This discontent has been aggravated by the growing recognition of the limits of global resources and the constraints these limits impose on efforts to foster growth and thus narrow the globe's grosser inequities. Most recently a series of particular emergencies—droughts, floods, food and fertilizer shortages, skyrocketing food and fertilizer prices, and almost incredible oil price hikes—has been battering the poorest countries.

All of this bad news catches the advanced economies, certainly the United States, in a time of self-doubt and of intractable problems at home. The impulse is to turn away from the poor countries—especially, perhaps, from the two most populous of the poorest, India, with a population of about six hundred million, and Bangladesh with seventy-five million. Americans feel that they have had a long, fairly expensive encounter with the Indian and (under its previous guise of East Pakistan) the Bangladesh developmental efforts. All they see now is a steady stream of depressing and/or perplexing reports from those places. South Asia, it is argued, is beyond our scope of responsible endeavor; it is now only of marginal strategic interest to the United States; as they are presently managed the Indian and Bangladesh economies are losing propositions and getting worse.

It is even becoming fashionable to apply the concept of "triage" to India and Bangladesh: in a world of scarce resources and limited opportunities for survival, some say it will be the part of global statesmanship to concentrate external

effort and resources on the more salvageable poor countries and accept a
Malthusian solution in South Asia. While the world averts its eyes, the scourges
of starvation, pestilence, and internal violence must be allowed to thin down the
subcontinent's population to a point where the transformed system of governance emerging can contrive a viable future for the survivors.

Intuitively, many American policymakers know that these canons of indifference are dubious guides to policy for the medium and longer term. Not only is
the "triage" proposition preposterous; even milder versions of the standing-aside
syndrome clash fundamentally with what many policymakers perceive will be
the dominant themes of transnational affairs during the balance of the century.

These latter are issues of global as opposed to narrowly national welfare: of
population control, environmental management, resources scarcities, resources
sharing, nuclear safeguards, and reduced inequity. Almost inexorably these
themes have been encroaching on the traditional "high policy" concerns of
international relations, and it requires no particular optimism or idealism to
expect the encroachment to continue. The condition of interdependence among
countries, including between poor countries and rich, is becoming more
pronounced and visible all the time. So are the forces that in due course will
tend to tilt policy responses in directions favoring the poor.

For one thing, there will be growing pressure from the poor countries
themselves; the following section refers to the swift emergence of reaffirmed,
post-OPEC, Third World solidarity and of demands for a "new international
economic order" since 1973. In the second place, a more subtle engine of
rich-country responsiveness to the global concerns may be at work: the
consciences of rich-country publics and, more particularly, of those making and
influencing public policy.

It is not that future policymakers in the rich countries will be morally
superior either to their forebears or to their counterparts in the poor countries.
It is simply that (a) they will be facing a world in which the requirements of
global interdependence will be clearer than ever, (b) it will be increasingly plain
that self-serving efforts by nation-states cannot cope with these requirements,
and (c) rich-country decisionmakers will view the world from a condition of
national affluence affording unprecedented scope for their consciences.

It seems to me fairly clear that a phenomenon of creeping globalism already is
infecting rich-country decision-making. Many of the gifted young Americans and
Europeans who have elected and/or recently embarked on careers in public
affairs provide the clearest evidence. On the average, the loyalties and values of
this new generation of public-policy participants are less sharply focused on their
respective nation-state jurisdictions than is and was the average case, not only of
their elders now but of those same elders when they were young. The diffusion
of the loyalties of today's young is not unidirectional. Part of the shift away
from the nation-state is inward to more localized jurisdictions and concerns but
part of their shift also is outward. Many more than was the case two or three

decades ago look at transnational issues through sets of preferences that relate more to planetary than to national interests, and they do so less with unction or self-righteousness than with an air of self-evidence. They are impatient with the antiqueness of nation-bounded decision-making.

These young people already find many like-minded seniors in Western decision-making communities—not just in the universities, foundations, churches, and public service organizations, but in national bureaucracies, parliaments, the press, and producer groups as well. Such people do not yet have reliable majorities, and most of them in most contexts still find it necessary to cloak their global-interest-promoting argumentation in orthodox national-interest terms. But globalists are common, and their numbers are growing.[a]

Creeping globalism is likely to be decisively reversed only by a worldwide disaster on the order of a nuclear holocaust, so devastating as to demolish the whole present system of interdependence. Regional disasters if they come—for example, a genuine breakdown of development processes and prolonged mass starvation in South Asia itself—will represent massive failures of the global imperative; but they will only accelerate the trend toward globalism subsequently.

One does not have to go overboard with this forecast. Certainly there is no prospect that global concerns will wholly submerge narrowly national concerns, any more than in its heyday the national interest wholly dominated state and local interests. Nor is it likely that the transition to a more sensible world order will be widely perceived as requiring anti-patriotism. It will be more a matter of reading new, broadening content into the "national interest"—at least for the long remaining time that the nation-state holds most of the power for dealing with transnational problems.

The need to be globally responsible is the central reason why American policy scarcely has the option of indifference to what happens in India and Bangladesh in the years next ahead. It is in the poorest countries, in what now are often called the countries of the "Fourth World" or, in the lexicon of the oil-food-fertilizer crisis, the "most seriously affected" countries, that the transcendent global welfare issues come most sharply and poignantly to focus. India and Bangladesh are not merely representative of this poorest country set; they account for two-thirds of the Fourth World's one billion people.

---

[a]The present hypothesis is partly at odds with one piece of conventional wisdom on which, as an introductory premise, most commentators on international affairs seem to agree these days—namely, that nationalism is on the rise worldwide. Certainly this is true of most of the poor countries, probably including China and of most or all of the oil-exporting countries; it may or may not be true of the USSR, East European countries, and Japan; but my guess is that, beneath the surface, the opposite is the case in most of the OECD countries including the United States. In this country, even the surface inclination toward international retrenchment is not at odds with the hypothesis in the text, since the cause from which we are retrenching was that of (albeit, in most of our minds, benign) American hegemony. To conclude that, after all, the United States cannot run the world is not to retreat into greater nationalism.

India, in particular, has other characteristics of interest to some Westerners. It is actually a multinational system with as much regional variety and almost as little history of national integration as all of Western Europe. The resilience of India's national integrity and the speed with which it has been acquired therefore are rather remarkable; they provide a useful standard against which to scale schemes for multistate regional economic and/or political integration elsewhere in the developing world. From 1947 to 1975 India's record of dogged adherence to constitutional-democratic processes of governance and change was unparalleled for a country so complex and poor. The related subservience of its military to civilian control and the related endurance of official legitimacy in the country (no change of government by force of arms since the eighteenth century) were also extraordinary.[b]

However fascinating many like myself find these features, neither they in the case of India nor their faint, less convincing, parallels in the case of Bangladesh, constitute the essence of the necessary American concern for these countries. Neither does the territory they occupy hold strategic importance for the United States. The essence is a matter of numbers. No program for a saner, more equitable world order can possibly write off a seventh (in the case of India) or a fifth (in the case of South Asia) of the world's people.

This is an uncomfortable premise for American policy, for the things that the American people and their government can do to affect South Asian outcomes during the next decade turn out to be comparatively limited. Nevertheless, the compulsion of the interdependency ethic is that we must try anyway. Hence the end product of this chapter will be a set of recommendations about the external, specifically American policies that should be attempted vis-à-vis India and Bangladesh. The necessary background for these statements will include a systematic sketch of the transnational policy situation in which the poorest countries now find themselves, identification of a number of the key problems facing India and Bangladesh, and the general policy choices faced by these two countries in the decade and quarter century ahead.

The Old Rich, the New Rich, and the Poorest Countries

In retrospect it is odd that for two decades after World War II expectations about economic growth in the poor countries were so euphoric. For the preceding century two massive problems that bore on the condition of the poor countries and their relations with the rich had been developing.

For one thing, to a degree wholly unprecedented, the planet was engaged in a surge of population growth that was by definition nonsustainable. In the quarter

---

[b]Some early reflections on the scale and significance of the break in the constitutional tradition marked by the emergency actions initiated on June 26, 1975 are offered in the section "Survival or Breakthrough?" (p. 121).

century following 1950, the population explosion has become far more dramatic. A further 1-1/2 billions have been added to the world's numbers with the great bulk of the increment coming in the low income countries. The world's rate of net population growth, which before World War II had been less than 1 percent annually (implying a doubling of population in 100 years) has risen to nearly 2 percent—which if sustained, would multiply our numbers six times over the next 100 years.

It already was clear in 1950 that the pace of expansion then underway could not continue for many decades. The only questions were how soon it would be stopped and whether by humane or inhumane means. The mechanism of humane slowdown, namely, the so-called demographic transition, wherein falling birthrates do begin to catch up with falling death rates, reducing net population growth toward zero, already was visible in some of the advanced economies. There was reason to hope (as there still is) that it would spread in due course to the poor countries, but there also was reason (a) to worry about the lag in this spread and its implications for the population problem and (b) to fear that, since the fertility-reducing transition evidently was linked to rising standards of living, it might not set in "naturally" or "automatically" at all in countries of low average living standards—where per capita income gains were being diluted, among other things, by the high population growth rate itself.

In the second place, for most of the same 100 years before 1950, the income differentials among the countries of the world had been widening to a degree that in its own way was as striking as the population explosion. These growing international disparities, caused by the degree to which the advanced economies had been running ahead of the rest, also were without counterpart historically. Before the 1950s were far advanced it was evident that the first (population) trend was fortifying the second: even when the poor countries achieved as high or higher aggregate economic growth rates as the rich countries, their populations grew so much faster than their per capita incomes tended to fall farther behind.

As I have written elsewhere:

Taken together, the world's population and income-disparity trends were a potent recipe for disaster. On a finite planet, a rapidly multiplying population was sure to run out of space, if nothing else, rather soon. And for all the world's ideological diversity, there was not a modern social ethic anywhere that could pretend to provide enduring justification for the existing, let alone worsening, inequality in international income distribution. The rich countries were living on borrowed time and the whole ship was getting crowded.[1]

Classic Development Strategy and Its Disappointments

Yet, after World War II, we embarked on a period of great optimism about poor-country development and rather quickly evolved the outlines of what can be called classic postwar development strategy. The poor countries themselves, most of them becoming newly independent, were full of heady new nationalism. Their leaders were keen for economic betterment. They were determined to borrow modern techniques and processes from the advanced economies aggressively, to plan and invest, to design economic accelerations along the lines of some mixture of Western and Soviet models, and to set their countries on paths of self-sustaining expansion that soon would achieve international self-reliance, while at the same time winning broadening benefits for their masses.

During the 1950s and early 1960s this agenda commanded growing support in the advanced economies. Aside from the cold war rationales that nourished it, the cause of overseas development offered the rich countries strengthened world markets and more productive sources of raw materials. In addition, "it salved their humanitarian consciences. And . . . did so 'on the cheap.' "[2]

The strategy was not a share-the-wealth program. Concessional transfers from abroad—foreign aid—were to play only a catalytic role. The poor countries were to tilt their growth paths upward mainly by self-help—borrowing technology astutely, practicing austerity, planning and investing wisely, creating capacities to meet their expanding requirements for savings and for foreign exchange. Aid, nicely timed to facilitate the launching of this self-help effort, was to play a limited, self-terminating, albeit key role in assisting the poor countries to establish themselves on fast growth tracks. The latter were to be enough steeper than those of the rich to catch up eventually. The external financial requirements envisaged for giving a succession of moderate, sustained but time-bound pushes to poor-country development were comparatively modest. In promulgating its strategy for the Second Development Decade in 1970 the United Nations General Assembly selected a concessional-transfers (i.e., official development assistance) target of 0.7 percent of donor countries' total products.

Thus classic developmental strategy spoke more of complementarities and mutual benefits than it did of sharing scarcities. People seldom put numbers on how long full convergence of rich-country and poor-country growth paths would take, and students of development worried that the expectations of the poor might outrun their performance and their patience. Yet the vision of each country sooner or later having the opportunity to attain a standard of material welfare even higher than the richer countries enjoyed presently was part of the mystique. The program was one of "creeping international economic justice."[3]

The classic strategy was not all wrong. The poor countries as a group during the late 1950s and the 1960s did make good the first Development Decade's GNP target of 5 percent annual growth in real terms, thereby matching, even slightly outpointing, the advanced economies' composite growth rate. Some did quite handsomely, also raising their per capita incomes substantially, boosting exports enough to make convincing progress towards self-reliance, and in a few cases like Taiwan and its huge Communist counterpart on the mainland, simultaneously putting welfare floors under their poorest groups. Even in most of the sluggish, slow-growth cases, development performance outdistanced the pre-1950 record.

Nevertheless, by the mid-sixties the Third World's development effort was generating a complex of frustrations and disappointments. The development policy community was dismayed at the degree to which burgeoning population growth eroded the gains in aggregate economic growth. Moreover, in the doing, the development process proved to be more complicated, time-consuming and error-prone than had been expected—in the cases both of the poor countries themselves and of external assistance agencies. As the sixties wore on, further-more, there was growing concern that the classic strategy had been aimed at the wrong goals, or, at least, an inadequate set of goals. In country after country evidence began to accumulate that the poor—both the rural and the urban poor, what Robert McNamara came sweepingly to characterize as the "lower 40%"—were sharing little if at all in development gains. By the early seventies these issues of intranational equity dominated development debate. The empha-sis was on the need to attack mass poverty and unemployment, to narrow national income distributions, at least to put welfare floors under low-end poor.

Meanwhile the disparities among the poor *countries* were widening alarm-ingly. No one had imagined that a classic strategy would cause all of them to move forward in lock step. But the dispersion of performance was extreme. Most, although not all, of the front runners were smaller countries. Many, although not all, of them had received exceptionally large per capita injections of foreign aid. Many of them had achieved notably good export performances and a few, of which Taiwan is an example, had combined rapid growth with improved equality. But cases of very sluggish expansion accounted for a large portion of the Third World—including the two countries of particular concern in this chapter.

Meanwhile, also, the classic strategy's catalytic instrument, foreign develop-ment assistance, was under increased attack. By the end of the sixties, donor governments had carried too many different briefs for foreign aid programs to their parliaments. They had promised too much too fast. Many in the donor publics as well as parliaments found that their aid had not bought as much political accommodation or overt gratitude as expected. Its economic benefits were arguable or elusive. From their side, recipients objected to political strings. They objected perhaps even more to donors trying to tell them how to run their own affairs for their own good. The aid relationship was complicated and prickly. In the case of bilateral aid it involved a transaction between two juridical peers in which, on the one hand, philanthropy could not serve as a sustaining psychological model but where, on the other hand, if the model were to be bargaining between equals, the value received by the donor was always subject to dispute. The relationship had a certain inherent illegitimacy. These particular difficulties were muted in the case of multilateral assistance, but the latter had problems of its own and, until recently, was not a vehicle to which many bilateral donors were willing to entrust large portions of their transfers.

By the end of the sixties, moreover, it became apparent that donors and recipients had collaborated in the creation of a kind of debt monster. By getting and accepting past aid on unrealistically hard terms—ones that assumed that the recipients would move rather quickly to conditions not just of self-reliance but of trade surplus—many of the poor countries were saddled with wholly unrealistic debt servicing and repayment burdens.

Scarcities and Development

Thus the cause of development already was in disarray when the world became reminded of its finiteness in the late sixties. The specific implications that the new concerns about environment and about natural resource and energy scarcities had for the poor countries were not all adverse. For example, the pollution-absorbing capacities of the most industrialized countries tend to be most overloaded and therefore to generate the highest environmental protection costs. In some manufacturing processes this should shift comparative advantage enough to cause outmigration of industry to the poor countries. Similarly, if scarcities do indeed now cause pervasive and persisting increase in raw material prices in relation to those of finished goods prices (a phenomenon long anticipated but, despite the flamboyant case of oil, not yet generally established), this will benefit those poor countries which own disproportionate shares of the world's natural mineral and energy resources.

Yet the overall implications of the new scarcities and environment awareness were unmistakably hostile to development, since they were hostile to growth worldwide. If one believed the most extreme and prominent of the macro-ecology tracts that appeared near the turn of the decade—the *Limits of Growth* broadside issuing in March 1972 from the Forrester-Meadows group at MIT under the sponsorship of the Club of Rome—the converging growth paths rationale of classic development strategy was totally demolished: global economic growth needed to be arrested forthwith; in the rich countries real per capita incomes probably should go into reverse; and even in the poor countries the goal of economic expansion should be set aside or greatly muted. Governments seeking uplift should look for it instead in cultural, spiritual, or other less scarcities-prone spheres.

Many of us take a much less apocalyptic view of global expansion prospects. We are convinced that to counsel the poor countries to settle for gains in their psychic well-being that are not dependent on increases in their aggregate output and income is supercilious nonsense. The case for zero population growth is far more persuasive than that for zero economic growth. Even so, the macro-ecological dimension forces some sobering changes into one's rich country-poor country perspectives. First, the finiteness of the planet's land, water, fossil fuels, and virgin mineral deposits does cast devastating doubt onto the forever-onward-and-upward-for-everyone mystique that underlay the classic strategy. Second, if this is so and if, at the same time, poor-country growth rates (for reasons of *intra*national equity) need to speed up, not slow down, the rich countries no longer can discharge their responsibilities to poor-country development "on the cheap." If the global imperative demanding that some consequential inroads be made on the world's welfare gaps is to be served, modest, temporary, self-terminating inoculations of foreign aid will no longer suffice. Some kind of continuing share-the-wealth program after all is required.

That there is a need for continuing net transfers in a vastly unequal world of limited resources is not really a very surprising conclusion. At the moment, however, the politics of such a program looks highly uncertain—in many aid-receiving as well as aid-providing countries. Thus at various points in the balance of this chapter and especially in the final section we shall need to revert to the political feasibility of different forms of transfers in different time frames. As we do so, it will be well to remember that two kinds of exaggeration should be avoided.

The worst exaggeration would be to imply that this matter of external transfers, important as it is, can dominate the futures of the poor countries. We shall see that in India and Bangladesh it can make a vital difference at the margin—but only if the bulk of the need effort, needed resources, and needed policy changes are produced by the Indians and Bengalees themselves.[c]

On the other hand, it would be wrong to exaggerate the underlying incapacity of the wealthier countries to implement a continuing flow of net transfers. Their growth rates may be dampened for reasons that have been partly suggested, but, especially in per capita terms, they will remain substantial. The "old rich" will retain plenty of scope for sharing resources with the neediest countries if they develop the will to do so.

The Third and Fourth Worlds, India and Bangladesh, and the Food-Energy-Fertilizer Crises

The latest set of jolts requiring us to rethink classic development strategy has been the rash of shortages and/or import price hikes—most notably in food, oil, and fertilizer—that has been afflicting the low-income countries since 1972. Although these need not be a kind of first-act unfolding of the doomsday,

---

[c]In this chapter I am adopting the convention that some in Bangladesh are promoting, namely, of using "Bengalee," with, as it were, an old nineteenth century British spelling, to differentiate the adjectival form of Bangladesh and the noun for nationals of Bangladesh from the genetic "Bengali," which applies to all of Bengal, including the Indian state of West Bengal. (Even though I am falling in line with the attempted new usage, I doubt that the Bengalees can make it stick.)

Limits of Growth scenario, they do, unarguably, sharpen the differentiation within the developing world and invite particular focus on its poorest, most beleaguered parts.

As noted, the diversity of performance among the developing countries has been well recognized for some time. Yet until recently the predominant tendency has been to emphasize the formal solidarity, the conceptual homogeneity, of all developing countries as a single category. In 1974 and 1975 the concept of Third World solidarity went through a period of most strenuous economic and political testing. Economically, there was no question that the differential impacts of the food and fertilizer price rises and, above all, of the oil price explosion at the end of 1973 had radically widened the disparities within the Third World.

At one extreme now were the oil exporters—the OPEC countries. They themselves were by no means undifferentiated. All of them still had difficult and interesting development problems. The oil-price bonanza had not yet lifted some of them (e.g., Indonesia and Nigeria) out of a condition of average poverty, and only a few of them with small populations had become genuinely "rich" countries, as that term is conventionally and sensibly construed. But all had experienced radically improved access to foreign exchange, and collectively the oil exporters had enjoyed a stunning expansion in their general power to bargain internationally.

In the broad middle of the Third World range now was a large group of oil-importing countries which rather plainly had good prospects for coping with the new food, fertilizer, and oil problems without any increment of notably concessional assistance from the international community. These were still poor countries by conventional standards; few of them had average per capita incomes of more than $500. But they shared some or all of the following characteristics: they had enjoyed rapid output gains during the sixties and early seventies; the volume of their exports had been rising briskly; the relative prices of their exports, including raw materials other than oil, had been moving favorably thanks to the boom in advanced economy markets in the early 70s; they had accumulated relatively abundant foreign exchange reserves, and/or they already had achieved levels of consumption that can be squeezed feasibly, even if painfully.

Such countries include most of those of Latin America, a number in East and Southeast Asia, and some of the non-oil exporting states of Africa and West Asia. In trying to sort out the implications that the explosions in oil, food, and fertilizer prices held for the Third World, one passes over this group briskly only with some trepidation. Just because a country can manage it, "coping" does not become easy or per se desirable. At minimum, it was widely concluded, the members of the middle-range group should be wound into whatever schemes for "recycling" nonconcessional petrodollars the more affluent countries, in concert with the oil exporters, developed for themselves. Moreover, if and as the thrust of the international community's antipoverty efforts shifted away from these countries, it was to be remembered that most of them still contain large numbers of extremely poor, disadvantaged people at the lower ends of their income distribution.

Yet in 1974 and 1975 persons of good will outside the Third World focused their predominant concern where, on the economic merits, it belonged: on those countries at the poorest end of the widened range. These nations lack either the wherewithal or access to supplies for importing the food and fertilizer they need. They do not have the export earnings or idle foreign exchange to pay the fourfold rise in oil prices since 1973 and they cannot reduce their consumption of imported oil without damaging their productivity. Even if these countries can find short-term suppliers' credits for patching across some of these basic deficits temporarily, they can do so only at the price of adding swiftly to debt burdens already too high.

The World Bank, the UN and such bilateral agencies as AID agreed that the populations of these "most seriously affected" countries number about one billion. They included most of what were officially the "least developed countries," but they also included India, whose population is many times larger than the entire "least developed" group and which is industrially much more mature than the members of that group. And they included Bangladesh and the rest of South Asia. Indeed it was clear that together India and Bangladesh constituted the bulk of the whole developing world's main problem area.

An emergency focus on the needs of the poorest, "most seriously affected countries was agreed upon by most governments participating in the April 1974 Special Session of the UN Assembly. But there and thereafter a strange thing (or so it first appeared in many Western eyes) began to happen to Third World politics. Whereas, with the best of intentions, the Overseas Development Council of Washington, for example, had begun to popularize the term "The Fourth World" as a device for dramatizing the urgently differentiated condition of these poorest countries, the usage began to be resented, not just by the rest of the Third World but by some in the poorest countries themselves. The signs had been evident in the first reactions of many of the poorest oil importers to the oil price hikes: they were remarkably muted and amiable. Even though the immediate implications were grievously costly to themselves, they could not suppress their glee at seeing some of their developing world colleagues twist the tails of the affluent.

However, more than sentiment was involved in the political turn of 1974-1975. The Third World did a great deal of counseling among itself and a bargain was struck—among the OPEC countries, the middle countries, and the poorest—that a solid Third World front was to be maintained; that OPEC's new-found muscle was to be used for bargaining with the "first" and "second" worlds on behalf of the whole Third World; and that, also, in some measure, OPEC's windfalls were to be shared with all in the collectivity, including the poorest countries.

This "bargain," obviously, is not graven in stone. Skepticism about its strength and durability are in order, and in no sense can it absolve affluent countries like the United States from their continuing (planetary) responsibilities vis-à-vis the poorest countries. Moreover, there is evidence that Washington is now beginning to understand that the new reinforcement of Third World solidarity is not just eyewash. Along with the politics of oil that prompted it, it requires some further examination in the next section.

Meanwhile, since there is no question about the more deeply differentiated needs of such "most seriously affected countries" as India and Bangladesh, let me make a last point about the significance of the oil-food-fertilizer emergencies from the perspective of this essay.

There is no question that India and Bangladesh are getting beaten up by the import price rises. The higher prices of oil, commercially imported food and fertilizer since 1972, mean that just to maintain the same volume of total imports, and therefore the same external inputs to the development process, India needs at least an extra $1.5 billion annually. This is six times the size of the recent *net* inflow of foreign economic assistance. The foreign exchange impacts in Bangladesh are comparable.

However, the whole exercise to which this essay belongs is concerned with medium- and long-term international problems. Are not the present crises irrelevant to our time frame? The answer is no—for two reasons. Firstly, some of the current impacts—deepened indebtedness, worsened malnutrition, frayed political fabrics—will bequeath legacies to the future. Secondly, the crises are symptomatic. The present difficulties reflect underlying, cumulative weaknesses in the Indian and Bengalee development processes.

It is true that India and Bangladesh have suffered worse-than-average weather in the first half of the 1970s, and that the establishment of Bangladesh drained real resources from both countries. For the most part, however, these countries have been hit hardest by the international price and shortage crises for reasons that have been endemic. India and Bangladesh were among the poorest. They had records of weak growth; they are slow-growth countries, moreover, in which grievous internal inequities have been compounding, not easing. They sailed into the current food-fertilizer-oil turbulence with few ready reserves of any kind.

The basic question the chapter addresses, therefore, is not whether these two countries can overcome the current crises but whether they can surmount the problems that the current crises reveal with new vividness. It happens that there is a further complicating twist: In both countries thoroughgoing revolution, particularly from the Left, probably is not in the near- or medium-term cards. So the question becomes, is it likely that acceptable results in economic growth and social equity will be achieved under a regime of nonrevolutionary reform, and what would it take for the rest of us to heighten the chances?

The question is not one that permits crisp answers. But the crudest error would be to bite off a quick, negative response. Before turning to look at India and Bangladesh from the inside out, however, we must put in place one final piece of the global framing within which their future development efforts are due to be played out.

The Old Rich, the New (Oil) Rich, and the Poor

Oil has been the first, and it is sure also to be the greatest, case of deliberate developing-country use of commodity power to extract significant transfers of income and wealth from the rich countries. In its degree of adaptability to this function petroleum was a sport; OPEC is not a model that other would-be raw-material cartelizers can copy literally, on anything like the same scale. But, as the preceding section began to suggest, the oil revolution itself has substantially altered the international context in which future Indian and Bengalee development efforts will be conducted. It has radically raised the costs of essential imports. But it also has altered the international power alignment and the array of external funding sources.

What is unusual about oil is the scale of its consumption (measured in value terms), its essential nature (in part because of the lack of ready substitutes), and the degree to which the heavy consumers had become dependent on a few developing-country suppliers. Once the latter awakened to the possibilities, their incentive to maintain discipline among themselves was extraordinarily high.

The degree of advanced-economy dependence on lesser developed countries which are oil exporters that had evolved by 1973, was partly the result of a technological accident, namely, that the most prodigious incremental demander of energy during the middle quarters of the twentieth century, the automobile, was oriented to a specific, comparatively scarce, energy source disproportionately deposited in a few poor countries. Moreover, the governments presiding over those oil deposits were backward and elitist. This helped the international oil companies (which provided abundantly for themselves) to pass along the oil to Western consuming countries and Japan (and, along with them, to the oil-importing LDCs) at prices well below its "true" scarcity value for at least a generation prior to 1973. Not only did the industrialized consumers become inordinately dependent on oil; they underinvested in and underplanned for alternate energy sources.

Especially since we may almost be within reach (in breeder-reactor, fusion, solar-generation, and other processes) of major energy sources that do not exhaust nonrenewable resources, there is no real reason to think that the race has lost its capacity for innovating new, acceptably cheap forms of energy a step ahead of its requirements. But by the early 1970s it was clear that at least briefly, for the next 10-15 years, the industrialized countries would be heavily dependent on imported oil, and it was on this vulnerability that OPEC seized. With shocking suddenness at the end of 1973 it moved to impose on its customers the full scarcity rent they had been avoiding together with a monopoly mark-up for good measure (how much was one and how much the other remains arguable).

The impacts of this action on Western Europe, Japan, and the United States (the OECD countries, at which, of course, the action primarily was aimed) were so traumatic as, at first, to obscure their vision of the spill-over on the rest of the by-standing, oil-importing LDCs. In terms of politico-economic power, the OECD countries suddenly found themselves confronting a giant born full grown. On their domestic economies the higher oil prices had the same effect as would sharp hikes in excise taxes unaccompanied by offsetting rises in government expenditures; at a time when all of the OECD countries already were struggling with different degrees and brands of "stagflation," the oil price increases retarded income, aggravated unemployment, and contributed to cost-push inflation. Internationally, the oil price upheaval not only threw the advanced consumer countries into a heavy trade deficit (because the oil exporters were not able to channel the bulk of the sudden surge in their collective earnings into indigenous consumption and investment that would have tended to raise their imports into line with the multiplied value of their exports); they had to struggle with the problem of adjusting the international monetary system to the resulting ballooning of oil-exporter liquidity.

The jury is still out on how well the advanced countries will cope with all these impacts on themselves. But meanwhile the question is what roles are to be played by the OECD countries on the one hand, and by the OPEC countries, on the other, vis-à-vis the emergency-augmented needs of such poorer countries as India and Bangladesh.

In early 1974, a number of Western liberals imagined a response scenario that instinctively still adopted a white-man's burden approach. The initiative, it was reasoned, was going to have to lie with the old rich who, rising above their own discomfiture, would need to make extra provision for the most seriously affected countries and, in the process of so doing, bargain, pressure, or otherwise induce some of the OPEC countries into following the OECD example. The actual scenario thus far has been quite different. The forecast underlying the early 1974 estimates, namely, that the most seriously affected countries were altogether likely to come up short, was right. As to initiatives, moreover, it is true that the multilateral institutions most directly involved, the World Bank and the International Monetary Fund (which, in early 1974, most Western liberals still regarded as mainly agents of the old rich) have been active and enterprising in trying to devise responses to the emergency problems of the "MSAs." Similarly, bilaterally and in their regional groupings, some of the OECD governments, notably the Europeans, have been quite forthcoming. But the indispensible lead of the United States has been missing. In late 1974 and early 1975, at and after the Rome World Food Conference, the American Government played a fairly positive and creative role in the area of food policy and food aid.

But in the realm of energy—with implications spilling over to other raw materials—possible pro-MSA initiatives by the United States throughout 1974 and much of 1975 were preempted by a preoccupying, almost surely futile, desire to roll oil prices—and oil politics—back to their pre-1973 position.

Meanwhile, as noted, the principal initiatives with respect to revised resource sharing in the post-oil revolution world have passed to a re-examined and reaffirmed Third World coalition. There is a demand for a New International Economic Order. Instead of the story line that some of us imagined in early 1974, where the good old rich would seize the initiative and browbeat (along with themselves) the OPEC countries into doing the needful vis-à-vis the MSAs, the operative line may come closer to one in which an alliance of OPEC, the MSAs, and the rest of the Third World browbeats us into greater action.

There is more to the new scenario than this, of course. As a group, the OPEC countries have been unexpectedly swift and sophisticated (and/or responsible) in reaffirming their membership within the developing country set. They are projecting lucrative exchanges of commodities, expertise, and capital—including a variety of promising joint ventures—within the set. Compared with other early aid donors (e.g., the Europeans in the late 1950s and early 1960s) they have been remarkably forthcoming with their concessional transfers, already raising their commitments of the latter to two or three times the UN percentage-of-GNP targets (of which the OECD countries are falling far short). Nor are they confining their distributions exclusively to their nearest neighbors and fraternal allies.

Nevertheless, much of the emerging scenario is indeed preoccupied with plans (1) for extending the oil-cartelization example to other commodities whose supplies are LDC-dominated and (2) for putting OPEC's oil-bargaining muscle to the collective Third World purpose of (a) securing more old-rich concessions vis-à-vis other commodities than the latter could win standing on their own legs and (b) extracting larger overt concessional transfers from the old rich to the poorest countries.

What will all of this reshuffling of international roles mean for the world trade and transfers context in which India and Bangladesh will be struggling to develop during the balance of the century? What, specifically, will/should it mean for American policy toward these countries? At present, unquestionably, many Americans are gagging on the new politics of the new international economic order. Indeed, from the viewpoint of the poorest countries, a politics of confrontation may often be counterproductive because of the reactions it provokes. Yet it may · also—let us be realistically cynical—sometimes work, extracting concessions that otherwise would not be forthcoming. At a minimum, however, continuing confrontation will be a tiresome, dispeptic diet, and for those Americans and the others of the OECD as well as for those Third Worlders who see the world whole, there will be increasing incentive to surmount it. Looked at through such eyes, what implications does/should the new 1974-1975

international alignment of things seem to hold for the 700 million Indians and
Bengalees? There are four factors that arise out of the preceding discussion and a
fifth that must be added.

The strategy of oil-simulating cartels holds very little promise for India and
Bangladesh. They are largely lacking in the raw materials and other supplies for
which this approach seems even superficially plausible.

It is entirely reasonable to expect both countries henceforward to find larger
portions of their trade and transfers needs within the Third World itself. These
will include the kinds of joint ventures, e.g., Indian iron ore will be supplied to
Iran for steel production, and India has begun to work out with Iran and the
Middle East trade in industrial goods, engineering, and other expertise that, in
exchange for commercial capital. However, the possibilities also include substantial inputs of OPEC capital on concessional terms. The facts that (1) a number of
the oil exporters are visibly awash in cash and will remain so for at least several
years, (2) the discretionary portion of their new, magnified incomes is now
higher than it will be when their own routinized uses of income have grown up
to the new levels, and (3) that they have voluntarily assumed special obligations
to share their windfalls with their less fortunate brothers elsewhere in the Third
World, all argue for some receptivity to well-wrought petitions from India and
Bangladesh.

There also will be scope for, and, from an Indian or Bengalee viewpoint,
advantage in channeling a larger fraction of OPEC transfers to the poorest
countries through the experienced, comparatively efficient and (as to distribution) even-handed multilateral institutions: the World Bank, IMF, and the
regional development banks. If so, the new (oil) rich are going to require a bigger
hand in the governance of these institutions. The senior managements of the
Bank and Fund have already understood this and have begun to make
accommodations for these countries. In the years ahead it will be important that
governments of such nations as the United States are prepared to share a greater
portion of the control of the capital-disbursing multilaterals, not only with the
oil exporters but with recipient countries.

The fourth implication of the new alignment is that the underlying distribution of wealth and income in the world has not in fact changed very much,
however. The emergence of the new rich has in no way, if one is concerned
about equitable sharings of burdens, taken the old rich off the hook. This is the
important and difficult lesson for Americans to draw at present. One can argue
that India and Bangladesh should find a higher portion of their external needs in
the Third World itself. However, those needs have been aggravated, and in
estimating any just distribution of responses to them, one must remember the
difference between liquidity, on the one hand, and income and wealth on the
other. Ability to pay is still primarily a function of the latter, and, although the
oil-price explosion has revolutionized the distribution of liquidity, it has (by
effecting transfers to the oil exporters equivalent to 1 or 2 percent of the

advanced countries' national products) barely nudged the world's distributions of income and wealth. It is no time, vis-à-vis the needs of the poorest countries, for the old rich to think of opting out.

There is a corollary to this fourth point. In addition to the OPEC countries' own genuinely concessional transfers to the poorest countries, in the case of other transfers it will make good sense then to provide the principal (which with their liquidity they can readily do) but for the old rich to provide most of the concessional elements in the financing. There are various such schemes on the International Bank for Reconstruction and Development, the International Monetary Fund, and other drawing boards whereunder rich-country donors would subsidize the interest rates that are charged to the poorest countries on OPEC-supplied loans. Such arrangements have much promise.

The final implication that the changes of 1974-75 hold for India's and Bangladesh's future international framework concerns the potential contributions by the "second world"—the Socialist countries mainly in the Soviet Bloc. This is a dimension that has not entered the previous discussion, and, unhappily, this is all too representative of the new-international-economic-order dialogue in the United Nations and elsewhere. The Socialist countries in general cheer on the Third World, but they also have managed to stand largely aloof from the oil-price and oil-politics revolution. The Soviet bloc countries tend to be collectively self-supplying in oil and fertilizer and were lucky or clever enough to escape the first and worst international food price rises. Their official intra-bloc trading and pricing arrangements have cushioned and slowed the impact of general international inflation on their domestic economies. They have somewhat increased their imports from developing countries, but not so much as from the OECD group, and while they report a recent rise in their commitments of development assistance the latter still are at low levels.

Any fair sharing of international burdens vis-à-vis India and Bangladesh in the coming period should include greater contributions by the Socialist countries— by receptivity to South Asian exports, through useful and flexible bilateral and/or Socialist bloc (CMEA) transfers, and by participation in expanded multilateral efforts. There have been signs, at the World Food Conference and elsewhere, that the Socialist countries may have a growing disposition to move in these directions. It will be the part of OECD, OPEC, and Indian and Bengalee diplomacy to press such claims vigorously in the years next ahead.

India and Bangladesh during the Balance of the Century: Some of the Problems

Bangladesh is everybody's most *in extremis* case. It is deep in food deficit. It is the world's most densely crowded large rural population. Population appears to be growing about 3 percent a year. The whole country barely has its nose out of water and every year is victimized by floods, which vary only in their spread and severity. Yet during much of the year many areas lack water for multiple cropping. As an alluvial delta, Bangladesh is so short of a normal complement of natural resources that ballast for road building is still routinely manufactured by baking conventional bricks, then breaking them into chips with hammers. Average incomes in the country are among the world's lowest. Its present export potential is precariously based on jute production and processing that since independence have been competing poorly with India. In industry, now mostly nationalized, as elsewhere, managerial problems are endemic. Corruption and inflation have been rampant. Most of the relatively small but vocal urban population is sorely distressed. In its first years, compared with its overwhelming reconstruction and development problems, the newly organized national government was grossly overmatched.

Nevertheless, in June 1974, after ten years of occasional trying, when I finally reached Comilla, eastern district town and site of the famous Bangladesh Academy of Rural Development, let me tell what I found. Comilla District (population about three million) and, more particularly, Kotwali Thana, the subdivision of some 200,000 that the Academy uses as a "laboratory," are among the most densely populated parts of this most densely populated rural country. In 1960, when Akhter Hameed Khan, an ex-civil servant, educator, and sometime theorist of rural-uplift, was set up in his Comilla Academy and given extraordinary discretion by the national Pakistani authorities and the government of East Bengal to experiment with practical measures, the area seemed to have below-average natural advantages. It was highly flood-prone, had little irrigation, was deficient in food, and suffered extensive underemployment. By 1974 food grains output in Kotwali Thana had increased about three times over. The whole Comilla District had become a food surplus area. A major irrigation facility and a good many farm-to-market roads had been built—labor-intensively and with local labor, although with provincial and central government finance, including American food-aid rupees. Many tubewells had been introduced and were being managed by village level cooperatives.

Multiple, overlapping, almost continuous cropping had become the norm; the period of peak wages for agricultural labor was said to have lengthened from about three to nearly eight months. The area has taken full advantage of the so-called "green revolution" technology (more fertilizer and higher yielding varieties of grain along with better assured water supplies). The regime of new cooperatives and of modified do-it-yourself agricultural extension radiating from the *thana* (roughly, rural county) center that Khan and his colleagues had worked out with the locals, was designed to favor the very small cultivators. It appeared to have done so—so well that the bigger farmers were now trying to take over the cooperatives. Most striking of all was the evidence that the Comilla reforms had managed indirectly to extend considerable benefits even to the landless: there were twinges of labor shortage in this most densely populated rural area. There was so much new work not only in agriculture but in the processing and other small-town urban activities that agricultural expansion had generated that Kotwali now was pulling in construction and field workers from other thanas.

None of this is to say that the "Comilla experiment" is without problems, let alone that Bangladesh rural development is easy. Although Comilla has used mainly local real resources, some imports have been critical and the area has made a greater-than-average draft on provincial (now national) funding. Furthermore, neither can Akhter Hameed Khans be sprinkled into each of Bangladesh's 400 thanas, nor has the Academy invented a magic formula that is self-multiplying. Yet since the time when, because of his West Pakistani identification, Khan had to leave in 1972, the Academy has continued; and the government has found its formulas sufficiently articulated and generally applicable that it is trying to propogate them to other parts of the country—along with other models of rural uplift against which they are being competitively tested. The Comilla story is a powerful sign that rural development in Bangladesh, while not easy, is in no way hopeless.

If one is looking for other encouraging notes in Bangladesh, one does not have to go beyond its large, high quality natural gas reserves, which thus far have been little exploited. India, many times larger than Bangladesh and far more varied, also has a much greater variety of obvious strong points. It has whole states—the Punjab most recently, Tamil Nadu (formerly called Madras), and Gujarat still earlier—that, had they been separate countries (each of them is larger than most developing countries), would be numbered among the developing world's success stories. The country has no one unexploited energy source as extensive, accessible and as capable of meeting its needs as Bangladesh's natural gas; but it does have massive coal reserves, great unharnessed hydroelectric potential (especially if North India can be symbiotically related to Nepal), perhaps a good deal of offshore oil, and a substantial part of the world's iron ore deposits. Probably more important than any of these, it has, across the whole northern Gangetic plain, the world's best and most abundant reservoir of ground water (still only moderately exploited). This plus good enough soils and hot, bright sunlight most of the year (the latter also has an obvious energy implication) means that, in terms of physical potential, the country embraces about as good a piece of real estate for year-round agriculture as the world knows.

Institutionally, modern India's most distinctive features have been the resiliency of its political system. The national integration that this enormous, varied, impoverished "multinational" system has achieved in the past quarter century is apparently irreversible.

Since independence in 1947 there also have been major economic achievements. After the government's launching of a planned development effort in 1951, average per capita incomes, despite accelerated population growth, have expanded at an average annual rate of about 1 percent compared with an aggregate growth of probably less than 5 percent from 1901 to 1921 and almost surely negative growth during the three decades following.[4] Food grains production during the 1950s and 60s grew nearly 50 million tons compared to no more than 10 million tons during the half century preceding. Modern sector industrial production (other than handicrafts and cottage industries), which already had increased 4-1/2 times in the first half of the century, multiplied a further 3-1/2 times in the two decades following. The national savings rate jumped from about 5 percent in 1951-52 to 11-12 percent in the middle 60s and has since remained at that level. Taxation as a fraction of national income has multiplied well over three times since the early 1950s.

It is customary, in describing the platform for further development that India now has in place, to emphasize the substantial physical infrastructure—railways, roads, communications, energy networks, the rather broad array of slowly started but now, in many instances, effectively functioning heavy industries. But the human infrastructure may be more important. Education, although of highly uneven quality, too much skewed toward the upper levels, and imperfectly matched with needs, has expanded. Since 1950, enrollments in primary schools have multiplied more than three times, secondary nearly five times, and university enrollments more than seven times. A number of institutions of excellence—a handful of the traditional universities, the five Indian Institutes of Technology, two Indian Institutes of Management, several of the new (state) agricultural universities—have emerged. Health training and delivery systems, although sorely inadequate to the need, have mushroomed, even in the countryside. The press, until June 1975, was freer than nearly any other in Asia, and was remarkably vigorous. There is a profusion of book publishing—in English, Hindi, and the regional languages. The country has become peppered with nearly 2,000 research institutions and units of all types and sizes, a number of them very competent. It has been estimated that, in terms of numbers, its pool of scientific and technical manpower is exceeded only by those of the United States and the Soviet Union.

India, in short, is more than an aggregate of mass poverty, much more than a culture of saddhus and old monuments. It is a complex, in many respects sophisticated, in some respects highly modernized, system with great varieties of potential for engaging its masses in much more productive and rewarding lives. It is a long way from its potential, but to write it off would be an act of ignorance.

The 1975 Political Changes

In January 1975, Sheik Mujibur Rahman, with parliamentary blessing, changed himself from prime minister to president, ending Bangladesh's brief tortured experiment with parliamentary cabinet government. In August, the Sheik was assassinated in a military coup that installed Khondakar Mushataque Ahmed as president, and he was trampled by yet another coup several months later. Meanwhile, on June 26 in India, Prime Minister Indira Gandhi persuaded the president to declare a national emergency, swiftly employed the police to lock up a large number of opposition leaders, other dissidents, traders, and alleged bad characters, denied the internees resort to the courts, and clamped tight censorship on the Indian press—as well as on those foreign journalists who remained in India.

The scrapping of the Bengali constitution attracted no great American or other Western attention, although, of course, the assassination of Sheik Mujib did. The three-year-long experiment with parliamentary democracy had encountered discouraging problems. If the January move to a formally authoritarian regime could mean greater administrative efficiency, diminished corruption, more effective management of nationalized enterprises, livelier promotion of agriculture, and the institution of some genuine egalitarian reforms, many internal and external observers could not deny it was worth trying. In July 1975, it was evident that a new system of governance was still very much in the process of being invented—bureaucratic power had been centralized in the office of the president, the single party had acquired a politburo, a central committee, and provincial cadres, field administration was being decentralized from seventeen to sixty-one districts to which had just been appointed a new set of locally originating governors who were admonished to be self-reliant, and the first central minister had just been fired for corruption. To this traveler, at least, there appeared to be a good bit more hopefulness (although not yet much more achievement) in the system than a year earlier, and no sign of an immediately impending collapse. Except for the new regime's explanation that it was necessary to remove the sheik because of his ineffectiveness in curbing corruption and mismanagement (subjects treated in the next section) it is not at this writing known how it will modify and/or extend the pattern of organization and of policy that had begun to emerge after January.

Mrs. Gandhi's June 26th so-called coup in India instantly triggered a wave of adverse Western editorial reaction. My own preliminary assessment is that the change has potential benefits as well as costs, that both are comparatively high, that the benefits might well exceed the costs although they are more uncertain, but that it is too early yet for confident forecasts of either side of the balance.

The events which directly led to the declaration of the emergency were a decision by a lower court judge seeking to remove Mrs. Gandhi from office for six years for two admittedly minor infractions of the election laws in her 1971 campaign, a decision by a review judge that failed fully to exonerate her, and a rash of rallies, demonstrations, and protest meetings in which the regime's opposition (whose popular appeal just previously had seemed to be diminishing) seized on the court ruling as an opportunity to revive itself by demanding the prime minister's resignation. In the last of these mass meetings, on June 25, the leading opposition spokesman, Jaya Prakash Narayan, came perilously close to explicitly inciting the police and army to rebel. The scale and suddenness of Mrs. Gandhi's reaction not only proved the extent to which, under its emergency provisions, the letter of the Indian constitution permitted the government to set aside of individual rights, it demonstrated how thoroughly the very submissiveness of the armed forces to civilian command exposed the system to authoritarian takeover by the highest constituted authority; and it revealed how quickly, once the police are ordered to begin such a repression, the fear engendered mutes and dampens resistance.

From the beginning, the burden of the repression, especially on those literate and sophisticated Indians who prized their legal freedoms, was painfully heavy. The Indian police are tough, and, like most police forces, potentially venal. With the reins of courts and press removed, their own propensity for escalating the repression is high. So would that of the leadership if it becomes nervous about the pace at which the emergency is delivering positive benefits and afraid that its initial disciplining effects will wear off. These risks will be greatly magnified as long as, thanks to its muzzling of the press, the regime remains largely dependent for its own information on its intelligence bureaucracy.

Even if these hazards are avoided, it will take a very long time to rebuild genuine constitutionalism. That is, it will be difficult to build trust in a set of ground rules such as those which operated prior to the emergency, within which workable accommodations were thrashed out among the plurality of interests and classes.

As for the potential benefits, one already has accrued: the extraordinarily sour, conflicted stalemate into which Indian public affairs had settled recently, especially from late 1972 onwards, has been broken. During the 1950s and 1960s, as noted, the Indian economy averaged a record of slow growth. Given the gross poverty and inequality of the system, the performance was not nearly good enough. But in an initially non-regionally-integrated and, throughout, elites-dominated system, the growth dividends were enough to keep things viable. They afforded some gains for most regions, for most of the rural and urban elites—considerable benefits even trickling downward, although precious little to the weakest classes.[d]

In the first half of the seventies the economy changed course. The combination of bad weather, a slowdown in the "new agriculture," food-policy mismanagement, explosive import price increases, and anti-investment fiscal and monetary restraints, turned India from a slow-growth to no-growth country. The nation was wracked by much the worst inflation ever, which originated in food

---

[d]Constitutionalism, which by blunting reforms and policy initiatives may have been a factor of retardation, was also a nation-building force. It mediated conflicts among contending regions and elites, but, by strengthening the resistance of the propertied elites, it probably also held down the poor. The latter lacked equal access to the courts and, in any event, were mainly interested in freedom from hunger and from such private masters as landlords and moneylenders.

shortages and import prices but was compounded by the scramble of the organized elites (which in India include organized labor) to preserve their shares of eroding money incomes. Inflation became entangled with an enormous escalation of the corruption issue—high and low, public and private. Reformers became cynical about the failure of the Gandhi government, after the signal electoral mandates it had received in 1971 and 1972 on the two sides of its triumph in the Bengal war, to press consequential antipoverty programs. A malaise of venality, malingering, disorder, and sabotage began to deepen countrywide. The regime was not candid in responding to criticism. The opposition was motley, indiscriminate in its embrace, fuzzy in its counter-program, often irresponsible. By the beginning of 1975, sessions of parliament had degenerated—not occasionally but regularly—into impossible shouting matches.

Such was the conflict-ridden stalemate that the trauma of the emergency has broken for better or worse. If the prime minister (whatever her mixture of motives) had not acted, this grinding, dead-ending condition could have persisted for a very long time while the economy went nowhere and the deficits of the poor mounted. As to positive effects of the emergency, the regime is cracking down on absenteeism, malingering, petty cheating, and bureaucratic inertia. These may be "cosmetic" moves but, given the country's recent approach to productivity, they are not trivial.

Beyond this, how much one expects turns heavily on his understanding of what will become a theme of this study—the paradox of egalitarian reform in nonrevolutionary settings. In such settings the principal agents of reform must be the official establishments that in large part are the political creatures of the very elites upon whom the reforms encroach. The paradox is especially sharp in India. Because of the dominance of the Congress party, one must mainly look for reform initiatives from within that party. More than that, because of the primacy of the prime minister within the Indian system (entrenched by Nehru, Shastri, Indira Gandhi), one must look mainly for initiatives to the sitting prime minister.

There are fairly good reasons to expect Mrs. Gandhi to press major growth and redistribution efforts in the new environment she now has created. To attribute her post-1972 failure to indifference is much too facile; the political and economic barriers to reform piled up very quickly. Now in the context of the fear it has established, the regime should, if it presses on such an issue as the serious taxation of prosperous farmers, find the reluctant elites more acquiescent. It will be running scared itself: Mrs. Gandhi has gone farther out on a limb than before and, if she cannot deliver worthwhile benefits, is likely to be displaced. On the whole, as to a strategy for arousing the nation's productive effort and attacking poverty, the government knows what it wants to do. Conceptually, if one can abstract from the recent political stalemate, the Indian program of development policy is in the best shape ever.

All of these positive possibilities, to repeat, could be swamped by mindlessly escalated repression, and it is too early to forecast the actual skill, boldness, and diligence with which efforts to stimulate the economy and promote equity will be pushed. However, there is a fair chance that most of the problems to which we now turn can be more effectively attacked in the post-June 1975 context than in the situation that preceded it.

Probity

For the most part there is no place for encapsulated or segregated discussions of politics in the present analysis. The political and economic variables are commingled. However, the outcome of two organizational issues will permeate the effectiveness of Indian and Bengalee responses to most of the selected developmental problems which occupy the rest of the chapter. One is corruption. The other is management.

Corruption is a subject that expatriate commentators usually do well to skirt. Almost by definition, they are cut off from representative and reliable data; and often, lacking knowledge of the subtleties of local mores, they wind up invoking standards they would never think of using in New Jersey or Maryland. Yet the issue is too inflamed just now in both Bangladesh and India to be passed over.

Bangladesh, still only three years old as an independent nation, seemed to plot a direct course to big-time venality. Suddenly installed as ministers and leaders of government, men with little previous experience either of wealth or of power busily employed the latter as an access to the former. India is a sadder case, because in a country where probity in high places had been the norm for two decades, and in which governments had appeared to be notably less corrupt than in most developing countries (for that matter, than in many developed economies), there has been great deterioration in the past half dozen years. Such is the vehement assessment of many knowledgeable Indians.

What is mainly corrosive, be it understood, is primarily high-level, essentially ministerial corruption. The provision of tips and gifts to petty bureaucrats has been part of the tradition of doing business in South Asia, as in the rest of Asia and most of the rest of the world. As the rates rise with inflation, the practice can become a growing irritant to the populace, and as inflation flourishes (and civil-service salaries fail to keep pace) the bureaucratic level as well as the per-unit scale of the practice escalates. But on the whole petty corruption is predictable; it can, in effect, be built into business cost projections; it is not flagrantly maldistributive; it is manageable.

In any event, in mounting an anticorruption campaign, it would be the worst kind of blunder for either the Indian or the new Bengalee leadership to focus chiefly on small-scale bribery. To do so would only deepen the cynicism of those senior bureaucrats who have sensed a proximity to but nonparticipation in high-level corruption—and such cynicism has become an alarming problem.

Another distinction is worth noting. In India, at least, although old-fashion, self-serving venality is not unknown, the recent surge of concern about high-level corruption seems mainly to have been a function of party finance. In 1969 when Mrs. Gandhi bested and ousted the "Syndicate"—the old regional bosses of the Congress party—party fund raising was centralized. At about the same time new legislation rendered illegal what had been legal corporate contributions. Thus, whether or not (under inflationary conditions) the total real volume of tainted fund raising actually increased, its practice in Delhi acquired a far higher silhouette.

Rooting out corruption has been proclaimed a goal of Mrs. Gandhi's June 26 emergency, and it figures prominently in the Bangladesh government's explanation of the liquidation of Sheik Mujib. It is doubtful that nonrevolutionary reform has much future in either country unless the salience of corruption is greatly diminished. This will take sustained effort. Part of the reform can be almost mechanical. Some scheme for public financing of political party costs can be adopted; at minimum, private business and other contributions can be brought back atop the table. In the discussion of domestic finance below, there is a reference to the "two-price system" as one of the principal generators of "black money." Its elimination, in so far as possible, will curb corruption at the same time that it tends to dry up black money. And in bureaucratic transactions generally, reducing the number of clearances that a licensee or applicant must obtain will reduce the number of tollgates at which bribes can be levied and that antibribery policing must monitor.

Once a serious cleansing effort is unmistakably launched, a machinery of sustained, aggressive but conspicuously just, enforcement will be essential. The determining question will be whether those at the very top have the stomach and stubbornness for such an effort. In the case of Mrs. Gandhi, who has been sitting at the top since 1966, this must also mean, presumably, the stomach for overriding personal loyalties to some senior associates—who will understandably ask, who is *she*, as their chief of longstanding, whatever her personal probity, to cast the first brick. But one sees no way around the conclusion that bricks nonetheless must be cast and that it will be a mark of leadership to persevere in such an effort, without sanctimony, without lack of self-criticism, but also without respite.

Management

"Management" is related to politics but is different. It extends to the realm of general public administration but also to the conduct of enterprises, public and private, and even to the incorporation of market mechanisms and other nonhierarchical, noncommand arrangements into the guidance of the whole economy.

Americans have been too inclined to see "better management" as the key to everything in South Asia, meaning too often management in the American style. In India, I do not see managerial reform as one of the sharply drawn, decisive issues of the next decade or quarter century. In a sense this is because I do not think radical changes will be forthcoming. Looking at Indian management through American lenses, I find much to complain about, but so do Indians about the style and ambiance of American management.

Modern India started with a stalwart Indo-British public administration system. The Indian Administrative Service continues to recruit people of remarkably high average ability; it continues to train them and imbue them with a common identity. Despite the litany of expatriate pundits to the contrary, the transition from a law-and-order to a developmental mentality is well advanced, and so is the shift from overwhelming reliance on superior generalists to the development and preferment of professional and specialist cadres.

Meanwhile, in enterprise management very substantial changes—many of them representing extensive but selective infusions from the West, especially the United States—are under way. A great many Indians have returned from American business schools. Two outstanding American-style Institutes of Management (at Ahmedabad and Calcutta) are going full tilt and a third is now starting at Bangalore. The country is replete with city-based management associations and by now has supplied high officers to the international chamber and junior chambers of commerce. It knows and has an appetite for all the new, including quantitative, management tools and techniques; it uses its computers well. The better and larger business houses in the private sector are moving away from nepotism and communalism to professional competence as a principle for selecting managers. More and more of the public sector is escaping from what Kenneth Galbraith called "post-office socialism." The ministries and the parliament may even be learning the need to establish an arm's length relationship with public enterprises, holding them accountable to profit and other performance standards rather than to members' whims. The spread of solid benefit-cost project analysis into the investment decision-making of the central and state governments as well as of enterprises is well begun—although not yet far enough advanced. In addition, the trend seems to be toward greater social reliance on market processes and allocations. None of this is perfect or complete, but India's prospect is for a gradually improving, Indianized kind of managerial competence.[e]

In Bangladesh the present contrast with all this is striking. There, in a nation without much experience in administering either its own businesses or its own

[e]The most serious problem is likely to be the development of efficient administrative capacity in the tens of thousands of local authorities which (it will be argued below) should be acquiring greater responsibilities. For the most part, with the help of the regional and local institutions available, this local capacity will have to develop from the ground up. Outsiders will watch the process with concern but cannot greatly contribute to it.

government at the top, the existing management deficits are enormous. Just as keenly as it needs an anticorruption effort and other various types of substantive reform, the government must (again, from the very top) project an explicit and comprehensive management development strategy.[5] Meanwhile the authorities—the preceding government and presumably also the current one—have indicated their readiness to welcome and give adequate managerial and technical discretion to expatriate enterprises in key sectors. This pattern is likely to be particularly important for a considerable period in order to exploit optimally the country's natural gas-fertilizer potential. For there the need will be, not just to build some fertilizer plants that operate, but to achieve enough efficiency to compete successfully in the export market.

The contrasting Indian picture, however, should be sufficient rebuttal to those who assume that Bangladesh is destined forever to remain a managerial desert. The notion that whole populations can be stereotyped by national caricature (". . . the Bengalis are great poets, orators, and intellectuals, but . . .") should long since have been laid to rest by the French, Irish, or Swedes. The Bangladesh population surely contains a full complement of foremen, managers, and administrators who, as soon as they can get some experience in a less chaotic environment, can perform just as capably as their counterparts in India.

Population

In both India and Bangladesh population deserves to stand at the head of any list of substantive developmental problems, but it is well to be clear about which of two quite different issues one has in mind. On the one hand, there is the question of how the countries are to cope with the further population growth that already appears unavoidable. This is what, in its so-called Second India Series, the Ford Foundation in New Delhi has been asking a group of able Indian analysts, drawn from a variety of disciplines, to consider the fact that, barring a resurgence of the death rate, the most careful and reasonable demographic projections now indicate that India's present population of 600 million will double by early in the twenty-first century, probably before 2010. Because Bangladesh's present annual growth rate of 3 percent is nearly a percentage point higher than India's, Bangladesh, even more impoverished than India, will, by similar calculations, double its numbers well before the year 2000.

While this question of how to cope with population growth obviously is all important, it cannot be differentiated from the whole composite development puzzle we are considering. Hence, my immediate focus is on the other (preventative) side of the issue.

First, it must be said that, overwhelmingly important as it is, the problem of population control cannot be given chronological precedence. It puts the cart almost squarely before the horse to say that population growth must be stopped *before* other inputs to the development effort make much sense. It is precisely now, when population expansion is still running full tilt, and when it will take a good deal of time for the most strenuous and cogent efforts to rein it in, that the other inputs are most needed.

The assessments of the population-control problems of countries like India and Bangladesh by most Western specialists and by most of the countries' own specialists have been converging and are not far apart. This was sensed, for example, by many of the participants in the 1974 World Population Conference at Bucharest, a circumstance unfortunately disguised by most reporting of the Conference in the American press. The latter dwelled too much on the distress of those hard-line, single-track Western population-firsters, who found themselves rebuffed by the developing countries, and it failed to distinguish the position of most developing countries including India and Bangladesh, both from the nationalistic, pronatalist views asserted by Brazil and a few African countries, and from the thoroughly cynical game played at Bucharest by China (which denigrated all international population control concern as craven imperialism while referring elliptically to its own apparently effective control program).

There is near consensus on the following points: (a) In India and Bangladesh the most rapid and feasible reduction of birthrates is indeed overwhelmingly important. (b) It would be folly to wait for a "natural" Western-style demographic transition dependent on the attainment of a level of per capita income so high as probably to be beyond the reach of the most ambitious efforts in these countries. (c) However, while the motivations and the social, economic, and health factors affecting fertility, especially in rural areas, are by no means adequately understood yet, fertility is plainly not a disembodied variable. It is intimately linked to improvements in maternal and child care, in the survivability of children, especially sons, in nutrition, education, old-age security, and in income distribution. Hence, while positive fertility control efforts must be pressed, they are only likely to have major impact if they are coupled with perceivable advances in these other dimensions.

As to the implementation of a nondisembodied yet positive fertility control strategy, few Americans have any conception of how substantial an effort India has been making for most of a decade. Bangladesh, in the middle 60s, had been included in Ayub Khan's strenuous single-tracked, semi-disembodied family planning push in Pakistan and then shared the political backlash against that program following Ayub's demise. Consequently, the early post-independence effort was weak. But India in 1966, following fourteen years of token official support, took up family planning in a big way. It has developed a massive bureaucratic-clinical structure of family planning services reaching unevenly but extensively into the countryside; it has, during much of the intervening time, been at the top of the list of developing countries in per capita financial allocations to population control, and has done more sterilizations than any other nation; it has run through the cycle of an all-out, if largely self-defeating, national IUD program; and has, with considerable vigor, promoted rural as well as urban mass marketing of subsidized condoms; and recently India has legalized abortion (albeit, by conceding the medical profession's demands concerning the qualifications of authorized personnel in a way that will discriminate against the rural poor).

The composite record is not unimpressive, and in some states and localities it has made a visible dent in birthrates. In other places, most strikingly now the state of Kerala, a substantial downward trend in fertility seems mainly to confirm the importance of such interacting welfare factors as female literacy, better health services, less rural-urban "dualism," more egalitarian distributions of rural incomes, public benefits, and political power. But even in this case it is clear that family planning services and campaigns have contributed to the result.

At the same time, it is plain that India's, let alone Bangladesh's, positive population control efforts have not yet been nearly effective enough. Recently, the Indian budgetary commitment was allowed to falter. The massive bureaucratic-clinical system has remained bogged in managerial problems (e.g., central government vs. state, administrative-generalist vs. technician). Too frequently the Health and Family Planning portfolio has been used as a parking place for superannuated Congress Party politicians.

Lately Mrs. Gandhi has become bolder in committing her personal prestige to the population control efforts, and in his last months Sheik Mujib was very outspoken, but earlier both were diffident. There has been too little promotion of modes of population restraint that do not depend on clinical delivery. Allocations to research and experimentation have been scant. In particular, neither government seems to me to have been sufficiently venturesome in experimenting with various types and designs of economic incentives—especially positive incentives—meant to bring private fertility preferences into line with social needs.

Population control, however, is an area of policy peculiarly ill-adapted to interventions by external actors. It is a personally sensitive, politically complex, subtle, conflict-ridden field. As evidenced at Bucharest, even poor country governments fully aware of the issue resent rich-country efforts that, to the exclusion of other dimensions of their development, seem to be mainly concerned to stop their breeding.

In India and Bangladesh the most useful thing international aid agencies can do regarding population policy is to get off recipients' backs so that official antifertility policies can be perceived as unmistakably homegrown. There are several positive things that international organizations and industrialized nations can do. Multilateral agencies, like the World Bank, should contribute to the funding of indigenous family planning efforts—at the request of the respective governments. It is important that the rich countries press their own research into reproductive biology and contraceptive technology and propagate the findings.

Further articulation of nonofficial population-oriented research networks world-wide can be useful and should certainly include Indian and Bengalee institutions. There still may be some place for selected technical assistance in the field, perhaps best dispersed through other than government-to-government channels.

Nevertheless, the most effective course for outsiders will be to contribute to improvements in the other dimensions of family welfare that interact with fertility. The outsiders then can hope that the governments of the two countries, as a matter of the most urgent self-interest (and at the cost of much less ideological backpedaling than was necessary in the Chinese case) will press innovative changes and higher priorities into their population control efforts to degrees that rival the recent apparent turnabout in China.

Food and Agriculture

There can be little doubt about the ready potential of both India and Bangladesh for sustaining vigorous growth rates in food grains and in total agricultural production for many years to come. In India, after a prolonged period of stagnation in per capita output, food production had a growth trend of about 2-1/2 percent annually during the 1950s and 1960s, growing a bit faster in the latter decade. Moreover, during the 1960s a much larger fraction of the gains came from advances in per acre productivity than from extension of cultivated area.

Those who argue that the new ("green revolution") agricultural technology introduced in the middle sixties was either illusory or a flash in the pan are wrong. What was changed lastingly was the methodology of agricultural expansion. The importance of the inputs "package"—of improved varieties, better water management, and fertilizer—was irreversibly entrenched. The facts that Indian cultivators respond to incentives and will adopt new technologies and demand the necessary inputs when the technologies pay off have been proven beyond argument. The appreciation of agricultural research, including its indigenous conduct, networking, funding, and application, has permanently increased.

It is true that in its first phase the smashing success of the "green revolution" was confined to wheat, of which India's output doubled from 1967 to 1971, and that the same pace of expansion cannot be maintained in that crop. In the case of the country's principal foodgrain, rice, comparable gains were prevented by the nonadaptability of the new varieties to the variable water-level conditions of the monsoon season. Although research and/or water-management solutions to the problem have not yet arrived, they appear to be within reach. Promising research thrusts have been launched with respect to rain-fed millets and pulses. For the most part the new methodology still remains to be applied to cash crops.

The opportunities for further improvement in Indian agriculture are enormous. Per hectare rice output still is only about 1.7 metric tons in India compared with about 2.0 tons in Thailand and 5.3 tons in Japan. The per-hectare use of fertilizer in rice growing is still only a small fraction of its level in Japan, Taiwan, and Korea—and apparently far below the current level in China. Still only about 20 percent of India's cultivated area is irrigated. There are some easy opportunities for extending irrigation and therefore multiple cropping (e.g., more tubewells in the Gangetic plain and implementation of the Narmada river scheme in Madya Pradesh, Maharastra, and Gujarat). Other larger opportunities are constrained by the problems of moving water either moving water either sideways (drainage) or uphill, i.e., by problems of energy. These also yield very big increments in farm output.

In Bangladesh, agriculture has not had the same lift from the wheat bonanza, and until the annual ravages of the Brahmaputra can be tamed, it will face higher average risk of flood damage than in India. Yet most floods are not all bad; they also bring fertile silt. As the Comilla story witnesses, the accessible opportunities for raising farm output are, like India's, very great.

Secondly, the conventional wisdom that the new "green revolution" technology, which continues to hold out the greatest technical promise for agricultural expansion in the decades ahead, is necessarily skewed toward the larger landholders also is wrong. It errs as to the technology proper. Packages of improved seed, fertilizer, and water can be applied just as effectively to small and large holdings. Tubewells too large to fit particular holdings can be shared through cooperatives or by the sale of water between contiguous cultivators; and effective smaller scale technology (e.g., bamboo tubewells) suited to very small holdings is being developed. Mechanization for the most part is not integral to the new technology. If the comparative prices of labor and capital are rightly set, mechanization will tend only to be used selectively, and, in any event, by means of custom farming or cooperatives, it too is capable of being divided up among the small users.

However, the conventional wisdom is right that in India, especially in the wheat areas of the northwest, the actual impact of the new agriculture thus far has been inequitable. Because of the peak-wage-lengthening effect of multiple cropping, some landless laborers have shared significantly in the income gains generated by expanded production, but the smaller farmers typically have not had ready access either to information about the new technology or to the credit needed for acquiring its inputs. In part this may be only the pattern of the initial spread; access may broaden gradually. Moreover, as the Comilla case suggests—and as the government of India has been attempting in its special "small farmers" and "marginal farmers" programs—the institutional tilts toward the rural elites can be offset by specific institutional counterpoises. However, in fact, during the past decade the welfare spread between larger and very small farmers has widened.

In both countries amplified efforts plainly are needed to broaden the benefits of progressive farming. Since paddy farming in India is dominated by very small holdings, better distributive outcomes may be in part automatic if, and as, the full extension of the green revolution to rice takes place. Moreover, explicit pro-egalitarian measures of the sort mentioned in the next section are needed.

Yet it is plain that distribution cannot take precedence over production. There is no medium-term policy goal more important in either country than the most vigorous promotion of agricultural production. Agricultural expansion is needed to lead general economic growth.[f] Failure to relax food-supply bottlenecks could abort any pro-egalitarian effort, for no matter what improvements in income distribution are accomplished, they will increase the pace at which food requirements rise. The potential for expansion is there, but realizing it will require the most effective government promotion—through research, the maintenance of incentives, the supply of inputs, and the facilitation and supply of credit.

Such are the key food and agricultural problems. In India in recent years there has been a separate and useful focus on "nutrition" *per se*—on the nutritional deficiencies of particularly vulnerable groups, notably infants, young children, pregnant women, and nursing mothers. However, while there are a few nutritional deficiencies, e.g., the vitamin A-eye disease linkage, which it is economically and administratively feasible to attack on a special-program basis, nutrition in India and Bangladesh still is overwhelmingly a problem of calories and incomes.

Similarly, in both countries there is lively and long-standing concern with public "food policy," by which is meant the regime under which the government collects food, distributes it at subsidized prices to some of the low-end, especially urban, poor, maintains reserves against famines, and uses reserves to stabilize food prices. This activity has been in a considerable shambles in India recently, because of miscalculations with respect to: (1) buffer-stock management, (2) the best modes and price policies for governmental procurement, and (3) the best means for exploiting complementarities between private and public trading in food. Without entering into these rather technical issues, it can be fairly said that the whole effectiveness of any such food policy is dependent on the central government's possession and control of substantial stocks. In the latter sixties, the government of India got such stocks from concessional food aid, while at the turn of the decade the surge in domestic wheat output allowed the government to build its stocks to a sizable (nine million tons) level.[g] If this essential program for a rational food policy is to be devised, almost surely it must come as a by-product of strong continuing gains in agricultural production.

---

[f]But it is also needed to create the conditions for improved equity.

[g]These were subsequently dissipated, in part in feeding Bengalee refugees in 1971 and in providing substantial food aid to Bangladesh in 1972.

Equity, Decentralization, and the Dynamics of
Nonrevolutionary Reform

The most fascinating dilemmas that development policy faces in both India and Bangladesh may be the following.

In the first place, improved equity is an urgent need in both countries—more so in India than in Bangladesh, which comes closer to being uniformly poor. But in both countries the low-end poor are the victims of an interlocked complex of unequal assets, incomes, and employment opportunities, of political power, social status, and of access to education, health, and other social services. At minimum they need some welfare floors, or the bodies politic will sicken incrementally. In both countries it is possible that this sickening could go on for a long time, worsening the dismal condition of nearly a twelfth of the world's people.

Second, in both countries, the putative agents of antipoverty reform are middle class regimes drawn from a variety of elite groups—the larger farmers and other rural oligarchs, private industrial and commercial houses, bureaucrats and other urbanized professionals, and now also, in Bangladesh, the military. A number of these politically influential elites are the very same groups whose relative positions would be weakened by strong antipoverty reforms.

Third, as previously noted, revolution from the Left does not appear to be a likely near-term option. Thus far, the events of 1975 do not seem to require a modification of this judgment in the case of India. The umbrella of the Congress party is wide, and as a political structure the party remains resilient. It tends to assimilate dissent and to accommodate as necessary turnovers in its subcomponents. The capacity of the system's constitutional structures for venting and mediating conflicts has now been drastically curtailed, and how and when it will be rebuilt is not clear. Meanwhile radical politics outside and to the left of the Congress are fragmented, being mainly effective from time to time in such particular states as Kerala and West Bengal. At the top of the system, there is much experience in putting out and/or damping down political fires.

The June 1975 emergency, as suggested above, probably has forced the dénouement of India's no-growth, no-reform-progress stalemate into a much shorter time frame. If the regime is genuinely devoted to consequential growth and equity reforms, it has strengthened its hand for effecting them. It also has exposed the nation to the risk of escalating repression and itself to that of earlier collapse. Even if the new scenario should fail, it is easier to imagine an overturn coming more or less from the Right than more or less from the Left. The likelihood remains that such egalitarian reform as occurs will be achieved in a nonrevolutionary context.

In the Bangladesh case events at the moment are even more turbulent. But there too, if the Mujib regime was (as it seems clearly to have been) essentially nonrevolutionary, that which has replaced it appears to be even more so.

The implication is that if there is to be more effective antipoverty reform in India and perhaps also in Bangladesh during the next ten years it is likely to come from the leaderships now in view or from others much like them. This will happen only if the leaders prove, not only that they are sufficiently declassed, but that they have sufficient strength, wiles, and stubbornness of purpose to push reform against the self-interested grain of the elites from which they are drawn.

Moreover, there is a further, aggravating complication: both countries must also try to decentralize official decision-making—in part "sideways" to the market and other self-adjusting mechanisms—but also downward within the official hierarchy. In India (which with Bangladesh shares the British colonial tradition of highly centralized administration), the latter means in part downward delegation (especially in development-related subjects) from central government to the states. Even more critically, it means delegation downward within the states, which typically are as large as sizable countries, and within which political-administrative authority has been heavily concentrated. Effective decentralization means more local self-government.

A pro-decentralization consensus may be building in both countries. As will be noted below, the change probably is essential if either country is to raise adequate resources for development. It is needed to overcome the sheer managerial clumsiness of excessive centralization in large-population countries. It is not, I think it can be shown, inconsistent with the maintenance of sufficient coherence in national development efforts (as central planners tend to fear).[6] Above all, it is needed for what elsewhere I have called the "arousal" of local energies, initiatives, and leadership.[7] Decentralization is necessary to contribute to the expansion of wage-goods production and employment upon which the feasibility of egalitarian reforms themselves depend.

The rub is that in passing more political power as well as financial and other responsibilities to localities, one typically is transferring them to local rural elites who are the least disturbed and least declassed in their adherence to the traditional society's inequities. Thus the recipe for nonrevolutionary reform must be amended to say that, in particular, against-the-grain reformers (together with the other declassed elitists in the press, universities, legislatures, and public service organizations who support them) must be at pains to do whatever they can early in the decentralization process to strengthen the hands of the weakly organized, underrepresented, low-end poor.

Such strengthening can be accomplished in part economically through public works and similar programs which permit income and employment benefits to flow disproportionately to the poor. It will also mean bargaining with the local elites and cajoling them into building types of public works which will result in benefits once they are in place, that are more pro-egalitarian than the elites would choose on their own; devising specific, e.g., credit reforms that break or weaken the traditional mechanisms that have reinforced the dependency of the rural poor on landlords and moneylenders; and promoting such class-specific organizations of the poor as landless labor unions, cooperatives reserved to smaller farmers, and low caste associations. Successful nonrevolutionary reformers must understand that almost surely it is necessary to stir up some class conflict in the Indian and Bengalee countrysides. Ultimately, with universal franchise formally available in both countries, reformers must rely on the ability of the poor to make their latent political power kinetic. Once the stakes attached to local decision-making have been raised, the poor, given some aids and encouragement, should be able to use their votes to act more effectively on their own behalf.

There is nothing impossible about such a scenario. Historically, in many countries it is through just such patterns that important reforms have been achieved. Nor, to become operative, will the patterns have to be pursued without respite or exception. Even if flawed and spasmodic, such efforts may move outcomes significantly during the next few years. In India, moreover, it is perfectly possible that major nonrevolutionary reform will proceed much further in some states than others—and then perhaps spread laterally. What must be understood by interested bystanders outside the subcontinent is that serious antipoverty reform will be a conflicted, uphill, necessarily risky business. It will indeed call for courage, skills, and considerable constancy of purpose on the part of leaders and upon the span of the resource options at their disposal.

General Development Strategy

There has been growing talk of the need for a "new development strategy"—in India, in Bangladesh, indeed in many countries of the developing world. What those who use the phrase have in mind has been given a variety of converging expressions.[8] It includes topics treated here under other headings—the needs for redressing the balance between growth and equity; for attacking mass poverty and unemployment; improving income distribution and, therefore, changing the composition of consumption; the case for decentralization and for revamping development's spatial design. At this point I wish to note only two of the revisionist strategy's pivotal themes. First, it is acknowledged that, in both India and Bangladesh, successful development during the balance of the century must be led by agriculture. The new strategists agree that agriculture does have strong expansion potential in both countries, must supply the most critical wage goods on which other development depends, and must for some time handle the bulk of the employment problems. With worldwide food shortages and the effects of income redistribution internally, demand constraints on its future growth should be less severe and slower coming than previously was expected.

The second of the new strategy's themes spells out the kind of agricultural-nonagricultural complementarity most needed, namely, efficiently labor-intensive modes of production in both sectors. Despite resistance among existing industries, mechanized farmers, and parts of the bureaucracy, these perspectives of the new strategy seem to me to be gaining acceptance in both India and Bangladesh. The problems for reform policymakers, therefore, are less those of reversing direction than of sharpening and emboldening changes already begun— plus finding additional degrees of financial freedom for implementing them.

Domestic Finance

Development is being inhibited in both India and Bangladesh by lack of external resources, but the more pervasive obstacle in both countries is that of domestic resources. It is not a problem that can be solved by taking up ready slack. In India, saving as a fraction of national income rose quite briskly during the first fifteen years of planned development, but has stagnated just above the 10 percent mark since the middle 60s—while general development has tended also to stagnate. To a limited extent this parameter of development can be worked on directly, by raising the interest rates that financial savings earn and by giving farmers better access to the financial institutions that can facilitate their direct investment. But in general it is hard for governments to push developmental activity by pushing private saving. More nearly, the needed sequence is to push development activity that in turn will pull savings into line with its requirements.

Recently, in both India and Bangladesh, however, would-be expansive budgeting has to confront the problem of virulent inflation. For fifteen years, until the middle 60s, India was known as one of the soundest money regimes in the developing world, but then things got out of hand and a period of rapid inflation ensued. During the fifteen months ending in September 1974, for example, the wholesale price index rose 30 percent. From August 1973 to August 1974 food prices increased 43 percent. The instigating factors were overwhelming—food scarcities, and as a result of the consequent rise in food prices, cost-push increases centering around modern-sector wages, with powerful augmentation from 1972 onward by increases in the prices of imports.

Yet, it is also true that during much of the latest decade, financial permissiveness has accommodated the inflation process. In India, the government's current-account (i.e., nondevelopmental) budget together with its (new-money-financed) deficit typically has run well ahead of target. State governments have avoided financial discipline by regularly running up large overdrafts at the central bank. The money supply for most of the decade has grown much faster than real activity. In Bangladesh since independence, the picture has been similar but worse.

Since July 1974, the government of India has taken a very firm fiscal-monetary grip on its inflationary problem, an effort that, with the propitious assistance of a very good 1975 harvest, has been remarkably successful. Both the Indian and the Bengali governments have rightfully concluded that henceforth new public developmental expenditures must be accompanied by anti-inflationary offsets—either taxation or its equivalent. However, this is a very tough requirement. On the one hand, the needs for additional resources are massive. Every program improvement that is mentioned here will cost substantial public-budget money if it is to be consequential, and these, of course, are not nearly all the budget headings that governments will need to fund. On the other hand, the national tax effort, at least in India, already is substantial. Every annual budget has imposed fresh taxation to the point that, even by the standards of considerably more affluent developing countries, the aggregate burden already is fairly high.

This overt side of the domestic financing problem is greatly complicated by the phenomenon, radically escalated in India and quickly full-blown in Bangladesh, of illicit, under-the-table, "black money" transactions that occur out of the sight and reach of the tax gatherer. Very obviously, black money and corruption are intimately related. As the announced intentions of the Indian government's June 1975 emergency make plain, an attack on one must become an attack on the other. A successful assault will strike a blow not only for probity but for development finance, for corraling such leakages not only broadens the effective tax base, it reinforces the government's whole financial disciplining capacity.[h] But plainly the mobilization of additional resources for development will need to go much farther than this.

In the first place, in both India and Bangladesh, the central tax structures are still capable of gradual augmentation. There is much scope for better enforcement. Managements of public enterprises can be pressed to shift from deficit to strongly surplus operations: in this regard, the Indian public sector has been delinquent, and in Bangladesh, the sprawling, recently nationalized, public sector is a disaster area.

There can be reallocations from current account to development account. Some of these, e.g., curtailment of famine relief outlays, will tend to be automatic if and as development succeeds. Some will require continued detailed

[h]Curbing black money is much less a matter of ferreting out and impounding stocks of already ill-gotten gains still in identifiable "black" forms than it is of curbing generation at the source. Plainly one source, the income tax, cannot be eliminated, but as the Indian government lately has been starting to do, the highest-bracket rates can be scaled down (reducing the incentives to escape) while at the same time enforcement is toughened. The other generic source is what I earlier called the "two-price system." This can be sharply curtailed in both countries by eliminating most regulatory and control mechanisms which yield "official" prices different from market prices. To be effective some anti-black-money reform may have to be radical. For example, because urban real estate is such an endemic and burgeoning source of illicit income, it would seem to me that in both countries nationalization of all metropolitan land may deserve a higher place on reform agendas than do the further rural land reforms that are so much advertised and so little implemented.

economizing of operating budgets. The largest possibility (in India)—a realloca-
tion away from the defense budget—would require reconciliation with strategic
assessments and policy. This last raises a range of questions that cannot be
explored here and that it is risky to treat summarily. Yet it may be noted that,
although the Indian defense budget's claim of some 5 percent of GNP may be
almost modest by comparative LDC standards, its share of total public resources
is very high. For both India and Pakistan there would be no readier source of
developmental reinforcement than the reductions in defense spending that a
secure accommodation between those countries would allow both governments
to make.[i]

In the second place, in India the domestic financial dilemma will require
pushing more fiscal responsibility onto state governments. The underlying issue
can be put more fundamentally in sectoral rather than jurisdictional terms, and
then applied to both countries: in both India and Bangladesh the tax system as it
has evolved from traditional origins imposes relatively little direct burden on
agriculture. Thus, when one is looking for increments of resources, the group
(aside from black-money tax evaders) best able to contribute are the better-off
farmers. On top of the other political difficulties that this poses, in India direct
taxation of agriculture is reserved to the states. If the necessary resources are to
be assembled for development, the central government will have to find some
way of its own around this impasse, and/or put more fiscal pressure on the
states. The only alternative is to put extra reliance on the third route, lower-level
financial decentralization.

To do what they need to do for growth and equity programs, both countries
may be forced to turn to the new sources, especially among better-off farmers,
that can be tapped by passing more financial responsibility along with more
self-governing authority to local jurisdictions. This, of course, is only the most
skeletal statement of an issue that also entails the expanded role of financial
institutions in the countryside, the use of user charges and other devices for
recouping the private benefits flowing from public investments, and the use of
matching grants (from the central government to states, and from the central
government and states to localities) to induce more self-help at the lower levels.
More than any one other policy line effective decentralization of financial
responsibility holds the key to the augmentation of resources for development.

---

[i]In passing, however, I cannot refrain from rebutting a related impression that presently is
widespread among Americans: namely, that India's decision to go for a nuclear explosion (in
May 1974) likewise represented a large, and, therefore, unconscionable diversion of
resources from development. This is not so. The incremental costs of getting the Indian
nuclear research and energy program also to make a bomb (or, in the Indian lexicon, an
explosive device for peaceful purposes) were trivial. The allocative argument would have to
be with the nuclear energy program as such, and, while the latter's economic case never has
been strong, it has been strengthened by the inflation of international oil prices. The
wisdom of India's move into the nuclear weapons club must be challenged on its own
merits, not developmental grounds.

Finally, the need to pursue this policy line raises a corollary problem in both countries: contrary to one aspect of their egalitarian rhetoric, higher govern-ments must remain somewhat insensitive to inequalities between lower jurisdic-tions. If decentralization is going to work, some local jurisdictions and some states are going to help themselves more than others, and matching grant inputs will only aggravate these differences. In both countries, of course, there will continue to be a partially countervailing flow of transfers to backward areas, but in a decentralized reform strategy the accent will have to be on the minimization of interclass and intergroup rather than interjurisdictional inequities. This should be accompanied by a policy of keeping open, nationwide, the opportunity for persons to move their work and their residences to places which offer more or better jobs and rewards to enterprises while at the same time enforcing greater demands on their people.

International Trade and Payments

In the later 1960s, most Western economists' diagnoses of India's policy needs dwelled, next to agriculture itself, on the case for industrial decontrol internally and for liberalizing and rationalizing the country's foreign trade regime. At the time many felt this was the sector of policy where the gap between Indian and Western perceptions was widest. Thus there is a nice irony in the fact that it was left to two economists who are Indian, albeit presently American residents— Bhagwati and Desai—to produce the definitive exposition of the liberalization case.[9]

That authorship symbolizes one reason why the priority of decontrol as an issue meanwhile has deescalated somewhat. It turns out that the legendary zest of Indian bureaucrats for managing all of the details of the economy's decision-making, and their contempt for all the free market institutions became exaggerated in the telling. The upper echelons of the Indian government, like most bureaucracies, were anything but monolithic. Many senior officials and advisers recognized, without Western nudging, that an accretion of expedient *ad hoc* measures over time had snarled the economy in a terrible clutter of bans, quotas, licenses, and artificial prices. They recognized that the market can be a powerful mechanism for socially efficient industrial guidance. They sensed also that the issue of controls versus market competition can and should be distinguished from that of public versus private sector industry—that, indeed, a market brand of socialism can be a perfectly coherent model. Provided markets abroad are reasonably accessible and supplies from abroad reasonably competitive, an import-export regime that encourages one to trade in accor-dance with one's comparative advantage is self-serving; and that competition, both internally and from imports (insofar as the latter is consistent with one's short-term foreign exchange constraints), can be a benign discipliner of industrial efficiency, thereby promoting export capabilities as well as benefiting indigenous consumers.[j]

Meanwhile India's behavioral pattern in the liberalization field has remained somewhat cyclical. After some regrowth of controls, since 1973 there has been some useful fresh pruning of the regulatory thicket, particularly as to industrial licensing. There is also evidence of a positive secular trend. The past half-dozen years have seen the mounting of a more serious and sustained campaign against private monopoly to promote internal competition. Moreover, invigorated export promotion has been a theme of the period. There has been a serious attempt to sort out and, in terms of official clearances and access to scarce imports, to give running room to those export items in which India has a genuine comparative advantage. Marketing efforts and organizations have been built on behalf of a variety of nontraditional exports including engineering goods—for that matter, including Indian engineering itself, which has made a considerable entree into the Indian Ocean periphery, especially the Persian Gulf area. The overall export effort has not been uniformly and fully implemented, but policy has been leaning in the right direction with reasonably encouraging results.

It may be too early to demote the general subject of decontrol and market rehabilitation from a high place on India's list of priority development issues for the next decade and the balance of the century. The whole subject remains fundamentally important, and aspects of it will continue to crop up urgently. Yet my guess is that an inclination toward market rationalization will tend to prevail when and as short-term foreign exchange constraints permit. The next time India unmistakably needs to devalue, the move should come with less trauma than in 1966.

There has been far less action to support a similar judgment about Bangladesh. However, Bangladesh's inherent circumstances (particularly, I shall be suggesting, vis-à-vis India itself) will tend to force that country to come to terms with the realities of the international market rather than attempt to escape from it.

In this present account, therefore, instead of marking down the whole matter of market policy as one of the more difficult and complex problems for the two countries during the balance of the century, the focus is on a few particular aspects of their international trade and payment prospects.

The most urgent matter, as has been emphasized already, is the huge oil, food, and fertilizer price increases with which India and Bangladesh have been assaulted in the past two or three years and which show no early signs of receding to their old levels. These pose a need for both governments to contrive

---

[j]Moreover, since the latter 1960s, many western observers of Indian (and, more recently, of Bengalee) development have become a degree less doctrinaire, particularly in their recognition of the practical constraints on liberalization and in fuller appreciation of how closely liberalization measures depend on the availability of some reliable current foreign-exchange elbow room for their implementation.

radical yet constrained adjustments in their trade strategies. On the one hand, there is no way that either country can retreat into trade isolation. At minimum each must continue to make substantial imports. Neither can afford defensive actions that, whether by impairing industrial efficiency or otherwise, damage its export prospects. On the other hand, there is no conceivable way the fairly encouraging but laborious recent growth in Indian exports can be stepped up fast enough to catch up with the old volumes of general imports plus the old volumes of oil, fertilizer, and food imports priced at the new prices. Most particularly, there is no chance of India's doing so at the same time every other oil-importing country in the world is trying to accelerate its export sales for the same reason.

The need therefore is for a new phase of import substitution—but of a kind that does not impair export capability. The obvious targets for such a drive are the bloated-price imports—certainly food, certainly indigenous energy production, and also, quite certainly, chemical fertilizers. It is possible that a sufficiently bold and concerted response to these import-substitution challenges in the food, energy, and fertilizer fields can be turned into a breakthrough for the whole pace of development in each country. In Bangladesh, the key to such a possibility is the country's reserve of natural gas, which may also be directly translatable into exports. In India, the pieces of the puzzle are more complicated, but they may be subject to assembly.

Fertilizer is enough of a special problem to warrant separate discussion. The upward surge in international fertilizer prices has moved in parallel with, and has been aggravated by, the rise in oil prices. However, the oil price increase has not been the principal cause of the fertilizer increase. Since the early sixties, when there was a shift in technology, which made existing fertilizer plants obsolete and helped to induce widespread investment in new plants, the industry worldwide has been in the grip of a massive trade cycle. Demand in the 60s, especially in South Asia, rose briskly, but the (uncoordinated) aggregate volume of investment in new plants around the world rose faster. Capacity outran demand, and by the end of the 1960s urea was a drug on the international market. Prices plummeted. Further investment plans were cut back or stretched out—again in an uncoordinated, worldwide way. As a result, from 1972 onwards, demand, pushed, for one thing, by the expanded acreages American farmers were planting, outran supply and urea prices soared. At present, the uncoordinated new investments now being undertaken around the world may well bring nitrogenous fertilizer into glut again by the end of the decade.

Nitrogenous fertilizers therefore form one component of the international inflationary binge that is due for a price reversal. Some observers conclude that India and Bangladesh, instead of building themselves more fertilizer plants, should wait for the international commodity to become abundant and cheap again. Some advocates of the new development strategy chime in: India and Bangladesh should import capital-intensive fertilizer, paying for it with labor-intensive products; the comparative advantage will lie with those new Persian Gulf plants that will make urea from all that natural gas now being flared (i.e., wasted) in Persian Gulf oil fields.

Planners in India and Bangladesh demur. They are anxious to expand fertilizer production in their own region. They reason, first, that they have available internal raw materials the real costs of which are competitive. Certainly this is the case with Bengalee natural gas. Taking account of the new levels of international oil prices as well as of international transport costs, it probably also is true that coal-based fertilizer production in India can be competitive. As I shall be noting subsequently, it may also be possible now in the Indian countryside to organize decentralized nitrogenous fertilizer production based on cow dung and other agricultural wastes that is competitive with the real on-farm costs of imported fertilizer. Secondly, given the critical importance of fertilizer availability to the expansion of indigenous food production, the Indian and Bengalee governments want a more reliable fertilizer supply than the fluctuating international market promises to afford. Thirdly, there is the generalized need for renewed import substitution that the whole collection of import price increases has forced upon both countries; even if imported fertilizer should itself become a better bargain, these nations will remain subject to oil-price and other pressures to save foreign exchange wherever with reasonable efficiency they can do so. The South Asian planners, I think are persuasive. The two countries should push ahead vigorously with expansion of their own fertilizer production—at the same time pressing for the kind of worldwide indicative planning of fertilizer production that in the past two or three years has begun to command widespread support.

The problem of future fertilizer planning in the two countries provides a nice illustration, however, of how renewed import substitution should not become brittle or hidebound. With its natural gas endowment, Bangladesh almost surely has the natural resource wherewithal to become a sizable, competitive net exporter of nitrogenous fertilizer in the international market. Given its locational advantage, it therefore also certainly has a comparative advantage for exporting fertilizer to India. Because of India's locational advantage as a supplier of a great variety of items that Bangladesh needs, there are the makings of a bilateral symbiosis here that does not threaten the foreign exchange constraints each nation faces. Fortunately, the two governments already are pursuing at least one joint, Bengalee-based fertilizer project that would begin to implement such a pattern.

This last suggests, for this eclectic listing of difficult trade and payments problems, the whole, complex subject of India-Bangladesh economic relations. It includes, beside all manner of trade issues and possibilities, the tortured matter of the division and joint management of "the Eastern Waters" (the Brahmaputra and the Ganges). More generally, it carries an emotional and political overload. Whatever Bangladesh's allergy to dependence on India, however, its future economic policies must come to terms with two basic characteristics of the Bengalee economy. The first is that Bangladesh has reached independence with an extraordinarily narrow array of products—because of its exceptionally narrow array of natural resources. It is quite true that Bangladesh must, as a succeeding agriculture stimulates a relative rise in nonagricultural activities, build labor-intensive manufacturing. But the latter will have a better chance of acquiring the efficiency it needs both for serving local consumers and for penetrating the international market if it concentrates on comparatively few product lines. Successful Bengalee development will almost certainly depend on the importation of a great variety of commodities—raw materials, intermediate products, consumer goods, capital goods—from a nearby compatible source, notably India. The second basic characteristic is the length and nature of the 1500-mile border Bangladesh shares with India. Short of building a picket fence of incorruptible custom agents around the whole frontier, there is no way to prevent abundant smuggling between the two countries.

Together, the two characteristics argue insistently that the two economies must become largely open to each other officially. The relative values of the two currencies (aligned more realistically since the Bengalee devaluation in the spring of 1975) together with the problems of the flight of Bengalee capital to and/or through Calcutta, of the loss of Bengalee rice to India, and of binational distortions in jute production and trade all must be worked out in this context. Moves toward opening the economies to each other will require political courage and common sense in Bangladesh, sensitivity and self-restraint in India, and more readiness on the part of both governments to accommodate national policies than either might prefer. There is no acceptable alternative.

Clearly, this cataloging of major development problems has not been exhaustive. I particularly regret the need to slight such issues as technological policy, spatial strategy, and educational reform. But enough particular facets of the Indian and Bengalee development puzzles have been sketched to allow us to proceed now to an overview of the critical choices those countries face, and then to the implications for external, especially American, policy.

Survival or Breakthrough? What Are Feasible Policy Targets for India and Bangladesh?

Most governments tend to worry about the quality of life they bequeath to their children and grandchildren—and then let their long-term objectives get pushed aside by current crises and politics. Such a pattern would be doubly sad in either India or Bangladesh during the next few years. A succession of accommodations to near-term realities is almost sure to yield cumulatively worsening outcomes. Moreover, shortchanging the future in this way could mean a costly loss of opportunity.

Economists typically cast up countries' choices of overall development strategy in a vocabulary of output and productive-capacity growth rates, income distribution, and employment goals. The present discussion will be less concerned with laying out such a panoply of targets than emphasizing the basic bifurcation of futures that India and perhaps Bangladesh face.

The Polarity of Choices

India by now has inspired a fair assortment of long-term economic projections. In one of the better of these futurology exercises, the Tata Economic Consultancy Services have spelled out four "scenarios" keyed to alternative possible rates of average annual growth in real GNP to the end of the century—3 percent (being about what India has averaged during her first twenty-three years of planned development); 5 percent ("a rate . . . set by the United Nations for the First Development Decade . . . and . . . achieved by nearly a third of the developing countries"); 7 percent ("a rate which a few developing countries have scored for nearly a decade" and which now more expect to achieve); and, to set an outer limit at once ridiculous and sublime, 9 percent (in which, say the authors, they imagine India doing "a Japan," as Korea, Taiwan, Singapore, and Rumania have done for nearly a decade).[10]

The analysis the Tata consultants present within this format is sophisticated and illuminating.[k] But in using the format, they entrench a set of impressions to which most official Indian macro-planning over the years has contributed. The implication is that the goals spectrum is a continuum; that the set of policy mixes to be used for seeking out chosen points on the goals spectrum is also a continuum; and that the targets in the middle of the range are in some sense the more plausible, reasonable, and/or feasible. Thus it is not surprising that the Tata authors, having lopped off the 9 percent scenario as being beyond the realm of plausibility, tend to focus on the five percent option rather than the three percent or seven percent patterns to either side. Every Indian five-year planning document has done essentially the same thing. Aggregate growth targets in the 5-6 percent range invariably have been their preference—and the economy has responded by making good 3 percent growth.

For reasons suggested, India's slow-growth syndrome has been more than

[k]For each scenario they have worked out a nice sequence of subperiod to subperiod dynamics within the total span of their projections; and they spell out the alternative implications, among many others, for investment and saving rates, industrial composition, and the availability of growth dividends for improving the low-end income distribution (under assumptions of official pro-egalitarian bias). Even at the simplest level their analysis provides an arresting reminder of the way (with comparable population-growth assumptions) a spread of aggregate growth rates fans out into a much wider spread of per capita gains (3 percent aggregate = 1.2 percent per capita; 7 percent aggregate = 5.1 percent per capita).

accidental. Probably it has reflected the system's size and complexity—and its constitutionalism. In the countryside, for example, new development initiatives have had so far to spread that typically, instead of snowballing, they have petered out. Transfers of resources from leading states and localities to backward states and localities have shifted inputs to areas of lesser dynamism. Constitutional processes have mediated disputes but they often also have vented, fragmented, or dissipated developmental energies. Because of the size of the country, external inputs, measured in per capita terms, in fact have been extemely thin.

The combined result has been a history of development by spurts. It has taken some special stimulus, challenge, or external injection (for example, the high foreign exchange reserves inherited at the time of independence, a Korean War connected spurt in exports, the launching of serious public-sector development and planning in the mid-1950s, the 1962 Chinese intrusion, the relative bunching of foreign aid in the 1960s, the green revolution's new agricultural technology) to push the system into something approaching vigorous performance. Some of these initiatives have had self-perpetuation propensities; indeed some, including the green revolution and a disposition toward economic-liberalization policy dating back to the 60s, are still much alive. However, none yet has had sufficient mass to set the whole system reliably on a new higher performance trend. Between stimuli the aggregate system has settled back into a sluggish, low-metabolism performance.

The broad development policy choice facing the government of India, therefore, is poorly conveyed by a graduated array of growth targets. It is more nearly a binary choice. On the one hand, the country can continue on its present course. Once again it can declare for 5 percent growth and perhaps get 3 percent. It can go for a resumption of the crabwise progress of the past quarter century. This is not an effortless, easy option. It implies the equivalent of all of the considerable policy effort that was made to shift India from pre-independence stagnation to post-independence slow-growth. Moreover, it will require a massive scramble by India itself and by the donor community outside simply to dig the country out of the foreign-exchange hole into which the oil-food-fertilizer price emergency has thrust it.

Even so, the more-of-the-same option will not be good enough. As long as the existing socio-political-economic structure persists, 3 percent growth will mean (no matter what egalitarian cosmetics and feints particular policies produce) a net worsening in the relative position, probably also in the absolute position, of the low-end poor.

Before the June 1975 emergency, India's political structures seemed to insure the probability of prolonged commitment to the alternative of slow, inequitable growth. Earlier it could be said that Mrs. Gandhi, with her virtuoso ability to cope with current political crises (unmatched, one fears, by equal readiness to risk political capital in behalf of grander long-term reform objectives), was likely to continue to cope, and cope, and cope—such was the nightmare. The emergency may now have disposed of that particular nightmare. It has increased the chances of an up or out result for the present leadership, but it certainly has not assured the country's escape from a pattern of bare, painfully inequitable, national survival leading nowhere. Indeed if the emergency fails in its larger purposes, and the present regime with it, precisely such a pattern might be the prospect under a successor regime.

Therefore, seizing the other branch of the binary choice which can be called the breakthrough option, will be anything but automatic. It will require deep and bold reform, skill, and a certain amount of luck. It means reaching for a very much more ambitious growth rate—say 7 percent in the Tata array—but more important, would be the commitment to a scale and quality of expansionist reform that once and for all would reorient the economy to a strongly cumulative growth pattern.

The real question is whether this high option really exists; but first, Bangladesh should be added into the discussion. Bangladesh does not fully share the size and complexity that have retarded India's growth, and it is politically less formed; it cannot bring to the cause of breakthrough as much stockpiled human and other infrastructure. Bangladesh's most probable economic future is worse than India's—significantly worse in per capita terms in view of Bangladesh's higher population growth rate. On the other hand, the physical resources nub, namely, natural gas, around which a breakthrough strategy might pivot is plainer. The concept of choosing between two markedly different strategies makes sense for Bangladesh also.

The Breakthrough Possibility

History has played some nasty tricks on India vis-à-vis the timing of development acceleration. Breakthrough, a whole new pace and quality of development performance, requires fairly massive financial implementation. Most of the latter has to be domestic, but an essential component has to be in the form of foreign exchange, and a fraction probably needs to consist of net transfers. In the late 1950s and 1960s, in the era of relatively abundant old-fashioned (mainly bilateral) foreign aid, when many smaller, less complicated, less constitutional countries were making developmental hay, India not only received a lean per capita aid input, but it was also not quite ready to make optimal use of development resources. Slow growth was its norm.

Now, behind the facade of resource stringencies and of the spreading frustration and cynicism of the 1972-1975 period, one can mark important changes: the establishment of a sustainable new thrust of agriculture, a greater appreciation of the social usefulness of market process, increased focus on exports, a more pervasive concern about underemployment and inequalities, more inclination toward decentralization and dispersed centering. Thus the Indian economy is riper than it was ten or fifteen years ago for a development performance breakthrough. Meanwhile old-fashioned foreign aid has gone out of fashion. For good measure, the country has been sandbagged by the price explosion in oil, food, and fertilizer imports.

Furthermore, in the longer run the world may well be entering an era of more substantial, regularized, and sustained net transfers, of which India, thanks to its size and poverty, will be entitled to a generous portion. However, in terms of the country's present needs and problems, this new bounty is likely to come too late.

There is, it seems to me, only one important way for confounding this irony that history seems to be perpetuating. The present food-fertilizer-oil crises give both India and Bangladesh powerful incentives to find new efficient import substitutes and/or exports. Both urgently need to raise food production. Both need expansion in regional fertilizer production. The other key to major agricultural growth in both countries is improved water management—both at the local, minor-irrigation level and with respect to major redeployments of water. In Bangladesh, the rivers (via joint efforts with India) need to be tamed and more groundwater needs to be raised to cope with recurrent off-season shortages. In India, the highest priority is to exploit the northern Gangetic plain's magnificent groundwater reservoir more fully, but this will require solving problems of increased drainage in a terrain that has the contours of a table top. Presumably part of the answer must be more positive and interventionist use of the principal rivers, with heavy pumping being employed to transfer part of the reservoir's abundance to water-scarce areas downstream during dry seasons, thereby increasing the reservoir's capacity to absorb the next monsoon.

This last brings us to the matter of energy. Most directly and obviously, of course, the oil-price explosion has posed the need for domestic energy substitutes for oil imports. In addition, energy shortages already had been seriously retarding agricultural production for several years, particularly in the tubewell areas of northwest India. Expanded rural electrification (especially in the context of higher diesel prices) is a key to further development of minor irrigation, and also is essential to the pattern of dispersed rural growth toward which both countries are inclining. New fertilizer factories will be heavy users of energy, and very large amounts will be needed for major water control and transfer schemes.

However, interrelated food, fertilizer, water, and energy problems are not new subjects in either country. What leads one now to imagine that fresh attacks on them can succeed, even trigger a general economic acceleration, under conditions of impacted financial adversity? There are three related bases for hopefulness. None comes close to being certainty, but together, given the dreariness of the slow-growth scenario, they warrant serious attention.

In the first place, in both countries there is a range of possibly high-return projects and ventures that until now have been relatively neglected. There are known or suspected high-yield resources with clear economic attractiveness which have not been exploited for one reason or other. Oil drilling off the shore of western India is one such case; just now starting, its desirability has been evident for at least seven or eight years. Attention has also turned to Bangladesh's offshore oil possibilities in the Bay of Bengal. The clearest example of this sort is the Bangladesh natural gas. It was discovered in 1955. Present estimated reserves are about 9 trillion cubic feet, i.e., almost thirty times as much per capita as India's. Prospects for future discoveries are believed to be bright. The gas is 95-99 percent methane. Its use thus far is very limited. The Planning Commission in Dacca has calculated that presently estimated reserves alone could, for the economic life of the generating capacity, support six times the national electrical generating capacity that it projected for the end of Bangladesh's First Five-Year Plan in 1978-79, still leaving the larger part of the gas for use as a raw material.[11]

In the case of other investment possibilities, the slackness of past effort has been the rational result of the cheapness of imported substitutes. However, now that import prices, especially oil prices, have skyrocketed, indigenous alternatives (coal-based fertilizer production in India, further hydroelectric development, much more coal-based electrical generation) have become more attractive. Yet in a number of such cases the lower priorities in the past have provided obstacles to expansion. In the case of Indian coal, for example, there is not now the rail capacity to move a quick surge in output. Moreover, the industry, both its erstwhile private and its public-sector components, has evolved a pattern of management that seems notably ill-equipped to lead a coalmining boom. Even in these turnabout cases, therefore, the change in price signals may not be enough to set up a process of corrective development, in train; they need a determined push from the top.

The most interesting set of cases of neglected opportunity may consist of potentially high-return projects (perhaps now still higher return thanks to the import price rises) that in the past have been shunted aside because they have looked too big or unorthodox. For at least ten years in India, and since independence in Bangladesh, investment decisions have been tightly constrained by financial, including foreign-exchange, shortages. The emphasis has been on sure-fire standard-technology, short-gestation projects. Many schemes have been ruled out of bounds before ever undergoing serious project appraisal: however good their benefit-cost characteristics might turn out to be, their absolute size simply was too large, given other competing claims on resources, to fit within annual domestic and/or foreign aid budgets.

No one knows how many genuinely good possibilities have been sidetracked for such reasons, since in most cases the detailed project designs and assessments have never been made. However, it seems fairly clear that in Bangladesh the apparent foreign-exchange constraints have inhibited the mounting of a multi-project program for exploiting natural gas on the scale which that resource deserves. In India one can list a number of mooted schemes: for example, the idea of deep pumping along the northern bank of the Ganges plus downstream transfer; the idea of joining the Ganges and Brahmaputra farther upstream; the suggestion of the former Irrigation and Power Minister, Dr. K.L. Rao, for a "water grid" that would be established during nonmonsoon months by pumping water from the Gangetic plain 1500 feet uphill into the dry river beds of the Deccan plateau; the various schemes for joint Indo-Nepalese hydroelectric development of the Himalayan torrents flowing into India, perhaps combined with the supply of Nepalese fertilizer needs from nearby Indian plants; and the proposal that the coal transport bottleneck be bypassed by building extensive generating capacity at mine heads.

The sidetracked project possibilities are not limited to those in which single, indivisible physical units are very large. The same inhibition has applied to highly decentralized, small-unit schemes that in aggregate generate unacceptably large financial claims. There are such examples in nearly every aspect of rural development. In the energy field the most interesting current example is that of proposed village-level bio-gas systems. The knowledge that, with the help of simple equipment, cow dung, which is now mainly used as a household fuel, can be converted into two parallel products—methane gas, containing most of the cow dung's energy, and a readily usable nitrogenous fertilizer that can return most of the dung's nutrients to the soil—has been available in India for two decades. The increase in oil prices recently has prompted technicians to dust off the proposition, add other vegetable and animal wastes into their designs, scale up the latter into serious schemes for village-level electrification, and tackle the problems of technological scale, adaptation to village and family mores, and motivation of effective waste collection. Compared to the costs of commercial energy delivered to dispersed villages, the possibilities appear to be exceedingly interesting.[12] However, if the schemes hypothesized were spread to a substantial part of the Indian countryside, the volume of investment required would be very large.

So much for the first strand of the case for the breakthrough possibility. It boils down to the likelihood that, in the food-fertilizer-water-energy field, to which the international price explosions have posed their most pointed challenges, there are substantial untapped potentials for innovative high-yield investments in both India and Bangladesh.

The second strand of the argument, if you will, invokes Albert Hirschman's theory of "unbalanced growth."[13] Caught as they are in history's ironical time bind, India and Bangladesh probably must eschew the comfort, which planners cherish so much, of projecting comprehensive, physically and financially balanced models of acceleration. They need to place their bets on a new-strategy-oriented core of activity that is most likely to induce extra effort both from their own people and from abroad.

Nothing else appears so likely to inspire strong and cumulative domestic responses as a set of major new agriculture-favoring initiatives in the energy, water, and fertilizer sectors. Expanded fertilizer availabilities, rural electrification, and better water management are the physical changes most apt to unleash the subcontinent's growth potential. No other steps would be better calculated to stimulate the expansion of dispersed, labor-intensive, agriculture-oriented processing and manufacturing. Coupled with a strategy of political-administrative decentralization, no other line of policy would have a better chance of arousing local participation and support—directly in the more decentralized food-energy-water-fertilizer schemes, collaterally in the building of supportive public-works infrastructure, financially, in the self-help funding of both. No other major policy initiatives could contain greater promise for the low-end poor, especially if distributive impacts favoring them were built into particular measures.

The third strand of the argument has to do with the possibilities for arousing extra inputs from outside the country. Here, just possibly, the prank that history is playing on the timing of Indian and Bengalee development can be inverted. A special opportunity for external funding of breakthrough projects in the subcontinent may be implicit in the same oil-price revolution that, more than any other external factor, has triggered this decade's development crises. The ballooned liquidity and particularly the reaffirmed Third World solidarity may cause some of the OPEC countries to be extraordinarily generous providers of concessional assistance during the next five to ten years.

As to donor obligations, the first task of the "new rich" will be to join with the old rich and the multilateral agencies in patching together something approaching adequate crisis relief for the poorest countries. In the realm of financial assistance, some of the OPEC countries may be persuaded to do more—if the governments of India and Bangladesh play their cards right in two respects.

Firstly, they will need to make their own direct approach to the oil exporters. Secondly, they should seek support for bold and attractive—and solid—projects. Like every new aid donor before them, the oil exporters are sure to prefer to channel their concessional assistance into concrete, identifiable projects that make good economic sense and also will serve the poor. These criteria, of course, also are necessities for India and Bangladesh. They can afford no building of monuments. Once the projects have been culled and ranked by the kinds of close analysis and careful design that is still largely missing, the types of food-water-fertilizer-energy investments suggested would have the maximum chance of appealing to OPEC donors on the one hand, and of delivering high social returns on the other.

This chapter does not conclude suggesting what growth, employment, and distributive targets a breakthrough-bent regime in India or in Bangladesh should set itself, nor does it sketch the sectoral and structural architecture that an overall plan should have. At this point even the most tentative such sketching would be unwarranted. For one thing, little of the necessary analytical detail yet exists for determining what the economic characteristics of the various schemes mooted as breakthrough possibilities might be, let alone for estimating how the Indian and Bengalee authorities, so informed, might rank their priorities. Second, since the external financing answers will turn so much on the complexities of bilateral diplomacy, only those same authorities, after they had pursued initiatives some distance, could make serviceable guesses of the possible scale of available resources. Thirdly, in any event, adoption of a challenge-and-response, unbalanced-development strategy would imply acceptance of a higher measure of uncertainty than that to which conventional macroeconomic planning is accustomed.

As it now can be argued, therefore, the breakthrough possibility is little more than brainstorming, but even in this form it looks far better than the alternative of continuing the "slow growth" pattern of the past and risking the potential catastrophes that may ensue. The Indian and Bengalee governments both would be well advised to undertake the homework and the legwork necessary for converting the approach into an actionable program.

American Policy

The thesis of the essay is that there is cause for the United States to adopt a more positive approach to development in South Asia than has been true of its position in this decade. The basic reasons are those of poverty and numbers. There is no way that centers of power, such as the United States will continue to be, can be responsive to the great transnational issues of equity, resource sharing, and environmental defense that will pervade world affairs during the balance of the century without addressing the massive poverty of India and Bangladesh. The United States will be pushed into more responsiveness to the needs of the poorest countries by the augmented strength of the Third World coalition. It may be pulled by creeping globalism within its own and other OECD elites.

It will be the part of executive-branch statesmanship in Washington to lead the American transition toward greater global rationality, rather than be overrun by it. In the cases of the two most populous of the poorest countries this will mean recognizing that contributing to the welfare of a third of a billion destitute South Asians is, *per se*, a reasonable and appropriate end for American policy, not to be easily displaced by our national strategic interests or noninterests. It will mean, in the case of India, surmounting the habitual sourness, into which our official perceptions of that country seem to have fallen. (The American and Indian governments may not be able to banish their capacity to be irritated by each other, but they can stop letting the superficialities of the relationship steer their policies.)

It is especially important at this juncture that Washington not let the condition of South Asian democracy swamp its priorities. We have every right to be partisans of constitutional processes in India and Bangladesh, and conceivably a condition of escalating repression could mean that the Indian or Bengalee government had lost all capacity to serve its own people. However, we have no right to assume that to most South Asians it is more important to be free of governmental encroachments than of hunger or private inequities, or that the value of freedom flatly outranks that of civil order. On the face of it, given the United States government's record in assisting non-democratic regimes, there would be a frightful irony in our turning away from India and Bangladesh because they have fallen from grace. The viability of the non-revolutionary Indian system probably requires the renewal of a modified but genuine constitutionalism. At the same time, the latter almost surely will be dependent on better growth and equity achievements. American policy that is motivated by some concern for the South Asian poor will not look at the subcontinent through simplistic, single-value lenses.

At the same time, should not the adoption of a more positive American approach to Indian and Bengalee development at least be conditioned on the vigor and cogency with which the South Asians attack their own growth and equity problems? The short answer is yes—on the practical ground that the relevance of our efforts will heavily depend on theirs. However, the issue can better be discussed in a more sharply defined time frame.

Necessarily, throughout the essay there have been references to the international community's short-run responses to the relief needs that inflated oil, food, and fertilizer prices currently are posing for the poorest countries. In trying now to suggest some directions for the longer run, I will pass over this nearest phase of policy and go directly to the very long run. The next section speculates about a radically altered pattern of relationships to countries like India and Bangladesh that might well be in effect by the last years of the century. Then the following section comes back to the medium term—to the more familiar but peculiarly difficult, peculiarly critical next five to ten years for India and Bangladesh. It is in this context that the question of interdependency between external and internal actions becomes most pointed.

In the Long Run: A More Equitable World Economic Order

During the balance of the century, I am hypothesizing, successive American presidents and congresses may find they can promote global economic rationality more and more openly. Long-term policies would not apply peculiarly to India and Bangladesh; yet throughout the balance of the century, however buoyant their breakthroughs, those two will continue to account for most of the people in the poorest-country set. Let me summarize briefly, therefore, what some of the outlines of an appropriate long-term American program vis-à-vis the poorest countries might be.

We should, in our own legislation and in multilateral forums, continue to facilitate the access of developing country exports, especially manufactures, to advanced economy markets. After long flirtation with the concept, we now must begin to supply genuinely effective adjustment assistance to American enterprises and workers in labor-intensive product lines which cannot meet the freer competition of developing country production. With such assistance available for cushioning the domestic impact, the United States government should accept and facilitate, not blindly resist, private decisions to shift some polluting industries to foreign locations where, because of lesser industrial density, the social costs of environmental protection are lower.

In the ramifying domestic and international reassessments of the role of multinational corporations that are now in progress, therefore, the American government should be slow to censure such corporations on grounds that they "export jobs" to poor countries. Similarly, it should recognize the value to developing countries that the multinational corporations can have as marketing networks for the export of less developed countries' components and other products. Enlightened American policy will, as it can, reinforce, not resist, the efforts that host-country governments are making to strengthen the contribution of foreign private investments to their exports—e.g., by disallowing clauses of past formation agreements wherein American and other foreign companies have sought to prohibit the host-country subsidiary from selling abroad in competition with its parent or other subsidiaries.

As to multinationals, there can be no pretense here of examining the issue in the detail with which it is beginning to be addressed both in the United States and by the international community. However, with respect to the poorest countries—at least South Asia, surely India—a guideline for long-term American policy probably should be not to exaggerate the importance or potentialities of the multinational corporations. They can have key selected roles, e.g., in Indian offshore oil drilling and in Bangladesh fertilizer. In such capacities they have a very good chance of making rewarding profits. They can be responsible local economic citizens; the host governments can treat them constructively and evenhandedly; and the United States government should be a partisan both of good behavior by and of good treatment of American firms. However, the multinationals show no signs of becoming major sources of the transfer capital that the poorest countries need. Many of them in their local operations practice a cookbook style of technological transfer, and as for taking charge and masterminding the local economy—at least in India—they have about the same chance as the Christian missionaries.

It would be a pity, therefore, if the United States government's approach to the poorest countries were either obscured by excessive reliance on the multinationals or obstructed by excessive zeal in defending their rights. The latter are essentially those of temporary visitors—visitors, moreover, whose investments usually pay out fairly quickly. In respresenting American firms to foreign governments the U.S. government does, to be sure, have the obligations of a conscientious attorney. But this is not a duty that preempts all others, and to avoid its becoming so is good enough reason for supporting the development of authoritative transnational machinery for settling host-government-multinational corporations disputes.

The foregoing pages have suggested the rudiments of a globally responsible long-term policy on resource transfers for the United States. For one thing, this country should accept without hysteria the prospect of a post-OPEC proliferation of efforts by scarce raw materials producers to extract economic rents from the old-rich consumers by cartel techniques. We can hope and expect that the United States and the OECD will react very badly to any attempts to implement "poor power" by roughhouse tactics. However, when the procedure is a civilized exercise of market power, ours should be a civil response. From the consumer's side of the market we should bargain hard, not indulgently, at least one reason being that cartelization is a very crude instrument for reducing international inequities: it deals most harshly with those other poor countries who have less than their share of rent-bearing resources. But strident reaction will prove counterproductive, and it should be easier to avoid than in the oil case, since no other possible producers' cartel looks even remotely as potent.

Most of the disparity-narrowing transfers during the next quarter century will have to be deliberate and official. The evolution, I have suggested, should be toward a system of concessional transfers heavily tilted to the poorest countries. Such transfers should flow through multilateral channels. They should carry grant terms or some very close approximation. Their allocation between areas should be far more a function of how many people inhabit an area than of how many separate nation-state claimants it numbers. The burden of supplying the transfers should, among the better-off countries, be graduated primarily in terms of per capita income and wealth, only secondarily in terms of per capita liquidity. The transfers should flow, not at the whim of donors, but reliably (for development planning purposes)—more or less as a matter of right and routine. They should continue to flow as long as important international disparities persist. They should work a good deal like a transnational progressive income tax.

It is not hard to conjure up vehicles that would have most or all of these characteristics. Some explicit proposals are in view right now: the so-called SDR "link",[1] a transnational oceans and seabed authority whose royalties and earnings of which would be distributed to nation-states in accordance with their

---

[1]The general notion of the "link" is that when the International Monetary Fund distributes new issues of Special Drawing Rights (i.e., the "paper gold" that governments are expected increasingly to hold as reserve assets) to meet the world economy's increased needs for international liquidity, the distribution would be skewed toward the poor countries so that rich countries, in order to get their wanted increased liquidity, would have to earn it by supplying a round of real transfers to the poor countries.

populations and poverty; a transnational tax on extractive industries the proceeds of which would be similarly allocated. The problem is not one of mechanics but of will. Very few of the old-rich countries are yet prepared to take most of these steps. The American government conspicuously is not, but we are talking about a gradual, piecemeal evolvement of policy over the space of two and a half decades. In that time frame I suggest that the kind of transfers system outlined need not be unrealistic. Indeed the number of senior Washington officials who would privately accept the preceding paragraph as statement of a sensible long-term goal may already rival the number who would see it as an itemized nightmare.

Finally, as to the long run, however, Washington's globalists will have to struggle with some very sticky problems of transnational procedure and governance. These, like the development of substantive policy, will be addressed piecemeal. They will arise every time a new or refurbished venture (whether the subject is a new mode of transfer, transnational multinational corporation regulations, or worldwide population restraint) is launched, and there is the possibility that the implementing agency, as it takes hold and functions, may build up some measure of supranational authority. The issue will arise most vividly when a multinational activity is to be given some sort of direct access to resources that does not require the mediation of nation-state budgets.

There will be conflict over representation. What, among the several nation-states, shall be the distribution of votes in the governing bodies of transnational agencies? At present the world has two models, both unacceptable, for the governance of a rational world economic order. In the International Monetary Fund-International Bank for Reconstruction and Development model, wealth tends to rule. The UN General Assembly model (which extends to most UN agencies and institutions) is even less acceptable. As a repository for transferred power and wealth, it not only is resisted by the haves, it lacks even the philosophical virtue that could begin to erode the possessiveness of the old-rich and now-powerful. In the UN General Assembly model it is not numbers of people which rule, but numbers of flags. Mauritius and Liberia cast the same votes as India and China. Such "government" does not attract serious assignments of responsibility.

On this final, procedural issue, the gap in which a missing answer must be found is still so wide that only prolonged and flexible negotiation is likely to yield a solution. If the United States government would promote a solution, therefore, it should become a tireless participant in such bargaining, not remain defensively arrayed on one side of the argument.

The Crucial Middle Run in India and Bangladesh

The kind of long-term program outlined cannot be implemented in time to deal with the unrequited needs of the poor in India and Bangladesh during the next decade. In that time frame the best hope for these countries may be the kind of high-risk, breakthrough strategy suggested above, "Survival or Breakthrough?" (pp. 121ff). It is clear that there is nothing consequential that the United States or, indeed, any other external actor can do to assist such an effort unless there is a very strong internal lead toward "breakthrough" by the governments of India and Bangladesh themselves. The latter's efforts necessarily will dominate the outcome. Moreover, as long as transfers still flow mainly at the discretion of donor governments (and not as a matter of "right and routine"), the donors will need to satisfy themselves, their parliaments, and their publics that their fresh inputs are adding momentum to committed indigenous efforts, not merely seeking to induce them.

On the assumption that such evidence does emerge in one or both of the two countries in question, the first thing to be said about the appropriate American response is that the preceding section's suggestion that India and Bangladesh might most appropriately turn to OPEC sources for "breakthrough" project funding during the next five to ten years in no way implies that the United States and others of the old rich should be morally exempt from such contributions. The judgment was about likelihood, not justice. During this transitional time, the old-rich countries, still preoccupied with their own oil-price traumas, will need to contribute (especially by debt relief) to the reestablishment and maintenance of India's and Bangladesh's old (pre-oil) aid base. The most likely source of major additive project funding will be transfers that come either directly, or through existing or newly contrived intermediaries, from some of the oil exporters.

At a minimum, however, a more positively inclined United States should be a diligent handmaiden of this process. It should encourage new-rich contributions, agreeing to changes in multilateral institutional governance that will promote them. It should encourage the old rich to engage in some measure of interest subsidy of OPEC funds destined for South Asian food-fertilizer-water-energy projects.

Most important of all for the medium term, the United States can recognize and plan for the continuing contributions that appropriately packaged American food aid can make to the poorest countries for some years yet. Fortunately, both the American administration and Congress during the past year have been evincing changing perceptions of this subject. It is clear, first, that for a long middle term, while Indian and Bengalee agriculture is advancing with all of the vigor earlier suggested, concessionally supplied food can loosen and speed up the expansion process. It can help remove the wage-goods constraints on big food-energy projects and on the labor-intensive processing and manufacturing that such projects will induce. It also can provide some of the real resources for the public-works and other employment-generating programs (many of them locally chosen and managed) that should be part of the breakthrough effort.

Second, it also is by now quite clear that properly programmed and administered food aid need not dampen indigenous agricultural development. Unquestionably (although the degree often has been exaggerated in the telling) it did have this effect in India at the start of the 1960s. But if there is any danger to which both Indian and American policymakers have become systematically sensitized since, this is it. Moreover, the priority of agriculture as well as an effective regime for implementing the priority have been entrenched in Indian policy—and, insofar as one can speak of firm policy patterns at all in Bangladesh, in that country also. Thus a sustained input of food aid need not change the prospect that in due course India, later Bangladesh, will become self-supporting in food and perhaps even become net exporters. However, for a substantial time concessional food can, with OPEC money, leaven the development process.

The third altered perception is simply an updating of what has been long evident: the United States has the same special competence to supply food aid that OPEC has to supply financial aid in these crucial middle years for the subcontinent. We are peculiarly "liquid" in food. That does mean that in the proper (income-per-capita) canons of aid-sharing justice we have a far greater obligation to provide food aid than does, say, Japan. We have a far greater facility for providing a disproportionately large share of transfers in this specific form—and the embarrassingly low level of our generalized per capita aid contributions now also adds moral incentive for us to do so.

An American program adequately implementing these perceptions would not be politically cheap. It would cost substantial budgetary and balance-of-payments dollars. Moreover, if it is to be a major new demarche in the projection of a more positive American approach to the poorest countries, it ought to be done right, in terms of eliminating the vestiges of the fire-sale mentality that had a hand in launching American food aid back in the 50s. The food should go in the form of outright grants or the effective equivalent, and it should go without U.S. protectionist strings, particularly those involving the rights of recipients to engage in agricultural exports.

Plainly this is a tall order politically. Yet carefully planned and forward-programmed, the reliable supply annually of two or three million tons of "investment food" to India and Bangladesh would not need to encroach painfully or abruptly on either America's domestic markets or foreign commercial sales. Probably something along these lines is the most important contribution that this country is capable of making to the subcontinent's pivotal medium term.

One last recommendation, a largely negative one, about the content of American assistance policy may be in order. As has been suggested earlier in this discussion, there may still be some scope for useful technical assistance from abroad in selected sectors in India. Partly because some of the previous technical assistance worked and contributed to the development of a variety of effective indigenous institutions, the remaining scope is very limited (it is somewhat larger in Bangladesh), vastly smaller than many slightly informed Americans imagine.

In particular, judgments recently broadcast in this country to the effect that what is required for resuming the advance of Indian agriculture is a massive further transplantation of American farm technology by American technicians are comically wrong. The useful technical transplants are largely in place. What are needed are a number of other things cited in these pages. By and large, classic, didactic technical assistance has seen its day in South Asia. What remains to be done should come through such multilateral channels as the United Nations Development Program or through nonofficial agencies.

Will It Play in Peoria?

The obvious complaint about a piece like this is that, under the guise of policy analysis, it has produced a set of recommendations that sound politically unrealistic. "How," one can almost hear any given assistant secretary or assistant budget director wail, "can you possibly think we could sell such a program to the Congress?" "How," any given congressman might chime in, "could I sell that to my constituents?" My principal reply to this challenge has been the argument throughout that a seepage of globally responsible thinking is underway, among other places in the United States, that already is penetrating the intellectual and bureaucratic elites and sooner or later will catch most of us. In conclusion, let me bolster this theme with two more points.

First, as to most particular foreign economic actions (trade actions that impinge on particular producer groups are an exception), the usual picture of the political constraints—namely that an apathetic public hog-ties the Congress, which in turn, hog-ties the president—is a canard. Any particular foreign aid or similar measure is of trivial importance to most of the constituents of most congressmen. There may never yet have been a congressman who lost his seat because of his favorable votes on foreign aid. This means that if some energy is injected from the center, this supposed constraining apparatus can become a permissive mechanism. In this field, a president who knows what he wants, and pushes, is very likely to get his way, because to the individual legislator the political costs of acquiescing are low. Such pushing requires spending some political capital and therefore may be inhibited by others of the president's objectives. Nevertheless, at a price, presidents (at least from Kennedy onward) have had more discretion in this field than they have been willing to admit.

Second, not only do presidents have the option of acting rather more boldly than we have been led to believe, it could just be that they would gain politically from so doing. I have spoken of Indian and Bengalee cynicism. The United States at present may be a more severe case. Americans have had a certain appetite for expressed idealism which seems genuine. It could be that, stagflation anxieties and all, if a president took a strong, uncompromising stand for the humanitarian obligations of this most affluent country—obligations to be discharged prudently, without foolishness but also without strings—and did so in the lead of creeping globalism, he would find the playback from Peoria surprisingly good.

Notes

1. J.P. Lewis, "Oil, Scarcities and the Poor Countries," *World Politics* 27, 1 (October 1974): 65-66. Parts of the present chapter draw on portions of this article.

2. Ibid., p. 66.

3. Ibid., p. 67.

4. Tata Economic Consultancy Services, *The Indian Economy in 2000 A.D.*, Second India Series of Studies, sponsored by the Ford Foundation, New Delhi (Draft, September 1974), p. 19. For consistency's sake the rest of the quantitative comparisons in this paragraph all are drawn from the same recent source.

5. Possible ingredients of such a strategy are discussed in J.P. Lewis "Some Notes on Decentralized Development in a Poor Nonrevolutionary Socialist Republic," Ford Foundation, Dacca, October 1974, mimeo.

6. Cf. J.P. Lewis, "Notes of a Rural Area Development Tourist," *Economic and Political Weekly* (Bombay), June 29, 1974, pp. A-42-A-54. Also "Designing the Public-Works Mode of Antipoverty Policy," paper for the Princeton-Brookings Income Distribution Project (Forthcoming.).

7. In the second of the papers (ibid.) just noted and also in "Some Hypotheses about Rural Development Strategy," the Ford Foundation, New Delhi, July 1974.

8. For example: In the well-known International Labor Organization "employment studies" of selected countries that began appearing in 1970, in a seminal speech at the 1971 meetings of the Society for International Development by the Pakistani (now senior IBRD) economist, Mabub ul Hag, in the 1972 through 1975 annual reports of the UN Committee for Development Planning, in a great many places in that quite remarkable merchandiser of scholarly research, policy analysis, and current commentary, the *Economic and Political Weekly* of Bombay, and partially, at least, in the more recent documentation of the Indian and Bangladesh Planning Commissions. One of the more comprehensive of the "new strategy" statements will be found in the forthcoming volume on Indian development by Professor John Mellor of Cornell.

9. Bhagwati, Jagdish, and Padma Desai, *Indian Planning for Industrialization: Industrialization and Trade Policies Since 1951* (London and New York: Oxford University Press, 1970).

10. Tata, *The Indian Economy in 2000 A.D.*

11. Planning Commission, Government of Peoples Republic of Bangladesh, *The First Five Year Plan, 1973-78* (Dacca, 1973), p. 330.

12. See Professor A.K.N. Reddy (of the Indian Institute of Sciences, Bangladore), *Bio-gas Plants—Prospects, Problems, and Tasks* (mimeo, undated, circa 1974); also the results of a July 1974 conference conducted, in company with Professor Reddy, at the Centre of Development Studies, Trivandrum (forthcoming); also the extensive treatment of the subject developed quite independently of the freshly interested set of Indian scientists cited in the Reddy paper by the American-trained Indian engineer Arjan Makhijani and Alan Poole in their book, *Energy and Agriculture in the Third World*, a report to the Energy Policy Project of the Ford Foundation (Cambridge, Mass.: Ballinger Publishing Co., 1975).

13. *The Strategy of Economic Development* (New Haven: Yale University Press, 1957).

IV

Progress, Stability, and Peace in Mainland Southeast Asia

Alexander Woodside

Introduction

It is difficult to predict the circumstances of mainland Southeast Asia by the year 1985 or 2000, although it is relatively easy to identify the problems and difficulties which confront Southeast Asian leaders now. The mainland Southeast Asian region—which includes Burma, Thailand, Malaysia and Singapore, Cambodia, Laos, and Vietnam—is famous for its baffling political and cultural complexities. Moreover, academic and nonacademic knowledge of its societies, in the United States and in other parts of the Western world, is very much inferior to our knowledge of China, Japan, and India, the three giant Asian countries which partly embrace Southeast Asia. Most generalizations about Southeast Asia are likely to be relatively primitive; many of the most ambitious prophecies about its countries are likely to be specious.

Making 1975 the starting-point of an analysis of mainland Southeast Asia's future, it might be added, has its own special perils. For the rise of a wholly Communist Indochina in the spring and summer of 1975 appears both to represent the most important bequest of the recent past in this region, and to provide the most commanding auguries about the region's future. Among the auguries themselves, however, some of the ones which possess the most clarity in the eyes of the general public may well prove to be the least valid.

For one thing, even the most callow and untutored witnesses of contemporary events must be aware that Indochina's communisms are not monolithic. The Cambodian Communist government, for example, rules a society where formal village organization and its mystique, and specific village loyalties, have never been a dominant historical force, and where control and manipulation of labor, rather than control and manipulation of land, have normally been the basis of political and social power. In these respects Cambodian history and society are very different from those of neighboring Vietnam (or China), and the Cambodian revolutionary government's desperate wholesale expulsion of urban populations to the countryside in May 1975, as a remedy for its agricultural crisis, therefore probably astonished the revolutionary governments of Vietnam every bit as profoundly as it astonished opinion in the West. There are no grounds whatsoever for believing that Cambodia and Vietnam will develop identical strategies of domestic reconstruction or of foreign policy in the next quarter century. There will be no single Indochina Communist "bloc" capable of imposing its will upon the rest of the half-continent.

For another thing, economic problems are now likely to take precedence over ideological confrontations in mainland Southeast Asia during the remainder of the twentieth century. Every Southeast Asian government is publicly committed to economic growth, to technological change and to at least moderate degrees of industrialization, and to the expansion of educational (and upward mobility) opportunities for more and more of its people. The Hanoi government, for instance, is building classrooms at a planned rate of 20,000-25,000 per year in 1975, even in the midst of its relative poverty. It has just abolished, apparently as a result of popular pressure, the payment of school fees by the parents of the nearly six million school children who are enrolled in general education in the DRV, despite the fact that it badly needs the revenues from these fees. All Southeast Asian countries, including Burma and Vietnam, and also I think Cambodia, recognize the necessity of export-led economic growth, and are increasingly concerned with the need to maximize both their international export opportunities and the prices which their raw materials receive on world commodity markets.

In June 1975, China accused the Western powers of seeking to "transfer" their own economic crises to Southeast Asia, by reducing their imports of Southeast Asian raw materials, thereby depressing the prices of these materials and making it difficult for Southeast Asia to pay for the industrial products of the West. This sudden, austere but opportune inversion of the central classical emphasis of the Leninist approach to imperialism—namely, that the hallmark of imperialism in 1975 is not the export of capital to underdeveloped countries, but rather the reduction of imports from such countries—is likely to have a most persuasive influence upon the minds of many Southeast Asian leaders unless Western governments realize that fair and generous access to the markets of the industrialized states is regarded in Southeast Asia as a life-and-death matter. Indochina politicans share these anxieties and they will continue to do so.

For a third thing, strategic and economic factors probably combine to make Malaysia, Indonesia, and Singapore—the states that border the Straits of

Malacca—more central (and more vulnerable) Southeast Asian actors in the future dramas of world history than any of the Indochina states, despite the admirable historic vigor of the Vietnamese people and their revolution. Economically, Malaysian and Indonesian rubber and tin still enjoy an unimpeachable significance in Southeast Asian affairs and on world markets that no product from the Indochina countries has yet attained. Strategically, it is perhaps enough only to observe that the Straits of Malacca themselves have become the crucial specific issue in the Chinese-Russian rivalry as it applies to Southeast Asia. In the Chinese view, complete Russian freedom of the passageway between the Indian and Pacific Oceans is indispensable to the presumed Russian dream of creating an unimpeded maritime "hegemony" based on the connection of Soviet naval activities in the Black, Mediterranean, Red, Indian, and west Pacific oceans and the Sea of Japan; and China further sees the Russian desire to obtain such freedom and to build such a "hegemony" as the explanation of all recent Russian activities in Southeast Asia, including Russian offers to the Malaysian government to help develop port facilities in Sabah, and Russian discussions with Thai officials about dredging a canal across the Isthmus of Kra.

Hence the great Communist victory of 1975 in Indochina is by no means as potent a key to the next few decades of Southeast Asian history as it may have seemed in the summer of 1975, either to its architects or to its enemies. In this chronically disturbed, casualty-ridden, highly variegated part of Asia, therefore, what should future American policy be?

This chapter will argue that there is a rapidly growing Southeast Asian fondness for a collective posture of complete political neutrality in the world of the great powers, and that no matter how ambiguous the potentially very elastic notion of "neutrality" may be, it is in the American interest to accept this tendency as the best of all possible prospects for Southeast Asia's future. No mainland Southeast Asian country regards political neutrality as a kind of meretricious camouflage for total isolationism, all Southeast Asian countries desire to expand their economic and social welfare by means of trade with the West, and it is in the American interest to contribute to this expansion by, at the very least, exercising suitable vigilance against short-sighted protectionism, against the arbitrary closing or narrowing of American markets to Southeast Asian products. All this is a very far cry from the creation of that morally cyclopean world administration to manage food, energy, and other economic resources which many analysts soberly believe is the real irreducible minimum solution for world tensions. In short, by most standards a warning against barriers to Southeast Asian trade is a shamefully modest prescription for improvement of American relations with the Southeast Asian sector of the Third World. Modest or not, it encompasses immensely troublesome questions. The Argentinian economist Raul Prebisch has observed that the poor countries which buy industrial products are the real victims of price and wage inflation in the industrialized world. Nothing is more likely to feed anti-American sentiments and reflexes among Southeast Asian elites in the next quarter century than painful, unbridgeable discrepancies between the results of such inflation and the market weaknesses of Southeast Asian exports.

Russian expansionism in this region may very well be a legitimate concern for American policymakers, but virtually all Southeast Asian Communist movements, including the Vietnamese one, are likely to remain quite independent of the Soviet Union and are unlikely to serve Russian interests. American hostility to left-wing or Communist political parties or governments in mainland Southeast Asia is dangerous and unnecessary because leftist regimes in this region are all both economically vulnerable and economically ambitious, and must, as a result of the interplay of their vulnerabilities and ambitions, sooner or later try to build bridges to the United States, once they are convinced that the effort will not undermine their political security.

If Russian expansionist influences have recently begun to manifest themselves in Southeast Asia, the best means of frustrating them is to make common cause with Southeast Asian nationalism, rather than to oppose it. Chinese policy in Southeast Asia, whatever it has been in the past, is increasingly sophisticated and effective in 1975, precisely because it obeys this formula. Peking has agreed with the leaders of Indonesia and Malaysia that the Straits of Malacca are not unconditionally "international" waters and that Russian invocations of international law to prove that they are, are deliberate assaults upon Southeast Asian national sovereignties. The Chinese government has also (in 1975) looked approvingly upon the joint efforts of Malaysia, Thailand, and Indonesia to control the quantities of rubber they offer to world markets and to create a united interstate Southeast Asian association for economic bargaining with Western-owned shipping companies in the Far East. The Chinese appear to believe that the Soviet Union has large ambitions but few real political assets in Southeast Asia, and that as long as the needs of Southeast Asian states remain, in the words of the Indonesian foreign minister, "different from those of India"— that is, so long as Southeast Asian states are not forced to confront regional rivals supported by superpowers from outside the region—they will not show any interest in Russian-sponsored "Asian collective security pacts." A genuine American reconciliation with the Communist governments of Vietnam would soon erode, to a significant degree, whatever practical Russian influences are now at work in eastern Indochina, and such a reconciliation is highly desirable for many other reasons, moral as well as strategic.

As for China itself, I shall argue in some detail that a chief international peculiarity of mainland Southeast Asia is that it is a region where the other superpowers are more capable of inflicting harm upon Chinese interests than China is capable of inflicting damage upon Russian or American interests. Geography and history have put China on the defensive in Southeast Asia, much as the United States is on the defensive—for other reasons as well as geographic ones—in Latin America. This condition will remain especially true as long as

China lacks the offensive naval forces of a superpower, as it has for the past five centuries. American fears of a massive and sinister Chinese intervention in Southeast Asia have always been grossly exaggerated, although it is only fair to admit that Southeast Asian states are, and will continue to be, chronically anxious about Chinese intentions, and have sometimes helped to encourage such American exaggerations.

Behind the anxieties of the mainland Southeast Asian states, let us remember, lie a host of unresolved domestic problems. The nature of these problems also inspires some of the recommendations just outlined.

Ideology, Politics, and Society in Mainland Southeast Asia

Authoritarianism Is More Likely than Democracy to
Prevail in Mainland Southeast Asia

This prediction is relatively easy to make. In the first place, nondemocratic patterns of government are likely to prevail for cultural and historical reasons. The tradition of Indian kingship, until recently very strong in Burma, Thailand, Cambodia, and Laos, and the tradition of Confucian kingship, until recently very strong in Vietnam, make rapid popular acceptance of Western principles of representative government and of a "loyal opposition" very difficult.

American politics, even today, are obviously shaped by the formulations of seventeenth century English philosophers like John Locke. It would be foolish to imagine that Southeast Asians, even in a period of unprecedented change for them, are not inclined to pay homage, consciously or unconsciously, to their own far more ancient political heritage. Burma, Thailand, and Cambodia were all the homes of royal governments whose kings or princes enjoyed absolute powers. Such rulers depended upon Brahman advisers, were surrounded by symbols like the white umbrella which indicated divine sovereignty, and gained the practical allegiance of their peoples, not by holding elections, but, in part, by promoting the Buddhist religion. Thailand and Laos still, in 1975, preserve modernized versions of this kingly or princely polity. Throughout the extraordinary vicissitudes of his career, part of Cambodia, at least, has remained loyal to Prince Sihanouk (who was actually the king of Cambodia until 1955); and the British destruction of the Burmese kingship in 1885 (the Burmese throne was even transported to Calcutta) did not eliminate all the political instincts upon which it had rested.

As a demonstration of this last fact, U Nu, the head of the Burmese government for most of the period between 1948 and 1962, functioned as an almost kingly patron of religion by spending millions of dollars upon Buddhist temples. He also toyed with the idea of converting President Eisenhower, commuted the prison sentences of all Burmese conficts who passed examinations in Buddhism, ordered government departments to dismiss civil servants thirty minutes early if they wished to practice religious meditation, and in general appeared to many to be recalling the style of a Burmese royal government which had hardly any parallels in the Western political experience.

Today, many of these countries—Burma, Cambodia, and Thailand at least until 1973—are in fact ruled by soldiers. It may be sad to admit, but these authoritarian military regimes do not contradict the values and expectations of their countries' political heritages as sharply as liberal parliamentary democracies would. On the other hand, neither are the military regimes all organic extensions of traditional political ideals. Moreover, they do not all fully express the aspirations of the more modern, educated nationalists in their societies. The outside world should not anticipate the emergence of democracy all over Southeast Asia, but it should also not assume that narrow military governments, incapable of invoking the rich religious mythology and of violating the religious patronage of traditional governments are likely to enjoy an undisturbed permanence. They are unsatisfactory halfway houses between the nondemocratic but humanistic past and the "mass society" future.

There is a second reason why nondemocratic patterns are likely to prevail in Southeast Asia, and it has nothing to do with the influence of tradition. Such patterns were not discouraged during the recent Western colonial era in Southeast Asia. Quite the contrary: the Western colonial powers habitually fostered the growth of cumbersome bureaucratic administrations in the Southeast Asian societies they ruled, and just as habitually repressed all but the most harmless and ineffective kinds of political parties. Nowhere was this more true than in Vietnam, under French rule until 1954.

Democratic political parties would have had difficulty flourishing on Vietnamese soil under any circumstances. Under the old Vietnamese monarchy, the word for political party in Vietnamese (*dang*) had the pejorative meaning of a selfish "faction," out to gain its own selfish ends by hidden subterfuges. For the traditional Vietnamese ruler justified his exercise of power by claiming to monopolize virtue, and he could not concede the usefulness or the necessity of an opposition party or "faction" in his country without countenancing the implication that his monopoly of virtue was imperfect and in need of repair. Nevertheless, the constitution of 1967, which was introduced into southern Vietnam by American advisers and by the veteran leaders of certain Vietnamese political groups, did proclaim the legitimate importance of political parties. It urged the south to ascend quickly to the blissful political plateau of a "two-party system." The world was subsequently startled to discover the existence, after 1967, of no less than twenty-four legally tolerated political parties in southern Vietnam.

Where did this plethora of political parties come from? Before 1945, most patriotic Vietnamese who were concerned with the fate of their country and with the improvement of the life of its people were virtually compelled by the

French colonial regime to organize secret parties—if they wished to remain alive and to gain political power of any meaningful kind. The colonial regime arrested and executed the leaders of some political parties and planted spies in the ranks of all the clandestine ones in order to destroy them. Protective secrecy became the first requirement of all political organizations, but it meant the frustration of most of the requirements of democracy as it is known in the West. Vietnamese party leaders could gain very little experience in publicly disseminating their programs; for that matter, they were prevented from being able publicly to ascertain the wishes of a large constituency about practical social and economic issues. Also, the colonial police prevented Vietnamese who were following essentially the same political path from getting to know each other and from combining into one organization. Instead, they found themselves scattered among a number of mutually distrusting groups, and since colonial Indochina's deceptive calm harbored an intense and growing Vietnamese interest in politics, generated by anticolonial feelings, it was inevitable that many such secret political groups would appear.

Why were these political parties unable to amalgamate after 1945, or after the overthrow of Ngo Dinh Diem in 1963? By this time, too much water had flowed under the bridge. Each party was jealous of its own "struggle accomplishments" under the French and did not wish to see its memory submerged. Each party had a different quantity of followers and a different mobilization capacity, and was fearful of those parties which had larger followings and capacities. Each party had developed a different leadership style, under the sweltering political blanket of colonialism; obviously it would become most difficult to merge a political party which had a relatively democratic internal structure with one which had much more autocratic command organs. Fragmentation became a way of life, and remained a way of life, under circumstances of revived repression after 1971, until the Communist victory in South Vietnam in 1975 wrote a virtual end to the story of Vietnam's ineffective non-Communist political parties.

There is also a third important reason why nondemocratic patterns of government are likely to prevail in Southeast Asia, and this reason breathes the fevered spirit of the post-colonial era. Southeast Asian governments must address themselves to economic and social tasks of an unexampled magnitude. Their leaders feel they must promote forced draft industrialization programs and, at the same time, unify societies which are typically potpourris (but not melting pots) of feuding ethnic groups. Like Milton's archangel, they must pause between a world destroyed and a world restored; they must ransack their pre-colonial pasts for inspirations that are meaningful to enough of their populations to hold them together, while they usher in economic development schemes which they hope will integrate (as well as enrich) their societies on a new basis.

One is reminded of constitution-building in Kuomintang China, whose constitutions usually had something for everyone, even though they failed to ward off a Communist triumph. The Kuomintang constitution of 1948, for example, tried to define laws, like the American constitution, tried to promote economic development, like twentieth-century Soviet Russian constitutions, and tried to exalt the Chineseness of the "Three People's Principles" of Sun Yat-sen, all at the same time. Democracy, with its encouragement of the expression of diverse points of view, often seems to Southeast Asian leaders to be, at best, an inferior thing to wish for. At worst, it seems to them to be a time-wasting threat to the achievement of necessary social and ideological unities.

The Armies. With decisive political party competitions absent from the scene, policy-making in most mainland Southeast Asian societies is dominated by the claims and the behavior of armies, bureaucracies, and educated intelligentsias which are often outside political parties. The role of the army in contemporary Southeast Asia may go well beyond such military concerns as the defense of the nation-state in time of war. For the passion to achieve equality with the former Western colonial powers has usually been expressed in military terms first. Army officers were among the first Southeast Asians to become partly Westernized. The army, in effect, has become a symbol of the drive for equality. At times, indeed, the fusion of military planning with international status-hunting may even affect the efficiency of the Southeast Asian army.

As Field Marshal Phin Chunhawan put it in a message to the Thai army in 1955, Thailand should have an army "the equal of the armies of independent nations of the same rank." Equality commensurate with rank was what counted; it apparently mattered less if these "independent nations of the same rank" were anywhere near Thailand, or in a position to threaten the Thai people.

As a better instance of such a Southeast Asian determination to make armies almost magical status symbols, without their necessarily having any intimate connection with their own precise environment, the non-Communist Cambodian army, which was created by Prince Monireth at the end of 1945, quickly became more Western than the Cambodian political system itself in the 1950s and 1960s. It acquired a taste for the most classical Western military doctrines, at the very time when Cambodia itself was threatened by guerrilla warfare. At the opening of the Cambodian military academy in 1955 the defense minister, Prince Sirik Matak, even strenuously complained that the omnipresence of guerrillas in Cambodia was regrettable because it had deprived his army of acquiring experience with "the management of units higher than battalions."

In so easily becoming a symbol of first-stage Westernization and of the desire for equality with the West, the Southeast Asian army risks becoming alienated from much of its own society. Consider the army of southern Vietnam between 1954 and 1975. Until the 1960s, its organization and training were based upon the French model. After that, until 1975, it was largely based upon the American. Trinh Pho, a former officer in this army, pointed out in 1969 that South Vietnamese officers were graduates of French and American military training programs which gave them good technical training but no training in political leadership, since "in America officers are regarded merely as fighting specialists." Whether or not this comment was correct, the South Vietnamese army exhibited quite clearly the deadly process of isolation through an excessive, equality-seeking fondness for foreign techniques. One of this army's defenders, Tran Ngoc Nhuan, even explained in 1969 that the army would have to be expanded to more than one million men despite the fact that such expansion would magnify its two shortcomings, untalented commanders, and "slovenly" organization. His reason for advocating a policy of expansion was suggestive. He said he feared that if the army contracted, and turned its tasks over to less costly village self-defense forces, it would not be able to receive and use the most modern American weapons. By this logic, the increasing "Vietnamization" of the war meant the increasing "Westernization" of the Saigon army.

Is it true that the more closely an Asian army enjoys the cultural and technological embrace of a Western power, the more problematic its social and political position will become in its own country? This depends upon the nature of the army's opponents, but contemporary mainland Southeast Asia provides much support for this hypothesis. The Ne Win military government of Burma, which came into power by a *coup* in 1962 and transformed itself into a nominally civilian regime by means of a new constitution ratified in 1973, has hung on to power by shrewdly cultivating a style of politics which reflects, not Sandhurst or West Point, but the code of life of much of the traditional Burmese village. There is an emphasis upon education, a belittling of economic individualism and of private business interests, a celebration of communal sharing organized by the state, and a hostility to foreign cultural influences. This experiment, it is true, has not yet performed any real miracles of integration; it has not, for example, won the irrevocable allegiance of Burma's subordinate ethnic states; but it has endured longer than some neighboring military regimes which have been more deeply Westernized.

The separateness of the Southeast Asian army, its potential difficulty of being exiled from much of its own civilization, is heightened by the apparent absence, much of the time, of strong competitive reference groups. The Thanom Kittikachorn military government in Thailand, which ruled by decree in Bangkok between 1971 and 1973, seems to have become too cut off to realize that if its troops openly clashed with students, other powerful segments of the Thai public would suddenly oppose it, as they did in the fall of 1973. In the spring of 1973, the ill-fated President Thieu announced in Saigon the creation of his own political party, the "Democratic party," even though he had never previously distinguished himself as a champion of political parties. But the three tasks he declared his new party would perform were, significantly, three tasks the army itself could never perform. They were also three tasks which must be performed for a political system to enjoy good health. They were the establishment of a two-way "transmission" of opinions between the people and the government; the creation of "exciting" political competition with other groups and parties (the boredom of most forms of army rule may ultimately be subversive); and the exercise of a critical supervision of the "machinery of state" (military rule can breed peculiarly uncontrollable corruptions). Because so many simple military regimes find it difficult to perform these three functions, they are, in the long run, totally undependable and subject to sudden *coups* from within or from without. A foreign policy which bases itself upon alliances with such regimes risks a great deal; I cannot think of any easily classifiable exceptions.

The Bureaucracies. To some extent, the problems of mainland Southeast Asian bureaucracies are very similar to those of the armies. In countries like Thailand these bureaucracies may encompass nearly all the people who find themselves in the upper reaches of society. The bureaucracy may employ virtually all the teachers and most of the doctors, lawyers, and other professionals in active service. It is not even uncommon for a Southeast Asian bureaucracy to arrange the genesis and the growth of futuristic new occupations which the West has taken for granted for centuries: the Ministry of National Information in Vientiane, Laos, taught pioneering courses in journalism to Lao bureaucrats in the early 1970s. But because it is a vast, all-embracing institution which makes major independent occupations and professions in the West into its own adjuncts and subordinate concerns, the Southeast Asian bureaucracy may be stimulated by abnormally few pressures and claims from outside. It lacks independent outside reference groups. One important result of this lack, as David Wilson has shown for Thailand's bureaucracy, is the dispersal of power to make policy. The bureaucracy has a tendency to break up into competing groups and cliques behind the scenes, partly because it is not made directly, formally, and repeatedly responsible to the demands and wishes of constituencies outside the government.

In northern Vietnam, the bureaucracy was much less able to avoid the orchestrated criticism of outside organizations and constituencies, all operating within precise Communist guidelines. Yet even there the malaise of bureaucratic detachment and fragmentation frustrates, at times, the ambitions of the revolutionary government in Hanoi. Colonial bureaucracies in Southeast Asia, including the one in French Indochina, were usually much more preoccupied with the defensive consolidation of Western rule in the region than they were concerned with economic development. (Most economic development was carried out by private interests, such as rice and rubber plantation owners.) The changeover from the colonial period to the post-colonial period in Southeast Asia has meant that national bureaucracies are now *expected* to plan and to carry out programs of economic change that their immediate ancestors, the colonial bureaucracies, would have regarded as being either vain or subversive.

The tensions of this rapid, forced transition can be enormous. If we look at

North Vietnam first, we find that the state machinery of the Ho Chi Minh government evolved on a piecemeal basis in the mountainous areas of the north before 1954, and then absorbed all the administrative workers of the colonial civil service who had agreed to remain in the north after the French withdrew. In 1955, when this piebald bureaucracy first began to function as the civil service of an independent state, a clear majority of its members, 97,550 out of 168,250, had nothing whatsoever to do with economic or industrial planning, research, or administration. By 1968, however, two-thirds of the members of the northern Vietnamese civil service were associated with what Hanoi now calls the "material production sector." On the surface, the center of gravity of the northern bureaucracy appeared to have been successfully shifted from defensive administrative purposes to the purposes of politically ordained economic growth—a revolution in the very conception of the bureaucrat's role—in just thirteen years.

However, institutional transformations do not really occur in mainland Southeast Asia quite so smoothly or so comfortably. While the *percentage* of civil servants in the north who played no role in economic development plans shrank from a majority to just one-third, the *numbers* of such bureaucrats actually tripled between 1960 and 1968, in spite of, or because of, the demands of the second Indochina War. Hanoi admitted in 1972 that it could not halt this undesirable expansion: the best it could do would be to force a slower "growth rate" upon this sector of the government. Swollen bureaucracies are not, of course, a phenomenon unique to Southeast Asia, but there are two features of life in much of Southeast Asia today which make this problem a more acute and disquieting one than it would be anywhere in the West.

First of all, in many Southeast Asian societies (Cambodia between 1954 and 1975, for example) the civil service has been the principal national industry. In traditional Vietnam, and also in traditional Cambodia, state service, rather than economic or commercial activity, was regarded as the chief source of prestige and of family advancement. Commerce was culturally deprecated; it was almost monopolized by outsiders (like the overseas Chinese); and it was subject to arbitrary taxation and harassment by the court. A gentleman did not become a businessman. Perhaps it is not surprising that North Vietnam's bureaucratic revolution has only been half successful. Perhaps it is not surprising that mandarin instincts surviving from the past may have helped to triple its numbers of noneconomic administrators against the wishes of the regime itself. Perhaps it is not surprising that the northern civil service still appears to undergo the same contractions and expansions as it did under the old Vietnamese dynasties—with trimmed bureaucracies being characteristic of the early years (as in 1955-1960) and swelling bureaucracies being characteristic later (after 1960).

The second reason for the importance of bureaucratic inflation in mainland Southeast Asia is that these societies are attempting to make up for lost time by embarking upon sometimes grandiose, state-directed industrialization projects. National bureaucracies are the authors and the foundations of these projects;

Southeast Asian societies lack the creative indigenous middle classes of the kind which were present in the industrializing West. North Vietnam, which is an exception in some ways among Southeast Asian states, may well be a paradigm of the future in this respect: it has large economic development schemes, but it must necessarily entrust the application of these schemes to a bureaucracy. Once bureaucracies are created, however, they tend to become rigid and conservative. They require masses of formal rules to coordinate their activities, to avoid random acts of favoritism, to control their spending, and to ensure their predictability. When they grow rapidly, they may become even more rigid, because their top officials try to preserve their diluted authority over increasing numbers of underlings by the issuance of more rules, and more demands for written reports. This vicious circle is quite capable of converting a revolutionary government into a most conservative one, undone by the very instruments it has created to advance its revolution.

Can a country like North Vietnam—or Burma—escape this deadly cycle of bureaucratic expansion and paralysis? The stakes are high; they are the very success or failure of the cardinal goals that post-colonial Southeast Asian states have set for themselves. As a consequence, an important focus of politics in some Southeast Asian countries may be the bureaucratic reorganization campaign, with its revelation (and its aggravation) of the rivalries among cliques both inside and outside the bureaucracy. Not all Southeast Asian states can afford to discipline their bureaucracies as directly as Hanoi did in 1962-1963, when it abolished more than 800 offices in government departments and state-owned companies, and transferred more than 3,000 cadres from the administrative center to production agencies in the provinces. One reason is that not all Southeast Asian states possess political organizations outside the bureaucracy which are sufficiently powerful to check its operations.

Three things complicate the problem of preventing Southeast Asian bureaucracies from drifting into states of predatory stagnation. The first, already mentioned, is that these bureaucracies do not receive enough prodding, or stimuli, from external constituencies. Another is that what little economic development does take place encourages civil servants, not to disown their traditional values and to become commercial entrepreneurs, but to make money as civil servants out of such development. Cambodia, before 1975, offered the worst example of this sort of dead end in contemporary Southeast Asian history: bureaucrats readily sold visas and import licences but neglected enterprises from which they could not make quick profits such as long-term agricultural planning. The third factor which may encourage the growth and the socially self-contained atmosphere of Southeast Asian bureaucracies, is that government service happens to be the most convenient source of employment for the thousands of educated job-seekers who have emerged in Southeast Asia since the colonial lid came off after World War II and indigenous governments permitted a dramatic expansion of educational facilities.

Education and Society. Colonial governments, until the eve of World War II, customarily offered little more than the most sporadic primary school instruction to the populations they governed. French Indochina (Vietnam, Cambodia, Laos) certainly lacked a broad middle school system, and contained less than 1,000 university-level students when the European war broke out in 1939. Once such societies regained their independence, their new rulers understandably set out to rectify this situation. North Vietnam now has thirty-seven universities and high-level technical colleges. South Vietnam, in 1972, had more than 40,000 university students. In Cambodia, Prince Sihanouk lavished a great deal of money and attention upon secondary and post-secondary education, opening "dozens" of universities as one of his critics (Douc Rasy) recently remarked. Even in non-colonized societies, the pattern was similar. In Thailand the number of middle school students increased by 43 percent between 1964 and 1969 (from 310,000 to 445,000), the number of government universities almost doubled in one decade, 1961-1972, and both these trends foreshadowed Bangkok's "student revolution" of 1973.

The graduates of these new institutions often became, with disconcerting rapidity, an embittered or clamorous species of unemployed (or misemployed) intellectuals or "semi-intellectuals." Apart from the bureaucracy, they have few places to go—Southeast Asia has not yet had its industrial revolution. Engineering graduates may be compelled to teach English; law graduates may be compelled to open laundries. Politically speaking, Southeast Asian states cannot afford to suppress their own transcendental bureaucratic growth, for the suppression of bureaucratic growth means nothing less than the suppression of the central job market for the ambitious sons of the urban upper and middle classes. At the time of his overthrow in 1970, some of Prince Sihanouk's most dedicated opponents in Cambodia were the surplus urban degree-holders his own educational reforms had produced, many of whom resented the lack of occupational opportunities, or the fact that Sihanouk's children were allowed to study abroad (in China, Russia, Czechoslovakia, and France) while they were not.

Another important source of unrest in Southeast Asian politics are Westernized or highly educated professionals and intellectuals which these countries possess, often have in greater number than the actual social demand requires. Accordingly, many such professionals and intellectuals, being underemployed, are discontented. The situation would not necessarily improve if economic change created a vast range of new opportunities for people with high level and middle level technical education. Southeast Asian intellectuals have an inbred fondness for humanistic and legal education, because of its correspondence to hallowed elitist ideals in their traditional cultures; they have far less fondness for the study of engineering and science.

U Nu, until 1962 the ruler of Burma, explained his decision to study law at Rangoon University in the 1930s by candidly admitting that he had no personal interest in the subject, but that his countrymen would not have "any man to be their leader who has no . . . Bachelor of Law degree after his name"; since his ambition was to become the leader of Burma, he felt that he "should try to satisfy their requirements of leadership" by becoming "a Bachelor of Law." Of the 36,007 university students on the rolls in South Vietnam in 1968, more than 65 percent (23,527) were in the faculties of law and letters, rather than those of the sciences, business, medicine, pharmacy, dentistry, architecture, etc. Lawyers enjoy an exaggerated prestige in modern Southeast Asia not because Southeast Asian societies have prominent traditions which cherish the supremacy of law and the solution of disputes through litigation—they do not—but because lawyers are seen as modernized versions of the old-fashioned mandarin or his equivalent. Occupations may enjoy an enviable prestige, during periods of cultural change, that has nothing to do with their economic suitability. When ancient cultural vanities help to produce an unemployable intellectual class, the stability of the political systems themselves may be jeopardized. Swelling bureaucracies try to buy time for such political systems by hiring more and more people.

It is plain that some mainland Southeast Asian societies have long suffered from a complete lack of coordination between educational programs and economic development. Since most of the manpower of these societies is employed in relatively small commercial and industrial enterprises, their educational systems do not need to purvey the knowledge of a "high" technology in order to be immediately useful. But they do need to supply a basic vocational and technical training to hundreds of thousands of middle school pupils, which such pupils can then apply in existing industries once they leave school. One measure of the great weakness of at least some Southeast Asian societies in this respect, can be provided by comparing South Vietnam with Taiwan. Whereas about *one-third* of all middle school students on Taiwan were receiving some form of vocational-technical training by the late 1960s, only 1 percent (25,000 out of 2.5 million) middle school and primary school pupils were receiving such training in southern Vietnam in 1967. In other words, even by more general Asian standards South Vietnam was backward.

Litanies of the difficulties which confront many Southeast Asians are easy to recite: problems of incompletely controlled bureaucratic growth, an absence of sufficient external counterweights to bureaucracies to make them more responsive, the pressures of underemployed intellectuals, a gap between education and economic development needs, armies which are sometimes too isolated from their societies. The outlook is one of instability within a context of nondemocratic polities, but of instability which threatens no one but Southeast Asians themselves.

Foreign military and political involvement in such a landscape is the greatest "destabilizer" of all. Foreign economic and cultural involvement, ranging from oil exploration to academic exchanges, need not be destabilizing and are likely to be welcomed, loudly or quietly, by most Southeast Asian states, including the governments in Hanoi and Saigon. One form of interaction between Southeast Asia and the outside world has been very common: the education of the children of Southeast Asian elites at universities in Europe, Canada, and the United States. Does the education abroad, of potential Southeast Asian leaders, contribute either to stability or to the greater well-being of Southeast Asians? In my view, ideological prejudices will be relatively unimportant in affecting Southeast Asian answers to this question in the future. The real touchstone of future American-Southeast Asian interaction will not be ideology, but rather the more ancient question for Southeast Asian states of how to reconcile their external cultural and economic relations with their political autonomy.

Fear of Excessive Dependence upon Foreigners Is More Important than Ideology in Governing Southeast Asian Relations with the West

Most of the regimes which govern Southeast Asian societies, from Hanoi to Rangoon, regard Europe and the United States as being both the sources of enslaving "colonial" relationships, past and present, and as the fount of an indispensable industrial civilization which they wish to adopt, at least in part. Their ambivalence has a peculiar historical pedigree, as well as a contemporary urgency. For the problem of how to borrow from another culture without sacrificing independence is an old one in Southeast Asia, much more so there than in China or India.

Indeed Southeast Asian history is filled with examples of states which borrowed extensively from other cultures but preserved their independence. The appropriateness or inappropriateness of these examples in the twentieth century is another matter: they all occurred, and flourished, before the age of nationalism. Thailand, Burma, Laos, and Cambodia borrowed religious creeds and political institutions from India and Ceylon; within the past century rulers have been crowned, in Rangoon, Bangkok, Luang Prabang, and Phnom Penh, according to Indian coronation practices. Malaysia is, and has been for centuries, a core of the Southeast Asian Muslim world, which stretches from Sumatra to the Philippines. Modern Malay literature takes its beginnings from the translation into Malay of an Egyptian Islamic reform novel in 1926. The father of the modern Malaysian nation, Tunku Abdul Rahman, leader for two decades of the United Malays National Organization, even chose to spend some of his political retirement in the early 1970s as the secretary-general of the Islamic Secretariat at Jeddah, Saudi Arabia. As for Vietnam, from the first century A.D. down to 1884 the Vietnamese borrowed their political institutions, philosophy, and writing system from China. This borrowing was so extensive that it is impossible to discuss politics or law or philosophy in the Vietnamese language today without using a host of Chinese-created words. The very term for "Westernization" in Vietnamese (*Tay-phuong-hoa*) is Chinese in origin, and in the twentieth century, the Vietnamese have borrowed much of their political thought, including some but not all of their communism from the Chinese revolution.

Hence Southeast Asians enjoy the potentially profound advantage of being able to think of themselves as astute, experienced cultural borrowers. This is no small asset in a world which is increasingly cruel to pretensions of self-sufficiency. Yet it still does not permit Southeast Asians to escape from the grip of a paradoxical psychology: they do not possess China's fabled (perhaps too fabled) "middle kingdom" aloofness, yet they *are* ultra-sensitive about their dependence on foreign cultures going too far. In December 1963, for example, the Hanoi Communist party publicly criticized a minority of its members for not "washing themselves clean of the mentality of servitude to foreign countries produced by the residue of influences of having been ruled for a thousand years by China. Here was an amazing reference to the early medieval Chinese suzerainty over northern Vietnam which lasted from 111 B.C. to 939 A.D., and which ended more than a century before the Norman conquest of England. Such a strangely extended memory of past states of dependency upon foreigners is most extreme in Vietnam, but it is not absent among other Southeast Asian elites. Its intensity, of course, is likely to astonish Americans.

Will ideology play a great part in determining whether mainland Southeast Asian states will want to borrow from the West between 1974 and 2000 A.D.? Available evidence suggests not. Practical perceptions of self-interest, firmly linked to perceptions of the social utility, or lack of it, of Western methods of technological and economic growth, will be much more decisive. "Leftist" regimes among the Indochina states, for example, have shown a variety of attitudes on this subject.

Prince Sihanouk of Cambodia, when he was in power, first solicited American aid and commercial investments. Then he terminated them. His reason for doing so was his fear that American aid was strengthening his enemies among the urban upper classes in Cambodia by creating a large group of import license holders with extensive business contacts with the United States, who were being integrated into the international commercial world on American terms, and who might question his power.

Behind this fear, it would seem, lurked the primordial and perhaps anachronistic political theories upon which the modernized Cambodian political system still based itself, especially the theory that the ruler's influence was most likely to survive in a relatively classless society. Such a belief would no doubt be laughed at by professional Communists, who nonetheless aspire to create such a society. In Cambodia, it was not really an unwarranted whimsy: the Cambodian social structure in the 1960s was much less undermined by the kind of social and economic polarization between absentee landlords and tenant farmers which characterized rural southern Vietnam nearby. (A survey of rural Cambodia in 1956 showed that of 727,000 landowners, less than 2,000 possessed "large" estates of more than 20 hectares; most land was distributed relatively evenly among thousands of peasants.) The Cambodian economic system, before the French conquest, had enshrined a "traditional socialism" in which the king and the Buddhist monasteries used the surplus lands they controlled as a social safety valve, devoting them to the subsistence of the poor. This non-Western approach to social management survived French colonial rule in Phnom Penh, but continued American aid, in Sihanouk's judgment, threatened it. For if this aid fostered the quick growth of an isolated urban business class, which then began to extend its commercial operations to the countryside, tensions might grow between the Americanized business class and the peasantry, and the Khmer monarchy might suddenly find itself disowned by both.

It is, unfortunately, impossible to predict how much of this perspective—the perspective that relations with the United States threaten the political and social stability of the country—will be inherited and applied by the Cambodian Communist government after 1975. Modern history might suggest that Cambodia, under almost any kind of government, would have a greater inclination to isolationism than any other Southeast Asian country. For it is certainly true that the extraordinary international fragility of the Cambodian state, both in the twentieth century and in the centuries immediately before it, has given Cambodian rulers good reason to be much more defensive and inward-looking, and much less willing to take foreign policy risks, than the rulers of Vietnam. The ideological predispositions of the two sets of rulers will continue to be less important in shaping their attitudes to the West than the degree of self-confidence in their own national histories—a degree of self-confidence which is large in Hanoi and tragically small in Phnom Penh.

The Vietnamese Communists, if we now consider them, came to power in 1954, in the northern half of their country, with a program which called for the securing of Vietnamese independence from the French and the removal of all social and economic inequities in the Vietnamese countryside. They not only linked French rule to the continued preservation of these inequities, they even suggested, at times, that all Vietnamese who associated themselves with Western culture and its products were invariably enemies of their own people.

Once the Communists came to power, however, they made their patented transition from agrarian populism to bureaucracy and to industrial entrepreneurship. Their nationalism remains constant, but it no longer makes targets and bogeys out of people who use Western products. To some extent, the Hanoi government is now, ironically, the most Westernized regime in Southeast Asia—at least in the sense that it worships industrialization and Western science, as well as the Western work ethic. In 1970, at the height of the war, the Hanoi State Science Committee's Physics Board published a 17,200-word physics dictionary in Vietnamese, Russian, and English. No effort was made to observe political niceties by publishing this physics dictionary in Chinese, and avoiding English. For that matter, the Central Science and Technology Library in Hanoi, which is used by factories and business enterprises in North Vietnam, does not reflect the static biases of political ideology, either. In the early 1970s, it possessed almost as many Japanese books (2,000 plus) as it did Chinese ones (3,000 or so). In the normal fashion of Communist states, this regime represses writers who circulate literature directly critical of it. But in the realm of science, there is no question at all that Hanoi permits relatively free inquiry and is highly desirous of improving its relations with the West, including the United States.

Hanoi particularly admires American agricultural science and American triumphs in such enterprises as plant genetics and animal husbandry. Westerners are probably unlikely fully to appreciate the reasons for such unabashed admiration. We take it for granted, and have taken for granted since the eighteenth century, that agriculture must make the production of fodder for livestock, and the planned cross-breeding of various kinds of meat and dairy animals, an integral part of its work. Mainland Southeast Asia, however, is just beginning to enter the "animal husbandry age." Until the very last years of French rule in Tonkin (northern Vietnam), Vietnamese peasants grazed their cattle haphazardly in deserted burial grounds, or on the tops of old earthen dikes, and failed (as had all their ancestors) to set aside special pasture resources for them or even to store fodder for the winter. One famous Vietnamese agricultural engineer estimated in 1944 that Tonkin required 500,000 oxen and water buffalos just to help plow its fields, that Tonkin actually possessed only 450,000 such cattle, and that Tonkin had pasturelands adequate to support and nourish only 15,000 cattle!

Many Southeast Asian countries are now compelled to devote awesome amounts of energy to emphasizing the care and use of livestock along scientific lines, an emphasis which seems as commonplace to Western farmers as the very need to harvest their crops. North Vietnam, whose pigs on an average weigh only 30 kilograms (as opposed to countries with more modern agriculture, which produces pigs that usually weigh more than three times as much), hopes to expand its program of importing foreign livestock. It seeks to borrow from other countries those industrial methods which are most appropriate to the production of animal fodders the raw materials of which are native to Southeast Asia. It faces the prospect of having to create, out of nothing, a whole structure of subsidiary animal husbandry industries (such as those making animal feed, vitamins, medicines, etc.). Recently (1971), one of Hanoi's leading scientific writers published an article, in a journal for Vietnamese readers, which praised the American farm revolution of the late 1800s and early 1900s as being a world prototype of its kind. To certify his own orthodoxy, however, he did carefully scan the works of Lenin in order to find, and quote, a favorable comment upon the American farmer's commendable preoccupation with animal breeding.

The point of this discussion, of course, is both to dramatize a most important if prosaic agricultural issue which concerns Southeast Asians, and to show that no Southeast Asian country, including North Vietnam, has a completely negative image of the American economy. Political ideologies, in the long run, make little difference where the raising of pigs and cows is concerned (except that farm collectivization can be damaging, as the Vietnamese may have discovered, to peasants' incentives for raising cattle). But it is time to make an uncomfortable return to the theme of Southeast Asian ambivalence. American knowledge and know-how are welcomed and studied everywhere, but American institutions and formulas which too obviously suit a mature industrial economy, or which too obtrusively reflect its social schisms, are feared and questioned.

In February 1971, Father Buu Duong, the rector of Minh Duc University in South Vietnam, held a strange press conference. It was one of the highlights of a crisis over "Eastern medicine" which rocked the Thieu government, but which very few Westerners were able to comprehend—as the weak coverage of this crisis in American newspapers demonstrated. The storm center of the crisis was the medical faculty of Minh Duc University. It had announced that it intended to teach its students both Western and East Asian medicine (i.e., acupuncture and the use of traditional local drugs, such as licorice). No sooner had this intention of the Minh Duc medical faculty become clear than a small oligarchy of doctors in South Vietnam, Vietnamese doctors who had been trained at the most expensive medical schools in Europe and America, immediately pressed the Education Ministry of the Saigon government to prevent Minh Duc University from teaching traditional Asian medicine. The Western-trained doctors argued, in effect, that they did not wish to see the prestigious modern Vietnamese medical profession become adulterated by the admission of swarms of primitive Vietnamese medicine men, whose credentials were surely contemptible by the standards of Paris or Harvard medicine.

In his press conference, Father Buu Duong, garbed in a traditional white Vietnamese tunic, declared emotionally that the Vietnamese people had chased after the French and the Americans long enough, and that it was now time to follow a purely Vietnamese road; Asian medicine was part of this "Vietnamese road." Vietnamese doctors, as he put it colorfully, should no longer concern themselves with the most fashionable methods for the care of "grape vines" (which grow in the West); they should concern themselves from now on with the proper methods for the cultivation of "banana trees" (which grow in Vietnam). If this sounds like the fire and brimstone of a backwoods nativist prophet, it should be remembered that Father Buu Duong himself studied at Harvard.

Why was this recent "Eastern medicine" crisis in Saigon so explosive? As of 1972, South Vietnam had 425 publicly employed doctors and 1,403 private doctors: that is, one publicly employed doctor for every 40,000 people and one private doctor for about every 10,000 people. The defenders of Minh Duc University publicly linked excessive worshipping of Western academic standards with South Vietnam's inability to provide medical care to the vast majority of its population.

An impoverished Southeast Asian society could not afford to cling to the American model of medical education, Minh Duc partisans claimed, and the more the Thieu government defended the right of an elitist group of Western-trained doctors to impose this model, the longer Vietnamese villages would have to wait for the arrival of elementary medical services. Of course the furor which this episode generated in Saigon is probably explained in part by the episode's remarkable marriage of nationalism to simple cost analysis. For a country in Vietnam's circumstances, Asian medicine is less expensive than Western medicine; it costs less to use local drugs and acupuncture than it does to use imported drugs and imported medical equipment from the West. Asian medicine, however, also attracts a strong patriotic love: the indigenous cultural tradition, which has been mocked and humiliated by contact with the West, is suddenly discovered to be the repository of some useful scientific lore after all.

The professional classes of modern mainland Southeast Asia are likely to be torn, in the future, by many similar conflicts between Western standards and indigenous realities. The education of future Southeast Asian leaders abroad, in the United States and elsewhere, is necessary. But it will have potentially disastrous after-effects if it deprives its recipients of roots in their own society, or does not encourage and equip them to solve the problems of village life, as opposed to those of upper class urban society.

To ask, therefore, whether the education of Southeast Asian students in the United States is a good or a bad thing, from the standpoint of world progress, really misses much of the problem. The problem is how to prevent such necessary and inevitable overseas education from becoming lopsided and culturally alienating to those who receive it, since mainland Southeast Asian societies do not all possess adequately powerful modern educational infrastructures of their own which overseas education can appropriately reinforce or supplement.

As long as Southeast Asian societies lack such infrastructures, overseas study is likely to undermine them almost as much as it helps them. It is certainly likely to exacerbate anti-Western nationalisms in the region, for the results of such overseas study may include the stimulation of a "brain drain" from Southeast Asia to the United States, the regular appearance of uprooted intellectuals who are not sufficiently attuned to their countries' most pressing social and economic issues, and the diversion of Southeast Asian funds from the building of (for example) small experimentation laboratories in the Southeast Asian countryside, to the financing of upper class sojourns at expensive American universities. European and Japanese overseas students can profit from studying in the United States much more unambiguously because of the strengths of their educational systems at home.

To the extent that American aid or educational programs for Southeast Asians impose goals, either of an economic or political kind, that their environments do not comfortably echo, such aid and such programs are doomed to failure, indeed to more than failure—to the fomenting of unnecessary crises. The developed nations may supply responsible assistance to goals which are set and tested in Southeast Asia; they cannot harmlessly devise and test such goals themselves.

The Southeast Asian environment, however, is hardly a classless uniformity with easily decipherable echoes. It has been said that the growing gap between rich and poor is the most momentous of world problems. But this gap exists within nations—including Southeast Asian nations—as well as among them. It is likely to be an especially critical internal fault line when it coincides, in part, with a gap between the cities and the countryside. Meaningful and accurate statistical testimony about this gap is not easily found for a half continent whose very population size is a mystery. However, it is significant that even the Socialist states of Southeast Asia are unable to control directly much of the supplies of the agricultural products in their countries—that government stores and a pervasive black market share the selling of the peasants' rice in Burma, and that Vietnam's government fruit and vegetable agency could supply no more than 65 percent of the actual market demand for fruit and vegetables in such cities as Hanoi and Haiphong in 1975, politically intolerable "free market" produce had to account for the remainder. The institutions of the nation-state which must resolve this gap in Southeast Asia are sometimes not only far from efficient, but are the prisoners of their urban settings.

The Gap Between Cities and Countryside Affects the Struggle for National Planning in Mainland Southeast Asia

Some analysts have argued that political stability flows from a situation in which styles of authority in politics, and styles of authority in society, fit or resemble each other. It would be challenging to apply this theory to contemporary Southeast Asia. One could certainly find a few realms where there was such a correspondence of styles, especially in Thailand, yet Southeast Asian societies are also greatly at odds with themselves. City-based elites are dismayed by the ways in which ancient rural practices and institutions contradict their visions. The populations of the countryside are ready to reciprocate this dismay, aiming it at the cities. To take an example from island Southeast Asia which would also suit the spirit of many people on the mainland, the Indonesian capital of Jakarta was described in 1957, by Sumatran dissidents, as a "leech sucking on the head of the Indonesian fish." There is no American parallel to this sort of thing—the skepticism which people in Montana or Utah might feel for the values of Manhattan would be mild in comparison.

As recently as 1930, indeed, half of rural Burma was affected by a peasant rebellion which attacked the entire apparatus of an urban-centered British colonial government with its supporting cast of English-speaking Burmese bureaucrats and lawyers. The leader of the rebellion suggested that Burma's ancient kingship be restored, and actually built himself a bamboo palace on a mountain in lower Burma. While North Vietnamese popular science journals discourse upon such subjects as chemical crop fertilizers and "wash and wear" clothes, provincial governments in North Vietnam are sponsoring campaigns (in 1974) to "invite" rural sorcerers, mediums, and fortune-tellers to go to their district capitals and "volunteer" to sign documents pledging that they will abandon their professions. Sometimes village-born politicians in Southeast Asia who gain national power become the most severe in repressing what they regard as embarrassing rural backwardnesses. Field Marshal Philbunsongkhram, whose pro-Japanese government was overthrown in Thailand in 1944, is a distinguished example: while he was in office he tried to forbid the production and consumption of betel nut by the Thai people, whom he also ordered to wear shoes, hats, coats, and ties.

Western colonial rule in Southeast Asia, which ended less than thirty years ago, depended upon essentially urban-based power structures. The nationalist movements or parties which succeeded these colonial governments in the 1940s and 1950s were often spearheaded by urbanized intellectuals. The bureaucratic and educational institutions which became the matrix of national life in these newly independent countries sometimes found themselves cut off from large rural-dwelling sections of their populations. (Northern Vietnam is, of course, an obvious exception to some of the foregoing—one reason for its resilience.) The colonial powers themselves had preferred to facilitate communication between the leading cities of their colonies (Saigon, Rangoon, Singapore, etc.); they were less interested in improving internal communications within their colonies. The Burmese made the rueful calculation, after they had won independence in 1948, that freight charges on a ton of equipment from Liverpool to Rangoon were normally cheaper than they were on the same ton of equipment from Rangoon to Mandalay.

All this became part of a vicious circle. Political discontent in the neglected countryside made it hazardous and uneconomic to locate new industries outside the leading cities. International aid programs which are aimed at Southeast Asia often have difficulty extending their real benefits beyond these cities, for such an accomplishment would require them to transcend the limitations of the existing political systems of many Southeast Asian nations. International diplomacy, for its part, has had to deal with Southeast Asian governments many of which cannot look forward confidently to solid, productive durability in the rural regions of their societies.

Some aspects of this problem have seriously worsened since the age of European colonialism ended. Before 1954, South Vietnam participated in a network of agricultural investigation and research which extended into the countryside and which helped to underwrite the vigor of the Indochina rice export economy. The Indochina Foods and Grains Bureau, which the French established in 1920, maintained a system of sixteen centers of crop improvement and plant selection. After 1954, the personnel and equipment of this bureau became scattered; the bureau itself was shut down in 1960; and by the early 1970s South Vietnam had reached the point where it was training administrative specialists in agriculture but very few, if any, rice research specialists. (The south began to depend upon imported Korean and Filipino research specialists.)

The decline of applied research by the Vietnamese themselves in southern ricefields could be attributed to a variety of causes. Lack of enough enthusiasm among Vietnamese elites for the resurrection of a decayed rice export economy which had been controlled by foreigners and which had been vulnerable to world price fluctuations, might be one. The disruptions of the war would be another. The static fortress psychology of a succession of military governments in Saigon between 1963 and 1975 would be a third. Whatever the reasons, this situation has become a symptom of the gulf between the operations of the government and the rational improvement of the rural economy. Another symptom of the same thing was the fact that the management board of the Central Farmers' Union in Saigon in the 1960s was filled, not with genuine representatives of provincial farmers' unions, but with Saigon politicians who controlled the union and used its resources for the profit of their own friends and factions. In this context, even corruption had an urbanized flavor.

In order to understand how this southern situation may change after 1975, we must look at the north—where even the Hanoi government has been unable, so far, to provide an ideological cement miraculous enough to unite tightly, the economic activities of the countryside with the planning of the national government. North Vietnam was vastly ahead of its pre-1975 southern rival in agricultural management and research: it has far more agricultural scientists, it has a system of state farms for crop experimentation, and it has a highly innovative Export Foodstuffs Research Station attached to its External Trade Ministry. Moreover, the Hanoi government is able to exercise its power in rural areas more effectively than any other government in Southeast Asia, thanks to its command of the activities of thousands of party cadres outside the towns. Without such cadres, the drastic transformation of the northern farm economy— by means of the forced transfer of most private family property to the ownership of more than 22,000 cooperatives, since the late 1950s—could not have taken place.

However, what we are talking about here is the struggle all over Southeast Asia to make national planning sufficiently effective to coordinate rising consumer expectations with tangible economic achievements, rather than outstripping them. Here Vietnam faces the difficulties of any Southeast Asian state. Hanoi's method of harmonizing relations between the peasantry and the government has been to permit the local village cooperatives considerable freedom in making plans for themselves, and many cooperatives have made use of this freedom by converting crop lands to "nonproductive" consumer purposes—such as the building of new houses. In just four years, between 1964 and 1967, the two coastal provinces of Thai Binh and Ninh Binh and the rural suburbs of the port city of Haiphong, on their own, converted some 12,000 hectares of agricultural lands to other purposes; between 1961 and 1967 the suburbs of Hanoi, and the provinces of Nam Ha and Hung Yen, took 24,000 hectares of land out of farming. Finally, in 1971, the Hanoi government was compelled to decree that any village which desired to convert more than 2 hectares of farm land from agriculture to building purposes, in a single year, would have to secure approval directly from the prime minister's office.

Rapid political and economic changes, no matter how necessary, are not usually sedatives. Vietnam, Thailand, Burma, and their neighbors are currently in the throes of building the basic infrastructures for what they presume will be modern societies. They would like to industrialize, on a national basis. If they turn to industrialization first, however, without seeking to improve notably the income and the purchasing power of the agricultural population, and the agricultural population becomes broadly aware both of its relative deprivation and of its secondary importance to elite planners, the future will be turbulent.

The First "Five Year Plan" of Thailand, in the early 1960s, was too much interested in industrialization, according to the analysis of the Bangkok Bank in 1967, despite the fact that more than 80 percent of the Thai people were engaged in work related to the neglected farm economy. In the late 1960s, under a second national economic development plan, the Thai government began to spend considerably more money upon agricultural growth, and to promote the vitality of local extractive industries like the making of castor oil, which is used in pharmaceutical and cosmetic products. (North Vietnam, interestingly enough, has also turned to local extractive industries in the "oil essence line"—resin, peanut-oil, castor oil, peppermint oil—as part of its effort to search for small industries, natural to an agricultural society, which do not require a high capital investment.) In the late 1970s and the 1980s, however, Bangkok faces the need to introduce a modern form of regional economic specialization into the future of Thailand. It may not have sufficient administrative and political power to answer this need dynamically. Specialized regional planning, like systematic animal breeding and the raising of fodder crops, is part of the twentieth century scientific apocalypse in Southeast Asia.

The Bangkok government is most on trial in northeastern Thailand—the landlocked Khorat plateau—where perhaps 38 percent of the farm households of Thailand live. The income of the people of the northeast is lower (per head) than that of the people of the rest of Thailand. The population of this region is, nonetheless, increasing relentlessly, making it difficult for the present agricultural system to continue to support it. In the 1960s, under the impetus of its two development plans, Bangkok built roads into the northeast. These roads linked the area more closely with the rest of Thailand and at least overcame some of the ghostly legacies of the pre-modern Thai kingdom (the political system of which exalted the capital city as the symbolic center of the universe, but did not cultivate any modern capacity to affect events in the principalities of the north and northeast).

However, roads may spread ideas more rapidly than they spread economic benefits. Thailand's new roads have helped to make the people of the northeast suddenly and acutely aware of their poverty. These people have acquired an unprecedented taste for such things as motorcycles and transistor radios. They cannot satisfy such tastes without transforming themselves into commercial farmers, yet they remain backward practitioners of the undifferentiated rice-planting economy of the more prosperous central Thailand. Some analysts believe that the economic salvation of northeastern Thailand can only come from the introduction of massive irrigation and a sensitive, politically-guided transition to the farming of a greater variety of crops, especially nonpaddy commercial field crops. (The soils of the northeast, to say nothing of the landscape, are better adapted to nonpaddy crops and to pasturing.) Is such salvation possible to arrange, and to arrange in a short time? With one eye on the clouded destiny of the northeast, Field Marshal Thanom Kittikachorn, the head of the Thai government during the 1963-1973 decade, declared in 1967 that "the government hopes that when the people are able to live happily, and their standard of living is better, they will not be easily deluded by the Communists."

Unfortunately, this statement concealed as much as it revealed about the factors which decide the future serenity of Thailand. The future of mainland Southeast Asia does not rest merely upon economic planning, and upon the political struggle to get the plans of city-based elites accepted in the villages. It also depends upon the question of ethnic reconciliation. There is probably no part of our planet in which this issue is more obstinately intractable than it is in Southeast Asia.

Ethnic Tensions Have a Central Importance in Keeping Mainland Southeast Asian Politics in an Unsettled State

In the traditional period, Southeast Asian societies were not polities with a belief in the sanctity of boundaries drawn upon a map. Early Vietnamese nationalists saw their first map of their country less than three-quarters of a century ago, when the Tonkin Free School displayed one in Hanoi in 1907. Nor were traditional Southeast Asian societies governed by a faith that all the people living within such map-drawn boundaries were equally the citizens of a single nation-state.

Instead, pre-modern Southeast Asian societies were cultural and religious clusters, ruled by relatively immobile kings or emperors or sultans from often grandiose capitals. Their rulers regarded the minority ethnic groups which attached themselves to these clusters, without fully sharing their values or their political life, merely as vassals or as tributary groups. But within the past century, the Western nation-state has arrived in Southeast Asia with a vengeance, bringing with it the twin gospels of ethnic self-determination and the sanctity of map-drawn boundaries. Unfortunately, these gospels are sometimes indigestible in Southeast Asia. They are, after all, quite capable of contradicting each other. Nowhere is this more true than in the geographical unit which the French casually drew boundaries around and called "Laos." The nation of "Laos" today harbors more than fifty different ethnic groups. Many of them have only the most tenuous links with the princely and aristocratic families which prevail politically in lowland Laos, and some of them live on both sides of the frontiers which "Laos" shares with such countries as North Vietnam.

Many of the minority groups of the Southeast Asian highlands practice a roving, and therefore frontier-defying, "slash-and-burn" agriculture. They are commonly (and most arbitrarily) regarded as economic and cultural primitives, when judged either by the standards of the dominant Southeast Asian peoples— the Burmese, the Thai, the Vietnamese—or by the standards of those "terrible simplifiers," the Western development experts. Yet such groups are far from being the apathetic relics of a dim, prenational past; they are organized into vigorous, richly memoried communities, and in some instances they are gaining ground rather than losing it in the ethnic competition for population growth which unfortunately characterizes contemporary Southeast Asian history. North Vietnam's 1974 census reveals, for instance, that the non-Vietnamese peoples of the north, who constituted 14.8 percent of the north's population in 1960, have risen to 15.6 percent of the north's population (of 23.7 million) in 1974. Westernized Southeast Asian leaders—whether Hanoi Communists or Rangoon army officers—are determined to make all the ethnic groups within their borders offer unconditional allegiance to the new nation-states which they govern.

Since the history of Southeast Asia until less than a century ago was a record of political and ethnic fragmentation unequalled elsewhere in Asia, crusades for national integration will probably create instabilities among Southeast Asian states for decades to come. If such instabilities are inevitable, the real question becomes one of finding ways to prevent ambitious but uninstructed great powers outside Southeast Asia from stumbling into this cauldron of ethnic perplexities and upsetting it. Furthermore, states within the region are probably all too internally vulnerable to risk aggravating these perplexities too sharply or too often themselves. The United States, and probably China, have been the chief culprits in the recent past. No doubt the abstention and the self-denial of the great powers depends to some extent upon the abilities of Southeast Asians themselves to keep ethnic tensions at the lowest possible temperatures.

Ignorance is certainly one factor in making the reconciliation of ethnic groups, on a modern nation-state basis, more difficult than it might be. In North Vietnam, for example, it was only in November 1973—nearly two decades after the French withdrawal—that a government conference held in Hanoi decided upon fixed names and categories for the north's minority populations. (The 1973 conference officially concluded that there were thirty-six different ethnic groups in the north, divided into seven different language clusters or families.) It is the relative lateness of the holding of this conference that is significant, although it is fair to say that Hanoi's approach to its minority hill peoples was at least much more knowledgeable than that of Saigon governments before 1975.

Until 1956, in fact, Hanoi even officially referred to the Yao people, who have lived in northwestern Vietnam for more than three centuries, as "barbarians" (Man). This followed traditional Vietnamese custom. Only in 1956, when the Zone Committee of the Viet Bac "autonomous" region in the north invited representatives of the Yao people living across the frontier in Kweichow, China, to come to Vietnam to attend its discussions, was Hanoi persuaded to begin referring to the Yao groups by their own name (Yao, or Dao in Vietnamese spelling.) Yet all Southeast Asian governments have the strongest incentive to familiarize themselves with their minority groups, for many of these groups are so strategically located that they can enhance or undermine these governments' influence upon their own frontiers. In a mountainous north Vietnamese province like Hoa Binh, for instance, west of Hanoi and on the borders of Laos, a majority of the Communist party cadres whom the Hanoi regime relies upon are non-Vietnamese. (In the "mass culture movement" in Hoa Binh in 1971, 46 percent of the cadres were recruited from the Muong people, only 14 percent were Vietnamese.) Their loyalty is crucial.

Thailand is well known for combining government ethnic ignorance with frontier vulnerabilities. Particularly high stakes are riding here upon the success or failure of the emerging multi-ethnic state. In the mid-1960s, Bangkok inaugurated what is called its "wandering dharma" program, an effort to send Buddhist monks on missions to the hundreds of thousands of minority hill people who live in northern and northeastern Thailand. The object of these missions was to immunize the hill people against "foreign" ideologies (such as Communist propaganda from Vietnam) by teaching them the modernized Buddhism of the Thai national church, and to recruit promising individual hill people for the Buddhist clergy. However, the reception of this "wandering dharma" program among the Karen, Meo, Yao, and other minority groups to which it has been sent has been damaged—once again—by ancient kinds of ignorance. For the program has been a relatively uniform one, neglecting to consider important differences in minority group cultures. Apparently assuming that all these minority groups are fundamentally similar—like the "barbarians" of northwestern Vietnam—Bangkok has tended to assign its minority clergymen to groups other than their own, thereby watering down their effectiveness. Behind all this, it is possible to detect a survival of the old fondness among Southeast Asian rulers for cultural hierarchy and for lord-vassal relations. Both these impulses placed the hill peoples in the shadows, and at the bottom of the ladder.

It has been stated that ethnic questions produce instabilities in Southeast Asia. This is true both in domestic politics and in relations among states. There is nothing obscure or mysterious about the inflammable forebodings which ethnic ambitions cause, and which become a political force in their own right. In fact, ethnic difficulties probably changed the course of Burma's history in 1962, more than almost any other factor.

Burma, like the other Southeast Asian states, is a patchwork quilt of peoples. The Shans, the Karens, the Kachins, the Chins, the Kayahs, all have a distinct major importance as well as long-descended cultural and religious traditions of their own that are often at variance with those of the plains-dwelling Burmans. Furthermore, British rule of Burma until 1948 did not provide an adequate chrysalis for a Burmese nation-state; the British ruled the Burmese directly, but permitted the upland peoples to keep their own hereditary rulers. In lower Burma, the agricultural Karens—regarded almost as "wild cattle" by the Burmese—had the instincts of an embittered separate community. With the arrival of British and American missionaries, the Karens—unlike the Burmese— readily became Christians, but they associated their new religion with a powerful new sense of ethnic identity. In 1881, the Karens formed their own "national association," and in 1947, on the eve of Burma's acquisition of independence, the Karen national union proposed the establishment of a separate Karen state.

To overcome such pressures, independent Burma evolved as a federation, whose "union" government was still nonetheless controlled by the Burmese. In 1950, Shan, Karen, Kachin, and Kayah rebels formed a "national liberation alliance" to frustrate the total "Burmanization" of Burma—that is, the imposition of the Burmese language and Buddhist religion upon minority peoples not desiring them. In March 1962, by a *coup d'etat*, the Burmese army overthrew the U Nu government, replacing it with the Ne Win government. The latter remains in power, having transformed itself on paper from a military government to a civilian one by a new constitution ratified at the end of 1973. The army's chief motive for this decisive action was its fear that the U Nu government would allow ethnic minorities a greater autonomy and might, indeed, even permit them to secede from Burma. Burma's 1973 constitution permits the existence of subordinate ethnic states, but makes them subject to one national elected People's Assembly.

The geographical home of Burma's most troublesome secessionist tendencies is probably the Shan states, which occupy 60,416 square miles of eastern Burma (one-quarter of the entire area of the country) and which borders on China, Laos, and Thailand. Before the British conquest, the king of Burma exercised a loose suzerainty over the Shan states, but his political rights in the region were vague and controversial enough to provoke wars with China (notably in the 1760s—the Burmese won). In 1961, Shan leaders demanded that Burma become a confederation of independent ethnic member states, each with its own constitution, legislature, judiciary and executive government. The Ne Win regime, however, can only accommodate a toleration of limited forms of ethnic autonomy in its vision of the future. In the creed which it enunciated in 1962 as "the Burmese way to socialism" it stipulated that "as the Union of Burma is a country where many indigenous racial groups reside, it is only when the solidarity of all the indigenous racial groups has been established that the socialist economy which can guarantee the welfare of every group can be achieved.

There is little evidence that this kind of modernizing evangelism has found enough admirers among the leaders of Burma's minority groups to ensure political tranquility in Burma in the 1970s and throughout the 1980s. This is ironic, for the minority groups who dream of political units based upon a single ethnic group are daydreaming themselves much of the time: "Shanland," for example, includes not just the Shans but Lolos, Kachins, Karens, Chinese, and Indians.

The "Burmese way to socialism," it is significant, makes ethnic solidarity a *precondition* of the achievement of an economy which can distribute benefits to everyone. In other words, the Southeast Asian situation is not remotely comparable to the situation in the industrialized West so far as the management of ethnic relations is concerned. The West's racial tensions occur within mature national economies which, in normal times, can survive such tensions and disturbances and even help to soften them. The encouragement of the rise of a prosperous black middle class in the United States is the outstanding example. Societies like Burma, on the other hand, do not have economic frameworks capable of enriching disadvantaged groups, ethnic or otherwise, yet they cannot build such frameworks if they are bedevilled by too much ethnic warfare. Moreover, they are afraid that private enterprise, rather than government-run "socialism" (which is a protean word in this region) will augment the disparities among different groups by giving them a class basis as well as an ethnic basis. This is perhaps the classic nightmare in mainland Southeast Asia.

The Overseas Chinese. The economic repercussions of Southeast Asia's ethnic riddles raise the question of the overseas Chinese communities. As of the early 1960s, there were an estimated 400,000 overseas Chinese in Burma, about one million in southern Vietnam, 2.6 million in Malaysia, and anywhere from 700,000 to more than 3 million in Thailand, depending upon such factors as whether or not children born within Thailand to ethnic Chinese were counted (as Chinese writers friendly to the Taiwan Kuomintang government were inclined to do). Southeast Asia is a statistician's nightmare: the total population of, for example, the entirety of South Vietnam is a mystery as of September 1975, to its rulers as well as to the outside world. It is clear, however, that the overseas Chinese communities, with their moneylenders and their businessmen, are the homes of a very special kind of Southeast Asian minority group. Their very existence has a conspicuous impact upon politics and development planning. The Thai and Malaysian governments, in particular, apparently shun the popularization of serious birth control measures among their people because they fear the overseas Chinese minorities in their countries will not abide by them, but will exploit the chance to change the population "balance" in their own favor. Ethnic Chinese represent nearly 12 percent of the population in Thailand, and about 36 percent of the population in Malaysia. The cultural separateness and the economic power of the overseas Chinese merchant world have been an issue in Thailand since the early part of this century, when one Thai king, with a mixture of bogus sociology and high-flying nationalism, publicly denounced the overseas Chinese as the "Jews of the East."

The separateness of the overseas Chinese, like the autonomy of the hill peoples, is regarded by contemporary Southeast Asian governments as a threat; it seems to inhibit the emergence of the broadly based national economies which Southeast Asian states require for the sake of prosperity and for internal peace. The nature of the threats is, of course, quite different. The hill peoples wish to preserve a political freedom which is anachronistic by the prevailing Southeast Asian standards, whereas the overseas Chinese wish to preserve an economic world which is more advanced and successful than those of their neighbors. Actually, pre-colonial Southeast Asian rulers helped to give the overseas Chinese their commercial superiority; they patronized them and used them as merchant go-betweens with other countries, thereby enabling themselves to keep their own subjects at home, safe and safely uncontaminated by dangerous foreign ideas. Unfortunately, this historical background of overseas Chinese economic power is not popularly appreciated in contemporary Southeast Asia. The result is that the overseas Chinese have become bogeymen, or the inspiration of neurotic speculation and festering pessimism which damage public morale. For example, Mahathir bin Mohamad, in his influential book, *The Malay Dilemma* (1970), charged the Malay people with being, comparatively speaking, a "fatalistic" people who were unwilling to struggle for "worldly goods," a people incapable of becoming businessmen as long as they were not "properly motivated."

The fact is that the Southeast Asian overseas Chinese possess crucial vulnerabilities of their own. They are, first of all, disunited. They are divided by guilds, by family businesses, by political parties, by lineages, and even by speech. The older overseas Chinese speak various regional languages of China; the younger overseas Chinese tend to speak Mandarin; and some most eminent overseas Chinese, like Tan Siew Sin, the Malacca-born finance minister of Malaysia in the early 1970s, can speak no Chinese at all. Lineage identities still overshadow communitywide identities; many of the Chinese students in Malaysian educational institutions are supported by lineage scholarships. Regional identities also frustrate any sense of Chinese togetherness in Malaysia: Hokkien Chinese dominate the rubber trade, Teochiu Chinese dominate the importing of Chinese goods, and Cantonese may find themselves excluded from Chinese enterprises sponsored by non-Cantonese. Recently, as part of a movement to induce a "mental revolution" in the conservative, culturally old-fashioned Malaysian Chinese world, various Chinese youth leaders have proposed the abolition of all lineages. So far there has been little positive response to this proposal. It goes without saying that the revolution in mainland China has passed by most of the Malaysian Chinese.

Hence a collision of mutual insecurities prolongs and colors the confrontation between the overseas Chinese and the majority of Southeast Asian peoples beside whom they live. This confrontation can be bloody, as it was in Malaysia in May 1969 when nearly 200 people, mostly Chinese, were killed in ethnic riots. It can, indeed, convert whole Southeast Asian educational systems into battlegrounds. To graduate from Malaysian schools, in order to go on to government jobs and higher education, Malaysian students must pass "Certificate of Education" examinations. In 1973 more than 14,000 of the 37,000 candidates at these examinations failed; most of the students who failed were Chinese; and most of the Chinese students who failed were undone by their lack of proficiency in the Malay language. At present the government of Malaysia, almost with the fervor of a mystic, is bent upon the creation of "a truly Malaysian middle class," as the indispensable foundation for any viable form of political democracy. But unless this "Malaysian middle class" can be brought into being without the simultaneous economic disestablishment of the overseas Chinese businessmen, stagnation and turmoil may well be the hallmarks of Malaysia's future.

The overseas Chinese are not in a position to affect interstate relations in Southeast Asia, however. They have been accused from time to time of serving as a fifth column, or potential fifth column, for China's ambitions in the region. Apart from the fact that most of them are far too conservative, politically and culturally, to do so, they are actually more like hostages than fifth columnists. The only exception to this generalization might be the smoldering confusions created by the decaying pockets of former Kuomintang soldiery in northern Burma, a country famous for its riots against its overseas Chinese traders (1931) and students (1967). The hill peoples, who live in mountainous frontier areas, are different: they make up for their lack of economic power by being in a crucial position to affect interstate relations.

Northern Thailand. The Thai government in Bangkok believes that it faces threats to its territorial integrity in both northern and northeastern Thailand. The economic and social circumstances of the northeast—its agricultural backwardness, its need for more crop diversification, the discrepancy between the circulation of new ideas over new roads and the stagnation of the economy— have already been discussed. Not surprisingly, the northeast is also the rugged mountain nursery of a rebellion of "insurgency" against the Bangkok government. This rebellion may have Communist leaders. Their identities and even their ethnic backgrounds are uncertain. High Thai officials, possibly with justice or possibly merely because of the sick man's appetite for unhealthy rumors about ethnic conspiracies which characterizes so much Southeast Asian politics, believe that as many as 80 percent of the leaders of the rebellion are Thai citizens of Chinese origin; they concede that the bulk of the rebels, perhaps 2,000 or so, are northeastern Thais.

What stimulates this rebellion is of course the northeast's obvious economic inferiority to the rest of Thailand, and the fact that it has received poor treatment—discriminatorily poor treatment—from the Thai central government for decades. This poor treatment can be explained in part, although only in part, by the lack of a long tradition of direct, interventionist rule by Bangkok in this area and by the general weakness of communications and transportation. In other words, northeastern Thailand—like eastern Burma, eastern Laos, and northwestern Vietnam—is peculiarly susceptible to movements of regional self-assertion. Thus far the Thai army has attempted to solve the problem by creating a host of "counterinsurgency" institutions similar in nomenclature at least to the ones which tried to thwart the Communist victory in Vietnam: "mobile development units," "accelerated rural development teams," "people's action teams," "volunteer defence corps," etc.

The threat to the territorial integrity of the Thai state in the north seems much more simple: it is a typical matter of ethnic dissent. Some 250,000 hill people have refused to be assimilated into this modern political system which seems so alien to them, ethnically and culturally. The hill people with the greatest taste for independence are the Meo (Hmong) people, who occupy the highest parts of the mountains in the north. In fact the Meo live scattered throughout southern China and Southeast Asia, displaying a sublime disdain for the recent Westernizing erection of "national" frontiers in Asia. There are, perhaps, four million Meo living in southern China; perhaps 250,000 Meo living in the mountains of North Vietnam; perhaps 250,000 more Meo living in Laos; and perhaps 50,000 of their cousins living in Thailand.

This astonishing fact of ethnic geography gives the politics of north Thailand a new dimension. Given the existence of this supernational, highly mobile Meo civilization, which unites China and Vietnam with Laos and Thailand at altitudes of 4,000 to 6,000 feet above sea level, it is not very difficult for conservative Thai army officers to imagine a Chinese or Vietnamese plot to use the Meo to subvert Thailand. The Meo are fragmented, linguistically and culturally, but many of them can read Chinese and do resent the incursions of land-hungry Thai peasants into hill country they have always regarded as their own. The Thai army, to repress Meo independence and dissidence, has moved large forces into northern Thailand. It has burned Meo villages and brutalized their populations. It has also mounted expensive operations against less accessible Meo enclaves. Such operations usually fail because these enclaves simply disappear into thin air—by temporarily migrating back to Laos.

What is the heart of the problem? To begin with, the alignment of Southeast

Asian states like North Vietnam and Thailand with superpowers outside Southeast Asia has exacerbated the Indochina hill country problem, magnified the destructiveness of the small-scale conflict it would normally breed, and converted a peculiarly prominent Southeast Asian difficulty—the difficulty of superimposing nation-state habits upon ethnic groups which regard them as an invasion of privacy, or which are not culturally prepared for them—into front-page news all over the world. Nothing would reduce the hill country problem to its natural proportions more quickly than the genuine neutralization of mainland Southeast Asia, or the practical removal of the region from superpower rivalries.

The point is that the political problem of the Meo highlanders looks strikingly similar to all Southeast Asian governments, whether it is viewed from Bangkok or from Hanoi. The keynote of the perspective, either in Bangkok or in Hanoi, is a sense of vulnerability. During the second Indochina war in Laos, for example, American special forces formed an alliance with groups of Meo highlanders hostile to the Hanoi-supported Pathet Lao movement. The Meo guerrilla army of Vang Pao, which received American supplies and training, was the chief instrument of this alliance. The Meo highlanders were one major ethnic force in the mountains of Laos whose loyalties the Pathet Lao had not been able sufficiently to monopolize or command. To recruit them, the Americans stepped into the role of a lowland Southeast Asian court; they patronized the Meo by supplying them with necessary lowland products like salt and cotton cloth, the way traditional Southeast Asian rulers had, but dropped these products to the Meo by airplane, a modern touch. Since the Meo people live in northern Vietnam as well as in Laos, and disregard Western-style frontiers, in Hanoi's eyes the American reinforcement and training of Meo armies in Laos encouraged subversion in North Vietnam itself. The repercussions of such American activities spread among Meo villages on both sides of the frontier.

Hence Thailand fears Chinese manipulation of the Thai Meo. Hanoi feared American manipulation of the Vietnamese Meo. With the departure of the Americans, and with the growing Chinese interest in cultivating good relations with the Thai government itself, as a means of constraining future Thai relations with the Americans and the Russians, the tensions just described may diminish. At their worst, before 1975, the result of the nearly symmetrical array of anxieties they caused was a deadlock, socially and psychologically debilitating to the Southeast Asians involved in it, while the two superpowers who were partly to blame for inflaming it looked on from outside.

Laos. In Laos, indeed, Hanoi struck back. After 1961, to match the American-sponsored Meo military groups, the Pathet Lao army began to acquire semi-independent Meo military brigades of its own, named after the Meo chief who had led Meo guerrillas against the French in a small Laos war in 1918-1922. By the mid-1960s, as part of this deadly competition for the loyalties of the Meo highlanders, each side was offering the Meo a hurriedly created writing script for their language, which had never previously been written. Popular magazines in Hanoi have even excitedly told Vietnamese readers that a Pathet Lao assistant province chief has devised a Meo writing script which is superior to the rival one devised by the Americans and their Lao confederates in Vientiane. Hanoi's efforts to offer the peoples of Laos some gifts of modernization, such as new writing scripts or medical dispensaries, are themselves a new extension of a very old tradition.

Nothing, indeed, will more surely shape the future of Laos than the belief possessed by almost every ruler of Vietnam, Communist or non-Communist, that Vietnamese governments have a permanent interest in Laos, because the political boundaries of the "nation" of Laos do not coincide with the actual geographic distribution of ethnic groups in Indochina. Just to control the peoples who live in northwestern North Vietnam—peoples like the Meo-Hanoi will almost certainly do everything in its power to maintain a sphere of influence in northeastern Laos. It will do this no matter how much hostility this earns it from the United States or from China, simply because ethnic groups like the Meo spill over the paper frontiers of the European colonial period and do not acknowledge their existence. The historical continuity here is striking. One hundred and thirty-five years ago certain provinces of northern and northeastern Laos-provinces like Phong Saly and Sam Neva—were part of the Vietnamese empire under the emperor Minh-mang, ruled from Hue. That these tracts of territory will be subject to influences from the strongest Vietnamese government today is inevitable, a counterpoint to Thailand's equally inevitable efforts to influence southern and southwestern Laos.

This means that the crisis in Laos has never been purely a drama of communism confronting anti-communism. Foreign powers, concerned with their own global chess games, have detected a greater "ideological" substance in this crisis than really exists. For the Indochina peoples themselves, three other elements have been important: the demands of regional ethnic politics, the cultural fragility in Southeast Asia of Western concepts like map-drawn nation-state boundaries, and, last but not least, a centuries-old struggle for hegemony in Indochina between the Vietnamese and the Thais. This struggle for hegemony may well continue after 1975, with neither side being capable of winning a permanent victory, particularly if the Pathet Lao movement in Laos develops factions which disagree about the extent of any Lao government's intimacy with Communist governments in Vietnam, and about the warmth or coolness of any Lao government's relations with Thailand. Such factionalism has not publicly betrayed itself to date, but probably only because massive American military intervention and the uncharacteristically simple-minded antagonism of past Thai governments inhibited its expression. The fact remains that factionalism of this kind has in the past been part of the bloodstream of Lao political history, even if Lao politicians have never shown the same intense antipathy to Vietnamese pressures that Cambodian politicians (probably including the current Communist leaders of Cambodia) have historically demonstrated.

Superpower abstention from Southeast Asian politics would not eliminate the bleak havoc which ethnic struggles bring to interstate relations in the region, but it would reduce the stakes for which such Southeast Asian ethnic political "games" are played. In 1972, an octogenarian leader of the Lahu people (90,000 strong) in the troublesome Shan states of eastern Burma, launched a revolt against the Rangoon government, apparently because the penetration of Burmese government administration to Lahu villages threatened his authority. Here was another typical Southeast Asian ethnic disturbance, compounded by nation-state rivalries: the son of the Lahu patriarch obtained arms from Thailand sources, and Thailand has maintained a traditional rivalry with Burma even longer than it has maintained one with Vietnam. But no outside power saw fit to make the Lahu insurrection a worldwide symbol of the expansion or containment of the "Socialist camp" or the "free world." The instability it caused was, therefore, relatively minimal.

Real stability in such situations depends upon keeping the superpowers out. It is possible that insurgencies like those of the Meo or the Lahu will become more common, rather than less common, in the next few decades. As lowland Southeast Asian societies modernize economically and technologically, and as their populations continue to grow, their encroachments upon the lands of the less advanced hill-dwelling minority groups within their frontiers may well become all the more devastating. The hill peoples are certain to react in their own defense with violence, whether they are mobilized by obsolete "holy men" or by chieftains using the most up-to-date American weapons. Vietnam will be no more immune to such disorders than its neighbors. Hanoi, indeed, plans to extend birth control programs to the minority peoples of its mountain regions, whose numbers are growing "unrationally," in the words of Duong Cong Hoat, the assistant director of the Hanoi state Ethnic Committee; indeed, they are growing at much faster rates than those of the Vietnamese people themselves. (The Thai population of northwestern Vietnam, for example, increased by 60 percent between 1960 and 1974.) Hanoi also plans to redistribute its lowland population among the midlands and the highlands, in "new economic zones," and to recruit highland minority workers to work on state farms and in factories. It would not be entirely surprising if such policies ultimately provoked ethnic unrest greater than that which the more economically advanced Communist states of eastern Europe, and the less significantly heterogeneous Chinese state, are accustomed to facing.

The least dangerous thing the outside world can do is to mourn the miseries of this increasingly cramped interaction of historic Southeast Asian communities; the most dangerous thing it can do is try to take sides. Fortunately, this game has its limits; it cannot be a major factor in reshaping the political complexion of the region. It is of real significance that because such ethnic tensions commonly occur in frontier regions, they make the interstate rivalries of mainland Southeast Asia unusually difficult to compose. They are difficult to manage, and, even worse, they create a morbid consciousness of great frontier vulnerabilities in the minds of lowland governments, quite unlike anything in the minds of European statesmen. No matter what ideological fashions prevail in this region, it seems safe to predict that rivalries and tensions among Southeast Asian states are likely to be nourished by this one factor.

Conflict and Accommodations Among Mainland Southeast Asian States, and American Interests in the Region

Historical Traditions and the Lack of Complementary Economies Make Southeast Asian Interstate Relations Relatively Frail

Most Southeast Asian societies are currently being compelled to invent completely new foreign policy guidelines for themselves. They cannot invoke tradition in foreign policy as Western nations can, or can they look back nostalgically to points of reference in their diplomatic past the way Westerners can look back to the American Monroe Doctrine or the European Congress of Vienna. This does not mean that Southeast Asia does not have a diplomatic past. The trouble with Southeast Asia's diplomatic heritage is not that it does not exist, but rather that its customs and reflexes are grossly inappropriate to national and international needs in the second half of the twentieth century.

As recently as a century ago, for example, the Vietnamese emperor in Hue regarded himself as a "Son of Heaven," ritually subordinate only to the emperor of China in Peking (whom he requested to intervene with an army to stop the French conquest of his country), and culturally and politically superior to a multifarious collection of "vassal" states (such as Cambodia and the Lao principalities). Like the emperor of Vietnam, the equally aloof king of Burma found it difficult to think of his country as a single state in an international system of national units. He regarded the spire of his palace at Mandalay as the center of the universe; even King Mindon (1852-1878), the most enlightened of Burma's nineteenth-century rulers, was apparently incredulous when Burma's correct size and location were demonstrated to him on a Western globe.

Each major Southeast Asian ruler—in Mandalay, Bangkok, and Hue—wrapped himself in his own unrealistic imperial mythology. What made these mythologies dangerous to the peace of the region was that they might be used to justify a succession of interstate wars as prolific and as exhausting as anything in the early modern history of Europe. When Vietnamese rulers invaded Cambodia—as they did in 1674, 1699, 1705, 1714, 1747, 1753, 1771, 1813, and 1834—they could publicly justify this activity by their need to protect their Cambodian "vassals" from the depredations of the Thai "barbarians" who just as frequently meddled in Cambodian politics. When Burmese kings invaded Siam—as they did in 1563, 1568, 1586, 1592, and the 1760s—they might present themselves as the architects of a Buddhist empire which divine providence had centered in Burma. Their egocentric pretensions even trickled drowsily down to their peasantry; many Burmese peasants have believed that the Buddha himself was a Burmese.

This Southeast Asian heritage in international relations is not, therefore, a very practical one. Modern Southeast Asian states must suppress most of it rather than use it as a quarry for inspirations, if they want to get along with each other. The Western colonial governments in Southeast Asia did alter this heritage, on the surface, in two ways. They deflated the credibility of Southeast Asia's relatively tiny pre-modern universal kingships, and they supplied Southeast Asian nations with precise boundaries. At the same time, however, relations among different Southeast Asian national groups, which had not been intense before the colonial period, did not really prosper much during the colonial period either. ("French Indochina" is an exception here, since it encouraged Cambodian and Lao leaders to study in Hanoi and Saigon.) Diplomatic intercourse and consultation among Southeast Asian politicians are not well-worn habits that can be taken for granted, as they can in Europe or in the Atlantic world. The Southeast Asian diplomatic universe is still in the experimental stage; it came into existence less than thirty years ago.

The resources of this quickly built laboratory of diplomacy must now be stretched to resolve, peacefully, such difficult problems as the ethnic and political contradictions of national frontiers which have already been described. Bernard Mandeville argued in *The Fable of the Bees* that nothing civilizes men as much as fear. In Southeast Asian interstate relations, however, fear has much more usually led to strife—or paralysis. Hence Bangkok's relations with Malaysia have stagnated unprofitably: the Thais have been unwilling to suppress the Malaysian Communist party, which uses southern Thailand as a sanctuary, because they fear that the Malaysian government will not suppress the Thai Muslim separatists who flourish in Thai provinces along the Malaysian border and who have ties with Islam in Malaysia. Burma has a 1,500 kilometer frontier with Thailand which is darkened by ethnic revolt and, more specifically, by the Free Shan State movement. U Nu, the former head of the Burmese government, took refuge in Thailand after 1962 and organized guerrilla activities against the Ne Win regime which took place until recently, from across this complex frontier.

Given the relative immaturity of modern Southeast Asian nation-state diplomacy, and given the magnitude of the Southeast Asian problem of making political and ethnic realities conform to existing frontier patterns, it is possible to draw two conclusions about the future likelihood of stability or conflict in the region. One conclusion is that stability will not be very likely unless the nations of Southeast Asia can find exciting goals of regional cooperation which will bring them greater progress than purely national efforts could, and to which they can sacrifice the insidious age-old temptations of confrontation and rivalry. The second conclusion is that stability will not be very likely if the superpowers continue to seek active political and military allies (or clients) in the region, on a basis of ideological selectiveness. The American defeat in the second Indochina War; the veiled but historic tensions between the Vietnamese and Cambodian Communist regimes; the publicly expressed desire of senior Vietnamese revolutionaries for better political and economic relations with the United States; and the competition between China and Russia for more useful diplomatic relations with existing non-Communist Southeast Asian governments, are all factors which do portend something of an "end of ideology" in Southeast Asia's relations with the outside world. This new condition will probably make superpower rivalries in the region more flexible than they were during the Indochina wars, but it alone will not be enough, unfortunately, to end such rivalries.

Let us consider these two conclusions in order. Within the Southeast Asian region, there is a pressing need to discover long-term objectives for everyone which are based on common aspirations, which can provide satisfaction to each state which participates in achieving them, and which can thereby transcend and soften interstate disagreements. Independence, and equitable economic growth, are desired by all the governments of mainland Southeast Asia. Presumably, therefore, these two goals, however elusive they may be in fact, are the ones to which regional cooperation should be dedicated. The only significant cooperative framework which exists in the region, as of 1974, is the Association of Southeast Asian Nations (ASEAN). It was formed in 1967, but includes only five countries: Thailand, Indonesia, the Philippines, Malaysia, and Singapore. The Burmese, the Vietnamese, the Cambodians, and the peoples of Laos remain outside its ambit.

At first sight, the economic potential of these five ASEAN countries is enormous: they produce 80 percent of the world's rubber, 90 percent of its abaca fiber, more than 60 percent of its copper and tin, more than half of its coconuts, one-fifth of its pineapples, and one-third of its palm oil. With the Vietnamese and the Burmese participating, these percentages could rise even higher. The food-producing capacities of Southeast Asia, with irrigation and scientific improvement, should be adequate to save the region from famine and even (if population growth could be checked) to nourish an export trade. (As recently as the 1930s, when its population was less, Southeast Asia produced 90 percent of the rice that was sold in global international trade.)

The trouble is that regional economic cooperation depends upon a great deal more than the existence of rich economic potentialities. Because of their climatic homogeneity, Southeast Asian countries produce the same kinds of agricultural and forest products; this means that they do not naturally complement each other economically, they rival each other. As of the early 1970s, only about 15 percent of the total trade of the five ASEAN countries is conducted among themselves. Their individual trading connections with the Western States which formerly ruled most of them and with Japan, are much more important. While economists (especially Western ones) would not find this situation irrational or surprising, it is nonetheless an impediment to the use of regional economic cooperation as a means of reducing regional political and military conflicts. The political reasons for cooperation are the most strongly legitimizing ones, not the economic reasons. The ASEAN nations are therefore faced with the political need to create an economic interdependence in their region, an interdependence which is scarcely a basic law of economic geography.

There is little question that if the Southeast Asian nations wish to industrialize themselves in any meaningful way—and most of them do—they must collaborate. Obviously no Southeast Asian nation currently has a home market capable of absorbing, by itself, enough automobiles to justify the establishment of an economically viable automobile plant, no Southeast Asian nation, by itself, has a home consumption of newsprint large enough to support the creation of a national newsprint mill so large that the newsprint it produced would allow it to be competitive in prices with the rest of the world. So long as the Southeast Asian nations do not collaborate in industrial planning and in state economic entrepreneurship, they must remain the importers of the more cheaply manufactured goods of Japan, China, India, and the West. And while economic autarky is obviously neither possible nor desirable anywhere, it is probably imperative for Southeast Asians to be able to produce at least some quantities of their own agricultural fertilizers, to say nothing of steel.

It is significant that the most realistic plan for Southeast Asian cooperation in limited forms of industrialization has come, not from the ASEAN capitals, but from the United Nations. A United Nations report of 1972 proposed that Thailand, Indonesia, Malaysia, the Philippines, and Singapore agree to distribute new industrial enterprises among themselves by politically contrived "package deals which might, for example, award Singapore the region's steel mill; Indonesia, the nitrogenous fertilizer plant; the Philippines, the region's newsprint mill; Thailand, factories to manufacture sheet glass and phosphate fertilizers; and Malaysia, the rights to manufacture compressors, typewriters, and engines. Each of these industrial enterprises would then promise to train citizens of the other four countries, if asked. The United Nations report also suggested that the five ASEAN countries resolve to create a free trade area among themselves, no later than 1990, and thereby eliminate all the tariffs and the quota restrictions which hamper trade among themselves. This United Nations report was modest and pragmatic; it did not look forward to some impalpable, fantasy-laden millennium; but it has not been acted upon. The difficulties of achieving economic cooperation in Europe are small in comparison with the difficulties of negotiating economic cooperation in Southeast Asia. Most basically, the United Nations report failed to build a traversible bridge between economic collaboration and Southeast Asian nationalisms.

This is the heart of the contemporary Southeast Asian dilemma. The governments of Southeast Asia (Thailand excepted) have just begun to savor the delights of political independence that some of their leaders risked their lives for as recently as the 1930s and 1940s. Now they find that their freedom to enjoy their political independence is circumscribed by the needs of economic expansion, which nationalism also consecrates. Political independence and economic progress are, indeed, pitted against each other in Southeast Asia much more sharply and cruelly than they are in the huge, relatively more self-sufficient neighboring society of China. Intimate regional cooperation with other countries is a necessity for significant industrialization in a country like Burma, or like Vietnam.

This fact places Communist Vietnam in a remarkable position among world Communist states. There is little question that the north and the south will soon be unified, much less painfully than is commonly recognized by Western analysts, who habitually exaggerate the importance of regional tensions in Vietnamese life. Throughout the war, the north was ruled by "southerners" from central provinces below the demilitarized zone, politicians like Le Duan and Pham Van Dong. The far more difficult tensions in Vietnam's present and future are sectarian ones, i.e., how to reconcile the Catholic communities in the south, or the Hoa Hao Buddhist communities, with the Communist revolution. Because of its smallness, Vietnam cannot combine self-sufficiency with economic progress as hopefully as can larger Communist states like the Soviet Union or China (which are themselves not self-sufficient, of course). Nor can Hanoi reasonably expect to be surrounded and reinforced in the future by other Communist-run societies of its own size across Southeast Asia—that is, it cannot expect to find itself in a situation similar to that of the Communist states of eastern Europe. Cambodia and Laos, for a number of reasons including sheer demographic weakness, will not make adequate partners for the Vietnamese in any Indochina economic commonwealth, which means that all three of these countries—but especially the ambitious Vietnamese, who currently luxuriate in masses of paper economic development programs—must look outward. Also, unlike North Korea, Vietnam is not isolated precariously among three much larger national powers. In other words, Hanoi has the opportunity—and ultimately, I believe, will experience the compulsion—to cooperate economically with a number of non-Communist neighboring states.

The Southeast Asian dilemma, therefore, is most acute in Hanoi, which must choose eventually between the economic promise of an ASEAN affiliation (which symbolizes an ultimate increase in power and influence for Southeast Asia as a whole, and to which Hanoi could contribute its impressive coal resources, etc.) and the prospect of a far less equitable private economic relationship with the two Communist superpowers. In 1971, Hanoi opened a trade mission in Singapore. Obviously it has not shut the door on the first alternative, nor can it afford to do so.

To resolve the Southeast Asian dilemma, the statesmen of the region will have to acquire a new willingness to dramatize the ways in which economic interdependence serves the purposes of nationalism, rather than subverting them. The economic sophistication of the city-state of Singapore is, in some ways, as much an obstacle to the gospel of interdependence as the somewhat cloistered behavior of the Hanoi politburo: an immediate cutting of tariffs among the five ASEAN nations would stimulate polarizations of industrial growth which favored Singapore rather than, for example, Indonesia. It is unrealistic to expect nationalism to decay in Southeast Asia in the next three decades. Many international relations specialists assert that technological revolutions have made the nation-state obsolete, and a threat to mankind's survival. But limited, nonaggressive nationalisms might be regarded more positively as a useful form of global decentralization, a legitimate means of ensuring human happiness for local majorities at least. The Thais, or the Vietnamese, have a much better idea of what is good for Thailand or Vietnam than do Americans or Russians or Chinese or Japanese. The persistence of dangerous conflicts and instabilities in Southeast Asia will be magnified, if not caused, by the intrusion of superpower ambitions. Can the superpowers learn to abstain?

The Prospects for "Neutralization" of Southeast Asia, and
American Policies and Interests in the Region

In 1971, the five ASEAN powers called for a neutral Southeast Asia, "free from any form or manner of interference by outside powers." There is no question that this search for the "neutralization" of the region will be a major theme, perhaps the major theme, of Southeast Asian foreign policies in the future. Special relationships between Southeast Asian states and outside powers are regarded by many—now including Malaysians and Thais, as well as Burmese—as being inimical to peace in the region. The nightmare of the second Indochina War has palpably increased the distaste in Southeast Asia for involvement in ideological "blocs," and has made the virtues of nonalignment more persuasive than ever before. My own view is that China has the most to gain from a nonaligned Southeast Asia, the United States has the next most to gain, and the Soviet Union has the least to gain, since Southeast Asian nonalignment would preclude fishing expeditions, ideological or military, in this region against Chinese interests.

However, the formation of an effective nonaligned bloc of Southeast Asian nations is, in practice, still remote. Economic circumstances do not favor it, and the trading relationships of many Southeast Asian countries seem to frustrate it. The difficulty of getting leaders in Hanoi, Bangkok, Kuala Lumpur, and Rangoon to agree upon what they mean by "neutralization" is enormous.

However, the idea, vague as it is, is far more popular now than it was in 1960. Its popularity means, for example, that multinational corporations may well be scrutinized (especially their lines of political responsibility) much more suspiciously in the future in this region, even though foreign capital investment is still welcomed by some Southeast Asian countries (notably Malaysia).

Even if there were unanimous agreement in Southeast Asia as to what "neutralization" meant, achieving it would not depend upon Southeast Asians alone. China, the Soviet Union, and the United States must all accept the idea, implicitly or explicitly. Burma, for example, which is not yet an ASEAN power, is most unlikely to join ASEAN unless Rangoon can be assured that *all* the leading international powers support its existence, and that Burma's neutrality in superpower rivalries will not therefore be compromised. This raises the question of what incentives the superpowers have for endorsing the notion of a "neutral" Southeast Asia.

Massive military intervention by outside powers in mainland Southeast Asia is, very clearly, a fool's errand. China has tried it four times in the past five centuries—an invasion of Vietnam in 1406, an invasion of Burma in 1766-1769, an invasion of Vietnam in 1789, and a military occupation of northern Vietnam in 1945. Not one of these invasions came close to achieving the political objectives the Chinese wanted to achieve; every single one of them undermined, in varying degrees, the political and fiscal stability of the Chinese governments which had sponsored them. American intervention in Vietnam in the 1950s and 1960s, designed to support one group of claimants to political power in Vietnamese society as against another group, may be regarded, from a Southeast Asian perspective, as a rather mediocre imitation of some of the earlier Chinese efforts to do the same thing. (The Chinese intervention in Vietnam in 1406 did, after all, seem to have worked for more than two decades; it only collapsed, finally and bloodily, in 1427.) The United States never had the long-term power to save southern Vietnam, or any other part of Southeast Asia, permanently from communism.

Given the sorry record of superpower intervention in Southeast Asian politics, it might be thought that proposals for the "neutralization" of this region would be received in Peking and Washington (and even in Tokyo, which also failed to "stabilize" the area by force of arms in the 1940s) with alacrity and relief. Unfortunately, what Southeast Asian states hope will be the *results* of such "neutralization"—domestic peace, a greater planned concentration of political power in the region, and a reduction of Southeast Asian economic subordination to outside powers—are much more likely going to have to be the *prerequisites* for attaining such a near-utopian international condition. For the current absence of domestic peace in Southeast Asia, the dispersion of political power in the region, and the economic dependency of the Southeast Asian states all make it far too easy for other governments to interfere in Southeast Asian life, and to attempt to seize competitive advantages there against world rivals.

Another very obvious obstacle to the triumph of "neutralization" is that such a scheme may benefit the great powers unevenly, serving the interests of some more than the interests of others. If, for example, a "neutral" Southeast Asia tried to make the Straits of Malacca domestic waters rather than an international highway, the capacity of the Soviet fleet operating in the Indian Ocean to move quickly against China might be seriously threatened. Through such an extension of the "neutralizing" dream, China would in fact cheaply gain an advantage against her arch-rival. Perhaps for reasons like this, the Soviet Union (judging from the pronouncements of Leonid Brezhnev, since 1969) would much prefer to entice the countries of Southeast Asia into joining an India-centered "system of collective security" in Asia. In present circumstances, and in the future circumstances most likely to prevail, no Southeast Asian state is likely to embrace such a proposal since it is far too obviously aimed against China, and will not truly insulate from power politics.

China, indeed, is the outside power most likely to welcome the "neutralization" of Southeast Asia. For one thing, persistence of fluid conditions similar to those of the recent past means that Southeast Asia will be seen by China more as a potential theater of operations against China than a promising theater of operations for Peking against her rivals. For another thing, as Lee Kuan Yew, the astute head of the Singapore government, observed in 1962, China can wield influence in Southeast Asia merely by her existence. Her strength and ambitions have psychological repercussions among the overseas Chinese, so that "there are almost no Chinese-educated political leaders in Malaya who have had the inclination to take a stand against communism, particularly of the Chinese variety." No other external power has the same capacity to maintain political leverage in this region even while practicing a kind of Taoist "nonaction" in the realm of formal foreign policy. Even Southeast Asian leaders who are well aware of the conservatism of the businessmen-dominated Chinese communities in their countries sometimes have blood-chilling public premonitions of a plot by Peking to conquer Southeast Asia from inside, by making the Southeast Asian Chinese the foundation of a conspiratorial pan-Chinese political movement. These premonitions are most likely to flourish in Malaysia, more than one-third of whose population is Chinese. In November 1968, the Malaysian prime minister publicly affirmed that he thought that China intended to take over the countries of Southeast Asia, directly or indirectly.

Nevertheless, these fears are more significant as reflections of Southeast Asia's acute ethnic tensions than as real omens of great power behavior. Indeed, the other side of the coin is that Southeast Asian governments may make anti-communism the pretext for new forms of sophistry in domestic ethnic politics. The anti-Communist activities act which the Thai government introduced in Bangkok in November 1952 was used to imprison overseas Chinese opponents of the Phibunsongkhram regime, many of whom had no connection at all with communism. It is safe to predict that as long as indigenous Southeast Asian

Communist parties remain feeble (as seems probable in the immediate future outside Indochina), and that as long as the Sino-Soviet split remains volcanic, China's first concern will be to preserve and develop harmonious diplomatic relations with existing Southeast Asian governments. For such relations must be made the cornerstone of a defensive Chinese policy in Southeast Asia, which has as its main purpose the prevention of encirclement by the Soviet Union through the acquisition of allies in Southeast Asia in the same way that they have been acquired in South Asia. In competing with Moscow for influence in Southeast Asia, China enjoys enormous advantages, but any subversive sideshow manipulation of "pan-Chinese" sentiments among the overseas Chinese would nullify these advantages and lead to ruin.

Furthermore, there is an ironic incompatibility between the fact that China is a Marxist-Leninist revolutionary power and the fact that the overseas Chinese are the dominant capitalists of Southeast Asia. As such, they are certain to be the leading economic victims of any Communist revolution in Southeast Asia.[a] In any kind of theoretical exhortation which Peking might make to Southeast Asia, pan-Chinese ideals and social revolution would not be harmonious elements, and the promotion of either one of them might prompt nervous Southeast Asian governments to fly into the arms of a superpower other than China. Nor can it be said that Peking is strongly interested in upholding the banner of Chinese culture in Southeast Asia, in the same way that France, for example, watches over the cultural prosperity of French-speaking areas around the globe. A succession of government-sponsored mass campaigns in mainland China have sought to overthrow, or at least modify, what many Southeast Asian Chinese believe to be the central essence of the traditional Chinese cultural heritage.

Chinese interests and inclinations, therefore, might be well served by the most realistic approximation of "neutralization" that Southeast Asian states can achieve; this will be especially true as long as the Sino-Soviet rivalry persists. Despite a history of sporadic invasions of Vietnam and Burma that is less pacific than some China specialists commonly suppose, China's reputation as the bogeyman of Southeast Asian politics, while not totally devoid of substance, has usually been grossly exaggerated. When China has become entangled in Southeast Asian affairs within the past ten years, it has been a futile kind of interference without the commitment of great resources: as in Burma in 1967, when Rangoon Chinese school children wore Mao badges to class, their refusal to remove them provoked anti-Chinese riots in which one hundred or more Chinese residents of Burma were killed, and the Peking government, at the height of the Cultural Revolution, responded by calling for the destruction of the Ne Win regime.

---

[a]Northern Vietnam after 1954 does not offer us a typical preview of this; the Chinese communities of Hanoi and Haiphong before 1954 were smaller, less upper and middle class, and less powerful financially, than their counterparts in Saigon, Bangkok, or Malaysia. The fate of the much larger overseas Chinese community in southern Vietnam will be far more typical and interesting; unfortunately, little information about this is available to me at this time.

Can the United States afford to accept a politically nonaligned mainland Southeast Asia? In the aftermath of the final collapse, in 1975, of American policies in Vietnam—policies which sought to enforce the continued partition of one of the oldest societies in the world, and which directly challenged the most dynamic and efficient heirs of a deeply rooted Vietnamese nationalist movement—the United States government may really have little choice in the matter. In 1954, the United States took the initiative in constructing a military alliance, the Southeast Asia Treaty Organization which was supposed to serve the same purposes in Southeast Asia that NATO had in Europe. Between 1954 and 1975, only two Southeast Asian states ever showed the slightest enthusiasm for SEATO—Thailand and the Phillippines. However, in the summer of 1975 the leaders of these two countries, Kukrit Pramoj and Ferdinand Marcos, formally proposed the abolition of SEATO, and it seems plain that the era when Southeast Asian states casually entered collective security alliances with larger powers outside Southeast Asia has come to an abrupt end.

This, I believe, will hold true everywhere. A Southeast Asian version of the Warsaw Pact is just as unlikely and inappropriate as a Southeast Asian version of NATO. A solid association of any kind between Russia and Vietnam, capable of influencing political trends elsewhere in Southeast Asia, is highly improbable. Economically, it is true there is a certain logic to the current friendship between Moscow and Hanoi. Russia, much more than China, is in a position to serve as a market for the agricultural exports which Hanoi hopes will increase its sources of foreign currency and thus enable it to finance its "Socialist industrialization"— specialists at the Institute of Economic Studies in Hanoi have even begun wishfully to plan for the export of 200,000 tons of DRV bananas a year to the previously unexploited Siberian market. Russia, much more than China, is also in a position to supply Vietnam with the technological equipment of industrialized societies it so highly covets—Hanoi imported its first Russian computer in 1968. Furthermore, Russia provides the opportunity for participation in international systems of advanced scientific research, such as plant genetics, at a number of far-flung Russian-sponsored research centers, including one which has been, or will be, built in Indochina. Yet the Western industrialized countries, to say nothing of Japan, could easily offer Hanoi equivalent or superior economic and technological relationships. They are in a position to diminish the importance of the economic foundations of Russian-Vietnamese relations at almost any moment they choose. I strongly recommend that they attempt to do so.

As for the political and military transactions between Russia and Vietnam, these will of course be haunted by the tensions between Peking and Moscow. Such tensions are unlikely to vanish after the death of Mao Tse-tung. Trotzkyism, an elaboration of Marxism-Leninism which has never been associated with the destiny and the pride of one specific nation-state, has nonetheless persisted as a political force for decades; Maoism, an energetic intensification of Marxism-Leninism which *is* the symbol of a powerful nation, is likely to prove a much more formidable and long-lasting enemy of the Russian state ideology, no matter what immediate policies are devised and followed in China by Mao's successors. After all, it is a commonplace that quarrels among co-religionists are more difficult to compose than quarrels among adversaries who are less socially or ideologically intimate with each other, and thus less totally engaged in their quarrel. If it is reasonable to assume the relative permanence of difficult relations between China and Russia, for this and other reasons, it is equally reasonable to assume that Hanoi cannot commit itself irrevocably to one side or to the other. It must also be clear by this time that the Vietnamese have a certain taste for their own independence. The granting, by Hanoi, of Vietnamese naval bases to the Soviet Union, would jeopardize the reputation of the DRV government in the eyes of its own citizens, just as inevitably as the Saigon governments of 1954-1975 were jeopardized by their all-too-conspicuous association with the American military bases they permitted on southern Vietnamese soil.

In sum, SEATO, the one system of military alliances which affected Southeast Asia's political evolution in the past, has disintegrated. No outside power is truly capable of creating a replacement for SEATO which it can dominate. Hence the immediate future of mainland Southeast Asia is likely to be governed by efforts by the United States and Russia to deal with individual Southeast Asian countries on an expedient bilateral basis, on the grounds that Southeast Asia is too "heterogeneous" to be approached as a single geographical or political entity. Similarly, it is likely to be governed by faltering counter-efforts by the Southeast Asian countries themselves to forge united political and economic policies in self-defense against the superpowers, in the hope of inducing them to withdraw their mutual competition from the region. American policymakers would be very wise to respect these Southeast Asian foreign policy ambitions, both because resistance to indigenous political trends in this region is costly and because the elimination of just one zone of competition on this planet betwen the two foremost nuclear superpowers would be sensible insurance, however modest, against unspeakable catastrophes.

Nevertheless, the great powers outside Southeast Asia will not be disinclined to respect the foreign policies of Southeast Asian states which are themselves contradicted and sometimes almost paralyzed by internal political problems and disharmonies. Tun Abdul Razak of Malaysia, for instance, is a leading exponent of Southeast Asia's "neutralization," which he hopes will be consolidated by great power guarantees. Razak has made improved Malaysian relations with Thailand a first step toward the achievement of an areawide consensus on neutralization; yet when he created his ten-party National Front Coalition government in the early 1970s, he was compelled to include the Party Islam, which has openly advocated the cause of Thai Muslim separatism, and thus made itself obnoxious to the Thai government. Establishing any kind of stable congruence between the needs of multi-ethnic political systems and the needs of regional cooperation among nations has never been easy in Southeast Asia.

For another thing, China will almost certainly welcome the efforts of Southeast Asian states to negotiate their own collective abstention from the battles of the superpowers. Yet China will probably remain skeptical enough of the long-term success of these efforts not to abandon entirely its own dual approach to the region, one approach being normal relations with the established governments and the other approach being continued ideological support for the Communist parties of countries like Malaysia and Burma. Once again, however, what must be emphasized is the Chinese sense of insecurity with regard to Southeast Asia, its fear that it has more to lose than to gain from the perpetuation of far-ranging, spendthrift rivalries with the United States and the Soviet Union on this particular half-continent. When Razak visited China in June 1974, the principal Chinese objective seems to have been the curtailment of Russian and American "hegemonial" influences in Southeast Asia. In return for Malaysian agreement with this, and Malaysian diplomatic recognition, Peking was quite prepared to recognize that all ethnic Chinese in Malaysia who had accepted Malaysian citizenship had automatically lost any right to be Chinese citizens.

This imperfect congruence of Southeast Asia's own foreign and domestic political policies, and China's nervous reluctance to ignore even the feeblest Communist parties of the region, work to discourage American (and Russian) acceptance of unconditional "nonalignment" for Southeast Asia. Yet the American government's acquiescence in, and support for, such nonalignment might be richly rewarded.

Nobody dreams of turning Southeast Asia into a kind of arcadian vacuum in international politics. Under no circumstances would nonalignment mean the economic exclusion of the United States, or any other power, from Southeast Asia. The Malaysian-ASEAN neutralization proposal of 1971 specifically permits and encourages great power economic and cultural involvement in the region. All Southeast Asian countries must look outward economically, in order to sell their raw materials; all of them, in varying degrees, intend to build their future societies upon export-led economic growth.

It is true that Burma and Communist Vietnam have sometimes, in the past, been described by Western analysts as examples of Southeast Asian states which are "introverted" and irrationally disinterested in international trade, but much of this description is exaggerated. The Burmese government now even allows private foreign companies (including Esso and European consortiums) to exploit its oil resources, as well as its mineral resources, provided that they accept the position of being contractors for exploration and production to a state-owned oil corporation. This formula differs very little from the ones in use in Malaysia and Indonesia. What Westerners must understand is that the infrastructure and resources of Burma's export economy—mines, roads, bridges, railways—were all devastated by the violence of Japanese-British warfare there in the 1940s and this country was not the postwar recipient of economically rehabilitating aid like that of the Marshall Plan in Europe. Chronic difficulties with distribution systems—Burma's railway network was still shorter in 1971 than it had been before World War II—have prevented Burma from exporting much rice and are preventing rampant inflation in the price of rice at home. These are some of the clues to Burma's supposed introversion.

Ideologies, or reflexes of introversion, are no more the problem in Vietnam than they are in Burma; once again, the effects of war, and structural problems, are acute. Northern Vietnam alone requires a minimum annual rice crop of 6.5 million tons to feed its growing population, which increased from 15.9 million people in 1960 to 23.7 millions in 1974. It has never, as of 1975, achieved such a crop, and thanks to its need for rice, it cannot afford to reserve too much prime agricultural land for the specialized production of export crops like tea, coffee, peanuts, vegetables, sugar cane, or bananas. In addition, the modern industrial plant upon which an export economy, even an agricultural export economy, depends, is only weakly developed in Vietnam. To expand its exports, one of its most important national goals, Hanoi must divert scarce resources, as it plans to do, to the construction of tea factories and fruit and vegetable canneries. Yet Hanoi has publicly affirmed its intention to increase sharply its exports, while holding down imports. By severe limitation of the domestic consumption of exportable goods, the DRV hopes to finance its industrialization through agricultural exports, and in August 1974 Khuc Dinh Van, of the Hanoi Institute of Economic Studies, even openly proposed that Japan be regarded as a future "essential market" for Vietnamese agricultural products.

No Southeast Asian state, therefore, views political nonalignment or neutralization as a means of facilitating an archaic withdrawal from the international economy. Virtually all Southeast Asian nations desire a greater participation in this economy. One advantage of the Southeast Asian combination of political neutrality with increased participation in the world economy would be that the political controversies associated with such participation might be softened within each Southeast Asian country. For example, the National Student Center of Thailand might not fear "Japanese economic domination of Thailand" as extravagantly as it did in 1972 (part of its fear was justified) if it could be assured that Thailand's political sovereignty was not being buffeted and undermined by great power political intrigues to which Japan was attached, however distantly. Japan would almost certainly enjoy more secure relations with a Southeast Asia which had been allowed to purge itself of extraneous global political tensions.

From the Southeast Asian perspective, neutralization—that is, a concerted effort by Southeast Asian countries to abrogate and ban all asymmetrical military agreements with big powers outside the region, whether or not this effort is accompanied by a formal "neutralization" treaty—would have the advantage of blocking an overly aggressive pursuit of great power rivalries in Southeast Asia, especially if American-Russian détente founders. Why should the United States not accept this perspective?

Critics of the formula might argue, firstly, that real neutralization in the past has worked only in extraordinary circumstances, such as those of Switzerland or Antarctica, and secondly, that the other great powers, China, Russia, and Japan, are competitively engaged in Southeast Asia, and that the withdrawal of the United States from the region would both jeopardize its position in world affairs and make the more anti-Communist Southeast Asian states, such as Indonesia, fearful of their future. Such critics may be found not only in high places in the current American government, but also in Southeast Asia itself: Lee Kuan Yew of Singapore would be the best example. But the criticisms, in my opinion, are not convincing. The Indonesian government's main reasons for fearing the future are domestic ones, no matter how many efforts may be made to disguise this fact. (It is worth recalling the elementary but significant historical fact that the Indonesian Communist party is older than the Chinese one.) In Southeast Asian societies where property ownership is widely diffused, as in Thailand, and where there are no domineering, sharply privileged social classes, as in Burma, indigenous Communist movements are feeble and will remain so. Burma's White Flag Communists have been unable even to develop effective relations with disadvantaged minority ethnic groups, and the Thai Communist party seems to have no more than a few hundred members.

Even if one accepted all the premises of the balance of power school of international relations, the fact must be faced that Southeast Asia is far less hospitable to even the most sophisticated great power "balance of power" maneuvers than other regions of the world, such as Europe or the Middle East, or—in naval terms—the Pacific Ocean. Chinese assets in the region, such as its proximity and its successes in "nation building," do not outweigh its liabilities, and in any event China's accomplishments cannot be duplicated on a long-term basis by the other powers. Russian assets in the region are almost negligible, provided that the Vietnamese honor their formidable traditions of national independence by denying the Soviet Union military bases, and are encouraged to do so by being politically and economically accepted by the Western world. Japanese assets in the region are also relatively small, and again are matched by liabilities. The fact remains that the United States has been the only foreign power to maintain a direct recent military presence in Southeast Asia. Even many non-Communist Southeast Asians regard this as imperialism, not as an attempt to supply some factitious form of military balance.

No doubt Thai-Vietnamese relations will be one of the first tests of the stability of mainland Southeast Asian politics after 1975. From the Vietnamese point of view, Thailand continued its centuries-old rivalry with Vietnam in the 1960s by supplying the American air force with bases. From the Thai point of view, Vietnam enjoys the services of a fifth column of 40,000-70,000 Vietnamese migrants who live in Thailand's politically troubled northeast, and Hanoi has continued its centuries-old rivalry with Thailand by scheming to extend its permanent political control over all of Indochina, an ambition that has never previously been realized by either side during the dark, stormy history of

Vietnamese-Thai relations. If the Kukrit government in Thailand does not soon succeed in palliating these relations, with some satisfaction to Thailand, the Thai military forces could return to power by a *coup*, as they did in 1947 and 1957. Yet Thailand and Vietnam are far too evenly balanced, militarily and economically, to gain long-lasting total triumphs at the other's expense. Nor is there any reason why the United States, China, Russia, and Japan could not enjoy equable relationships with both these potentially feuding states at the same time. There is very little to gain by not doing so, and in certain circumstances much to lose.

If China has the most to gain from the political neutralization of Southeast Asia, it is still always possible that China may not at first, quickly and publicly cooperate with other powers in agreeing to certain ground rules. China's strong desire to differentiate itself publicly from the United States and the Soviet Union—as expressed in its strategy of "deeply digging holes, broadly amassing provisions, and not being called a hegemon"—is almost reminiscent, on a grander scale, of the American desire before 1939 to separate American policy and postures from the presumed intrigues of the old, corrupt European states and their League of Nations. In addition, China, and many other Asian countries, for that matter, are sensitive to their own poverty status in the world of Western-Asian diplomatic relations, to the fact that diplomatic activities and initiatives that involve both them and the Western states are usually broached or devised by the West, and have been since Western powers first forced the Chinese to create their own semi-modern foreign relations ministry in 1861. However, neither of these things—the desire for differentiation or the sense of a history of being subordinated to Western international diplomatic energies—is a fatal obstacle to cooperation. What these things do mean is that even in circumstances where the United States and China have common interests, the wrong diplomatic style of crystallizing and maximizing these interests—such as an American pronouncement of the desired policy in public followed by frenzied efforts to get the Chinese to agree to it—would be quite self-defeating.

In conclusion, therefore, I recommend that the American government recognize that mainland Southeast Asia is not an Asian replica of Europe; that it is neither necessary nor desirable for superpowers from outside Southeast Asia to try to pursue, or underwrite, their chimerical dream of a perpetual "balance" between two or three ideological systems there; that since the states of mainland Southeast Asia are increasingly likely to resist having the status of pawn or of partner thrust upon them from outside, the region may prove the most promising part of the world for the USSR, the United States, and China to disengage from political confrontation. Southeast Asia could even be made a practical laboratory for the premeditated reduction of great power rivalries. For the stakes in Southeast Asia have never been as disconcertingly high as they are in Europe, the Middle East, or on the Inner Asian frontiers between Russia and China. The American government should indicate its general friendliness to the limited political "neutralization" the ASEAN countries seek and should help to formulate guarantees of this neutralization that all great powers could accept. In addition, it should on the whole thus work to disprove, if it can, the Chinese charge that the United States is one of two compulsive "hegemons" engaged in a global competition with the Soviet Union without a clear sense of priorities.

Leftist, even Communist, regimes in Southeast Asia do not imperil American political or economic interests the way they might in Western Europe, and that many Southeast Asian politicians who have loudly advertised their fears of communism before American audiences in the past have often had more than one motive in doing so, including the very natural desire to mask their own political inadequacies. Diplomatic relations between the United States, and Vietnam and Cambodia should be established as quickly as possible, in the interest of allowing these states the opportunity to develop a greater flexibility in their foreign and international trade policies, and the opportunity to tap American technology, if they so wish, in furthering their domestic reconstruction. Strict neutrality should be followed by the United States in any controversy or conflict between Vietnam and Thailand, as long as these two historically antagonistic countries are the only two states directly involved. In addition, the recent American proposals for trade concessions to Third World countries, and the right of these nations to participate in the consumer-producer forums, should be extended to Vietnam and Cambodia whenever they are extended to other Southeast Asian governments.

Obviously, the complexity and the magnitude of the task of planning for peace have increased almost unimaginably since Leibniz and the Abbé de Saint Pierre, in the early eighteenth century, dreamed of persuading the European courts to renounce war and to keep no more than 12,000 dragons per nation under arms as proof of their good faith. The idealism of contemporary academic "peace strategists" has probably increased almost to the same degree. Nevertheless, I suggest that with provident and subtle statesmanship (and luck) the United States can still overcome its own recent past in Southeast Asia, and make the next few decades of Southeast Asian history the possible harbingers of the more general history of a more conciliatory, peaceful planet.

V

The Evolving Role of Asia in American Policy

Robert J. Pranger

This chapter is an analysis of Asia's evolving role in American foreign policy. Emphasis will center on Asia as a highly prominent actor in United States global activity, and on the changing nature of this role in the past and future. In other words, Asia will be treated as a factor or force within a broader calculus embracing not only a generous range of policy on matters external to everyday American life, but including also domestic considerations very much part of this life. Rather than looking principally at United States policy toward or in a given country or region, the focus is on a region's changing position within American calculations about foreign affairs.

Hopefully, these distinctions will not seem too pedantic. In Asia's case the idea that it might have a role to play in American policy, much as an actor would play a part, is not farfetched. Harold Isaacs has observed that despite "vagueness" about Asia's lands and peoples, even among educated Americans, there is a real sense in which "America's emergence as a major world power has been peculiarly linked to Asia and its rise as a primary setting for decisive world events."[1] A contrast between cultural distance and strategic proximity, so typical of United States policy toward Asia for most of this century, does make of Asia an actor of some prominence for Americans, without necessarily establishing any widespread sense of intimacy. Another way of stating this is that, for most Americans, Asians have been "in" but not "of" U.S. foreign policy, closely intertwined with matters of life and death urgency yet curiously

Views expressed here are the author's and do not necessarily represent those of American Enterprise Institute.

far away. Unlike Europe and the Middle East, there seem to be no deep-rooted American attachments to Asia, no powerful ethnic constituencies that might bridge the gap between foreign involvement and domestic sentiment. Whatever economic ties exist, and there are significant ones with Asia, are probably more pecuniary than sentimental; in any case, the capabilities of trade to knit peoples together are slow working and have more to do with the convergence of mutually beneficial interests than with intrinsically compatible ways of life. Indeed, with the exception of defeated Japan, no long-term American consensus has ever legitimated the United States defense treaty ties in the Far East in the same way that such legitimacy has been bestowed on America's formal military commitments in Europe or even its more informal defense ties with the Middle East. Yet, paradoxically enough, during the Second World War the United States spent more time in Asia than Europe and has since engaged in its only major military actions in the Far East.

As a result of this curious Asian role in American policy, the Orient has not occupied a consistent place within U.S. worldwide calculations. Tied to America's rise as a world power but not deeply connected with domestic politics until Vietnam, Asia has tended to exercise an exotic and sporadic influence on Washington's world efforts. In fact, one is tempted to picture the condition of Asia in American policy in economic and psychological terms: it has been boom-or-bust from one perspective and schizophrenic or at least ambivalent from another. Before World War II, leaders of American foreign policy could relegate Asia to something less than a strategic necessity, even when faced with the spectacle of flagrant militarist aggression in the region. On the other hand, Washington also committed itself to far-reaching and enthusiastic political-military commitments.

Perhaps as nowhere else in the world, American foreign policy in Asia exhibited—and still exhibits—an acute ambivalence toward the use of force. On the one hand, we have made heroes of the violent: on the other, we have championed the causes of peace and world community through law. In turn, Asia has played—and continues to play—a very prominent part in perpetuating this split in American thinking. If policymakers hope in the future to fashion a foreign policy that can rest easy with a fairly consistent role for force in world affairs, then perhaps an examination of Asia's evolving role will benefit not only American policy in Asia but its activities worldwide. Asia has proved and may continue to prove to be a *deus ex machina* in American foreign policy, a premise for idealism and a pretext for intervention. It has pushed into the open latent American impulses toward the world that come from quite different cultural roots. And it has continued a proving ground for United States power, power that drew very little of its breath from Asia's peoples and resources: in no other part of the globe have Americans spent so much time at war in this century as in Asia, yet no other region has so small a role to play in America's domestic constituencies.

All of these disparities beg the question, "Why Asia?" Perhaps if it had not existed, it would have been invented as a place and time for a nation, as heavily bound to domestic values as the United States, to find its place in world affairs. A successful foreign policy must somehow differentiate a nation's narrower provincialities from its wider international interests, and the extreme domestic isolation of the nineteenth century American republic seems to have channeled the nation's foreign policy toward Asia. Asia constitutes a region of the world in which the United States could be engaged across a spectrum of political and military choices that had no relation to this domesticity—no deep historical ties before independence and no substantial immigrant representation afterward.

This study will examine Asia as *deus ex machina* in American policy, an actor whose role it was to bring the United States into the world as a great power without sharing any cultural intimacy with the United States. Although Washington scarcely recognized it, Asia played the role of mentor. We shall also look into the future, noting that with America's disengagement from Vietnam and Saigon's collapse, Asia has discontinued its historic role for the United States, in that it has no more elementary lessons to teach. Any relations in the future will have to be on a higher plain of maturity or else American influence—as contrasted with the sheer presence of American power—will wane in areas of vital interest. If Americans have wearied of Asia, Asians may well become exasperated with the United States.

Asia and America's Rise as a World Power

Beginning as early as 1844 when the first Sino-American treaty was signed, American involvement in Asia has produced a policy that Asia itself could not have originated. American entry into Asia in the nineteenth century was founded on a supreme belief in the vitality of institutionalized, constitutional authority and democratic community as ultimate political values for mankind, even though still secondary aspects of world politics. While the century was relatively peaceful, the ideals of world order and freedom were not the principle driving forces of international relations from Waterloo to Sarajevo (any more than they are today). On the contrary, the great powers were solidifying their empires abroad and pacifying populations at home. In fact, the fairly tranquil nineteenth century was already planting fertile soil for the violent century to follow. Underway were tendencies that would bear spectacular fruit: the worship of science and technology, the growth of liberalism and democracy in Europe, the dawn of the age of the common man and mass society, the belief in secular messianism, the development of totalitarian ideas, the accumulation of private and national wealth, the heightening of intellectual consciousness in the areas of economics, politics, psychology and social thought, and the intensifying of despair over the limits of reason. Yet Asia was, for all the great powers, a domain for imperial exploitation, a region of contention and potential war, not tranquility. Into this picture came the United States, with minimal involvement in European trends, but seeking to introduce liberal democratic values into Asia.

American strategy in Asia during the nineteenth and early twentieth centuries was part business, part ideology, and part religion. In addition to the virtues of democracy and constitutional order, the United States would bring missionary zeal and trade. In saving China for Christian faith, China's integrity against rapacious foreigners came to be seen as elementary in America's "Open Door" policy, a policy that coincided nicely with American interests in the China market. Yet this combination of Christianity, democracy and trade seemed remote from China's own ascendancy to national independence, free from outside domination.

Eventually, however, the entry by the United States into world politics was bound to involve American policy in the more standard international experiences of conflict and force. This was particularly the case after World War I. Following the war, the United States held a very real military presence in China but was extremely reluctant to use force as a tool of policy. This was borne out by repeated American accessions, despite official protests, to the demands of the Japanese beginning with United States acknowledgement of Tokyo's claims on all German possessions in China in the aftermath of Germany's defeat in the war (Treaty of Shantung).

When Japan invaded and occupied Manchuria in 1931, the United States role in world affairs was reactivated after a period of "normalcy" following Woodrow Wilson's presidency. Asia played the role of catalyst for America's rise to great power status. Secretary of State Henry Stimson held to two objectives: the prevention of Japanese expansion on the mainland of Asia (what the United States had protested against since 1917), and the retention of the system of collective security behind the Open Door. However, the United States did not confront Japan directly and alone, but rather attempted to bring world opinion to bear on the crisis, with little success.

As military events in Asia developed during the 1930s, the United States still appeared reluctant to use force against the Japanese, even after it was clearly stated by President Franklin D. Roosevelt that American national interests were threatened by Japan's expansion. On July 7, 1937 it might be said that World War II began in earnest, on the Asian mainland not in Europe, with the "China Incident." In this incident a clash occurred between Japanese and Chinese forces at Lukouchiao near Peking, thus giving pretext for Japan's full-scale invasion of China. On December 12, repeated Japanese dive bombings sank the American gunboat, U.S.S. *Panay*, near Nanking. The American public was outraged; Japan later apologized and paid an indemnity.

After nearly three years of Japanese expansion in China proper, including capture of China's two principal seaports, Tokyo turned its attention to Indochina. On September 4, 1940, Secretary of State Cordell Hull warned Japan of possible unfavorable American reaction to Japan's aggressive moves toward Indochina, but on September 22 Japanese forces began to occupy northern Indochina. For the first time since 1917, the United States reacted to Japan's aggrandizement with unilateral and forceful measures by declaring on September 26 an embargo on scrap iron and steel for Japan. Twenty-three years had passed after the first tangible evidence of Japan's designs on acquiring control of the Asian mainland before the United States took direct action against Japan, despite the presence of sizable American military forces in China and the Pacific and in spite of very substantial American commitments to business, democracy, and religion in the Far East. It is difficult to argue that the sheer presence of these commitments *blocked* U.S. military action or *thwarted* careful assessment of more specific American national interests. Perhaps Washington's reluctance was based on contradictory impulses toward Asia, on a lack of cultural intimacy coupled with substantial strategic and ideological commitments. And possibly the United States, because of its strong allegiance to the secondary factors of institutionalized authority and democratic community in world politics, found it difficult to use force even when it was manifestly in the American interest to do so.

On October 8, 1940, Japan declared the American embargo an "unfriendly act." With American encouragement Winston Churchill reopened the Burma Road on October 18 in order to supply Chiang's forces from the south, a road he had closed three months earlier under pressure from the Japanese. Japan's assets had been frozen in the United States on July 26, 1941 in retaliation for the spreading Japanese occupation of Indochina. Less than a month later, President Roosevelt issued a sharp warning that further attempts by Japan to dominate Asia would compel the United States to take appropriate steps to safeguard American rights and interests. Negotiations started between Japan and the United States, in Washington, to restore trade and reduce tensions.

Only in the period from September to December 1941, however, did the United States take any military steps in China, and these on an extremely indirect and modest scale. The "Flying Tigers" were organized under command of retired U.S. Army Air Force Captain Claire L. Chennault, with American supplied P 40s (to the Chinese) and with tacit U.S. government approval. Yet no mobilization was called in the United States and no special steps were taken to prepare American forces in the Pacific for possible war.

On October 7, 1941 a new militaristic government in Japan, under Lieutenant General Hideki Tojo, was installed. Tojo issued his secret war plans a month later, calling for simultaneous offensives against the U.S. Pacific Fleet at Pearl Harbor, British Malaya, the American Philippines, and Netherlands East Indies at the end of November. While Hull proposed an agreement on restoring trade in late November that the Japanese could never have found acceptable (requiring their complete withdrawal from French Indochina and recognition of the National government of Chiang Kai-shek as conditions for resumption of trade), still no special mobilization plans were made by the United States. Making matters worse, from the standpoint of America's willingness to face the hard realities of force in world politics, Japanese war plans were well-known to American authorities, although the main thrust of their invasions were thought likely to occur in the Philippines and Malaya. During the period from the breakdown of negotiations on November 26 to December 7, American intelligence knew that Japan was on the move in the Pacific, save for the presence of the First Air Fleet which was to attack Pearl Harbor. Nonetheless, on December 7 no special emergency footing had been ordered for Hawaii; only the absence of all three American carriers of the Pacific Fleet from Pearl Harbor prevented complete disaster.

By December 7, 1941 the reluctance of the United States to be in readiness for war with Japan, despite possession of the latter's secret war plans and a complete breakdown in relations, bordered on pathological. Perhaps underlying this inability to alert onself to manifest danger was an ideological allegiance to forms of world politics that remained secondary for all other great powers in the period from 1918 to 1941. The United States had already entered the European conflict through military assistance and lend lease programs, including the beginning of American convoys to Europe in September 1941. Yet Asia had been of greater American concern, to the point of marines in China, years earlier. American failure to accept force as a primary and legitimate aspect of world politics, in the absence of effective world organization, was ideological.

It took the shock of Pearl Harbor to bring the United States into direct military confrontation with the Japanese. One only wonders whether Washington would have taken such action had Tokyo invaded only British Malaya and the Dutch East Indies. Once in the war, however, America may have learned its lessons too well. What was to be the prominent role of Asia in the postwar era of American policy would prove quite different than before 1941. After 1945, Asia was alternately mentor to American idealism and realism, still a repository of high hopes for a world ruled by law, not force, but now also a battleground for all significant military actions. World War II conditioned Washington to the utility of force in world politics. The great issue for the postwar would be how to adjust America's traditional allegiance to secondary features of world politics to this new found military power. This adjustment could not be easy, nor would the ambivalences disappear. Indeed, the ambivalences would intensify. Only with the withdrawal of America from Vietnam in the early 1970s did the issue of a proper balance between law and force in America's Asian policy appear as the primary issue for future American involvement in Asia's affairs.

An explanation for American reluctance to use force in Asia, despite much provocation and a long-standing attachment to China's welfare, can be sought on a number of levels. In world politics force is more than apparent, it is one of the prominent features. To some extent such force is legitimate and measured, since it is exercised *by* sovereign nations with finite capabilities. On the other hand, force in world politics is also exerted *against* nations and thus has a tendency to move from careful application to unrestrained violence, because there are only very weak institutional boundaries for its international use. This is quite evident, for example, in the vagueness of rules of war governing treatment of civilian populations, and even in the imperfect execution of the much more specific rules covering conduct toward prisoners of war. In the twentieth century, each war has brought greater insecurity for civilians, and now the nuclear doctrine of mutually assured destruction rests on the threat of killing hundreds of millions of noncombatants within a matter of hours.

There is really no need to belabor the prominence of force in world politics today. In one sense, it provides a cement that binds nations together in the absence of institutional authority: it is a court of last resort, so to speak, in the absence of any institutionalized courts at all. One does not have to argue that "might makes right" to see the prominence of might in "making right" the differences between nations. Hence, force may take the place of law in the absence of such law, in the process becoming a kind of litigation with an ultimate verdict, however illusory this verdict. One could add that even today, in the midst of nuclear danger, many nations see limited conventional force as efficient for achieving certain political ends.

For the United States, two kinds of objections against treating force as legitimate policy in the absence of institutionalized authority have been made. First, there has developed the highly realistic doctrine that in a nuclear age, with strategic parity between the superpowers, war becomes less significant, pragmatically speaking, for achieving political aims. Such conflict may even be highly dangerous. Unhappily, this view does not cover limited conventional wars between nonnuclear states, except to the extent such conflict might prove escalatory. Yet the doctrine has worked as a brake on overt military engagements between the United States and Soviet Union.

A second American objection to force is more traditional: the world would be better off if force were deemphasized and authoritative institutions for nonviolent settling of conflicts were established. This view has provided a nice extension of American sentiments for a stable domestic society under law with a lively sense of common citizenship. If this second antipathy to force has erred, it is not on the side of excessive idealism, as some have criticized Woodrow Wilson. The error has not been committed in pursuit of idealistic purposes, but in its ambivalence toward force that alternately and sometimes even simultaneously, treats military power as an unclear means toward higher ends or as the ultimate arbiter of international affairs. This American ambivalence has involved either idealistic disdain for military dimensions of policy or ultrarealistic admiration of its potentials in world affairs. That force is prominent in world politics cannot be denied, nor can the possibility that it can be made less dominant. But here one is dealing with more and less, not either-or. Contingent doctrines of more and less underlie mature foreign policies, whereas ambivalences express immaturity, the unsteadiness of inexperience.

Over the first three-quarters of this century and especially the last thirty-five years, Asia's role in American foreign policy has been to make this policy evolve from one where force was alternately deprecated and celebrated, to a possible threshold where force can be accepted as relative to and relevant for world politics. At the same time that this realization may now be possible, however, Asia will itself have to be seen in a new light by the United States. Asia can no longer teach lessons of maturity. Having accepted this relativity of force and having seen that its position in world politics is still very prominent, American policy may now move to work for an evolving relationship between force and other political factors that might ultimately make the military dimension of international affairs secondary if not extinct. Whereas Asia's evolving role in American policy before Vietnam was to make the United States confront its own ambivalence about force in world affairs, Asia's role after Vietnam may well be to assist—in the sense of partnership—the United States in changing the relative positions of force and institutional authority in the international order.

The Role of Asia in American Policy after World War II

Official American policy in Asia after 1945 focused on four components thought necessary for a peaceful world order. Two of these components, China and Japan, had already played significant roles in the rise of the United States as a dominant world power, with Korea now ready to enter the stage for its part in America's international ascendancy. Still later Indochina would appear in a crucial role.

Without the strong stimulus of a consistent external threat, however, United States policy in Asia quickly lapsed into a familiar ambivalence about the use of force in world affairs. No such self-doubts existed for American policy in Europe after the war. But in 1949, the year of NATO's founding and less than one year before North Korea's invasion of South Korea, the Senate Foreign Relations Committee and Armed Services Committee jointly provided only 2 percent of the total authorization for the Military Assistance Program of 1949 for "Iran, Korea and the Republic of the Philippines." The highest military authorities saw little strategic significance in Korea, and recommended against committing defense resources there. This was seconded by Secretary of State Dean Acheson in his speech of January 12, 1950 before the National Press Club, "Crisis in China—An Examination of United States Policy." In it, Acheson drew his famous "defensive perimeter" excluding Korea.

The outbreak of war in Korea in June 1950 changed all this. Now the ideological spell of containment would operate under the official sanction of National Security Council Resolution 68 (NSC-68), adopted as basic policy by the U.S. government in 1950. This allowed that Soviet interests in world domination must be counterbalanced, by force if necessary, through an American interest in an environment in which free societies could survive and operate.

However the old habits of mind that grew out of American allegiance to secondary features of world politics and ambivalence toward force would not die. Public and even official uneasiness, over a new emphasis on building defense, persisted. In the fall of 1950, as United Nations forces stopped North Korea near Pusan and began their own drive northward, Dean Rusk was articulating the official fundamentals of America's Far Eastern policy. There were six goals, none of them really "strategic" in the sense that tangible American national interests were served by anything going on in Asia; that is, there was scarcely a hint of Asia's role in American foreign policy. The list of objectives rang familiar indeed: (1) freedom—political independence of nations; (2) equal partnership—full and equal participation by Asian nations in the international community; (3) security—secure nations from both overt and covert aggression; (4) material well-being—economic self-sufficiency and welfare; (5) cultural exchange and (6) good neighbors—stable and positive relations with the United States. All six had a traditional American sound, while perhaps two—security and material well-being—might be considered common interests for most nations.

In this combined policy of traditional American capitalistic, democratic and religious attachments to Asia and the postwar containment doctrine, at least four profound changes in Asia since 1945 were being obscured. All four should have been elementary for an American strategy of national interest that broke cleanly with past ambivalences. First, after 1945 there was the objective fact of the central presence and paramountcy of the United States in Asia. Toward Japan this supreme power was first displayed through devastating nuclear power and then through a proconsular dominance in its internal affairs and foreign affairs to the point of complete Japanese dependency. Both America's nuclear power and imperial political position were everywhere else in Asia obvious as well. The Communist Chinese and their friends would become obsessed with the imperialist devil; Indians would recoil into neutralism; Southeast Asia would pass from French to American suzerainty; and Northeast Asia would become a military protectorate.

The second major change after World War II in Asia was the lively presence of communism *in Asian clothing*, in China, North Korea, and North Vietnam. Under the doctrine of containment, communism would always be outside Asia, threatening the Far East. Because of this bias, American policy would lose sight of the incipient Sino-Soviet rift for at least ten years, save for a few analysts who could not be heard over the din about "monolithic" communism.

Third, after 1945 all prewar empires had fallen or were doomed. The Japanese, of course, were destroyed in 1945 and their expansion eradicated everywhere. The British, Dutch, and French were to follow. Because of its primacy in the Asian-Pacific sector of World War II and its role as liberator, the United States did not so much inherit a power vacuum as create it. Even the

Communists in China sent peace overtures to the Americans before 1945. If ever democratic idealism (Jeffersonianism) could have an audience, it was among the newly independent throughout Asia. Yet American aims in postwar Asia seemed too much tied to past ambivalences: nothing exciting and befitting a revolutionary tradition was conveyed. For once, aggressiveness in the field of political ideas might have established American paramountcy in the minds of Asians as well as in the realpolitik of their newly emerging governments. Instead, they were served with moderate policies, the peace of a generous victor *and* tired warrior.

The disappearance of prewar empires, together with the presence of Communism in Asia, promised an era of new violence in the Far East. Not only would budding national aspirations bring war between new states, but internal unrest would likely be a constant feature of Asian politics after 1945. American policy was to have great difficulty with this prolonged violence. Either it was treated as antithetical to a world ruled by law, a traditional American ideal, or it was constantly identified, sometimes wrongly, with Communist threats to the security of countries allied to the United States. As time passed, United States policy tended to emphasize counterrevolutionary strategies such as "internal security" programs and "counterinsurgency" forces. Jeffersonianism would have appeared a genuine American response to Asia at the end of World War II, when the future seemed open, but later the battlelines had been drawn with the United States usually found on the side of conservatism and stability.

As a fourth major change, the termination of the war with Japan by nuclear weapons at Hiroshima and Nagasaki ushered in an era of foreign policy underwritten by atomic power. In terms of impact on postwar world politics, Asia had played perhaps the most significant of all roles it has played in American policy: it provided the space for demonstrating the terror of nuclear force. Hiroshima and Nagasaki underscore the horrors of mutually assured destruction and thereby stand at the base of contemporary foreign policy, a fact not recognized by American policy at the time.

Had the United States seen the truly revolutionary significance for its foreign policy of these four major changes in Asia after World War II, and oriented its approach to Asia (and the world) accordingly, a much different American policy might have emerged. Instead of the familiar ambivalences repeating themselves in the litany of force and freedom, there would have been greater openness in the United States and Asia's evolving role in American policy. In place of a flaccid expression of good neighbor policy toward Asia, might have come frank recognition of the responsibilities of the first truly paramount *world* power in history. The presence of communism in Asia, having grown out of violence in that region, might have been seen much earlier for the unique facets that many now take for granted, thereby eliminating the need for the transfer of containment from Europe to Asia and the dreary defense policy that drained the United States' capacities for some twenty years. An exploitation by American policy of the postwar collapse of empires might have provided a kind of success for democratic ideals in Asia that was denied before the war by great power rivalries. And a more serious American appraisal of the significance of Hiroshima and Nagasaki, not as definitive military advantage but as a radical departure for the role of military force in foreign policy, might have led to less optimistic views on security-oriented policies in Asia and elsewhere throughout the 1950s and 1960s.

The six points said to be fundamental to American Far Eastern policy by Rusk in 1950 do not reflect much appreciation for the four new conditions in Asia. By 1950 it was probably too late, because the basic policy positions of Rusk's superiors veered sharply from these realities to a target considered more fundamental, the threat of Soviet Russia. Yet even this threat, so coldly pictured in NSC-68 and then so simplistically preached to the American public, was seen in typically ambivalent terms. In his National Press Club speech of January 12, 1950, Secretary of State Dean Acheson voiced a familiar American altrusim toward Asia:

Throughout our history the attitude of Americans toward the peoples of Asia had been an interest in them not as pawns in the strategy of power or as subjects for economic exploitation, but simply as people. For a hundred years some Americans had gone to Asia to offer what they thought was the most valuable thing they had—their faith. They wanted to tell the Asians what they thought about the nature and relationship of man to God. Others had gone to offer what they knew of learning; others to offer healing for Asian bodies. Others, perhaps fewer, had gone to learn the depth and beauty of Asian cultures, and some to trade. This trade was a very small part of American interest in the Far East, and it was a very small part of American interest in trade.... In China, the Philippines, India, Pakistan, Indonesia, and Korea [this American interest] had strongly, even emotionally, supported people working out their own destinies free of foreign control.

Vietnam

American experience in Indochina represents the historical death of Asia as a *deus ex machina* for the growth of the United States as a world power. Acheson's sincere belief that Americans had always treated Asians as people not pawns was belied by U.S. machinations in Indochina. All semblance of missionary zeal disappeared after a decade of intense American involvement there. One could not even call commercial advantage a reason for the United States' commitments in Southeast Asia.

Approached from the standpoint of military force supporting the bipolar conflict posited in NSC-68, Vietnam was anomolous. Defense of freedom against aggression furnished official justification for America's involvement, albeit aggression of "a new kind." Surely Vietnam expressed the quintessence of the United States' forward defense and counterinsurgency doctrine to contain communism. At the same time, however, the bipolarity basic to policies in 1950 hardly pertained to the mid- and late-1960s. Furthermore, the communism to be contained was *in* Asia, not external to it. And there was not a little suspicion that this communism was so interlaced with nationalist sentiment that what American policy was "containing" might well be part of the very "self-determination" it had traditionally supported.

Finally, if defense of free institutions was a justification for an American role in Indochina, the same issues that had much earlier confronted the United States in China applied. While American policy had sought to protect the progress of Chinese democracy, progressive forces in China were hardly democratic in any sense understood by Americans.

It has been noted earlier that a split in American policy toward Asia, between a strong predilection for promoting institutionalized authority and democratic community, on one hand, and a peculiarly uneven temperament toward military force, on the other, has produced curious results in terms of American reactions to world events. At times, in the face of the most patent provocation, the United States has moved timidly, but once determined to use force, American power could mount a violence of awesome proportions. All the while, however, force has been treated as an unclean means toward lofty and perhaps unrealistic goals of building ambitious world institutions. Under these circumstances, the ends could justify the means, not out of any cynicism but from belief in the purity of the ends.

Vietnam was a historical culmination of this split in American attitudes toward the world and Asia's role in American policy. Contrary to some of the criticisms leveled against America's part in the Vietnam War, American power moved neither too hesitantly nor too brutally in Indochina. Washington's chief failing was that it could not make up its mind between "people" and "power" in Vietnam. So its policy encompassed both. At once American measures were humanitarian and draconian, healing and destructive. Every contradiction in America's traditional imagery about Asia was magnified and distorted.

As the war in Vietnam dragged on into the late 1960s, there appeared no way to heal these splits in images and action. On the contrary, they only grew more apparent and less amenable to meaningful correlation. On the one hand, there was a consistent ethic of economic and political intervention that recommended nonmilitary means for containing the Communist threat. Yet such means seemed inevitably to express themselves in military terms: economic assistance served to prop an economy largely geared to war, while political methods came to include the ironies of "pacification" implemented with a mailed fist. At the same time, military action was both highly politicized (for example, in counterinsurgency operations) and yet uncontrollable by ordinary political methods (for example, in the so-called "secret wars").

Confronted by an involvement mired in complicated ambivalence, the Vietnam War, there seemed only one way out and that was out. Although there were many who either wanted to continue the struggle among warring opposites or else end the dialectic by drastic political or military methods, the general American consensus seemed to support a withdrawal careful enough as to maintain the illusion that somehow the United States had a consistent policy in Vietnam. At least during the withdrawal from mid-1969 to 1973 the American position appeared patiently orchestrated with political and military efforts working in harness. One must use the expression "appeared," because the relationship between negotiations and war was highly politicized.

The American withdrawal from Vietnam, "Vietnamization," was made to do symbolic duty for America's worldwide policy as well. The broader umbrella, for what was taking place during America's retraction from the muddy ambivalence of Asian containment, was called "the Nixon Doctrine." As a device for smoothing out some of the more glaring disparities between aspiration and capacity in American policy, thereby extricating the United States' military forces from Vietnam with safety and honor, the Nixon Doctrine worked. Beyond this strictly American aim, however, the war in Indochina did not end. Eventually South Vietnam fell before Hanoi's armed assault, as it probably would have a decade earlier, had not the United States intervened, with none of the ensuing bloodshed.

Until the bitter end, Vietnam, as part of Asia, continued to play a role in the maturation of the United States as a world power. Significantly, the chief lessons of American involvement in Vietnam were not in its beginnings, as some have tried to argue, but in its ending. As long as the ambivalence between nonmilitary and military interventions continued, and the tension between our aspirations and capabilities persisted, nothing could be learned since this simply repeated American experience in Asia for over 100 years. It eventually became obvious to America's leadership and public opinion, however, that any "lessons" would have to be found at some distance from the past, almost as if the United States had to become a "participant observer" of its own policy. This could be accomplished only through debate—inside and outside the government—as withdrawal from Vietnam took place. By deliberately and unilaterally withdrawing, the United States would put distance between itself and the object of its attachment, thus seeing the situation more clearly as it gradually came out from under choices imposed by containment and earlier policies. Obviously, containment itself would be questioned, with especially careful reviews of American policies toward the Soviet Union and People's Republic of China.

In this process of Vietnamization and formation of the Nixon Doctrine, the *relative* roles of politics and force, negotiation and strength, aspiration and capability could be reassessed in American policy. Perhaps it was even possible that the experience from this withdrawal would be translated into other areas of American foreign policy. Hence, in the years between 1969 and 1975 Asia played a role it had not played before in American policy: while it seemed to support America's curious democratic identification with the Far East until the full flush of America's action in Vietnam, the trauma of the war and the painful realism of the withdrawal were directed at removing this. It was with a peculiar combination of bitterness and relief that the American public and its leadership learned the ultimate lesson of our involvement in Indochina: what may lie beyond our capacity may not serve our interest, even when this interest is as lofty as human freedom itself.

U.S. Policy and Future Trends in Asia

Perhaps in no other area of American foreign and defense policy is it as important to view the present and future in light of the past as in Asia. Tendencies that can be traced back over a century have exercised enormous influence and may continue. Growing out of a combination of cultural distance and strategic proximity, America's policy toward Asia was a good deal more ambitious before 1941 than conventional stereotypes about U.S. isolationism would suggest. But such ambition contained in identification with Asians that saw in the American involvement a strong ideological mission to make the world a lawful community. Nonetheless, the rise to world power status by the United States could not help but bring America into strategic choices that invited the use of force. Ambivalence was an outgrowth of America being compelled to use military might, which it loathed and yet admired, in service of ideology and tangible interests. As Asia pulled the United States further and further into the realm of overt force, Americans also began to have mixed sympathies for Asia. Vietnam epitomized these divided loyalties and in Vietnam's aftermath there is a natural tendency to try to find "mistakes" where the problem may well have been of much longer duration. Under these circumstances, historical understanding is important and not a mere embellishment.

In looking at the future after Vietnam, it has been inevitable that American policy choices would be seen as having something to do with "intervention." While this approach is understandable in a way, since the United States did intervene in Vietnam, it has a tendency to avoid the historical context in which the American involvement in Vietnam occurred, a context that stretched back into the nineteenth century. By combining the problem of intervention with the question of mistakes in Vietnam, a literature has developed that attempts, in various ways and degrees, to prescribe American military disengagement from Southeast Asia and even East Asia. This literature tends to agree that, in the past, pursuit of American security interests in Asia has led to a primary reliance on military might. On both moral and pragmatic grounds this is considered wrong. Frequently the chief American failure has been its high flown aims and its limited power, so this line of thinking argues.

What is disturbing about the intervention-mistakes-disengagement approach to America's Asian policy is that the contrast between high political principles and low military means persists. Only now the nonmilitary options should be given even higher esteem, while the military should be minimized. This is what disengagement means in light of the "mistakes" of Vietnam. As long as the dichotomy remains stated in these terms, the *relative* values of military and nonmilitary means in foreign policy cannot be either appreciated or adjusted to each other.

As reviewed earlier, Asia's postwar role in American policy developed in three phases. In the first or immediate postwar period, the future for American policy in Asia was quite open. Drastic changes became evident in 1945, but were largely ignored by the United States in any profound sense: the central presence and paramountcy of the United States in Asia as part of its unprecedented *world* dominance; the presence of communism in and of the Far East rather than alien to it; the demise of all prewar empires in Asia; and the dawn of the nuclear weapons age. Instead of carefully examining these new tendencies, American policy quickly entered its second phase, that of resuming older democratic aspirations for Asia but combining these hopes with a militarily fortified containment doctrine in 1950. With a heavy American security emphasis in Asia after the start of the Korean War, the historical American ambivalence between altruism and power was accentuated rather than eliminated. The third phase of American policy did not occur during the origins of Vietnam *per se*, but in the lessons of withdrawal which called for a reassessment of *both* altruism and power, democracy and containment. The question now is whether the lessons of the third phase will be seen as necessitating a clear break with the past, or whether the familiar ambivalences of engagement-disengagement will reappear. If the second choice is made, it is unlikely that containment will be part of the picture, at least not in Asia.

This study recommends the first choice, that of making a clear break with the confused past. Much as in 1945, trends are occurring objectively in the Asian picture which might conceivably provide some focus for American policy. In most cases these long-term features will not be quite the same as those of 1945, but it is surprising how World War II set in motion tendencies which, if slighted by American policy, have nonetheless persisted in spite of America's strenuous efforts in the Far East. Tendencies today resemble earlier ones without being identical. In this sense, it is meaningful to speak about the limits of American power.

Major future trends in Asia may be divided into economic, political, and military tendencies. It may be assumed that they will continue through 1985 and out to the year 2000.

Economic Trends

In the economic area, the proliferation of new states in Asia has led, first to complexity in developmental policies. A good deal of experimentation has taken place. In some instances, such as the People's Republic of China, the experiments have been purely socialistic. Some nations, like Malaysia, have put heavy emphasis on a market economy. Still others stand somewhere between, often enmeshed in conflict among opposing points of view.

A second economic trend in Asia is the emergence of transnational economic issues in juxtaposition, if not opposition, to strong nationalistic (and autarkic) tendencies in the same areas. One thinks here immediately of energy, food and population. With the breakdown of prewar empires in 1945, food and population became issues for most newly emerging states in Asia. In fact, the most noticeable efforts to deal with these pressing problems have come in the two population superpowers, both Asian, India and China. Nevertheless, these economic and social issues, as well as others such as oceans policy, have also reached the center of international attention, with significant attention directed toward Asian countries. Economic growth itself (including inflation) is now conceived in both national and international terms. These transnational issues tend to be survival problems, and they represent world divisions along North-South as well as East-West geographic lines.

Political Trends

Among various political trends that are likely to continue and perhaps intensify in Asia through the remainder of this century one stands out as evident even in the early postwar era, instability between Asian nations and insurrection within certain states. As noted earlier, American policy has experienced difficulties with this fragmentary tendency in Asia, resorting to various methods for "stabilizing" the region. In the recommendations for American policy that will conclude this study, an effort will be made to sort out the wheat from the chaff among these remedies. There seems little doubt any more that American capabilities to manage violence in Asia are extremely limited and should generally be confined to war *between* states rather than spread very far into the field of internal unrest.

A second political trend will also become more pronounced, this one a result of successful democratic development rather than its failure. American policy has also had a difficult time appreciating this tendency in the past. There is the tendency of Asian and Pacific electorates to shift toward greater independence from American policy. In turn, United States policy will confront one of those paradoxes for which it has become famous: authoritarian regimes may actually be friendlier to the United States than democratic ones. To support democracy in Asia, however, Americans must live with its consequences. This means, in effect, that "friendship" should be in all cases confined to mutual interests, whatever the regime, and that under no circumstances should regimes that favor the United States be accorded special protection if that is all they offer. More of this later.

Fluidity in Asian international relations will be a third political trend, following rather naturally from the first two tendencies. This shifting of forces and opening of policies constitutes a worldwide phenomenon, something I have called elsewhere "international indeterminacy." What it portends for American policy in Asia and Asia's role in American policy can scarcely be contemplated. The structure of containment possessed fixed commitments and defenses, veritable ramparts against the Communist threat. As will be noted below, the issue for American foreign and defense policy during a time of international and regional fluidity will not be whether to intervene or disengage, but how to resist or accommodate. Within an on-going process of constantly shifting world relationships, the chief questions for the United States to decide will be why, when, where, and how to place sizeable diplomatic and military weight in a given area of contention thought somehow relevant to American interests. While this surely presumes that national interest criteria will be rather clearly established, it is a necessary but not sufficient condition for adequate decision-making in fluid political situations. An interest in a given area of conflict may be quite explicit or implicit, but as long as there is any interest at all, the critical choices in foreign and defense policy will be: why should we become involved? when should we lend our weight to the conflict? where should we exert ourselves? and how should we apply our weight in the scales of conflict?

The last political trend that will most surely continue through 1985 and beyond relates to an economic trend already discussed. Contradictions will continue between Asian interests in autarkic and cooperative behavior. "Regionalism" has been a key concept for American policy, sometimes for want of any other measure to induce states friendly with the United States to be friends with each other. Realists have tended to point at the importance of atmosphere in these relations: the stronger the American pressure the more likely regionalism will emerge. This has seemed to some Americans a good enough reason to continue intense American involvement in Asian affairs, for the peace and stability of Asia itself. There is not much evidence, however, that Asian countries see such American backed cooperative schemes in quite the same way they see American backing for each nation separately. In typically narcissistic fashion, the "peace and stability for the good of Asians" school of thought tends to treat as primary what many Asians may well see as secondary.

Military Trends

Four trends in Asian military relations will probably continue, each of which deviates somewhat from traditional American views of the ideal defense picture in Asia.

First, political instability—external and internal—will continue to assume military or paramilitary forms. The list of possible horror stories for stereotyped American dreams of Asian peace and security are dreary. Just to get some idea of what lies ahead, one can mention the Sino-Soviet dispute, North and South Vietnam, insurgency in the Philippines, a nationalist revival in Japan, military coups in India or other places, total Australian nonalignment, another war between North and South Korea or India and Pakistan, and so on. This itemization is meant only to give some samplers of external and internal military crises lying down the road toward the year 2000.

A second trend likely to continue is that of nonalignment along East-West lines, though this may be superseded by North-South military blocs. The major changes after Vietnam will most likely be in the defection of former defense partners to nonaligned, not Communist, positions. While this is not a very credible path for, say South Korea, it is more likely for Australia and perhaps Japan. Problems with the latter two nations have grown out of Vietnam, in the case of Australia because of the war in the first place, and in Japan as a result of the general retrenchment of American power. Japan's situation is additionally complicated by its economic power, which requires that it sometimes take positions independent of the United States to sustain its own economy. Nonalignment among former allies will generally proceed from democratic trends leftward, a matter discussed above. While authoritarian regimes may well become more friendly to the United States than democratic ones, key states in America's *military* calculations could move into positions of nonalignment.

Increasing general defense competence, not necessarily under American patronage, will be a third military tendency. This trend includes medium powers, such as India (with Soviet assistance and nuclear power), as well as additional countries that may procure arms from sources other than the United States. In addition, the long-term prospects for substantial and continuing American arms aid to Asian forward defense countries seems bleak, not only in Southeast Asia but in the northeast as well. However, growing competence in defense is a two-edged sword. On the one side, this should make it less likely that the United States will have to supplement the military capabilities of *weak* states in the future. On the other side, however, the United States might find itself drawn into a conflict between *strong* nations in Asia. As in the Middle East, there seems little likelihood that the presence of growing volumes of arms and improved competency in using them will lessen the risks of war. To argue otherwise is to indulge in one of those confusions so endemic in America's Asia policy in the past: the means of force, it was held, would actually serve the cause of peace by decreasing the danger of outside aggression. Few asked what relationship there was between the danger of aggressive external forces and the incidence of wars. So rational a reason as a genuine threat to one's security is only one possible explanation for why nations go to war. But whatever the reason for fighting, possession of a capability to wage war effectively lends more credence to one's use of that option. Credence builds confidence and confidence can make war more attractive.

The final change in Asia, not directly connected with the Vietnam War, will have important long-term effects. This is nuclear proliferation. Of six nuclear powers, two are Asian, China and India. Despite an acute allergy to atomic weapons, Japan only recently ratified the Nuclear Nonproliferation Treaty and still has the capacity to develop such armaments on short notice. Pakistan could acquire nuclear arms as a counter to India's program. The Soviet Union has a formidable nuclear force in Asia along its Chinese frontier. Speculation has centered on the possibility of a "surgical" or "preemptive" Soviet nuclear strike against China as a prelude to full-scale war. In the United States, there might be future pressures to deploy tactical and strategic nuclear arms as the core for a military presence in Asia and the Pacific, thus drastically cutting down on manpower and other conventional force expenses.

Sheer facts of nuclear proliferation in Asia do not tell the whole story. With the exception of Japan, tensions have run high between the various other powers armed with atomic weapons, and the causes of these disputes have not been settled. Pakistan fears Indian nuclear attack; China obviously feels nervous about a nearby Russian threat; and China and India could still confront one another. United States nuclear power in Asia is widely dispersed, but the possibility of using nuclear weapons could arise in defense of some of its allies, especially South Korea.

Five Future Strategies for American Military Force in Asia

With American withdrawal from Indochina and the defeat of South Vietnam has come some confusion about what, if any, future military strategy the United States should have in Asia. Given the central role of force in world politics, as well as the complicated treatment of force in past American policy toward Asia, it would seem premature to rely on the rather comforting promise by some influential Americans that the United States is finished with war in Asia. No sooner did Saigon fall than Washington was wrestling with the *Mayaguez* incident and the divided Korea problem. Even without such events to remind us of Asia's sensitivity in America's global policies, however, it appears essential that the United States make some effort, after the last traumatic decade, to adjust its future global military strategy to accommodate realistically Asia within our broader defense capabilities.

The prospects for future use of American military force in Asia must be stated very bluntly: in the wake of a serious setback in Vietnam, the United States is searching for a coherent global strategy to protect its national security interests, but presently lacks such a consistent defense posture in Asia and beyond. Surely the fall of Saigon must signal the end of the United States' containment policy in Asia, just as the defection of Greece and Turkey from strong attachments to American military presence indicates the erosion of cold war positions in southern Europe. These reversals of old policies have been accompanied by a somewhat premature belief, on the part of some, that the United States will never become involved in Asian land wars again. Such relatively "objective" factors as these have not been faced fully by the American defense establishment in its planning. Official military rhetoric still seeks to contain the Soviet (and Chinese) threat, even while events continue to undermine such containment.

One indication of a certain drift in present national security planning is the current controversy over whether the United States navy should have smaller ships, thus increasing quantity, or more of the large nuclear-powered carriers and support elements with a correspondingly smaller number of ships. Vague references are made to the relative strategic virtues of one or the other naval option, but either these virtues are spelled out only in terms of the Soviet navy's growing size, or in reference to possible operations, such as the Middle East, which are patently designed to provide propagandistic footnotes for bureaucratic positions. Outsiders to this controversy can devise, of course, good strategic reasons why one or the other option should be followed, but one has the feeling that it is not strategy that is guiding the controversy so much as the lack of it.

Similar considerations apply to almost all other areas of present American defense planning. We are to build more ICBM missiles of bigger size and quality because the Russians are doing so; or we are to improve accuracy of existing missiles for the same reason. The Middle East War of 1973 revealed the importance of antitank weapons, so accelerated development should take place in the United States. The Soviet Union is calling on ports in the Indian Ocean, so America must increase its naval elements there. And Moscow is building a base in the same Indian Ocean area, so the United States must imitate the Soviet Union (the inception of Diego Garcia, in U.S. naval planning, predates Soviet activities at Berbera).

When all is said and done, however, one has a strong impression that with the decline of cold war containment doctrines, spelled-out officially in NSC-68 of 1950 and discussed earlier in this essay, no global strategic conception has yet replaced it in American policy and nothing is on the horizon. Defense planning seems adrift in a morass of bureaucratic and congressional politics, toward ever higher budgets and lower proficiencies, while some parts of the national security apparatus promote détente and others warn of confrontation. It is doubtful that, without a better adjustment between military and political planning than now exists, the United States will achieve neither a safe peace nor a proficient defense organization.

Unless the decline of containment in places like Ankara, Athens, and Saigon is seen in its most significant light, as the end of a globally consistent American policy, there will be no urgency to reconsider global strategies and hence no military policies for Asia that are effective for American interests, over the long term, within this region or beyond. The end result of not engaging in this reconsideration will be that the United States must continue to live in an unsafe peace with an incompetent defense apparatus, no matter how many missiles and ships we have.

This essay now turns to five possible strategic alternatives and corresponding forms of military force in Asia during the post-Vietnam era. These strategies are: (1) revised containment; (2) neo-Mahanism; (3) selective engagement; (4) strategic disengagement; and (5) futuristic planning. There are partisans today for each; some argue for a mixture. Table V-1 provides an overview of all five Asian strategies and their force planning requirements. Not only does it roughly indicate the magnitude of required commitment, but the table also gives some idea of what strategies are implicit in any force decision. By not paying attention to the strategy-force linkage, one could well develop a defense that fulfills contradictory or inconsistent policies, with resulting decline in one's credibility.

Defense Strategy Number 1: Revised Containment

All five of the alternative defense strategies to be outlined for Asia have two things in common: they provide security for the fifty states of the Union, at a minimum, and *all are applicable in global as well as Asian terms.* This last feature is taken as essential for future American policy, since it is assumed that one token of superpower status is that there be a globally consistent foreign and defense policy so that a nation can be *identified* as a global power. Such symbolic consistency is precisely what is threatening the superpower status of the United States at present. In fact, this threat is much more dangerous than improved Soviet military capabilities, because by operating inconsistently on a worldwide basis the United States could find itself facing war in one region without sufficient resources for maintaining its posture elsewhere. Under these circumstances American credibility, as a superpower, would suffer. Something like this seems quite possible in scenarios now being proposed for American military action in, say, the Middle East, in order to gain access to vital oil supplies or to intervene on Israel's behalf during a fifth round of fighting. This is not to say, however, that global consistency constitutes, in and of itself, a virtue. Some of the possible strategies to be discussed will be analyzed in their negative as well as positive aspects.

Revised containment, our first strategy, has the virtue of representing an emendation of policies of the past. It is an extension of the cold war, but in more up-to-date proportions. The Soviet Union is seen as expansionist and adventurist, with a growing propensity toward spreading its conventional and nuclear forces globally. This policy alternative views the Soviet Union as even more dangerous than in the past, now even threatening its former ally, the People's Republic of China. Needless to say, those who espouse revised containment have no affection for détente.

As far as Asia is concerned, an interesting aspect of revised containment is its

Table V-1
Force Planning For Five Asian Defense Strategies, Contingency

Strategy	Nuclear Deterrent	Other Nuclear Options	Naval	Air Force	Japan	Korea
1. Revised Containment	Expand	Expand in quantity and quality	Expand along present lines	Continue where feasible	Continue as 1975	Continue as 1975, but use U.S. troops for counter-insurgency support elsewhere also
2. Neo-Mahanism	Expand	Doubtful except for naval	Expand for protecting all key sea lanes—access points	Continue where feasible	Continue as 1975	Doubtful save regarding Japan
3. Selective Engagement	Continue as 1975	Expand modestly to allow "selectivity"	Continue as 1975	Continue where feasible	Continue as 1975	Continue as 1975
4. Strategic Disengagement	Continue as 1975 or reduce modestly	None	Continue as 1975 or reduce	None	Continue as 1975 or reduce	None
5. Futuristic Planning (Possible only)	Continue as 1975	Expand to include non-Communist nuclear powers	Expand for two navies	Expand to cover access/sea lanes	Continue as 1975 or reduce to save Japanese rearmament	Continue with expanded roles for U.S. military forces in Korea & in Asia (contingencies outside Korea)

changing view of Peking. The People's Republic, so feared by past containment policies in Asia, would not be put into perspective as a curable hegemonic power, still far from superpower status, which rests in the vice of Russian expansion eastward and southward into the Pacific, South Asia, and the Middle East. At least it is in the American interest, revised containment would argue, to

Southeast Asia	South Asia	Southwest Asia (Persian Gulf)	Indian Ocean	Military Assistance (including arms sales)	Sino-Soviet Dispute
Expand defense against new Communist states; continue other	Expand to include "mini containment" against hegemonic powers	Expand, including encouragement of Iran-oriented "mini-alliances"	Expand	Continue as 1975 but improve quality in South Korea	Expand U.S. military interest preparations
Reduce to key bases	Doubtful save regarding key sea lanes in Indian Ocean	Expand to protect access to resources	Expand	Doubtful save to buy access	Doubtful
None	None	Continue as 1975	Continue as 1975 or expand modestly, avoiding naval race with Russians	Reduce modestly but improve quality in Korea	Doubtful
None	None	Continue as 1975	Continue as 1975, avoiding naval race with Russians	Reduce significantly	None
Doubtful, save waterway access	Doubtful, save access (includes nuclear danger)	Expand for full access	Expand	Reduce	Doubtful

encourage the Sino-Soviet rift and to consider contingencies which would cause American forces to rush to China's aid in case of Soviet attack. Such protective forces might even include conventional forces in Asia, such as the Seventh Fleet formerly assigned to contain Peking's designs on Taiwan and Southeast Asia. North Korea, as North Vietnam, would be envisaged as still largely a product of

Soviet machinations aimed at achieving Russian hegemony in Asia. All efforts would be made to keep Japan away from Moscow, even if this means rapprochement between Peking and Tokyo.

From a military perspective, revised containment would require extensive American force in Asia and its environs, conventional and nuclear, both to counter expanding Soviet armed might and to keep a circle of nuclear fire tightly constricted around the southern and eastern frontiers of the Soviet Union. Revised containment would require significantly enlarged American naval and air elements in the Indian Ocean, continued offshore presence of all military types in Southeast Asia and the South Pacific, strong naval forces near the Chinese mainland, along with complete conventional and nuclear security guarantees for Japan and South Korea including American troops in Korea. What a direct American presence could not accomplish would be supplied by generous military assistance programs.

While much of this force would resemble that now present in the Asia and Pacific region, revised containment would entail significant changes, all toward an expanded American presence. Firstly, the Indian Ocean would require enlarged forces, with operations facilities at Diego Garcia, Subic Bay, and elsewhere, including perhaps use of Simonstown, South Africa (this strategy would put considerable emphasis on white Africa, notably Rhodesia and South Africa). Secondly, the new possibilities in Micronesia at Saipan would be expanded drastically to provide conventional and nuclear strike forces against prepositioned Soviet forces in the Pacific and Indian Ocean. Thirdly, the entire American military presence would be more oriented, than in the past, toward possible deterrence and/or intervention against any Russian attack on China. Fourthly, this ring of force, at sea and on islands offshore as well as in Korea, could lend support—overt and covert—to counterinsurgency operations by indigenous non-Communist states and to protection of American interests against Communist nations of Southeast Asia. And fifthly, certain non-Communist countries with regional hegemonic ambitions, such as India, might be part of a mini-containment or containment-within-containment strategy operated by the United States, especially when they move, as India does, with Soviet blessing. Such mini-containment could include a kind of miniature nuclear deterrence by the United States, if any of these so-called medium powers were to threaten the use or actually use nuclear weapons. Surely mini-alliance systems could be encouraged in accord with mini-containment strategies; for example, an Iranian-Pakistani linkage aimed at Indian expansionism.

This strategy has all the advantages of adhering to the dictum that the United States should avoid further involvement in Asian land wars by withdrawing from a permanently based presence on the mainland. In a sense, therefore, this strategy can be described as *revised* containment, since it puts little or no premium on the kind of "forward defense" concept developed by American planners in the fifties and sixties. No two and one-half war global plan would be necessary; that is, the United States would not have to prepare for fighting two full wars at the same time; as well as mounting preparations for another subtheater conflict.

When all is said and done, however, the revised containment strategy is somehow both too ambitious and not ambitious enough. On the extravagant side, as far as military expenditures are concerned, it would likely be trimmed and argued over at home, while subject to a good deal of criticism abroad. Indeed, the current global policy of the United States, aimed at alleged increases in the proficiency of Soviet forces ("alleged" because they have not been tested in combat as American forces have), still has one foot in the cold war and one in a vaguely designated "generation of peace." This policy represents the results of having your cake and eating it too, a program that ambitiously strives to contain Russian advances with a sieve.

Yet in a very profound sense, revised containment is not ambitious enough, despite the fact that, in full flower, it would well double the present defense budget (because it would actually have a double task, to contain and to confront expansion). This strategy would constitute an essentially reactive, negative posture, aimed at matching numbers of Russian ships, filling so-called "power vacuums," and anticipating far-out contingencies, but not necessarily serving tangible American interests in Asia. For example, one would think that next to getting along with a populous People's Republic of China and a wealthy Japan, America's long-term goals in Asia would include amicable relations with India. Revised containment could well result in even more trouble with influential India (a country destined, perhaps, to have even more influence, now that it has exploded the twin myths of its pacifism and democracy). Similarly, whatever the virtues of détente with the Chinese, eased relations with the Soviet Union would seem ever more essential for a policy of global peace. Revised containment would not really serve such a policy, whatever the rhetoric employed, because it aims so frankly at counterpressures against a Soviet Union that is much stronger in foreign affairs than it was in the period for which containment it was originally designed.

In the balance, therefore, revised containment with its attendant psychology of "the Russians are coming, the Russians are coming," does not seem adequately designed for what the United States may likely face in Asia—and globally— over the next two decades. It is at once too ambitious for our capabilities and yet falls too far short of protecting our interests. One might say that the over-achievement/under-achievement workings of containment, in any form, furnish a basic rule for all future American defense planning in Asia (and globally): what may be too demanding of our capacities may not protect our interests. This surely is the most important lesson of Vietnam, and provides a fitting epitaph for American experience in the cold war period.

Defense Strategy Number 2: Neo-Mahanism

Our second alternative strategy, drawn freely from the teachings of Admiral Alfred Thayer Mahan and applied in contemporary terms, is a counterpart to the containment school. Neo-Mahanism would urge that the United States set out to do what containment alleges the Russians are up to, a frank American expansion of its interests by economics, politics, and the sword in Asia as well as elsewhere. Here flag and trade would operate in concert throughout the Pacific basin, in something like the old manifest destiny-great white fleet days of the late nineteenth and early twentieth centuries. Choices for the last decades of the twentieth century would be framed with materials from Admiral Mahan's linkage between a strong domestic industrial base, vigorous trading networks, overseas possessions, and naval power. Underlying this strategy would be a solid faith that this is still an American century, in that no one can match our skills in trade and war.

From a military perspective, neo-Mahanism would require a revitalized naval force, on patrol in all essential sea lines of communication; on station for finely tuned offshore conventional operations; and on alert for a wide variety of nuclear missions. We would constantly demonstrate our doctrine that trade and force are interlocked, by suffering no impediment to vital supplies such as petroleum. In turn, force planning of whatever description would be oriented toward the Mahan vision of authentic military power; defense would gravitate to basic economic interests and would unapologetically promote imperialistic expansion. One could also call neo-Mahanism an "armed multinationalism."

Since the expansion of economic interests abroad would, in the American case, be capitalistic, it follows that the United States defense would have an anti-Communist as well as pro-interest orientation. Indeed, revisionist historians tend to see American cold war policies as motivated by this linkage between economic capitalism and political anti-communism, but the connection has been overstated. A number of areas of American policy in the fifties and sixties did display this close relationship between economics and defense, but others did not. Neo-Mahanism, however, would suffer from none of the altruism of the past. Yet this second strategy is discussed after revised containment, precisely because it would still retain cold war features almost by definition. At the same time, small non-Communist states would be no more immune from American military reprisal than large Communist nations, if they sought to frustrate the industry-trade-overseas linkages vital to American prosperity.

It is hard to imagine the exact nature of American military force in Asia required to meet the demands of neo-Mahanism. However, it would have to possess interventionist capabilities of limited duration in order to secure necessary access to vital resources and perhaps even to onshore markets. This would mean a naval force in the Indian Ocean of at least the revised containment size, as well as plenty of smaller naval vessels to protect lines of communication throughout this region and the Pacific. Given the inevitable linkages between neo-Mahanism today and anti-communism, a strong nuclear deterrent would be called for (which would not stop neo-Mahanism from favoring détente on strictly *economic* grounds). On the other hand, contingencies such as the Sino-Soviet dispute or even a fight between North and South Korea would be less interesting to neo-Mahanism, except as they would impinge on Japan's security (since Japan is a major capitalist economic power and trading partner of the United States) or trade with China (should this expand at the rates some are predicting for the near future). In summary, therefore, neo-Mahanism would probably involve a smaller force commitment in Asia than maximal containment would require, but probably would necessitate an increase in present American defense capabilities, especially naval, around the Asian littoral including the Indian Ocean.

It is no accident, of course, that present arguments in the United States to expand and refurbish the post-Vietnam navy have revived the shades of Admiral Mahan and Theodore Roosevelt, as well as citing the menace of Soviet Russia. There is evidence that these two arguments for a strong navy and national defense were intertwined as far back as the first secretary of defense (and former navy secretary), James Forrestal. The close connections between trade and naval power were, of course, dramatically present in the imperial rivalry between Japan and the United States leading up to World War II, and could easily be sublimated today in competition between the United States and the Soviet Union.

Neo-Mahanism has the virtue of a certain practicality—and honesty. There seems a close connection between domestic prosperity and unhindered international trade, a central thesis in economics since early attacks on mercantilism. Surely the United States has long stood for free commerce abroad, in tangibles as well as ideas. When focused on all assaults on open commerce, a strategy that closely links economic and military power has the value of great consistency and specificity. This explicit linkage is not alien to Soviet conduct in world affairs.

Unfortunately, neo-Mahanism would appear in the context of revived containment, since in protecting capitalist expansion it would automatically lead to confrontation with a Soviet Union armed with its own vision of how economics and military power should work together. Leaving aside trouble with the USSR, conflicts could develop with other major capitalist powers, a realm of competition well-known to Mahan and Roosevelt, who both had their own imperialistic predilections. Hence, Mahan may have appeared to be prescribing a linkage between free trade and seapower, but in fact his historical model was mercantilist England and his own milieu comprised nineteenth-century imperialist rivalries. Something of neo-Mahanism could have been introduced into the Nixon Doctrine as well, with predictable abrasions between capitalist allies rather than with the Soviet Union.

The major deficiency of neo-Mahanism as a global defense strategy, aside from its high political and military costs, is the same general weakness found in revised containment: neo-Mahanism would not serve American interests of domestic prosperity, if it would involve the United States in adventures (including wars) that might prove beyond our capacities to pursue successfully. This is, in fact, one of the chief criticisms of those who advocated use of American force in the Persian Gulf to secure oil supplies: in pursuit of the golden egg, neo-Mahanism is a military strategy well designed to kill the goose.

Defense Strategy Number 3: Selective Engagement

In the wake of Vietnam, it is said that these are times for modest strategies in Asia and on a more global scale. As noted earlier, in a sense the Nixon Doctrine proposed such modesty some time before the fall of Saigon. It has also been observed that the so-called lessons of Vietnam include one, that the United States cannot play world policeman. Why not, then, select certain areas held vital for the defense interests of the United States and invest military effort in these alone, a strategy of selective engagement? Those holding to the principle of selective engagement usually rule out a major American defense role in Southeast Asia's future. At the same time, they cite the critical linkage between Japan's security and South Korea's future, and the primacy of both for American defense planning. In addition, there appears to be some margin in selective engagement for modest efforts in the Indian Ocean, ANZUS (U.S.-Australia-New Zealand) and the Philippines, with watchful attention, but no solid military commitment, to the dynamics of the Sino-Soviet dispute.

Selective engagement seems more compatible with a general détente policy toward the Soviet Union than do either revised containment or neo-Mahanism. While this strategy usually sees several confrontation areas remaining with Russia, most notably in the Mediterranean and NATO, it would keep active defense policy in Asia within the general Northeast Asia area alone, with even this on a relatively low key compared to past efforts. Gone are the broad aims of containing Russian expansion, an expansion that selective engagement tends to see as partly a function of American cold war policies anyway, and most surely the ambitious plans to thwart Chinese interests in Southeast Asia and Taiwan have also disappeared. Generally speaking, military assistance will have a role to play where direct American involvement no longer does, but even here the emphasis will be on a modest scale with attention to encouraging others to prepare for a defense within their own capacities rather than under American dictates.

Present American defense policy seems a hybrid of containment and selective engagement, one foot in the well-organized past and one in the incongruous present. Heavy naval and air contingents are still poised in the Central and South Pacific areas, as if Washington continued to have an interest in the fortunes of

Taiwan and SEATO; indeed, official declarations still make such avowals. At the same time, however, the mood of Congress and public, as well as the letter of the law, forbid American intervention in Indochina, while warming relations with Peking have raised doubts about American willingness to take on the defense of, say, Quemoy and Matsu. In the 1960 presidential campaign the last two islands provided a major issue for debate, one readily understood by the American public: today, one might as well talk about defending lunar landscape against invading Chinese modules.

At the same time that American defense rhetoric still bristles with talk about counterinsurgency and selective nuclear war as part of an Asian strategy, official pronouncements also make clear the unequivocal commitment of the United States to Japan's and South Korea's security alone, with an admonition that "Vietnam is behind us." And we are apparently prepared to live with raised rents in the Philippines, while President Marcos pursues rapprochement with the Chinese.

Selective engagement surely does not require the defense force in Asia that either a revised containment or neo-Mahanism would. Some naval presence (with appropriate air cover) in the South and Central Pacific, a nuclear umbrella over Japan, troops in South Korea as token of our commitment there, and a modest patrol in the Indian Ocean are all that would be required. Regarding the last area, if more force were necessary for some contingency connected with the Middle East, it could be taken from Atlantic and Pacific units. Since no necessary linkage is envisaged between one engagement and another by selective engagement, it is thought that American military force could safely be spread thin in any emergency. Events in the Persian Gulf would not necessarily spark problems in Asia, especially given American nuclear deterrent strength, so Asian forces could be diverted with impunity.

Selective engagement obviously has the virtue of a certain economy and efficiency, much admired in times of fiscal strain. Also, there is some merit in thinking *and* acting modestly after over two decades of defending the "free world." There was a time when every new president of the Philippines felt it mandatory to journey to Washington—the center of containment—to speak before a joint session of Congress about the solidarity of Asian and American democracies against the Communist peril, meaning both Peking and Moscow, but especially Peking. Such rhetoric was duly applauded by Congress, which somehow felt it was master of Asia's fate. Defeat in Vietnam may have brought the American government to some understanding of Asia's essentially alien cultures and indeterminate future. Now the Philippine president must make his peace with Peking.

In subduing hubris, however, selective engagement leaves everyone guessing, including Filipino leaders. Since politicians generally gravitate toward no-lose policies wherever possible, there is a natural tendency for the elites of non-Communist states in Asia to place bets on as many numbers as they can.

The idea, for example, that the United States will defend those who help themselves, sounds a bit like "every man for himself." An invitation to help oneself can quickly lead to selfish and unpredictable behavior on the part of erstwhile allies ostensibly joined in altruistic love. Once the bets have been laid across the board and deals struck with former adversaries as well as friends, it is a little late for the United States to complain about selfishness among its allies or to deplore "growing Soviet influence."

Especially difficult is the practice of selective engagement when part of one's allegiance is still to systematic containment. Such an inconsistency may be seen by some American policymakers as their own kind of no-lose game at home (gestures to the Right and the Left), but to other nations it could look confusing. While the United States can withdraw from forward defense strategies in Indochina and still talk about containing Russian or Chinese expansion in Asia, a small nation like Thailand cannot have it both ways. Once the United States rules Thailand out of its forward defense perimeter—and selective engagement bears striking resemblance to our perimeter thinking in the late 1940s—Bangkok can hardly find any other way to oppose the Russians or Chinese or perhaps even the Vietnamese. It must make peace with them, with a possibly negative impact on the United States.

Selective engagement does recognize the full value of the ultimate lesson of Vietnam: what may be too demanding of our capacities may not protect our interests. What this strategy has difficulty with, however, is the idea of "too demanding." American policy might have been *too* demanding, but it now runs the risk of overreacting to this experience by not demanding *enough*. This rather familiar pendular swing in American foreign policy is particularly true today in the area of alliances in Asia. The war in Indochina may have been partly based on artifice concerning SEATO commitments, but this hardly has much logical connection with the issue of what future alliance commitments are important for American interests in Southeast as well as Northeast Asia. And disregarding formal alliances, the overly demanding imperatives of the cold war did contain an important, historic American dedication to the self-determination of states as well as to the expansion of representative forms of government. In the historic perspective of 200 years of history, isolationist and internationalist, America has committed itself to freedom in the international as well as domestic sphere. Selective engagement, particularly when it includes military commitments to a South Korean dictatorship and not to the shaky parliamentarism of a Thailand or a Malaysia or a Singapore, seems short on vision. If selective engagement means that the United States will have no more interest in the future of a non-Communist Southeast Asia, then it may be a very inconsequential policy indeed, surely not one that would give much credibility to America's pretensions as a global superpower.

Defense Strategy Number 4: Strategic Disengagement

As a defense strategy, strategic disengagement is the simplest to plan and operate. Basically, this approach to national security policy would rely on nuclear forces to defend the United States proper, but foreswear military intervention in Asia. The arguments for this strategy are both ideal and pragmatic.

From the standpoint of American ideals there is little in Asia to recommend an American commitment of military force, strategic disengagement argues. With the exception of Japan, which is both democratic and can afford to defend itself as it deems appropriate, most of Asia is alien to American political experience. Indeed, it is not at all clear after over three decades of American military involvement, that Asia is any freer, in its governmental forms, than it would have been without our intervention. As noted earlier, so much of what Asia represented to the United States was a function of our own needs and not those of Asia. And a case could be made that the people of Vietnam, who are now all under Communist control anyway, would have fared better for not having to live through all those years of devastating war. Democracy, as we know it, has not prospered in areas where Americans have died by tens of thousands or where the United States has pumped economic assistance by the tens of billions.

As a pragmatic position, strategic disengagement also makes a certain sense. Rushing to fill "power vacuums" and to restore "balances of power," America's military force has exhausted itself chasing phantoms of our own invention. As in nature, a vacuum in politics may display certain properties and functions worth preserving; for example, working for neutrality through diplomacy in the Indian Ocean. If such diplomacy does not succeed and the "vacuum" is filled by an unfriendly power, perhaps it is the fault of the diplomats that neutrality was not achieved, and in any case, a situation not correctable by military force. Similarly, it is well known that classical balance of power policies, wherein preponderant military force can be used to seize special advantages and thereby change the equilibrium of forces, has little or no utility in an age of nuclear weapons. In fact, even before atomic arms, the pursuit of such advantages by force led as often to disastrous anxieties as to success, a matter adequately revealed in Europe's bloody history during the first half of the twentieth century.

The central issue then, for a policy of strategic disengagement, is how to resist military interventionism and all the rhetorical ploys used to overstimulate imaginations in the national security apparatus. "Lead us not into temptation" may require a new "best and brightest," known not for the chances they take but for the opportunities they avoid.

In order to minimize interventionist temptations, strategic disengagement would drastically trim the wherewithal to intervene. Severe deprivation of the defense establishment would become the rule, on both ideal and pragmatic grounds. The United States would be better *and* stronger if it could stop squandering its defense resources in fantasies of world power.

As for the cold war's fight against communism, strategic disengagement would see this in highly revisionist terms: while communism was surely no political phantom, neither was it the threat alleged by the United States. And in any event, where national Communist movements have captured the fully legitimate means of force within countries—the regular armed forces—they have often prevailed against outside armed intervention (overt and covert) by the United States. In other words, the real battleground between communism and capitalism is in the arena of domestic insurrection, before capture of an official state apparatus, and in this arena any outside power would be at a disadvantage over the long term. What American policy seemingly failed to grasp was that even where *national* left-wing movements might succeed in becoming established governments, the same inhibitions might apply to Soviet external influence as to American.

With almost a puritanical code of self-abnegation, strategic disengagement would provide the least costly American defense in Asia. Indeed "in" Asia would be the wrong preposition, for with the exception of a nuclear retaliatory force on station in the Pacific in event of armed attack on the United States (and perhaps on a disarmed Japan), no force would be necessary at all. This would allow for a drastic American pullback to mid-Pacific island redoubts.

The strength of strategic disengagement as an overall plan for American defense is the same as that of its opposites, revised containment and neo-Mahanism. All have the virtue of consistency, though in quite different directions. In addition, strategic disengagement exhibits a certain compelling honesty, an iconoclasm that is valuable whether or not one accepts the full defense implications of disengagement. Politics, and one suspects a good deal of international politics, has a propensity to fantasize about that will-o'-the-wisp, power. Despite Machiavelli's warning that politics is but one part rational excellence, with two parts fortune and necessity, there still persists a tendency among very high decisionmakers (and their critics) to see political activity as a form of highly conscious control over collective life. Accident and fate tend to be minimized, whereas the political figure becomes a kind of grand architect for the destinies of many. Strategic disengagement questions these assumptions which underlie military intervention in the affairs of others. In a way, such disengagement is the best of defense strategies from the standpoint of what is actually known about war, where the elements of freak happening and unintended consequence tend to dominate. Under such circumstances, one errs on the side of overestimating one's capacity to influence events, and boldness is most often associated with defying the odds one knows are *against* a daring operation.

At the same time that one can appreciate the good sense implicit in a policy of strategic disengagement, there is no doubt that political and military success are sometimes associated with bold action. Military intervention by a power equipped to bend another's will by force is one form of daring. Cold war strategies may have overestimated military capabilities and squandered defense resources, but there was a boldness that impressed others and often tipped the balance in favor of, what were deemed at the time, vital interests. Without the capacity for military intervention, a critical piece of the puzzle of international power may be missing, a puzzle unclear in its ultimate outlines and a piece that must be carefully employed. But boldness and risk are political virtues, when used judiciously. The anti-interventionism of strategic disengagement would disarm these virtues and accordingly diminish American capacities in international politics, including the capacity to make peace.

Defense Strategy Number 5: Futuristic Planning

Ranging from the most to the least expensive to least among defense postures in Asia and worldwide are revised containment, neo-Mahanism, selective engagement, and strategic disengagement. The most ambitious force planning, perhaps requiring a doubled defense budget, would be revised containment with its twin priorities of containing the Communist giants through deterrence directed against their homelands and at the same time countering these superpowers as they reach out increasingly away from home with prepositioned military forces. All four strategies have global applications. Each would defend the United States proper from direct attack by another power, chiefly the Soviet Union.

It has been the thesis of this analysis that, in the post-Vietnam era America is without a globally consistent defense strategy, save for technological organization of its forces, so it is time to look at strategic alternatives. All other talk about the status of national defense policy only leads to interminable disputes about how American forces compare with those of Soviet Russia. What purposes American force will serve in the next few decades remains unclear, and for this reason present the United States military capabilities are neither adequate nor inadequate in any classical sense of a military power that serves the broader considerations of national interest. Weapons-for-the-sake-of-weapons is no policy at all. Except for technocrats fascinated by the latest status of military hardware, it is meaningless to talk about how good or bad or indifferent present American defense capabilities are vis-à-vis developments in the Soviet arsenal. Capabilities for what?

The last defense strategy to be discussed addresses future trends in world affairs, and is, therefore, somewhat more open or "indeterminate" than the other. Issues under futuristic planning center not on values or mistakes in the past, but on radically changing outlines in world politics for the future. Among such trends are shifting global alignments from East-West orientation to North-South. There are also a host of new transnational issues already with us and increasing in importance such as food, oceans, energy, population, and the distribution of wealth. Steadily developing in competition for primacy in foreign policy with traditional geopolitical considerations are economic ones. All such trends may require a national security policy that is geared to the next few decades rather than tied to lessons given by the past.

While history is surely a key to wisdom in any field, including politics, it is also true that large sectors of mankind are shaking off their past and creating new histories; in some cases, their policies are in revolt against international practices of long standing. Surely questions such as how energy shall be controlled and world wealth distributed have taken a different direction since the founding of OPEC, an organization deliberately established to shift past international patterns in these areas. This "rejection of all that history has taught me," as Camus put it, is a hallmark of twentieth century politics, for good or evil, and if anything this process of rejection promises to accelerate in the next two decades.

Under these circumstances it may be well to put Vietnam behind us in defense as well as political terms. As noted previously, defense planning today has one foot in past containment strategy and one in the present selective engagement policy, an amalgam that will produce neither a safe peace nor a proficient defense in the new policy areas noted above. Any American plan to use force in the future, in Asia or elsewhere, had better account for futuristic planning that involves the kinds of alignments and issues entailed in these newer problems.

If North-South rivalries over survival issues that involve political and economic matters of great consequence will dominate the rest of this century, *then* the roles, missions, capabilities and threat assessments of the present American military establishment are not prepared for the future. In Asia this does not imply that nuclear postures should be relaxed; that is, for targets in the Soviet Union and People's Republic of China. It does mean, however, that threats against American interests will have to be perceived as involving North-South controversies as well, with both deterrence and war-fighting strategies developed to cope with these threats. Constraints on unilateral use of force, within the context of conflicts that transcend national boundaries and involve multilateral decision-making, should also be clearly understood. Survival issues may well be transnational enough as to make one nation's military power inadequate to cope with them; or perhaps force itself may not only be irrelevant in certain instances, but disastrous if used. Futuristic defense planning would require, therefore, the most careful attention to both the roles and limits of military power under changing circumstances.

By focusing so much attention on *Soviet* military capabilities, some defense specialists have failed to see the full range of threats possible to vital American interests in the next few decades. These dangers may spring from actions by medium as well as great powers. Such threats may or may not have Russian backing; in some cases, such as on matters related to law of the sea controversies, the Soviet Union may even be on the American side.

While it is impossible to specify exactly what a new futuristic defense force would be like that would conform to a more indeterminate strategy, the following outlines for Asia seem plausible. These forces would have their counterparts in other geographical regions.

Firstly, a nuclear force armed for deterrence against both the Soviet Union and other nuclear powers in Asia should be present.

Secondly, several task forces of large, nuclear-powered carriers, with associated amphibious elements, should be on constant patrol in areas where armed intervention with *definitive* American power would secure access to vital resources and waterways, should these be closed by the force of any power. Such task forces would operate in deterrent and war-fighting modes. They should be independent of major base requirements.

Thirdly, operating out of bases and homeports, naval elements with smaller vessels than in the large carrier forces should cruise well-traveled sea lanes to and from resource-rich areas. These forces should have base support in the Indian Ocean and in Western and South Pacific.

Fourthly, air force units should be strategically placed at bases where they can engage in reconnaissance, antisubmarine warfare, and strike missions.

Fifthly, American army forces in South Korea should remain there, but with added missions, including airborne operations, in support of forces engaged in North-South confrontations.

Admittedly, this futuristic planning would not come cheaply. Leaving aside the question of expense, however, the chief problem is to reorient defense thinking away from the idea of fighting wars against Communist forces, to the notion of protecting vital interests against Communist and non-Communist nations alike. In such a strategy as this, there is some amalgam of other strategies: revised containment; a dash of Admiral Mahan; a good amount of selectivity; and yet some disengagement in the sense of recognizing explicit interests rather than vague rhetoric. But futuristic planning has a different spirit as well as unique assumptions. For the longer term, this strategy will require some maturing of the American public's ambivalent view of military force. Force is neither glamorous nor criminal, but one very prominent way in which world politics operates, which involves a taking or defending of something by power of one's physical strength; there is no ultimate legitimacy for this mode of political activity save its own success. It should not be used frivolously, but it has a key role in foreign policy. For vital national interests, force should be used only when it is usable, which is another way of saying that only force within our capacities can possibly be effective. It is my view that only a futuristic planning strategy that accounts for emerging realities in world politics will allow us to employ military force, over the next few decades, with some confidence that it will be both wisely used and successful.

Of course, the futuristic planning suggested here is only *illustrative* of the kind of force structures that may be required. And the magnitude of this force in no way implies that the United States should use muscle rather than negotiation as the primary emphasis in its foreign policy in North-South controversies. On the contrary, military force will have severe limitations when it comes to survival issues, for all sides will develop their most proficient defense for such contingencies. Diplomacy will become, therefore, all the more important, and force should occupy its rightful place as a court of last resort. Yet this new diplomacy, occupied as it will be with life-and-death questions, should have all the support it can obtain. Military preparedness can supply an important element in America's future international strength, providing it is geared to new realities.

Note

1. Harold Isaacs, *Scratches on Our Minds: American Images of China and India* (Westport, Connecticut: Greenwood Press, 1973), p. 38.

VI

Alternatives for the International Order in Asia

Robert A. Scalapino

Not since World War II has the future course of international relations in Asia been more uncertain. Significant political changes including the major American defeat in Indochina, and complex socioeconomic problems now plaguing much of the world have combined to produce far-reaching reverberations throughout this vast area. Whether we stand on the edge of a new age, or are merely witnessing important but confined readjustments remains to be seen. Nor can one assert with assurance today that the current Asian scene is more unstable than that characterizing Europe. There can be no doubt, however, that all of the states of the Asian-Pacific region, large and small, face a wide range of decisions reflective of the challenges of the contemporary world.

Given the many variables and uncertainties, it would be foolish to posit a single future course for the domestic and international politics of Asia and its subunits. Rather, our effort here is to explore the basic alternatives available, but in so doing, to analyze the critical variables and when the evidence seems to warrant it, to advance certain probabilities. Since domestic trends have a direct bearing upon foreign policies, some preliminary effort must be made to assess these.

This work deals primarily with nation-states because while the nation is by no means fully sovereign in the modern world, the truly critical decisions respecting international affairs are still made by this unit. Moreover, our concentration is upon the major powers, a term requiring a brief definition. A major power is a nation which by virtue of some combination of economic, political, and military capacities has the ability to influence in a substantial fashion the policies and

227

attitudes of other nations and nation-states. Such powers may be essentially regional in their scope, or their power may extend more broadly. Our primary concern here is with six nations. Three of them, the United States, the Soviet Union, and Japan, can be considered international powers, albeit in a different sense insofar as Japan is concerned. The People's Republic of China is a regional power, but one having a certain international reach. India and Indonesia are regional powers in the more classic sense, with the former having gained near hegemony in its region, the latter possessed of much more limited influence.

One other introductory note is in order. Since Asia represents nearly one-half of the world, whether measured in area or population, regional divisions are critical to any analysis. This is the more true because in some cases, regionalism itself has socioeconomic or political potentialities. For our purposes, the area can be divided into five regions, with some overlapping essential, since a number of states are involved in more than one region:

1. The Pacific, its center encompassing the vast mid-Pacific complex of water and islands currently dominated by the United States, its peripheries including the sizable array of states bordering upon the Pacific Ocean.

2. Northeast Asia, with its vortex being Japan, and including the Korean Peninsula, Siberia, and Taiwan, consequently being of direct concern to the USSR and China, and to the United States also, given the nature of American commitments.

3. The Continental Center, overwhelmingly dominated by the two major Communist states, Russia and China, with all of the states in the immediate vicinity deeply affected by the course of their relations.

4. Southeast Asia, defined classically as encompassing the continental states comprising the old Indochina, Thailand, Burma, Malaysia and Singapore, and including the Philippines and Indonesia, with Australia and New Guinea-Papua also being involved.

5. South Asia, with India now the controlling force, but including the other nations of the subcontinent: Pakistan, Bangladesh, Sri Lanka, and the Himalayan states.

References to these regions will be interwoven into our analysis of the alternative policies confronting the six major societies with which we are concerned, and we shall also deal with them specifically in our final survey.

Japan

It is fitting to commence our study with Japan, a nation that in certain respects bridges Asia and the West. As the area's leading industrial nation, and also its foremost open society, Japan is closely interrelated with the major Western societies both in economic and in political terms. Even Japanese culture has become uniquely hybrid. On the other hand, the Asian component in Japanese society remains strong and geography makes special involvement in regional affairs inevitable. Potentially at least, involvement in Asia could grow as this vast part of the world undertakes a sustained developmental drive. Thus, to treat Japan as an appendage of the West represents a major error.

In recent times, projections of the Japanese future have undergone frequent reevaluations. In the earlier part of this decade, domestic trends in Japan were the subject of pessimistic speculation. Economically, the golden age was seen as coming to an end. The costs of energy sources and raw materials, together with a growing labor scarcity and Japan's extreme vulnerability to various forms of economic nationalism were regarded as constituting crushing blows at the old economic order. Economic difficulties in turn, together with the numerous side-effects of incredibly rapid social change were viewed as likely to produce political instability in the near future. Thus, the end of conservative dominance was widely predicted, with coalition government taking its place. The rise of the Left was assumed to be certain with repercussions upon foreign as well as domestic policies.

By 1975, trends seemed to be moving in a direction opposite to that predicted by the pessimists. Among all of the highly developed nations, Japan was among the early ones to experience an economic upturn after the steep 1974 recession. The onset of recovery was a product of a tough anti-inflationary program, a major drive to expand exports, and more generally, that close interaction between government and industry which characterizes the Japanese economic system. By 1976, the goal of a stabilized growth rate of 6-8 percent did not seem fanciful.

On the political front, after the fortunes of the Liberal Democratic party had sunk to a low ebb under Prime Minister Tanaka, a new figure in the person of Miki Takeo took the helm. While Miki was expected to be an interim leader pending the resolution of the power struggle between stronger personalities, he proved to be more durable, buoyed by reasonably good LDP showings in the April 1975 elections. Then came the Lockheed scandal, however, and renewed signs of fierce internecine warfare within the LDP rendering political predictions once again hazardous.

Despite their current troubles, the conservatives continue to be powerfully aided by the disunities and weaknesses of the Left—nor is there any indication that these problems can be easily resolved. On this side of the political roster, only the Communists display a combination of able leadership, excellent organization and a shrewd grasp of issues. Even they may have peaked in terms of voter appeal, however, barring some dramatic new turn of events. Meanwhile, the fact that Miki represents the "progressive" wing of the LDP may be a harbinger of the future, irrespective of his personal fate or that of the party as presently constituted. The need for greater attention on the part of the government to social welfare policies has become increasingly apparent. One must also recognize that among the younger elements of the LDP, many individuals of talent are to be found, and in some combination, they are likely to become more prominent.

Will the Japanese conservatives defying numerous predictions and the political law of averages, hold power indefinitely? To make such a flat prediction would be dangerous, especially in the light of recent events. Some of the critical economic issues which confronted Japan so formidably a short time ago can be considered alleviated and quite possibly, the Japanese economy can adjust to a new economic order better than had been assumed—but few of the big problems have been "solved." The competition for raw materials and energy sources is likely to grow sharper. The future pattern of international monetary, trade and investment policies remains to be shaped. And the very capacity of open societies to survive is being brought into question globally. On the strictly political front, meanwhile, serious challenges lie immediately ahead. The old factional leaders with few exceptions appear less capable of adjusting to the electronic age, or to new constituent pressures than may be necessary. Nevertheless, the immediate political future in Japan appears to be one in which the conservatives will play the dominant, if not the exclusive role, assuming that no major, unforeseen disaster strikes. Some restructuring of the LDP, or even a coalition government certainly cannot be ruled out. A dramatic shift to the Left, however, remains much less probable. Whether that will continue to be true as the 1980s dawn cannot be predicted at this time. Thus, in thinking about middle-range possibilities, we should not ignore some consideration of Japanese foreign policies under a Left government or Left-leaning coalition.

Let us commence, however, with an examination of the basic alternatives that confront Japan today, a Japan under the governance of moderates. These alternatives would seem to be four in number, and they can be expressed in their "pure" forms as pacifist nonalignment, Gaullism, a new alliance and the continuance of special ties with the United States. Each broad policy has its special appeals and drawbacks, strengths and weaknesses, viewed from various Japanese perspectives.

Pacifist nonalignment is most attractive to those who envisage a world that imposes no obligations of a political or security nature upon Japan *and* presents no threats. A pacifist strain has run deeply in Japanese society since World War II. That war was so devastating that for many Japanese involved the very concept of war became unthinkable. From the early postwar years, idealistic concepts like those of Nehru thus had a strong emotional appeal. Socialist leaders, indeed, still live in that era, having never accepted the need for armaments or alliance. If the Japan Socialist party were to come to power, therefore, the bent of Japanese foreign policy might well be in this direction, with a strong emphasis upon Japan's identification with the Third World, and particularly with Asia.

Are the Socialists truly prepared for nonalignment? The Left Socialists, currently dominant in the party, are decidedly unneutral, being strongly anti-American and very pro-Chinese. Their recent efforts were to see if Chinese attacks upon the Soviet Union could be reduced, and when they failed in this effort, they signed a joint communiqué that in many respects, aligned them with Peking. The Communists, on the other hand, are bitterly anti-Chinese at this point, reflective of a break with Peking during the Vietnam War. They reflect a Left nationalism that might be more in keeping with the future political configuration of Asia, one devoid of any pacifist notes. Indeed, unless and until basic changes can be affected in the personnel and policies of the Japanese Left, unity in foreign policy will be as elusive as in domestic affairs.

For Japanese conservatives of whatever hue, pacifist nonalignment has a very limited appeal. Japan's vital economic and political interests are much more closely identified with open societies, in their view, and particularly with those of the advanced West. The resource-rich underdeveloped areas are of near-equal importance, to be sure, and increasingly, Japan can be expected to cultivate these—with the critical balance to be struck between the West and elements of the Third World. In striking this balance, however, neither pacifism nor classic nonalignment is seen as of value. How could a Japan, both defenseless and alone, defend its interests adequately, the Japanese ask. And they see a number of interests subject to challenge from diverse quarters: maritime rights, access to markets, and territorial claims among others. What would prevent other states, even small states, from taking advantage of an unarmed, nonaligned Japan? Could such a Japan expect to receive the treatment in international gatherings accorded a major society, one with a vital stake in the outcome? Already, Japan has had a sufficient experience with the travails of the weak in a balance of power world to make these questions highly germane.

Gaullism represents another form of nonalignment, one coupled with the acquisition of substantial military power, and dedicated to reestablishing the prestige of Japan in international circles. It is a natural expression of a people whose culture has been rooted in independence and aloofness, a people intensely private, whose commitments center upon the small inner group and are strongly hierarchical in nature. Japan comes to alliance with difficulty, and to equality with the greatest of conceptual and practical problems. This is a society built upon inferior-superior relations, and naturally these carry over into the international realm. Now, after a long period of accepting inferiority, a rising number of Japanese, particularly among the younger generations, are questioning their international status.

Thus, one can perceive a rising nationalist tide in Japan, one emanating from diverse quarters. The trend is not an entirely new one, but currently it seems to be garnering strength. Nationalism finds expression in the media, in political circles of both Right and Left, and within the powerful bureaucracy as well. As yet, perhaps it partakes more of sentiment than of policy—although for some years it was manifest in Japanese economic policies and went largely unrecognized. It is presently being abetted by various developments. Is there another major society in Asia that has not displayed strong nationalist proclivities in recent years? India—once the spiritual home of Japanese pacifists—now has a victorious war to its credit, its own nuclear program, and a new militancy at home under Mrs. Gandhi. China, under communism, reflects the determination to become a modern, powerful nation, and one with special interests in Asia. Even in the small states in Japan's neighborhood, the spirit of nationalism is rife, such as with the two Koreas.

All of these developments have been observed, and with observation has come a growing sense of uneasiness. Many current trends in Asia do not seem favorable to Japanese interests. Specific problems, including important territorial issues, remain unresolved with the Russians—and Russian power in Northeast Asia is due to increase greatly. Similar issues exist or are potential in relations with China and the two Koreas. The pressures from the People's Republic of China wax and wane, but they are never absent, and in very recent times, they have once again been on the rise. Difficulties with the Koreans—both South and North—seem endemic to the Japanese. And above all, the sharply declining credibility of the United States in Asia greatly complicates the picture.

It is thus not surprising that voices demanding the reassertion of Japanese power and authority are being heard in somewhat greater volume. The recent divisions within the LDP over whether to ratify the Nuclear Non-Proliferation Treaty (finally bridged for the most part) is but one manifestation of the trend. A debate, still muted and tentative, relating to fundamental foreign policies appears to be commencing, and if this is the case, Gaullism will have its adherents.

Nevertheless, the disadvantages of Gaullism for Japan remain very formidable. It may be doubted, incidentally, whether Gaullism has provided France, its homeland, with any significant gains either in security or prestige. In any case, one of the secrets of Japanese success to date has been the ability to take advantage of the American security umbrella, thereby obviating the deep divisions and high costs that would ensue in the country were a forward military posture to be assumed. There has never been any basic consensus within Japan on foreign policy, it is true, but the low-risk, low-cost foreign policy pursued has made it difficult for the opposition parties to use this as an issue. Gaullism, however, would produce a militant opposition and might seriously threaten internal order, at least if undertaken under present circumstances.

Similarly, its repercussions abroad would almost certainly be adverse on balance, at least initially. Even in the absence of military and political roles, Japan has induced substantial resentment in such vital regions as Southeast Asia through its exercise of economic power. A Gaullist Japan would heighten fears and anxieties—and in all probability, these would extend to the major Communist powers as well. If Japan were to undertake a nuclear weapon program, for example, it would find herself quickly targeted by both Russia and China. Given its extreme vulnerability as a small, densely populated, extensively urban community, could Japan possibly achieve a credible nuclear deterrent against these continental societies? And how does a nation protect its sea-lanes, markets, and investments by military means in this age?

If the problems with Gaullism in its pure form seem overwhelming, it is nonetheless likely to have an influence upon Japanese attitudes and policies in the years ahead, a point to which we shall soon return. Meanwhile, what are the possibilities of a new alliance, either with China or Russia? If the influence and interest of the United States in Asia is truly waning, is there another source from which Japan might seek protection and patronage? An alliance with the Soviet Union could conceivably offer security were the primary threat from China (or the United States), and its economic benefits, at least theoretically, could be substantial. The development of Siberia, as we shall note, is a prime Soviet objective and few nations are better equipped to aid (and benefit) economically than Japan.

Yet an alliance with the Soviet Union is extremely difficult to envisage under any likely circumstances. Russian-Japanese relations have been marked by a lengthy history of hostility, suspicion, and betrayal. Culturally, the two peoples are totally different, and thus, each seems very foreign to the other. Politically, also, the differences are major ones, and even now the Soviet Union is continuing the tough policies that have characterized its position toward Japan throughout the twentieth century. The issue of the northern islands, eagerly exploited by China, blocks progress toward the normalization of political relations, but economic ties are also inhibited by other issues. Meanwhile, the growth of Russian power in Japan's near vicinity causes increased apprehension. Public opinion mirrors these facts by consistently recording in polls an emotional dislike of the Soviet Union.

An alliance with China, on the surface, would seem more plausible. Throughout modern times, two schools have contended for control of Japanese foreign policy, the pan-Asianists and those identifying more strongly with the West. The former group, playing upon cultural and ethnic factors, and frequently positing "Western imperialism" as the central threat, have argued for a Japan identified primarily with Asia. Inevitably, in one form or another, this requires a special relationship with China. In the period after World War I, the pan-Asian movement ultimately took on messianic, expansionist form. Today, one sees a resurgence of that movement in certain respects, the product of the extensive interaction with the West for the past thirty years, and particularly with the United States. Parties like the Kōmeitō and the Japan Socialist party take pride in being Asian, and seek an identity separate from that of the West. China thus beckons as a nation rich in past cultural associations and pregnant with new potentialities for interaction.

In the historic competition between the Japanese pan-Asianists and Western-oriented elements, a synthesis was repeatedly effected. Japan used ties outside of Asia to forward its policies in Asia. There is no reason to believe that such efforts will cease. Japan, against the wishes of certain Westerners, *is* an Asian nation even as its fate is closely linked with an international order in which the West plays a critical role. But an alliance with China seems highly improbable when all of the factors involved are closely examined. These two nations are at very different stages of development, and they currently rely upon radically different values and institutions to forward their goals. Thus, culturally as well as politically, Japan and China are moving away from each other at a rapid rate.

Potentialities for interaction, especially in the economic field, do exist and will probably be exploited. Even here, however, inhibitions are posed by the systems and goals of each nation. For the present at least, Chinese Communist leaders continue to place a high premium on self-reliance and very conservative economic policies. Moreover, they are not likely to want any nation, including Japan, to control more than one-quarter of their trade, a figure close to the present one. Thus, despite the pledge of oil and the prospects for continued trade expansion as the Chinese economy grows, China's economic potential for Japan will be limited for the foreseeable future. Notwithstanding the rapid gains of the recent past, China trade still accounts for less than 4 percent of total Japanese trade, and direct investment is not possible.

In the political realm, China can easily become a divisive factor in Japan since its various pressures can be interpreted as undue interference in internal Japanese politics, as is once again being done. In the final analysis, moreover, China has a limited capacity to protect Japan against any superpower threat.

One broad alternative remains, namely, the maintenance of special ties with the United States. This policy is clearly not without its costs and risks, and these may be rising. As noted earlier, the Japanese Left has never accepted the American-Japanese alliance, and the Mutual Security Treaty (MST) in particular has aroused stormy controversies on several occasions, as is well known. Foreign bases are generally a political liability, especially in the absence of a clearly felt threat—and that has proven true in Japan. In recent years, moreover, both the prestige and the credibility of the United States have declined in Japan, with the Vietnam debacle raising the gravest doubts thus far. Would the United States really come to Japan's aid in the event of a crisis? A large number of Japanese think not. The other side of the coin is the fact that many Japanese regard the MST as essentially designed to forward American interests in Asia, not to protect Japan. Thus, they fear involvement in a war not of their own making or choice, and few see a correlation between the defense of another Asian state and their own security, although this may be changing.

Thus, the military aspects of the alliance engender controversy and division. In recent years, this has been muted to some extent because both the Russians and Chinese have given evidence of not wishing to see American-Japanese relations disturbed, taking into account their own limitations and the uncertain course of a self-reliant Japan. Recently, however, the People's Republic of China in a joint communiqué of May 12, 1975, signed with Japanese Socialist leaders, publicly stated its support for the abrogation of the Mutual Security Treaty, thereby seeming to revert to a pre-1971 position. This may have been only a verbal concession in exchange for Socialist acceptance of an antihegemony statement aimed at the Russians. Indeed, on subsequent occasions, Chinese leaders have repeatedly indicated privately the importance of a Japanese-American security relationship *for the time being*, being careful to avoid any permanent commitment to this condition, and positioning themselves for a shift if Japanese domestic developments of international trends so warranted.

Economic relations with the United States also face uncertainties in the future. Here are two dynamic societies, moving in the same broad direction in their economic development, but with significant differences in the relations that prevail in each society between government and business, and other differences of a cultural-developmental nature that engender misunderstandings and antagonisms. Competition, in any case, is destined to vie with cooperation in the American-Japanese economic relationship.

On the other hand, the benefits of the American alliance have been far-reaching. By accepting the American security guarantee, a savage debate over military policies has been largely prevented. Pursuing a low profile foreign policy, Japan has been able to reap unprecedented gains. Increasingly, moreover, the United States has proven tolerant of Japanese efforts to separate economics and politics, even accepting Japan's separate policies toward Arab nations and toward certain Communist states such as North Vietnam and North Korea. Today, all alliances have become looser, more flexible, allowing greater latitude to the parties involved. The age of exclusive, all-encompassing alliances of the cold war type is over, at least for the present. Hence, Japan can potentially partake of the advantages of special ties with the United States while still pursuing a more independent course.

Unquestionably, Japan faces problems at this stage in its development, but the broad policy direction appears fixed. On the economic front, it hopes to continue advances and equal, if not surpass, the United States as a truly universal economic power. Its efforts will doubtless continue to be those of seeking the widest possible diversification of economic ties. No opportunity, however small or seemingly unpromising, will be overlooked. This dictates the effort to separate economics and politics wherever possible, as is the present course of action. The charge of being "an economic animal" may wound Japanese pride, but in a highly troubled, dangerous world, being merely an economic animal— particularly if one is successful—has its compensations.

Ideally, Japan would be best served by being able to improve its relations with both the People's Republic of China and the Soviet Union, keeping these relations in tandem, and still maintaining special ties with the United States. The latter ties would not be allowed to interfere with the creation of certain independent positions vis-à-vis the Third World. Through these policies, once again, Japan would be utilizing ties outside Asia to forward its policies within Asia.

It is also in the Japanese interest to see the political status quo maintained, especially in Northeast Asia. Any change, especially a change brought about by force on the Korean peninsula or with respect to Taiwan, could only heighten Japanese feelings of insecurity, and affect Japan in other respects as well.

As has been noted, however, ideal policies and developments are not easily achieved. Keeping relations with the two major Communist states relatively equal has proven to be impossible up to date. At this point, Peking is clearly ahead of Moscow, albeit with the recurrent possibility of overplaying its hand. The Chinese have seen two major objectives with respect to Japan accomplished up to date: keeping the Soviet Union and Japan apart, and containing Japan politically and militarily. Today, Japan is politically isolated from even her near neighbors to an unprecedented extent, not merely Russia but also North Korea, Taiwan, and even South Korea. Moreover, Peking has also signalled its interests in ultimately weakening Japan's ties with the United States.

Can that too be accomplished? Unquestionably, as noted earlier, the American defeat in Indochina added to earlier doubts about American credibility and capacity—even among those Japanese who had strongly opposed U.S. involvement in Indochina. Korea or Taiwan may well prove to be the next issue bearing upon these questions. Meanwhile, despite the seeming American-Japanese intimacy of the past thirty years, true communications remain extraordinarily fragile, and the element of trust surprisingly weak. Consequently, a strong sense of being alone pervades Japan, her "special ties" with the United States notwithstanding.

Thus, it is not surprising that a period of soul-searching has commenced in Tokyo, a reexamination of future possibilities. The imbalance between economic power and political impotence has never seemed greater. Even in military terms, Japan is weaker, quantitatively at least, than all of its neighbors, including the two Koreas and Taiwan, not to mention the Soviet Union and the PRC. Nor is there any evidence to suggest that the morale of the Japanese defense forces is high. Thus, in the event of a serious dispute with any of these states, from what degree of strength could Japan bargain? Can economic power alone be turned into a successful negotiatory weapon, and with whom? The vulnerabilities of economic power as an international instrument seem greater to many Japanese as a result of the events of the last several years.

To re-examine basic policies, however, is not necessarily to change them in some dramatic fashion. The probability is that Japan will continue to opt for the fourth alternative, that of special ties with the United States, albeit with some increase in what might be termed Gaullist propensities. This will not be done with great joy or ease of mind, but primarily because the risks or infeasibilities of all major alternatives are too apparent. There are several critical variables, however, the outcome of which could have a substantial influence in either supporting or undermining this probability.

On the international front, the continued absence of a perceived threat from another state or coalition of states, and the absence also of any significant change in the current political balance within Asia, especially Northeast Asia, are of vital importance. So too is the capacity of the United States to regain a greater measure of credibility as guarantor and ally. In this connection, the thesis that American support for Japan *alone* will suffice if properly demonstrated is fallacious. Japan will insist upon being an Asian as well as an international state, one deeply concerned with and interrelated to developments within Asia. To this matter, we shall return later. On the domestic scene, the major and probably interrelated variables are the capacity of the moderates to remain in power, whether through the LDP alone or in some coalition, and the success of Japan's economic game plan for the future.

Certain outcomes with respect to these variables could advance Japanese foreign policy alternatives other than that just outlined. For example, the combination of a serious, perceived threat and continued low American credibility would certainly give added impetus to Gaullism, with or without a nuclear program. But it is also conceivable that the course of events might lead to a serious polarization within the nation between "Pan-Asian pacifists" and "Gaullists," resulting in Japan's immobilization. Under such circumstances, Japan's ultimate course might be determined by a combination of economic developments and the political reactions of the major Asian-Pacific powers to the internal struggle.

Thus, although Japan's current foreign policy course has short-term promise, the state of the world, especially the Asian international situation, is so troubled and unstable that some substantial modification seems probable over the next decade.

China

The People's Republic of China, now in its third decade, presents a picture of political transition and uncertainty. This massive nation is in the last stages of the Maoist era, and efforts are currently being made to insure a relatively smooth transition through "collective leadership," using the formula of bringing together the old, middle aged, and young, and in functional terms, uniting veteran party-administrative cadres with the military and mass representatives. The latter group represents the New Socialist Men and Women recruited via the model worker competitions, and from local factories or communes.

Will these major efforts succeed in providing China with political tranquility in the years immediately ahead? While no absolute answers can be given, the likelihood is that this important society will face recurrent instability during the next decade, with the primary question being whether that instability can be contained at elitist levels, as it was in the case of the Lin Piao incident, or whether it will spill over into the society at large, affecting productivity and the social order. The elements that have been hastily put together in recent years are too unintegrated, the political institutions too fragile, the wounds of recent factional struggles too fresh to warrant any other conclusion.

It would be a mistake, however, to base policies on the presumption of a political disintegration—or even a degree of sustained crisis sufficient to immobilize the PRC as a regional power of significance. More probable are periodic crises, possibly serious but not threatening to the survival of the nation, or of Communist rule. It should not be forgotten that China's new leaders have conducted a massive campaign to instill nationalist sentiments into their people—including their elites—and there seems little doubt that this campaign has had its effect. Moreover, the capacity of the state to move military forces to any rebellious quarter has greatly improved, making the warlordism of the past vastly more difficult. It is clear, however, that China will be governed by a new top group within a very few years—and the indications are that they will be a mixed civilian-military team, strongly China-oriented rather than internationalist in outlook, of varied but generally limited formal education, rich in revolutionary experience in some cases, but with a growing number of New Socialist Men who are presumably dedicated to Mao's vision of a revolutionary China, yet who will be forced to make major compromises in the name of necessity—as Mao himself has done.

As in the past, the economy will be a factor of critical importance in determining China's future course. Here, performance has been relatively good considering the enormous obstacles faced in recent decades. Nevertheless, China remains desperately poor, and even under optimal conditions, well-rounded modernization will take decades. The key remains in agriculture, as the leadership recognizes, and in this field, capital inputs must be greatly increased if the next stages of development are to be successfully achieved. In the industrial arena, successful progress requires the handling of a number of problems, among them the issues of relative centralization-decentralization, management, resource-manpower allocation, economic incentives, and research-development strategies. Naturally, political stability will be one vital factor in the success or failure of economic programs, as will be the question of whether serious errors in policy such as the Great Leap Forward can be avoided in the future. Military expenditures will also be of significance. A cautious optimism appears warranted, but the tasks remain prodigious ones.

If we assume that the magnitude of the internal challenges facing China on both the political and economic fronts is very great, does this not suggest the likelihood of a minimum risk foreign policy? In very general terms, the answer is affirmative. Clearly, China wants to avoid war with either the Soviet Union or the United States, and it is not likely to take actions that would provoke such a war. Nor is the PRC apt to engage its armies in direct military action beyond its own territories unless it feels its security immediately threatened. As we shall note, however, old fashioned aggression—the open movement of national armies across state boundaries—is not the principal means of expanding one's influence or even control in this era. The PRC gives every evidence of intending to display "a special interest" in Asia, an interest which some would insist will lead it toward a sustained effort to develop a buffer state system and create its own sphere of influence.

To explore this matter further requires a concise summary of the current Chinese view of the world. While official organs set this forth in a manner reflective of the strong ideological element that presently pervades Chinese politics, it also represents a pragmatic, highly nationalistic assessment geared to China's immediate policy goals.

For Peking, the world is currently divided into three unequal parts—the superpowers, the Second Intermediate Zone, and the Third World. Toward the superpowers, China exhibits a hostility betokened by the epithets "imperialism" and "social imperialism," which it uses in defining the United States and the Soviet Union respectively. Assuring everyone that China will *never* seek hegemony, it charges America and Russia with being the twin enemies of all people.

Within this broad framework, certain distinctions have been articulated, and tactics have also been altered from time to time. The attack on the Soviet Union currently remains at a higher decibel rate than that on the United States. Under Mao, Peking has not only written Moscow out of the Socialist world, but has denounced the Russians for a long series of crimes against mankind, bringing this campaign home via school texts, study groups, and all other means. In the most critical sense, the Soviet Union is regarded as the foremost enemy because it is "a rising power"—whereas the United States is a "declining force," its peak passed.

Recently, Peking has launched with renewed vigor an effort to depict the primary threat of the Soviet Union as lying in the West, not in Asia. Chinese leaders have announced that conflict between the United States and the Soviet Union is inevitable and signalled its primary locus as being in Europe. Simultaneously, Peking has strongly championed European unity against the Russian threat, supporting a strengthened NATO and a continued American military presence in Europe.

Do these policies carry over to Asia? Is the Soviet charge correct that Peking now supports "American imperialism" in Asia, and curries favor with any "reactionary force" that repeats anti-Soviet statements? Setting aside the form in which Russian polemics are expressed, the facts appear to be more complex than in the case of Europe. China's balance of power foreign policies are clearly dependent in some degree upon the fashioning of a united front against the Soviets, in Asia as well as on a global scale. Thus, an American presence in this region, strategic as well as economic and political, is essential. So is a Chinese relation with a range of non-Communist Asian societies that is competitive with that of the Soviet Union (as well as the United States and others).

At the same time, it is now clear that Peking wants a *selective* not a universal

American presence in Asia, and in general, China's interests lie in seeing the United States play a temporary role in regions where the Chinese cannot currently have a strategic reach. Thus, security relations between the United States and Japan, and also between the United States and the Philippines are desirable at this point. Concerning continental Southeast Asia, however, the PRC attitude is equivocal at the very least, with few indications that Peking regards Washington as a necessary element. Moreover, the Chinese Communist leaders naturally want American ties with Taiwan drastically altered and Peking has made it unmistakably clear that an American presence is not desired in Korea.

Indeed, since the Indochina debacle, Chinese policy toward the Korean issue has hardened perceptibly, with the current commitment to Kim Il-s̃ong being very strong. The joint communiqué of April 26, 1975, issued at the close of Kim's visit to Peking, proclaiming that "completely identical views" had been achieved on all questions discussed, asserted that the DPRK was "the sole legal sovereign state of the Korean nation," fully underwrote Kim's reunification formula and demanded the removal of all U.S. troops from Korea. In this communiqué and in subsequent pronouncements on the Korean issue, moreover, Peking clearly signalled that it is prepared to treat the Korean and Taiwan issues as demanding similar solutions.

As noted previously, even with respect to Japan, the PRC has left an alternate door open for possible future use. The joint communiqué of May 1975 signed with Japanese Socialist party leaders, not only condemned both Soviet and American policies in Asia in very sharp tones, but expressed the "admiration" of the PRC for the "just struggle conducted by the JSP, together with the people of Japan" for the abrogation of the Mutual Security Treaty, the dismantlement of military bases *and* the recovery of the northern territories.

In essence, the People's Republic of China currently finds it advantageous to ride two horses in East Asia. One horse might be labelled "independence," and trends in the direction of a separate and hopefully dominant position for China in this, the region of its primary presence and power. Like other major states enroute to prominence, the PRC cannot avoid thinking in terms of a sphere of influence and a buffer state system, however much it may deny any hegemonic ambitions. Within the region, it would prefer small, non-aggregated units and a minimal presence of other major powers. In the near term, however, China needs an American presence in East Asia, given her multiple weaknesses. Thus, the other horse is "united front," and moves in the direction of limited détente with Washington and select other non-Communist forces in the region.

Before exploring this matter further, and the other available alternatives for China in dealing with the Superpowers, let us examine the policies currently in vogue with the "second intermediate zone," namely, the countries of western Europe and Japan, "capitalist states," but ones not necessarily destined to remain within the orbit of the two superpowers. Here, Chinese foreign policy underwent major changes in the years after the Sino-Soviet split. At an earlier point, only France was considered worthy of attention, primarily because De Gaulle was correctly perceived as a thorn in the American side. The other West European countries were regarded as "puppets of American imperialism," enemies to be scorned or challenged. Japan was also seen as a candidate for the American role in Asia, with the high risks of remilitarization emphasized. In recent times, however, the nationalism of both West Europe and Japan have been cultivated, firstly against the Soviet Union, secondarily against the United States. The perils of war, as noted above, are stressed, with the indication that China can be counted upon for at least moral support. China's meager current resources, however, limit its capacity to interact on a major scale with these societies, particularly those of West Europe.

Meanwhile, the PRC now defines itself as a member of the Third World and makes it abundantly clear that it hopes to influence that world, shaping its attitudes and goals even while helping it to become the critical political force in a balance of power world. China's Third World policies are not without their major elements of contradiction, to be sure. The Chinese seek to pose both as a leader of international revolutionary forces *and* as a nation-state dedicated to its own power and wealth, acutely conscious of its prestige and rights. Since the Third World is seen as a crucial element in China's balance of power strategy, moreover, "reactionary" as well as "progressive" elements of that world are cultivated at the state level to offset Soviet containment efforts. But efforts at the state-to-state level are not allowed to obliterate people to people and comrade to comrade relations. Peking, varying the mix, chooses to operate on each of these levels simultaneously. It is not without reason, therefore, that especially among the small states neighboring the PRC, China is seen not merely as an emerging society but as an omnipresent major power, capable of wielding its own carrot and stick policies with significant effect.

When Chinese capacities and propensities are matched, what basic alternatives confront the People's Republic in this troubled, transitional era? Let us commence by setting forth the alternatives in terms of Sino-Soviet relations, with the implications for Sino-American relations to be specified shortly. Four "pure" alternatives exist: conflict; a renewed alliance; continued competition and confrontation short of war; and a limited détente.

A Sino-Soviet war has been widely predicted in recent years, often as a result of hints or fears expressed by the major actors themselves. On balance, however, a full fledged war between these two neighboring giants seems improbable. While there is no absence of issues, nor of cultural-historic separatism—even racial hostility—it is difficult to conceive how such a conflict would possibly be other than a disaster for both parties. One can conceive of military assistance given by the Russians to a faction—national or regional—engaged in a life and death struggle, possibly even limited direct military intervention in this event. Indeed, this is the possibility that has most worried Mao and his adherents in recent years. For the Russians to conduct a massive assault, followed by occupation, however, would defy elemental common sense. Under far more propitious circumstances, the Japanese failed in such an endeavor, even with the aid of the Wang Ch'ing-wei government. A frontal attack by the Chinese upon the Soviet Union is far less conceivable, given the great disparity in military strength between these two nations—a disparity that is not diminishing.

Is it possible to return to the era of alliance? Here too, the probabilities seem very remote. Not only is great bitterness present among the leaders on both sides amidst rising nationalist tides, but major issues, impossible of resolution, exist and will survive into the foreseeable future. In the most general terms, moreover, the odds are adverse: the Soviet Union and the PRC are destined to live cheek by jowl with each other, buffer regions rapidly disappearing under the drive to populate Central Asia with Russians and Han (Chinese). Thus, the geopolitics of the Sino-Soviet relation are greatly different from those conducive to détente in Europe. Nor does the common commitment to communism neutralize the vital differences between the two countries with respect to timing of revolution, stage of development, and degree of power—differences leading directly to rival interpretations of national interest.

If the probabilities incline neither toward war nor alliance, which of the less dramatic remaining alternatives, confrontation short of war or limited détente, seem more likely? A strong case can, in fact, be made for each of these alternatives, and the odds are nearly even at present. In addition to the factors making for confrontations already noted, the indications are that both nations intend to play a major role in Asia, with the military power of each being augmented in the years immediately ahead. Nearly every year has brought new issues—from maritime jurisdiction to the future of Indochina. Nor can one anticipate that the old fears, suspicions and hatreds, fortified by the words and deeds of the last fifteen years, will be easily or quickly dissipated.

Yet it is clear that throughout the stormy period since 1959, some Chinese have questioned the wisdom of their nation's foreign policies toward the superpowers. They have argued that one does not need to love or even trust Russia in order to realize the great risks and costs of a high level of tension with this major state. The Soviets are both near and very credible. The United States is a distant, unpredictable state, limited in what it can or will do at this point. To sacrifice rapid military modernization with Russian support, to immobilize hundreds of thousands of Chinese troops on the 4,800-mile frontier, to undertake the expenses involved in a multipronged defense effort on a crash basis—all might be avoided by limited détente with the Soviet Union.

The logic of this argument increases in the aftermath of the American defeat in Indochina and the precipitous drop in American credibility. Limited détente between the PRC and the United States was not the result of convergence, either ideological or institutional, but came from a pragmatic decision on the part of Peking's leaders based upon the belief that the United States could play two roles: it could help China end its isolation and at the same time, serve as a counterweight to the Soviets in Asia. The former function has now been accomplished, and for the latter function, America's will may be lacking. Some accommodation to the Russians, therefore, would enable the improvement of state-to-state relations, reduction of troop concentrations, and increased trade— as well as a softening of the divisions that have recently wracked the Communist world.

The number and complexity of the variables make any firm prediction concerning future Sino-Soviet relations impossible, as noted earlier, especially as between the last two alternatives. It should never be forgotten, however, that American policies, including the extent to which the United States remains a credible Asian-Pacific power, constitute one of the critical variables.

Alternative Chinese policies with respect to the Second Intermediate Zone are more easily assessed. In general terms, Japan is of much greater import to China than West Europe, politically and strategically as well as economically. In recent years, as has been indicated, China has been very successful in its primary objectives with respect to Japan: to contain that nation strategically and to move it closer to the PRC via economic, cultural, and political ties. Japan's political ties at present are primarily with the United States and China, relations with most other neighbors being minimal and troubled. Economic intercourse with the PRC has increased, with Japan currently accounting for 24 percent of China's total trade. Cultural relations have also advanced, some with strong political connotations.

For Peking, however, an element of risk exists in relations with Japan, and also some uncertainties. Difficulties have emerged in securing ratification by the Japanese Diet of the Sino-Japanese Treaty of Peace and Amity, largely because Chinese leaders insist that the treaty must contain an antihegemony clause, thereby edging Japan further toward an anti-Soviet stance. These difficulties may be overcome, but it is clear that Peking can appear very heavy handed on occasion in dealing with the Japanese, leading to a deepening concern in various quarters that it is prepared to interfere sharply in Japanese internal affairs when its interests are involved.

Chinese affections also seem fickle on occasion. After an earlier period of hostility to LDP spokesmen and alignment with the Japanese Left, Peking came to the decision that a limited future lay with that course. Consequently, a cultivation of the conservatives followed, with the Left generally given short shrift. This general pattern may still prevail, but the pro-PRC Japan Socialist party recently received a warm reception as noted above, and meanwhile, pressure has been greatly increased upon the LDP in an effort to influence its policies, with the Chinese not hesitating to pay homage to their "friends" within the party and slight their "enemies," thereby making themselves a growing issue in LDP factional politics.

From a Chinese perspective, is cooperation or competition more likely to prevail in Sino-Japanese relations? Tightly knit cooperation of the type that would approximate an alliance is most improbable. Despite a strong potential for economic interaction, these two societies are significantly different and growing more so. China cannot provide Japan with credible security guarantees, now or for the conceivable future. Politically, the gap between Chinese authoritarianism and Japanese openness remains huge. In cultural terms, "socialist realism" has little to offer to an avant-garde society, one thriving upon intellectual diversity. Finally, the PRC in its present stage is not geared to alliance with another major society—any major society.

Hostility, on the other hand, will be avoided if possible. China does not want to see a situation develop that might be exploited by a rival, especially the Soviet Union. Undoubtedly, in the long run, Peking would like to see a situation whereby Japan was essentially an Asian-centered nation, with Asia as a whole increasingly a Chinese sphere of influence. In this fashion, the tables of the 1930s would be turned, with China, not Japan, at the helm of a powerful new pan-Asian movement.

Can this be accomplished by ties with the Japanese conservatives or at some juncture, will another turn to the Japanese Left be required—and in line with Japanese political trends? Clearly, this constitutes a dilemma for the Chinese leaders. Decisions relate in part to Sino-American relations, in part to trends within the major Japanese parties, notably the LDP. The Japanese Communists currently represent a serious problem, being vigorously anti-Mao, but the Socialists are almost embarrassingly available, and the Kōmeitō can also be wooed. Thus, Peking has the option—with risks—of closer identification with "friendlies" of the Left, and at some point, if their electoral chances look promising, this is very likely. Indeed, as we have seen, recent feints in this direction have been made, whether to demonstrate their pique at the United States, to put pressure on the LDP, or as an indication of a more fundamental shift in policy.

In sum, Sino-Japanese relations will in all probability contain elements of both cooperation and competition in the years immediately ahead. The former will come primarily in the form of a mutually beneficial economic interaction; the latter as a product of the profound diversities earlier signalled, including the different type of Asia—and world—to which each nation is dedicated.

China's interaction with West Europe—indeed, with East Europe as well—is largely psychological and political, although economic relations are growing. It is clear that Peking hopes to keep the European front a troubled one for Moscow. "The world is in great disorder," the Chinese assert, with both conviction and hope. The suspicion cannot be erased that Peking would be overjoyed to see the cold war renewed, or even to witness a major conflict in the West, both to provide a further alleviation of pressure upon China and greater opportunities for expanded Chinese influence in Asia. Peking's impact upon Europe, however, is likely to be marginal, and Chinese objectives fairly transparent to the nations directly involved there.

In the Third World also, China is far from subtle at present. Here, successes have been substantial, however. On many issues, China is able to mesh its own interests with those of various "emerging" states. In certain respects, the PRC is entirely credible as a developing society and this lies at the root of some of the problems in its relationships with similar states. China is able to offer only limited concrete assistance, economic or military. At the same time, the closer the geographic proximity to the PRC, the more the image of China as an emerging nation becomes blurred with that of China, the major power.

In Asia, moreover, China does little to discourage the latter image. It is true that Chinese leaders constantly vow with emotion that the People's Republic will *never* seek hegemony outside its borders. At the same time, the slogan oft repeated internally is the same as that governing Japan in the decades after the Meiji Restoration, "A rich country, a powerful soldiery." Thus, most Southeast Asian countries retain private reservations about Peking even as the post-Vietnam climate moves them toward "normalization" of diplomatic relations in the hope that the dragon can be restrained.

As we have already indicated, the signs increasingly point to the fact that China intends to be a regional power of significance, its protestations notwithstanding. In South Asia, the PRC has viewed India as a foil for the Soviet policy of containment in the recent past. Instead of seeking to loosen Indian-Soviet ties, Peking has largely ignored New Delhi's interest in rapprochement to date, although the recent exchange of Ambassadors may augur the beginnings of a more subtle policy. Nevertheless, at this point, the PRC continues to give strong support to Pakistan, and seeks to cultivate the various small states on the Indian border. In the past, at least, this has been because Peking views Mrs. Gandhi's regime as unstable and hopes at some point to find the Indian political climate a more compatible one. In part also, China cannot bring itself to fear India, despite the latter's victory in the Bangladesh War and its nuclear program.

In Southeast Asia as in South Asia, the Chinese profess primary concern about Soviet expansion. Yet, the problems of the immediate future may revolve more around the deeply divided indigenous Communist movements and regimes of the area. Will Hanoi continue to seek its own hegemony over Indochina, and what will be Peking's response? Logically, the Chinese should not be pleased with any large political unit or bloc emerging in this region, whether it flies Communist banners or not. Hence, it might be expected to aid those forces within Indochina seeking to maintain an independence from the North Vietnamese. There is some preliminary indication, indeed, that this is precisely Chinese policy with respect to states as Cambodia—with the Soviets continuing to view Hanoi as important in containment of China.

In this region, however, the Chinese have some very powerful advantages. None of the Southeast Asian nations, singly or collectively, are likely to be able to match the PRC in military strength or political capacity. The Russians are very distant and very foreign. If the United States plays a relatively low posture role, as is now likely, China's opportunities for greater influence are increased.

In sum, Chinese foreign policy in the years immediately ahead, strongly conditioned by internal developments, is likely to display two somewhat different aspects; on the broad international stage, the PRC will play the role of weak, emerging state, seeking to align itself with the new global majority, thereby substituting political strength for economic and strategic weakness. At the same time, in Asia, taking advantage of its natural assets and the handicaps of potential competitors, China will mount a sustained campaign to increase its influence. Under whatever label, this campaign will represent an effort to establish a buffer state system or sphere of influence not dramatically different from that which other major nations enroute to power have sought. To achieve this goal, Peking will continue to use a mixture of state-to-state, people-to-people, and comrade-to-comrade relations, with the mixture being changed periodically, depending upon circumstances. In both of these policies, the international and the regional, the elements of tradition, nationalism and communism—Chinese style, will remain the interactive forces shaping Chinese foreign policy. If the Chinese leaders are successful, the PRC will combine a growing global presence with enhanced regional power.

India

India, long labeled "the world's largest democracy," is currently in the throes of a political crisis many would consider the most serious since the recovery of independence. Does political openness have a future in India? At this time, no firm answer can be given, but the prospects cannot be considered encouraging. Prime Minister Gandhi's use of her emergency powers to crack down on political opponents and restrict civil liberties is not entirely without antecedents. On occasion, the government has used similar powers to take over state governments. In scale and scope, however, the action does set a precedent, one available for the future even if the old measure of freedom should ultimately be restored, the prospects for which currently seem slim.

Mrs. Gandhi's rationalization for her stringent policies was that "a deep and widespread conspiracy" against her government was underway. Setting aside the hyperbole, she had a point. As in many new states, the line between parliamentarism and taking to the streets has frequently been breached by the government's opponents, and in India, the distinguished Gandhian tradition of nonviolent resistance was recently used with growing effect. Opponents were also winning state elections, finding a mixture of tactics effective.

The fundamental causes for the present crisis, however, go much deeper than the immediate challenges issued to the prime minister from the courts and her political rivals. Once again, we are confronted with a nation beset by multiple problems, the product in considerable degree of the relatively early stages of nation-building and economic development characterizing this society. The experiment with political openness has naturally stemmed from the British legacy, with the effort to adapt British political institutions and values to the needs and nature of Indian society. A major asset has been the strong commitment of a preponderate majority of the elite to the democratic way. Even the Indian Communists, particularly the CPI (Communist party of India), have been strongly influenced by their British training, setting them apart from most Asian Communist movements.

In recent years, however, the careful observer could discern the emergence of a new type of leader from within the Congress party itself, especially at state levels. As a "pure type," he can be described as coming from the provincial town rather than the capital; less well educated than his predecessors, and having no direct contact with the British educational or political system; less committed to parliamentarism and more concerned with action—social, economic, and political. It would be a mistake to project this type of leader forward in a dogmatic fashion as the coming generation of top Congress figures. The future of the party—and the nation—is likely to be considerably more complex. Nevertheless, such younger elements have been emerging, many of them heavily dependent upon Mrs. Gandhi's favors—but possibly exerting some influence upon her in exchange.

The Congress party, it must be remembered, is still a movement in many respects, one seeking to represent the whole of India—reflective of its earlier role as spokesman for the drive toward independence. Thus, heterogeneity and contradiction abound. Radical in the cities, conservative in the countryside, Congress faces the perennial problem of bringing and holding together a vast, diverse population. To do so, it has developed many images, with the danger always that of falling between various stools. Mrs. Gandhi herself epitomizes the problem. Like her father, a consummate politician in many respects, she has also been a mediocre economist. Thus, it has been easy to interact with the temptations that democracy itself advances: extravagant and unobtainable promises are made to win elections, followed by less than satisfactory policies. In recent years, India's mixed economy has been badly mixed from every vantage point. The public sector has been mismanaged by a bureaucracy that is both inefficient and subject to various types of corruption. The private sector has been stunted by governmental policies, and partly as a result has developed its own forms of mismanagement and dependency. In the agrarian sector, urgently needed reforms have been minimized or ignored, reflective of the Congress party's connections with the rural affluent classes. Indeed, Mrs. Gandhi's recent spurt of populist promises and measures in an effort to gain mass support are the clearest possible indication of her own recognition of past deficiencies. It remains to be seen, however, whether a new path can be established and sustained.

If it is too early to predict India's precise political path of the future, one reason lies in the multiple weaknesses of elements that might succeed the

Congress. Looking first at the political parties, the forces of the "Left" remain badly divided, testimony to Mrs. Gandhi's skill on this front. Having earlier humbled the "right-wing" forces of her own party, and established herself as leader of the Congress "Left," she proceeded to forge an alliance with the CPI, the most moderate of India's Marxist parties. At the same time, she did not hesitate to use a combination of force and political maneuvers against the CPI-M (Communist party of India-Marxist) and the Naxalites to keep them under control. None of these parties today is a truly national force, nor do current leaders and policies augur well for that prospect. The CPI seems bound to Mrs. Gandhi's authority, now more than ever. If other Left elements seek to operate as an underground or in a quasi-legal fashion, they are likely to find government police and military power to be more formidable than in the past.

In some respects, the "Center" and "Right" in Indian politics (and like the term "Left" these are often dangerously misleading appellations) had recaptured a considerable political momentum prior to the recent crackdown. Playing upon a variety of sentiments and causes, these forces were capitalizing upon governmental weaknesses and the sentiments of significant numbers of citizens. Localism and nativistic proclivities; the corruption and officiousness of bureaucrats and politicians; and unrest in such socio-economic classes as the small businessmen and petty agrarian proprietors stemming from current policies—all of these and many other issues have been grist for the oppositionists' mill.

Here too, there have been strong elements of contradiction and paradox. The disabilities of the "Right" do not stop with confusion over policies. Nationally known leaders—particularly of the Old Congress—are now advanced in age, lacking in the vigor that is demanded in trying times. Nor can it be said that any of the forces on the moderate side of the Indian political spectrum has a truly national reach in the fashion of the Congress. They have—or had—some powerful enclaves of strength, including certain regions and metropolitan centers of special importance, but—having had to operate under the shadow of the dominant branch of the Congress party—an all-India image has escaped them. And now they must face further handicaps given the sharply restrictive measures that have been put into effect. With some of the leaders imprisoned, their press confiscated or censored, and their rallies prohibited, they can neither retain their organization nor their clientele easily.

The present crisis also reveals the fact that the Indian masses remain on the political peripheries, not yet mobilized by any political party or cause, at least on a significant, sustained basis. Prime Minister Gandhi's gamble is that she can once again swing the masses to her immediate support, as was the case after India's victory in the Bangladesh War, this time by combining repression and populism. In the meantime, Indian politics continues to be a contest of elites, with the average citizen showing limited concern over civil liberties and responding far more readily to any economic or social measures that might benefit him. In that setting, the advantages of Mrs. Gandhi and her Congress party appear formidable, now and for the near future at least.

However, could a force external to the parties challenge Congress and its leader? The bureaucracy, of course, constitutes a special type of challenge. Its power is immense, and without question, its capacity to sabotage or ignore programs will remain high. But no bureaucracy seizes power—it only wields power in varying degree, depending upon the capacities and instincts of the prime governors.

What of the military? The traditions of the Indian military are strongly against political intervention, reflective both of the low esteem in which the armed forces have generally been held and the British traditions upon which they were nurtured. However, one can envisage a scenario in which military rule might become a reality: repeated political crises requiring police and military intervention; a general disillusionment with civilian politics and the current leadership; and finally, the spector of a serious breakdown of national unity, or the threat of some "extremist" victory. While this scenario certainly cannot be ruled out, it does not seem on the immediate horizon.

The probabilities are that Mrs. Gandhi and the Congress—or more accurately, her branch of the Congress—will continue to hold power in India, whatever the precise character of that government. This prediction could be overturned, however, by one of several posssibilities: the passing of Mrs. Gandhi herself; disorders so serious as to require repeated police-military intervention, leading to a general breakdown of order, and the advent either of military rule or a change in civilian leadership; the progressive weakening of the center, and the corresponding development of strong autonomous regional governments based upon cultural-linguistic and economic diversities. The latter possibility assumes an inability of the center either to govern effectively or to retain the primary allegiance of the critical elites that comprise this very heterogeneous people. It posits a reversal of the trends toward centralization, and the advent of regional power, even the possibility of "warlordism," Indian style.

Clearly, none of the above alternatives can be disregarded in a situation frought with uncertainties. The safest prediction is that India is destined to experience political instability in the period immediately ahead, because the present situation is too paradoxical to be extended into the indefinite future. We see at present a government based upon extensive constitutional guarantees and still insisting that its commitments to democracy and to the law are intact, taking "emergency" actions that point in the opposite direction. If Mrs. Gandhi were removed from the scene—and in all probability, this could occur only through illness or assassination—new forces engendering instability would be released, especially given the deep divisions within the Congress party itself at this point. In any case, this is a variable dependent upon chance or accident. We have already assessed the possibilities of a military *coup d'etat*. Strong regionalism has deep roots in India. Yet one should not underestimate the force of Indian nationalism, and the stout resistance that would be put up in a genuine secessionalist movement were to emerge.

Some of the above developments could easily cause a change in aspects of

Indian foreign policy. Mrs. Gandhi, for example, has put her personal imprimatur upon foreign relations, notably in her particular brand of anti-Americanism.
The disintegration of India as a unit, or even the substantial weakening of the
Center, moreover, could have serious repercussions on relations with both the
neighboring major powers and peripheral small states. To date, however, trends
have not substantially affected Indian foreign policies, and as long as Mrs.
Gandhi together with her alliance dominates Indian politics, that is likely to
remain the case.

Within the past decade, one of India's major objectives has been attained,
namely, the achievement of hegemony over the subcontinent. Today, it is
unrealistic to think in terms of a balance-of-power approach to the politics of
this region, whatever may have been the case earlier. The Bangladesh War served
as the final turning point. Pakistan at present is only another minor state on the
Indian border, totally incapable of matching India in military terms. Indeed, it is
now in the Indian interest to see that Pakistan does not further disintegrate,
since that could pose the Indians with new problems. It would almost certainly
mean the increase of Soviet power—directly or indirectly—and this has already
become a matter of growing concern, even within Mrs. Gandhi's circle. Thus,
while the Indian government resents any effort to strengthen Islamabad
militarily, it would like to see the status quo preserved here.

Similarly, India's current relations with the other states of the subcontinent
are generally satisfactory from an Indian standpoint, and no major changes are
desired. This does not mean that the reverse is true. The small nations
surrounding India feel varying degrees of resentment or apprehension concerning
the giant on their borders. None, however, can afford to ignore New Delhi with
respect to its own domestic as well as foreign policies. In truth, the Indians face
the same dilemma as that which confronted the British in their era of hegemony
in this region. In order to protect the Indian "heartland," it is necessary for New
Delhi to exercise some degree of control over developments on the peripheries.
British rulers did not necessarily want to intervene (and ultimately dominate) in
such areas as Afghanistan, Tibet, Ceylon, and the Himalayan states—but the
stake in India itself pushed them in this direction. Similarly, India cannot
tolerate the breakdown of order, or a hostile alignment on the part of
neighboring states. That is the lesson of Bangladesh and Sikkim. It is the reason
for the ultimate concern over Tibet, the factor instrumental in the deterioration
of Sino-Indian relations.

Given the volatile, changing nature of politics in most of the small states of
the subcontinent, and the uncertainties surrounding India itself, India's energies
in the arena of foreign policy are likely to be heavily occupied with regional
relations. Regional issues, however, automatically involve India in major power
relations as well. Despite the fact that nonalignment continues to be a symbol to
which homage is paid, India has not been nonaligned for some years. Indeed, the
close ties between India and the Soviet Union have influenced both domestic

and foreign policies. They have made more natural the coalition between the Left Congress and the Moscow-oriented CPI, the union upon which Mrs. Gandhi's power has rested and also the alliance establishing the general thrust of her economic policies.

Let it be said quickly that although some of the prime minister's key advisers have been Soviet-oriented, neither the government's economic policies nor its political ideology qualifies in Russian eyes as Socialist. Indeed, from time to time, various Russians have expressed private apprehensions about the thrust—or lack of thrust—of Gandhian policies. Nor has total harmony prevailed in this alliance on the international front. Indian sources reveal that only after some very tough talk did Mrs. Gandhi obtain full Soviet backing for Indian policies in the course of the Bangladesh War. Nevertheless, the Soviet-Indian relationship has been a vital one for New Delhi. Not only did it enable the Indians to intervene successfully in Bangladesh, but in more general terms, it has both underwritten the Indian drive for hegemony in the subcontinent and provided a decisive offsetting force to any Chinese threat.

All alliances today are less exclusive and all-encompassing than in the so-called cold war era, and that is true of this one as well. Moreover, as suggested earlier, with hegemony established and a situation thus basically favorable to India achieved, New Delhi would like to see relations with the other two major states of consequence to it improved. If the estrangement between India and the People's Republic of China could be ended, the relations with the United States bettered, the "overreliance" upon the Soviet Union could be ended, and hopefully, a general acceptance of the new order could also be obtained.

To date, however, this goal has fallen considerably short of achievement, and recent political developments may pose additional handicaps. The United States, as we shall later note, is not likely to regard South Asia as a region which in itself rates a high priority in terms of American vital interests. Thus, no substantial American commitment is in the offing, and the retreat from democracy—especially if it proves to be a long-range trend—will only strengthen present American inclinations. On the other hand, the United States has in essence accepted Indian hegemony over the subcontinent as a fact of international politics, and permanently abandoned its earlier efforts to assist in the creation of a political-military equilibrium between Pakistan and India.

For several years, meanwhile, New Delhi has hoped that Peking would see the wisdom of coming to a similar position, and shifting toward a policy of rapprochement. In some respects, indeed, it has been difficult to understand China's policies of continued hostility toward India. The opportunities exist for loosening the Soviet-Indian tie, or at least creating additional problems here. Nevertheless, China has seemed the least reconciled to the status quo in the South Asian subcontinent, and the most critical of Indian policies, domestic and foreign. Why?

Historically, the Chinese have held Indian military capacities in low esteem, and even the advent of India as a potential nuclear power has not altered that appraisal. Consequently, the element of fear is low. At the same time, Peking has regarded the overall political situation in South Asia as unstable, and destined to change—to India's disadvantage. Thus, it has seemingly preferred to await a more propitious time for new forms of political action, meanwhile castigating India at once as a Soviet puppet and an imperialist force, dangerous to all its small neighbors. From these attitudes and policies follow the present Chinese efforts to remain friendly and available to the small states of the region, hoping to provide an alternative or at least a neutralizing element in counterpoint to the Indian presence.

While the return of ambassadors to the two capitols may signal some shift in Indian-Chinese relations, New Delhi's quest for greater equidistance is not likely to produce any large dividends at this point, and the ties with the Soviet Union will continue to be close ones. India's primary concerns, moreover, will be regional even if it joins the nuclear club. Here, prediction concerning India's precise policies is difficult because of the many variables. The alternatives range from outright annexation as in the case of Sikkim to involvement of a more benign, but nonetheless important character such as providing economic and military assistance. Clearly, it behooves states important to India's security such as Nepal and Bangladesh to keep their own houses in order, and this could also be said to apply to Pakistan, Bhutan, and even Sri Lanka.

India's preoccupation with its internal problems and with regional relations will not preclude the possibility of a growing interest in those regions directly adjacent to South Asia. Already, New Delhi has turned to Iran both for economic and security reasons, and there are strong indications that Iran intends to be a regional force of significance in its own right. Potentially at least, India's interest in the Arab world will also increase as its energy needs and general financial requirements continue to expand. Similar factors could stimulate a growing interest in Southeast Asia. Burma has always been of concern since it represents a potential security problem. Naga dissidents from India's northeast frontier have been trained in small numbers in China. A more general Chinese threat—possibly expressed through such forces as the Burmese White Flag Communists—has also concerned the Indians in the past. India's identification with North Vietnam is not unrelated to the quest for a power balance, and fits rather naturally with the Soviet ties. Increased economic relations with non-Communist Southeast Asia could be of substantial benefit, given the resources of this region. Closer political ties might follow. Nothing approaching Indian leadership is likely to ensue in this region, however.

Japan also represents a potential resource of importance to Indian development. To date, however, this resource has been underutilized, largely because of Indian economic policies. Japan remains very foreign to the Indian elite, reflective of the tremendous cultural and developmental barriers that separate various parts of Asia. Changes in Indian policy could make an economic relationship of steadily increasing magnitude possible, and that might provide New Delhi with a dynamic source other than the Soviet Union in India's drive for economic development in the coming decades.

With hegemony in South Asia attained, economic development becomes critical, not least because upon success or failure hinges the Indian capacity to hold to its foreign policy gains. Logically, India should be a primary booster of truly international approaches to the basic issues of food, population, and resource management that cut across ideological and developmental lines. It should provide maximum cooperation with multilateral approaches as the most feasible method of reducing dependency upon any single power and encourage nations like the United States in continued bilateral assistance. Whether internal politics—and capacities—will permit the development of the requisite attitudes and policies attuned to these ends remains a critical—perhaps the most critical—variable in India's future.

In sum, India is not destined to be a major international power, irrespective of its ultimate decision regarding nuclear weapons. Its internal fragility, plus the tremendous challenges involved in keeping its immediate regional relations under control will continue to shape the priorities of Indian foreign policy. Its very regional concerns, however, dictate the necessity of an intricate set of relations with the major powers, especially Russia and China. As we have noted, the ties with the Soviet Union will remain paramount, particularly given the inabilities of the PRC to contribute in positive fashion to India's economic or security needs, and the improbability of any major shift in the American decision to regard South Asia as a region of secondary importance. In the former case, however, the initiatives lie with China, and a shift in Chinese policy would meet with a positive Indian response, since it would provide New Delhi with greater leverage and lessened dependence. Such a development is not totally out of the question in the post-Mao era, as has now been indicated. At the same time, it is by no means foreordained. Indian initiatives could provide greater diversity of external involvement in its economic development by encouraging Japanese and Western investments—but that hinges on political decisions that would reverse past practices.

If the broad outlines of Indian foreign policy appear set for the foreseeable future, the great, uncertain variable relates to India's own domestic stability. Should the Indian nation undergo a prolonged, severe set of economic-political crises or even some form of disintegration, its regional role would certainly be diminished, and its dependency upon an alliance with a powerful external force greatly heightened. Under present circumstances, that force could only be the Soviet Union—unless the political upheaval were to tilt the nation sharply toward "radicalism" or "moderation," thereby attracting the attention of the PRC or the U.S.

Indonesia

"The situation is critical—but it's not serious" was a comment often made semi-jocularly about Sukarno's Indonesia. It signified the fact that under Sukarno's reign, and particularly in his final decade, military adventurism dominated the scene with the economy increasingly stagnant, even retrogressive. Yet all predictions of Indonesia's imminent collapse floundered on the rocks of a heavily self-reliant peasant economy largely impervious to inflation, scarcities and other urban-centered ills.

Today, some observers would turn our opening remark around, asserting that while the situation is not critical, it is serious. To understand the implications of this latter statement, one must appreciate the dilemma that surrounds the economic and social policies of recent years. To move a stagnant economy, the new military leaders, who came to power following the abortive 1965 Communist coup, halted the emphasis upon grandiose expansionist policies abroad and concentrated upon internal development. Turning to the advanced industrial societies, and notably the United States and Japan, they sought foreign assistance in exploiting Indonesia's rich resources and utilizing its limitless labor market.

Economic growth has ensued, but the pattern has had familiar flaws. Much of the development has been urban-based and in particular, has centered upon Jakarta, the capital. Rural programs have generally been meager and inadequate. Meanwhile, population growth continues largely unchecked, with the rural overflow tending to pour into the towns and cities, creating ever more difficult social problems. A very high percentage of the indigenous capital, moreover, remains in the hands of Indonesians of Chinese ancestry, a small but affluent minority. The resentments thereby created boil over periodically in racial riots and restrictive legislation. To add to the catalogue of problems, corruption has steadily risen among the political-military elite in recent years, keeping pace with development. This fact, together with the disparities in income that have become ever more obvious, fuel a growing resentment. Its first manifestations have come in the form of student-intellectual protests, protests that caused sufficient concern in governmental circles to provoke retaliatory measures—and some new orientation. A tougher approach to foreign investments and a heightened nationalism followed the demonstrations during Prime Minister Tanaka's visit to Indonesia. Fundamental reforms relating to basic development plans, however, have not yet been undertaken.

Is Indonesia another country destined for rising political instability? Once again, prediction is very difficult, partly because as in the case of India, there is no necessary correlation between severe socioeconomic problems and the proclivities of this society for political change. If strongly authoritarian societies can contain political unrest even under the most adverse socioeconomic developments (and the history of both the USSR and the PRC show this to have been the case at times), quasi-authoritarian societies are not without their instruments of control too.

From what quarter might the present government expect a challenge sufficiently formidable to threaten it? The political parties are not likely candidates. At one point, to be sure, several of the parties had impressive grass-roots organizations, especially in Java. The PKI (Communist party of Indonesia) and two Islamic parties—Nadathul Ulama and Masjumi—penetrated deeply into the countryside as well as the urban areas, indicating the potentialities for mobilizing the masses. The aftermath of the 1965 coup, however, witnessed the bloody extermination of the Communists, with only a handful of leaders surviving, and they mainly in exile either in Peking or Moscow. There is no indication that the PKI has yet been resurrected in any meaningful fashion, despite the periodic warnings of government spokesmen. The old PNI (Nationalist party of Indonesia) being Sukarno's personal instrument, fell under similar, if less bloody disfavor. Toward the political Islamic elements, the government has shown a combination of begrudging respect, wariness, and opposition. Recognizing the potential importance of such groups, it has occasionally made concessions to the Moslems but maintained its guard against their political activities. Despite its strong reservations concerning political parties—or perhaps because of them—the military have formed their own political organization in a move both to compete with and to "coordinate" all political forces. In sum, there is no current indication that a serious challenge could be posed to the present government from any of the old political parties or their possible successors.

In several Asian nations, the students have served as catalysts for political change, notably South Korea and Thailand. Is this a possibility in Indonesia? As noted earlier, there can be little doubt that student circles are rife with unhappiness, testimony both to their general economic lot and political trends of which they strongly disapprove. Behind them, moreover, stand a number of well-known intellectuals and journalists, many of them formerly affiliated with the old PSI (Socialist party of Indonesia). While these groups represent a worrisome force, not least because they attract international attention, alone they can be easily controlled. Only if sizable elements of police and military were to join them, passively or actively, could they pose a grave threat.

Thus, if political change is to come, in all likelihood, it must involve elements within the military itself, if not as initiators, at least as supporters. It should be remembered that the Indonesian armed forces have never been fully united politically. Sukarno and even the Communists had their adherents within military ranks, some of them in high positions. Today a number of military men are unhappy with aspects of the current scene and once again they represent a wide range of ranks and stations. Suharto is not unaware of this situation, and increasingly he has operated without long-continued dependence upon any single individual or faction. By using various men and groups for a time, then relegating them to the outskirts of power, he has abetted a competition for his favors and kept any other individual from rivaling his position. In many respects, Suharto is a traditional Javanese ruler, as was Sukarno, mysticism and all.

If Suharto were to pass from the scene, a struggle for power might well ensue, but it seems likely that some military dominated coalition would again emerge, with the probability that a single individual within it would gradually gain primary power, as has been the case recurrently in Indonesian politics.

Thus, change is most likely to come from within the military, whatever the timing and the means. This does not necessarily preclude radical alterations, domestic and foreign, but at the moment these do not appear on the horizon. And one central fact must be kept in mind: unlike some of its neighbors, Indonesia can afford a fairly extensive developmental program, given the rich array of natural resources which it possesses. What is needed are the qualities of commitment, vigor, and a capacity to learn from past mistakes—the qualities that are at a premium in every society.

Against this background, what are the alternatives in Indonesian foreign policy likely to be considered in the years ahead? Whoever governs in Jakarta, Indonesia's primary concerns for the foreseeable future are likely to be regional ones. First and foremost, this elongated, heterogeneously populated nation is intimately connected with Southeast Asia, and developments there—especially in the Malay world—will have a decided influence upon it. Broadly speaking, regional policies pose three "pure" alternatives for the Indonesians: an effort to play a dominant role in Southeast Asia; a heavy reliance upon regional cooperation and reciprocal responsibilities through ASEAN (Association of Southeast Asian Nations) and similar groupings; or minimal regional ties and commitments, with primary attention devoted to domestic concerns.

Those familiar with the recent history of this region know that an activist policy by Indonesia is not without precedent. In the 1960s, prior to his overthrow, Sukarno was pursuing policies profoundly worrisome to his non-Communist neighbors. Not only was Jakarta engaged in a hot war with Kuala Lumpur and hostile relations with Singapore, it was also seeking to confront other states of the region via an alliance with Peking, an alliance that even had as one goal the development of a global union of newly emerging states which would challenge the Western-dominated United Nations.

In a great many ways, those days seem part of a distant past at this point. Nevertheless, one can envisage circumstances under which Indonesia might be sorely tempted to remount an activist approach within the region. Assume that Malay political control was threatened in Malaysia by a Chinese-led Communist movement, or even that this nation—culturally so close to Indonesia—suffered from a sustained political crisis. Assume also that some such event spilled over into Singapore, a Chinese city on Indonesia's doorstep. Under such circumstances, the possibility of calls for intervention would be high. At the same time, the risks of activist policies have been clearly implanted in the minds of the present generation of leaders, and they are not likely to be forgotten. In a broader sense, moreover, Southeast Asia is too divided politically and too evenly balanced militarily to guarantee any such policies' success. One must assume, therefore, that only under very dire circumstances would Indonesia take that route.

Currently Jakarta is attempting to make ASEAN an instrument of effective regional cooperation. Not only has it supported increased economic cooperation, but it has suggested political and security roles for ASEAN members as well. Without doubt, Indonesia would like to see a stronger regional force, one capable of turning Southeast Asia into a zone of peace and neutrality, and toward this end it is prepared to take certain initiatives and offer some leadership. The most optimistic supporters of regionalism, however, generally recognize that many obstacles lie in its path. First, the basic cleavage between the Communist and non-Communist states of the region remains to be bridged. Linkages are not inconceivable, particularly of an economic character, but given the intricate political configuration of the Communist elements themselves, including the preoccupation with Chinese and Soviet relations insofar as foreign policy is concerned, a close-knit unity seems unlikely.

There are the multiple problems within the non-Communist Southeast Asian states. The nation-building process is still unfolding throughout most of this region, with various racial and ethnic problems unresolved. Fragmented states, having problems of internal unity, are not normally good candidates for effective regionalism. Economic competition is at least as prominent an element marking this region as economic cooperation, and across national boundaries there is also a lengthy legacy of hostility.

The path toward Southeast Asian regionalism is thus likely to be slow and painful. One should be careful not to write the movement off, but merely to record that its effectiveness will be partial, as well be its membership. For enthusiasts, as some Indonesian leaders are, there will be periods of depression and resentment. And when all factors are considered, Indonesian foreign policy is most likely to comprise a mixture of the second and third alternatives. Together with the commitment to regionalism will be a continued sense of priority of Indonesian development. On some issues, this will make for friction as well as cooperation with neighbors.

Whatever the precise course of Indonesia's regional policies, Southeast Asia is not and cannot be self-sufficient. The major powers will be involved in one form or another and, thus, as the Indonesian leaders now recognize, policies toward these powers must be kept under constant review. This has not been an easy task. Let us look first at relations with the two major Communist states. Toward the PRC, Jakarta has adopted a very cool posture, and (with Singapore) will be the last to reestablish diplomatic ties with China. The reasons are not difficult to discern. First, Indonesia's present leaders firmly believe that the Chinese Communists were involved in the abortive coup that killed a number of top military leaders and came close to a success that might well have ended their lives also. They are well aware, moreover, of the continued presence of certain PKI leaders in Peking, and the Chinese support that is given them. Of equal importance, however, is the fact that Suharto and his associates are deeply concerned over the impact that a reestablishment of formal ties would have upon their own Chinese community. On this point—as well as upon the question of Communist party relations—they will be watching the results of Thai and Malaysian normalization closely. To date, their position has been "we can afford to wait."

Relations with the Soviet Union, while normal, remain relatively cool. Once again, the perceived needs have been minimal whereas the possible adverse impact has been carefully noted. As a result of past experience, Indonesian leaders do not have a strongly favorable impression of Soviet goods, military or civilian. They have found Japanese and Western products more satisfactory. There are also PKI exiles in Moscow, and their angry words against the Jakarta government are sometimes echoed in Soviet organs. Indonesian leaders, moreover, perceive that a Soviet presence of greater degree might accelerate a Sino-Soviet dispute in their immediate vicinity, a development much to be avoided.

Repeatedly, spokesmen for Indonesian foreign policy have insisted that their domestic anti-Communist policies do not preclude a normalization of relations with Communist states. Indeed, the recognition of North Korea and North Vietnam, undertaken in the Sukarno era, although put on the back burner, was never rescinded, and East Europe has been actively cultivated on occasion. However, the tilt away from the major Communist states in recent years is likely to continue for the near future at least.

The obstacles to improved relations with either China or the Soviet Union do not signify an absence of problems with Japan and the United States. In the initial drive to attract foreign capital, Indonesian authorities dealt with a range of investors. Certain Japanese firms who came into the scene were less well established and primarily interested in a quick profit. Some of the deals consummated were of limited advantage to Indonesia and in not a few cases, they were lubricated with money and gifts to officials. Corruption and a loss of national control gradually became issues of importance, particularly to the student-intellectual community, with Japan a major focus of attack. In the aftermath of the 1973 Tanaka visit, the Japanese government is now well aware of the antagonism aroused and some remedial efforts are underway. Here and elsewhere in Southeast Asia, however, Japanese economic power—as well as Japanese business methods and the general aloofness of the Japanese community—will continue to present problems for Tokyo. There is little indication, however, that these problems will be sufficient to interfere with Japanese economic primacy in the region as a whole.

Some of the same issues touch Indonesian-American relations, but in this case the central questions are political and strategic rather than economic. A few specific differences exist, such as the Indonesian position on control of the Malacca Straits and its attitude toward Middle East issues. The overarching question, however, relates to American credibility in the aftermath of the Indochina debacle. Indonesia, after Sukarno's overthrow, had consciously tilted toward the United States in political-security matters, providing training to the Khmer Republic forces, agreeing to the onerous assignment of serving on the ICC in Vietnam, and speaking out against Communist activities in Southeast Asia. The extent and nature of the American defeat in Indochina came as a major shock, and evoked some sharp words in Jakarta. "Who can trust the United States as an ally?" was a question here as elsewhere. A new testing of American intentions and capacities has gradually gotten underway, with President Suharto's trip to the United States in the summer of 1975 one part of this operation. If any advantage has come from the events of the recent past, it is an awareness that a greater degree of self-reliance is essential, and also, that the time to tackle serious problems is now.

In summary, Indonesia in all probability will be a regional power of rising significance in the years ahead, but it will not play the dominant role that India plays in South Asia. Neither Indonesian capacities nor the political configuration of Southeast Asia permit such a development. Jakarta will render active support to the growth of regionalism, but as we have noted, the emergence of meaningful regional institutions and policies will be slow and incomplete. Under certain circumstances, Indonesia might be caused to intervene in the affairs of its nearest neighbors, but this is not its present desire, the priorities upon internal development being primary ones.

The Indonesians recognize that any plan for making Southeast Asia a zone of peace and neutrality must have the active support of the major powers, and that in any case, this is not a self-sufficient region, one that can develop without the participation of external forces. It hopes that a broad equilibrium involving the United States, the Soviet Union, China, and Japan will ensue, one underwriting neutralization and foreclosing the hegemony of any single nation. Its current concerns in this connection are several: first, will the United States be willing and able to play its role in making possible an equilibrium; second, can China be contained in the region, or will its ascendency constitute the main trend in the years ahead.

The Indonesians cling to nonalignment as an official position, and there is little likelihood that Jakarta will enter into an alliance with any state external to the region. Neither national security nor other needs are likely to be served via this route. If the American presence in the region becomes more uncertain and minimal, Indonesia will undoubtedly clasp the cloak of nonalignment around it more firmly. In any case, its military strength is likely to grow, now that it recognizes the greater need for self-reliance. In the final analysis, however, it trusts that détente will work sufficiently well to permit major power agreements that advance the security and development of Southeast Asia. If that fails, its minimal desire is for a de facto balance-of-power among the major powers, one sufficiently distant not to involve Indonesia directly, but sufficiently close to prevent the hegemony of any single power, with Indonesia's current fear being China.

Soviet Union

Like the United States, the Soviet Union faces in two directions. In the decades immediately after World War II, its western front commanded primary attention. Politics, economics—above all—security dictated that Soviet foreign policy direct its priorities toward Europe. In recent years however, the Russians have increasingly turned their attention to Asia, and it is safe to predict that the importance of the Soviet eastern front will continue to rise as the twentieth century moves toward its close. The Soviet Union intends to be a Pacific-Asian as well as a Western power. The premium upon the development of Central Asia and Siberia testifies clearly to that fact, as do the plans for expanding Russia's Far Eastern military, naval and air strength. Can this be reconciled with the interests and goals of the other major powers, and particularly the People's Republic of China?

Once again, it is important to examine the Soviet domestic scene briefly so as to place foreign policies in perspective. On the surface at least, the Soviet Union appears to be a more stable society today in political terms than any of the states thus far discussed. Undoubtedly, certain issues produce divisions within Russian leadership, and the removal of important figures from power continues. Nevertheless, Brezhnev not only seems reasonably secure, but more importantly, a sufficient consensus regarding policies appears to exist so that a transition to a new leadership need not be fraught with great trauma. Some would argue that the Soviet Union in its own way is achieving constitutionalism, with succession and other political events increasingly institutionalized.

This may be too sanguine a view of contemporary Russian politics. Serious reverses, whether on the home front or in the realm of international relations, might well produce or exacerbate cleavages at the top. A Communist system is generally able to obscure its internal divisions until a veritable explosion occurs. Frequently, that explosion has been building up over a considerable period of time, and often it centers around an issue difficult to reconcile or resolve, of which there are no small number in the Soviet Union. In broader terms, moreover, Russia today is a more porous society than in the past, subject to growing influences from abroad. Comparisons are thus possible. This abets the rise of consumer pressures which, together with more specialized interest groups, appear to be of increased importance.

In summary, the Soviet Union manifests certain signs of stability lacking in the other major Communist society with which we are concerned, China. Russian institutions appear more deeply implanted, and political processes more regularized, in part a product of the fact that the Russian revolution is now nearly six decades in the past. These signs may be illusory but in any case the passing of Brezhnev from the political scene will probably not make a significant difference in the Pacific-Asian policies of the Soviet Union.

Given the extensive interests of the Russians in Asia, it is appropriate to examine Soviet policies and attitudes on a regional basis initially. To commence with the continental center is logical, moreover, because relations with China remain the critical determinant for policies elsewhere. From a Soviet perspective, the problem of China is that of a highly nationalistic, xenophobic leadership that has warped Marxism-Leninism into an instrument for Chinese power. Russian spokesmen insist that the initial break came largely because Mao demanded a Soviet-American confrontation, and would not countenance détente. The facts were probably considerably more complex, but there can be no doubt that in the late 1950s, Peking was enormously unhappy with what it regarded as Soviet weakness in the face of American "imperialism."

Whatever the precise origins of the dispute, a deep bitterness now pervades Sino-Soviet relations, evident both in the polemics and policies of each party. The Soviets are less tense regarding the China problem today than was the case a few years ago. This may be the product of their striking—and growing—military supremacy, and also their assumptions—correct or incorrect—concerning the prospects for China's internal evolution. Yet the issue of China is never far from Russian thoughts as leaders survey the long-term future. Here, history and ethnic consciousness intermingle with contemporary issues to induce a continuing uneasiness.

Moscow's optimal goal would no doubt be the reestablishment of relations with China approximating those of an earlier era. But the chances of this must seem very slim to those presently involved in decision-making, and a more modest goal is set forth privately: relations akin to those which the Soviet Union currently has with Yugoslavia. Presumably, this would mean "correct" and "friendly" relations between equals, with cultural and economic exchange growing, and a widening arena of agreement or cooperation on political matters. In a phrase, "limited détente" is the prime Soviet objective.

To obtain that objective, the Russians are currently pursuing a stick-and-carrot policy, as noted earlier. The stick is a sizable one, with nearly one-half a million men and some of the most modern Soviet weapons on the Chinese border. Nor have the Russians been prepared to make any concessions on boundary issues or other matters. It has been a "hang tough" policy at all points. At the same time, Moscow has signalled its interest in improving relations from time to time on a step-by-step, reciprocal basis. In fact, this is a policy similar to that pursued by the United States for some years, and it is quite possible that the Russians hope for a similar outcome.

What are the prospects? As noted previously, neither war nor alliance seem a likely development, but the odds with respect to conflict short of war versus limited détente are so even as to preclude confident prediction. Under present conditions, each side must bear substantial costs and risks, especially China. Yet the factors making for competition and hostility remain high, and may actually be increasing at this point. It is also clear that the Mao-Chou team have done everything possible to insure that the present policies of confrontation are continued after their departure.

Whatever the future, current Soviet policies in Asia are largely based upon the containment of China. Turning to Northeast Asia, we can observe that here the competition over Japan is intense and at this point inconclusive. A stalemate now exists. Improvements in Soviet-Japanese relations are blocked by the Russian refusal to make any concessions on the four northern islands, economic questions relating to Siberian development, and perennial controversies over fishing rights. In Japan, the Soviet Union is generally perceived as rigid and harsh, and Soviet specialists in turn see the Japanese as "anti-Russian." On the other hand, Peking may have overplayed its hand in insisting that its treaty of friendship with Japan contain an explicit antihegemony clause. Japan, as indicated earlier, does not want the tilt in its relations with the two major Communist states to be too pronounced.

North Korea also represents a problem for the Soviet Union. Since the late 1950s, Moscow's relations with P'yongyang, and more specifically with Kim Il-sŏng, have been troubled, and at times, hostile. It is doubtful that the Soviet Union would favor a Korea unified by Kim, partly because it distrusts the North Korean dictator and suspects that Peking can have the greater influence upon him and his cohorts. At present, however, the Russians have retreated from an earlier stance that pointed toward the recognition of two Koreas, primarily one may presume, because Peking has accepted Kim's line, thereby giving him the necessary leverage to apply upon Moscow.

If there is no surge of enthusiasm in the Soviet Union for the unification of Korea, it may be assumed that a similar attitude applies to the China-Taiwan issue. Russia could not possibly want to see the PRC annex Taiwan at this point, given the relations between these two powers. It is unlikely that the Soviets will take an open stand on this matter, however, because their intent is to play for the next generation of Chinese leaders, or the following one, and any stand favorable to the independence of Taiwan might complicate the success of that endeavor. If Chiang Ching-kuo were to show any interest, nevertheless, it is conceivable that the Russians might toy with the issue.

Thus, in a survey of the Soviet position in Northeast Asia, two facts stand out: firstly, the Soviet Union is currently not doing so well in this region, its relations with all of the states indigenous to the area being either minimal or cool; secondly, the Russians favor the territorial status quo here, principally because no changes that are likely would be beneficial to them. Given their problems, and the importance of the region to them, the Russians can be expected to increase their military power in Northeast Asia, with Siberian bases being strengthened and the Pacific fleet being augmented. Political initiatives toward Japan could pay handsome dividends, but the Russian track record on this score is poor, and quite possibly, will remain so.

With respect to the Pacific region, the Soviets are not likely to challenge American superiority, but neither are they likely to permit this region to be a monopoly of American power. One can anticipate that the Russians will not only increase their military capacities but also insist upon sharing Pacific resources. In some degree at least, this places them in contention with both Japan and the United States, and in the longer time framework, with China too.

Peking is now loudly proclaiming to all who will listen that the Russians have their eyes fixed on yet another part of Asia, the southeast. The Chinese assertion is that with one superpower defeated and retreating, the other is seeking to take its place. Various Southeast Asian leaders have been warned not to let the tiger in the back door while forcing the wolf out the front. Unquestionably, the Russians would like to exercise an influence in Southeast Asia greater than that which they currently possess, partly to contain the Chinese in this resource-rich, strategically situated region. Limited progress has been made, however, and in truth, this region is of secondary importance to Moscow compared to both Northeast and South Asia.

What are the problems? First, the Russians are very foreign to the region, differing radically in culture and outlook. Here, as elsewhere in East Asia, the Chinese have an innate advantage which they have exploited to the utmost. Even with respect to the Communist movements of the region, the Russians have fared badly. In addition, Russian ventures of the past with such states as Burma and Indonesia have generally been failures, leaving a legacy of mistrust.

If the Russians are to succeed in containing China in Southeast Asia, they will have to act through surrogates in all probability, and the most promising candidate is Hanoi. Although relations with the North Vietnamese have not been intimate, the Russians were critical to the military success of the Vietnamese Communists, and they will continue to be of importance both in military and in economic terms. In all likelihood, Hanoi will seek to avoid undue dependence upon Moscow, and hope that she can play the Chinese and the Russians off against each other. Should serious problems with China emerge, however, whether over the control of Indochina or other issues, the Russians represent the most feasible counterweight. To a lesser extent, the same opportunities for the Soviet Union might apply under certain conditions with respect to Singapore and some other Southeast Asian states. On balance, however, the likelihood of an extensive Soviet presence in this region is limited, Chinese warnings notwithstanding.

In South Asia, the picture is very different. Here, as we have noted, the Soviet tie has been of vital importance to India. South Asia represents a region of risks for Russia, given the magnitude of the problems there and the political uncertainties. From a Soviet perspective, getting too deeply involved in the Indian morass could be both unrewarding and dangerous. Nevertheless, the dividends have been considerable to date, and the costs less than might have been anticipated. Moreover, the Russians on occasion have sought to make the limits of their commitment clear.

Soviet policies toward the other states of South Asia stem from the requirements of the Indian alliance. Moscow has generally not cultivated relations with Pakistan and the Pakistani remain wary of the Russians, particularly in light of close Soviet ties with Afghanistan. With respect to the other states of the region, the Russians generally have a low profile, although they have naturally been supportive of Bangladesh, and fairly active there.

South Asia forms an important element in Moscow's effort to contain Peking, and it is here that the Russians have enjoyed some of their most impressive successes. Given the volatility and uncertainties of the region, however, Soviet fortunes could change rapidly. Clearly, this is a region much too vast and heterogeneous to be manipulated by any external force. In recent years, moreover, Soviet-Indian ties have seemed to be weakening, as we have noted. New Delhi has shown signs of wanting a broader, and a more equal set of foreign relations. The recent Indian political crisis may make the Soviet connection more important to Mrs. Gandhi, and therefore strengthen the alliance, in the short run, at least, but much hinges upon what basic socio-economic policies are pursued. There is some evidence, for example, that in an effort to stimulate the economy, Mrs. Gandhi has recently adopted a more friendly attitude toward the private sector. Will this last—and will the Soviet model seem progressively less attractive?

It remains to speak briefly of one all-Asian policy emanating from the Soviet Union, namely, the proposal for an Asian security agreement. Here, the parallels with Soviet European policy are apparent. For some fifteen years, against great odds, the Russians doggedly advanced a similar proposal for Europe. Their efforts were finally crowned with success, as the Helsinki Conference of 1975 illustrates. Moscow can thus be expected to show a similar determination to continue its drive for an Asian security pact, although the demands in this respect have recently been muted. Understandably, this concept is very vague at present. When asked about the specifics, the Russians assert that these are to be developed by the Asian community as a whole. The reasons are clear: Moscow knows that Peking would assault any given proposal of a specific nature as made-in-Moscow and deliberately anti-Chinese.

Indeed, vagueness has not protected the Soviets from precisely these charges. Peking has made it abundantly clear that it regards the scheme as another Moscow-directed effort at the isolation of China. Most Asian states, consequently, have been reluctant to show great enthusiasm for the concept. Such is the influence of the Soviet Union, however, and the desire of Asian states to avoid offending either of the Communist giants, that a number of states have issued non-specific but generally approving statements, stressing their support for Soviet *objectives*, but carefully refraining from underwriting a conference or pact at this time. Privately, moreover, enthusiasm is extremely limited.

How should one summarize the position of the Soviet Union in Asia today, and the prospects for the short- and middle-term future? From a Soviet perspective, recent trends are decidedly mixed. On China, the pendulum swings between cautious optimism and considerable pessimism. Moscow's leaders hope that Mao is ultimately succeeded by "reasonable men," individuals who will put China back on the path of "correct Marxism-Leninism." They conjure up various scenarios whereby this can happen, and under certain circumstances they are undoubtedly prepared to help the process along. This, indeed, is the precise concern of the anti-Soviet faction today, as we have seen. But there is clearly no certainty that trends in Chinese politics will benefit the Soviet Union, and the contrary possibilities are at least equally strong. Thus, the containment policies, those involving both a stick and carrot, will continue.

The Soviet Union's regions of primary concern—apart from the continental center—are those of Northeast and South Asia, the Pacific and Southeast Asia being of secondary importance. In the Northeast, as we have seen, Soviet policies are not enjoying great success. In the competition with China, up to date, the Soviet Union is coming out second best in this region, with Japan the key target, but Korea also of importance. To compensate, the Russians are likely to increase their military strength here, although new political and economic initiatives are possible, since these could so clearly serve longer-range Russian interests.

In South Asia, the general situation is reversed. Here, Soviet policies have enjoyed considerable success up to date, and the Chinese have witnessed humiliating setbacks, particularly via the Bangladesh War. But this is now a highly uncertain region, one subject to huge problems, hence possible dramatic changes. Consequently, any major power that is deeply involved from the outside must watch events with considerable trepidation.

In Southeast Asia also, momentous events have occurred, including a major political-military defeat for the United States and the non-Communists. Each nation of the region is now seeking to take the new situation into account in adjusting its foreign policies. Generally, the gains have been scored by China, and it cannot be denied that China's long-run advantages with respect to influence in this region are very considerable. A Soviet presence—and Soviet influence—hinge on the degree to which the states of the region want a counterweight to Peking, and find the Soviet Union suitable—or indispensable—for these purposes. Naturally, American policies are an important variable in this connection. Here, as we have noted, the nation of greatest importance is North Vietnam, and an intricate game is now unfolding throughout Indochina, one involving both major Communist powers as well as Hanoi, with its outcome extremely uncertain.

Two general observations are also in order. First, to a greater extent than at any point in the past—and much more so than China—the Soviet Union favors the status quo for Asia at present. This is not to say that it would be unhappy with the emergence of Soviet-oriented Communist movements or states. It is merely to record that Moscow sees few if any changes in the political landscape that are probable which would advance its own interests.

At the same time, the Soviet Union—having witnessed generally favorable trends for it in the West—now regards the Asian front, and most particularly its China problem, as of critical importance. Consequently, the Russians intend to become a stronger, more impressive *Asian* power. This goal will be underwritten first by placing a high premium upon the development of Siberia and Central Asia—Russia's vulnerable eastern frontiers. That development will include the type of expansion that has military implications, direct or indirect; the double-tracking of the Siberian railway; the emphasis upon new industries and an increased permanent population; and the augmentation of present military facilities. The Soviet Union thus looms up as a larger component in the Asian political scene, and this could place it in continued confrontation with a militantly nationalist China that considers Asia *its* proper sphere of influence. As we have emphasized, the costs of Sino-Soviet confrontation are such as to make accommodation attractive, but given current trends, it will not be easy. Moreover, expanded Soviet power might increase tension vis-à-vis Japan and the United States. In balancing off the respective goals and capacities of Russia and China in Asia as they relate to Japanese and American interests, China—not the Soviet Union—may pose the greater long-term challenge.

United States

Until recently, it would have seemed foolish even to raise the question of the political stability of the United States, and the related issue of American credibility in the world. Friend and foe alike regarded the United States as the richest, most powerful nation of the world, capable of exercising its influence or asserting its will at almost any point in the international scene. A portion of this judgment may still be valid, but a new phenomena can now be witnessed: all concerned nations through their leadership are raising questions about American political stability and the capacities of the United States as a global power. In general, the issues relate not to capacity but to will, and to such basic questions as whether the American nation can any longer act as a unified force, even when its vital interests are at stake.

In many respects the United States has been the most revolutionary society of our times, not in the sense of bloody seizures of power but as a result of a steadily accelerating process of socioeconomic change that has profoundly affected the living standards and life style, and hence the values and behavior of almost all Americans. This rolling, interconnected revolution has opened up a new world of exciting opportunities, but it has also bequeathed a series of fundamental problems. For example, it has loosened the consensus upon which, in the final analysis, democracy depends. It has opened or reopened such issues as these: centralization versus decentralization of power; the appropriate balance between authority and freedom—hence, the proper role of government as against that of the private sectors; and the priorities that should be accorded various domestic and foreign commitments.

In connection with the last issue, how to direct the American revolution into constructive channels and, at the same time, accept responsibilities in an international order constitutes the supreme challenge for the United States today. Can that challenge be met effectively? At this point, the answers being given vary. "Optimists" assert that a national consensus will shortly be regained, especially with relation to foreign policy. They assert that recent developments, including the Vietnam debacle, were essentially healthy because they have caused the United States to slough off unnecessary or undesirable international commitments, enabling it to focus on the truly crucial relationships. For the most part, such assertions come from those with Europocentric or "trilateral" tendencies, individuals who believe that the United States should confine its strategic commitments to the advanced, industrial world of West Europe and Japan. Thus, they see involvements such as that in Southeast Asia and most other parts of the world (Israel being normally granted an exemption due to domestic considerations) as not in the American interest.

"Pessimists" divide into various schools. In general, however, they project a higher level of political instability in the United States than in the past, in part, the product of economic and social problems to which there are no easy solutions. Confronted with grave internal problems, America—in their view—may well constrict its international role to a quite minimal one, even if its rational interests dictate otherwise. They doubt that a satisfactory consensus will be forthcoming, and they thus have a grave concern about the American will— regarding the issue of will, not that of capacity as the critical one. Nor do they necessarily agree that it will be sufficient to make America's primary commitments to the advanced world, or to purely regional concerns. Rejecting the concept of "global policeman," they nonetheless place a much higher premium than some upon the importance of linkages in the international realm.

Without predicting Armageddon, one can easily foresee difficult times ahead in the process of adjusting to continuing changes both in the domestic and international environments—particularly since many of those in the global arena will run counter to the values and policies of the United States. This is no time for a complacent optimism. Before seeking to venture any predictions concerning general American foreign policies toward Asia, let us examine alternative policies at the regional level.

The Pacific

The issues of the Pacific Ocean revolve primarily around two concerns: security and resources. Recently, a plebiscite involving the people of the northern Marianas was held, with an overwhelming majority voting for incorporation into the United States on the basis similar to Commonwealth status. Following this vote, the U.S. Senate accepted one portion of Micronesia as an integral part of the United States, with a status similar to Guam. Meanwhile, the future of the Carolines and Marshalls remains unclear, due partly to internal differences among the islanders. These regions, or portions thereof, may opt for independence—but with certain ties to the United States, at least for a stipulated period of time.

In any case, Washington can be expected to aim at the maintenance of its primacy in the Pacific, given the proximity of this region to American territories and the enormous wealth of the resources under Pacific waters. If a consensus exists in the United States today, it is to be seen on the importance of the Pacific Ocean region to America. Granting this fact, however, will it be possible to retain American dominance here? Neither the Soviet Union nor the People's Republic of China consider the Pacific Ocean off-limits strategically. Currently, Peking is inhibited by virtue of the limits upon its military capacity—but certainly not by any doctrinal restraints. On the contrary, a commitment to the development of modern naval and air forces exists, and the most recent trends with respect to PRC defense expenditures are once again upward. Moreover, the campaign to annex Taiwan, whether successful or not, serves as a powerful stimulus for an expanding Pacific presence. Much of this lies in the future, however. The Pacific Ocean activities of the Soviet Union are of the present, and these can be expected to increase, as we have noted. While it is unlikely that the Soviet Union will seek fixed bases here, its augmented Siberian facilities are but one indication of the future thrust of Soviet policies.

Meanwhile, Japan will continue its march toward economic expansion, with the Pacific Ocean region one prime target. Already, the Japanese have regained much of their old economic supremacy here, and there is no indication that their efforts will slacken. In sum, the United States will probably remain dominant strategically in the Pacific Ocean as a whole, but it will be forced to share the region in increasing measure, militarily as well as economically.

Northeast Asia

It is in Northeast Asia, however, that the challenges to American policy seem more immediate and more serious. Here, economic, political, and strategic issues are intertwined in such a fashion as to make this region one of critical importance to all of the major powers. Viewing it from an American perspective, what are the alternatives? Central to the United States is its relationship with Japan. While this is widely regarded in America as a critical relation, it is not a noncontroversial one. One problem, perhaps more of the past than of the future, has been that of reconciling two dynamic economic systems which, while seemingly similar, are in fact quite different, especially with respect to governmental-business relations. Some earlier Japanese advantages which abetted astronomical American trade deficits with Japan may have disappeared or declined. There will always be a strong element of competition here, however, as well as sizable potentials for interaction. There are no guarantees against future crises on the economic front, especially if monetary, trade and investment policies suitable to this era cannot be devised on a multilateral basis.

Meanwhile, Washington looks at defense relations with Japan ambivalently. On the one hand, it acknowledges the security of Japan to be vital to its interests and those of the world with which it is affiliated. Moreover, it does not wish a shift toward Japanese Gaullism, nor any movement into nuclear armament. But there has also long been an undercurrent of American resentment that Japan bears no responsibility for regional security, even for countries vital to its own future. Nor has Tokyo had to bear the normal expenses of defense, costs that have strained the American economy.

Contradictions in American attitudes are not likely to disappear, but a concatenation of events will probably cause an ever greater premium to be placed upon elements of equality or reciprocity in the defense field. This could come about as a result of increased Japanese responsibility for defenses in neighboring seas and skies, combined with the transfer of all Japanese bases except naval repair-dock facilities to Japanese control, to be kept in a readiness status if necessary. At a minimum, American defensiveness concerning security relations with Japan—and other countries—will disappear, replaced by a new attitude that if these are not considered desirable by those involved, they can be abrogated.

An even larger issue confronts the United States, however, with its epicenter focused on Japan. As suggested earlier, some influential Americans espouse an enclave policy for Asia. They would confine American strategic commitments primarily or wholly to Japan, coupling this commitment to that of West Europe. Indeed, the more Europocentric elements of our society only regret that Japan cannot be moved physically into the Atlantic, preferring not to regard it as an Asian society at all.

The enclave policy has the advantage of reducing U.S. commitments, focusing upon regions admittedly vital to Washington, and in so doing concentrating upon some of the key issues of these times. Moreover, it may well accord more closely with current American attitudes and capacities than the policies of the recent past. The enclave concept, however, has one fatal weakness. It is unrealistic, and hence, if applied rigorously, it will fail.

This is not to say that Japanese-American-West European relations are unimportant or should not be given special attention. Some key issues that must be resolved *do* primarily concern these three parties, and progress in multilateralism on this front *is* important. To make this the exclusive American commitment or consider it the only important set of relations, however, or even to make a strong thrust in that direction would be counterproductive. This is apparent even when we consider the other triangle with which the U.S. must be concerned, that of Sino-United States-Soviet relations. But the problem with the enclave thesis is more serious. Japan is as much an Asian as an advanced industrial society. There is no legerdemain whereby this state can be made essentially an Atlantic nation. Its political requirements, its economic health, and above all, its security hinge at least as much—in some instances, more—upon developments in Asia as upon those in the West. Japan cannot ignore what happens in Korea or Taiwan, nor be oblivious to its relations with China or the Soviet Union—all near neighbors. Nor are developments in Southeast Asia of scant significance, given the huge Japanese economic stake there. A mere recital of these facts underlines the importance of accepting linkages, of having an *Asian* policy.

In passing, two issues critical to the future of this region and to major power relations have been mentioned, namely, Korea and Taiwan. What alternatives exist here for the United States? Regarding Korea, the starkest alternatives are those of withdrawal or continued commitment. The argument for withdrawal is that the United States has no vital interests involved in the Korean peninsula, that the risks of conflict here at some point in the future are high, and that we cannot and should not fight another war on the Asian continent. To these themes is added the thesis that given domestic trends in South Korea, the United States is put in the position of upholding an undemocratic political system, with the implications that there is little to choose between Seoul and P'yŏngyang at present.

Those favoring a continued commitment assert that to abandon the Republic of Korea after the Vietnam debacle would end American credibility in Asia and throughout the world, produce a major disequilibrium in East Asia, and particularly in Northeast Asia, and seriously affect Japan. Indeed, it is submitted, if Korea were to be forcefully unified under communism, the pressures upon Japan for either Gaullism or a pacifist-neutralist stance yielding to other major powers in the vicinity would be irresistible.

A careful study of Kim Il-sŏng's pronouncements and actions strongly suggested that he is now committed to a modified Vietnam approach which he entitles "peaceful unification." Every effort will be made to isolate South Korea from the United States and Japan while consolidating the North Korean position with China—and using this as leverage to obtain the most favorable possible treatment from the Soviet Union. Kim, encouraged by the Chinese, is now ardently seeking to establish a close relation with the "Third World," hoping to parlay this into victories at the United Nations and elsewhere. Meanwhile, a southern "revolutionary" movement will be seeded and fed from the North, labeled "a Liberation struggle by the Korean people," with the hope that the line between a civil and international war can be thoroughly blurred. Then, as in Vietnam, the North will both fuel and man the struggle. The risk lies in the likelihood that Kim may be tempted to use incidents to speed up the timetable since an insurrectionary process will be even slower and more difficult than in the case of Vietnam.

Under these circumstances, South Korea's future hinges both upon Seoul's domestic policies and the attitudes and actions of the major powers, especially the United States. Clearly, Pak Chung-hi has drawn his own lessons from Vietnam, the chief of which is that a weak government and a divided people become easy prey for a monolithic opponent. This together with growing uncertainty about Washington's credibility as an ally, have constituted two major factors in the restrictive measures taken recently in the South. Meanwhile, as we noted earlier, Kim has apparently scored a significant gain with Peking. The Chinese now appear to be strongly committed to the North Koreans, with the Russians more ambivalent—but feeling the pressure to cooperate. Japan, on the other hand, deeply concerned about the turn of events, is treating overtures from P'yŏngyang with caution while seeking to improve its rocky relations with Seoul.

Confronted with these developments, the United States has reiterated its commitment to the Republic of Korea in the aftermath of the Indochina defeat, and asserted that any potential aggressor should understand that in fulfilling that commitment, America does not rule out the use of tactical nuclear weapons. In this fashion, Washington sought to signal that it did not intend to be drawn into another protracted limited war, but that it could maintain its pledges if forced to do so without taking that route.

For the time being, this position has evoked only limited challenge from within the American political arena. Those inclined toward a relinquishment of all commitments to Korea realized that in the aftermath of Vietnam, the time was not ripe to push that view. With the passage of time, however, the issue of Korea has become more controversial. What are the alternatives? The withdrawal of all security commitments to Korea would remove the United States from strategic involvement on the continent of Asia, a position long advocated by a number of Americans. It would also eliminate the issue of military support for a government now anathema to many due to its repressive policies. However, such a policy would also have further adverse repercussions upon American credibility in Asia, potentially affecting the policies of friend and foe alike. Its impact upon Japan in particular would be severe, especially if the ultimate result were a unified Communist Korea, with unification coming via violent means. Other risks cannot be ignored, including the possibility of a nuclear South Korea. Certainly, at this point, it would be an act conducive to destabilization within Northeast Asia.

Another alternative would be to maintain the American military presence intact, thereby making it unequivocally clear to North Korea and to the big Communist powers that the United States had no intention of abandoning South Korea. Such a stance would certainly deter any overt military attack for the foreseeable future, since none of the Communists want to risk a conflict with the U.S. It would also go far toward reassuring Japan concerning American intentions in this region, and might encourage the Communists to engage in meaningful negotiations—both in terms of South-North talks, and broader major power discussions looking toward a peaceful resolution of the Korean problem. On the other hand, such a policy is likely to come under increasing attack from within the United States, with predictable political and strategic arguments being advanced. In some measure also, it is in variance from the thrust of the Guam Doctrine which placed a high premium upon American allies assuming the primary responsibility for their own defense.

In all probability, American policies toward Korea will continue along a path already sketched in recent months, one that represents neither total withdrawal nor a maintenance of the status quo. The military forces of South Korea, and particularly the air and sea forces, will be modernized in the course of the next few years, to guarantee that the Seoul government will not lack in the means to defend themselves against any threat from P'yŏngyang. American ground forces will be repositioned away from the front lines, and with the completion of the modernization process, largely or wholly withdrawn. However, the basic American commitment will be retained, and some air and sea forces will be present to give that commitment substance. From this vantage-point, various negotiations will be encouraged to test possible alterations in the positions of North Korea, the PRC and the Soviet Union.

To date, such explorations have not been hopeful. South-North talks are at an impasse, and the fault lies overwhelmingly with the North. In contradistinction to its domestic policies, the foreign policies of South Korea have recently been marked by realism and a considerable degree of sophistication, albeit, with limited success. The South has seen reunification as a distant possibility, and to be approached on a step-by-step basis, commencing with exchanges among divided families, moving to expanded cultural and economic relations, and achieving political dimensions only when some degree of trust has been established. In contrast, the North has insisted upon major military-political acts at the outset, acts clearly bearing little relation to the current state of affairs. Similarly, the South has indicated a willingness to enter into diplomatic relations with all states, including Communist states, and to accept the admission of both South and North Korea into the United Nations and other international bodies at this point, with no barrier to future unification. The North has condemned such a policy as a "two Koreas plot," and has prevented the South from normalizing its relations with the Communist states while trying to drive a wedge between Seoul and Washington and Tokyo.

As we have noted, recent PRC policies toward the Korean problem are far from encouraging. The Soviet Union is clearly less enthusiastic about Kim Il-sŏng at this point, and has engaged in some limited cultural contact with the South Koreans. Moscow remains inhibited, however, from moving very far in this direction because of possible repercussions within the Communist world. Meanwhile, North Korea gives evidence of fairly severe economic problems and a rising amount of domestic political intrigue. The chances seem reasonably good that in the years immediately ahead, the South will grow stronger vis-à-vis the North, at least in economic terms.

The United States must couple its commitments to South Korea with continued efforts to achieve some major power agreement on this thorny issue, the currently dismal prospects notwithstanding. American proposals should include the effort to get universal recognition of the existence of two de facto states; the importance of allowing these states international contacts on the widest possible scale, including United Nations representation; a definition of "peaceful unification" which would include strong strictures against the interference by either of the two existing states in the internal affairs of the other; and agreements concerning the thorny problem of arms transfers. It is particularly essential to have the closest consultations with Japan on the Korean problem, and to work toward joint policies.

Meanwhile, Washington should be in continuous discussion with Seoul, both with respect to these matters and concerning those domestic issues that affect our security ties. The importance of distinguishing between Communist subversives and democratic oppositionists lies partly in South Korea's image abroad, and not least of all, in the United States. The impact of repressive governmental policies in Korea upon public and Congressional attitudes is a cumulative matter, inhibiting to the type of relationship that must underwrite any firm commitments. Thus, it is more than merely an internal concern of the Korean government. It relates directly to the security issue for which the United States bears a joint responsibility. When it seems necessary, moreover, the U.S. should not hesitate to make its displeasure known via carefully devised measures. Such measures should not be of the type that injure the whole Korean people, or represent irreversible steps. It should be kept in mind that the democratic opposition is strongly opposed to such American actions as military withdrawal or massive reductions in military assistance. But there are ways of showing displeasure—both in words and in actions.

At the same time, it is now essential to challenge those individuals, including some Americans, who have long been applying double standards in dealing with Communist and non-Communist states, or equating quasi-authoritarian governments with strictly authoritarian ones of the Communist or Fascist mold. Seoul is *not* P'yŏngyang with respect to the rights of self-expression, just as New Delhi today is not Peking. Anyone who has talked with intellectuals or observed the general atmosphere in these cities knows the difference. The dramatic dissimilarities with respect to privatism are but one index. Moreover, the potentialities for political evolution in the direction of openness are certainly better in the long run in those states committed officially to parliamentarism, whatever the transgressions of a given period, than in those where rigorous, exclusivist, one-party dictatorship is both preached and practiced.

Recently, we have had an awesome illustration of double standards in operation. The critics of the Lon Nol regime—highly vocal during its existence—watched in silence as millions of Cambodians—including the old and sick—were marched out of the capital and certain other urban centers into the countryside in one of the most ruthless measures taken in recent times. Yet one heard few voices of protest from those who had so remorselessly criticized the previous government.

If the United States were truly to insist that governments in order to qualify for aid or defense had to be replications of the American system, few nations would qualify, and they grow fewer each year. This is admittedly a period of crisis for democracy everywhere, including in the United States itself. It thus becomes important to be able to make distinctions of degree as well as of kind in determining American interests and commitments, and to rely upon quid-pro-quo policies rather than the rigidities of the all-in or all-out approach. Simultaneously, there should be an end to the mechanistic equations and double standards that have so distorted the true political spectrum of today.

Taiwan

No less than Korea, Taiwan poses a serious policy issue for the United States. The Chinese have played Taiwan variously. At times, it has been pushed forward as a matter of primary importance, made into a litmus-paper test of Sino-American relations. At other points, it has been relegated to a secondary position, with the indication that the PRC can be patient, waiting decades if necessary. In fact, Taiwan is not likely to be the major determinant of Sino-American relations, just as it was not the major determinant of the movement toward limited détente. Relations with the Soviet Union are for China the crucial variant, and correspondingly, the credibility and presence of the United States in Asia assume vital, if unspoken importance.

Regarding Taiwan, a number of alternatives present themselves in theory at least, but the realistic choices may be much more narrow. One obvious possibility would be to accept the position of the PRC, with the United States severing its political, economic and military relations with Taiwan, and recognizing the People's Republic as having sovereign control over the island. Washington might urge and even aid the Taiwan authorities in negotiating what the Communists have sometimes referred to as an autonomous status in the manner of Tibet. Such a development would have the advantage of ending the largest immediate political issue between the United States and the PRC, according to some, would thereby reduce the chances of a limited détente between Russia and China. The argument has been made that some settlement of the Taiwan issue during the lifetime of Mao is essential since it is his imprimatur that upholds current policies toward the United States and the Soviet Union.

The case against this first alternative, however, is truly formidable. First, it would be widely interpreted as another abandonment of an ally, and in the aftermath of Vietnam particularly, it would constitute a devastating blow at American credibility, not merely in Asia but throughout the world. Once again, it would be likely to have very serious repercussions in Japan, and upon Japanese-American relations. Further, there is no indication that it could be "delivered." Explosive developments might well occur on Taiwan, ones causing the United States deep embarrassment and anguish. Finally, the major argument on behalf of such a policy, namely, that it could help prevent a later Sino-Soviet détente, can be turned on its head. If in helping to turn Taiwan over to the PRC, the United States performed the last major act beneficial to the PRC of which it was capable, and in the course of so doing, diminished its credibility in Asia to the vanishing point, would the case for reaching an accommodation with the Russians not be strengthened rather than weakened?

A second alternative would be to seek from the PRC an explicit statement renouncing force in the solution of the Taiwan issue, and using this, reverse current political relationships, establishing full diplomatic relations with Peking and creating a political relation with Taipei similar to that existing with Peking today, meanwhile continuing economic and cultural ties. If such a formal statement were made, there would be no need for the Mutual Security Treaty, it is argued, but military assistance to Taiwan could be continued. The central problem with this alternative is that Peking to date has signalled very clearly that it has no intention of renouncing the use of force in determining the Taiwan issue. Among others, Teng Hsiao-p'ing has asserted that force may well have to be used if other methods fail, and that since Taiwan is an internal issue, China proposes to make no guarantees on the matter.

Under this situation, several variants upon the second alternative have been advanced. The most commonly discussed is a formula whereby some Chinese leader, presumably Mao, would issue a statement urging the peaceful settlement of the Taiwan problem, and without further comment on either side, a political exchange would be undertaken, full diplomatic recognition going to Peking, a Liaison Mission to Taipei. This would be done with "the understanding" that American economic interaction with Taiwan could continue and that military assistance, at least in the form of arms sales, would be maintained, but with the Mutual Security Treaty ceasing to be in effect.

The supporters of this formula argue that it represents a case of having one's cake and eating it too, namely, of reconciling a Chinese insistence upon having the sovereignty issue settled without turning Taiwan over physically to the

Communists. They assert that in this fashion, the status quo would be preserved for many years. Critics insist that such a formula ignores the political realities in China, in Taiwan, and in the United States. How long would any Chinese government submit silently to a situation whereby one of its provinces (in its view) and a territory now defined by the United States as a nonstate, received economic and particularly military assistance from a foreign power? How long would the American people and Congress support such an anomaly? And would not international opinion be swift in its condemnation of this situation as "unwarranted interference in the internal affairs of another state?" The thin veil of not having formally declared Taiwan a province of China would certainly not be sufficient under these circumstances to prevent such developments. Would this not be a surrender on the installment plan with even more painful consequences than the first alternative? And would it not be so perceived in Taiwan, with uncertain repercussions, particularly among the vast majority of Taiwanese who have no desire to be annexed by the mainland?

Yet another alternative would be to do nothing at this juncture, continuing the current relations with both the PRC and Taiwan, and awaiting developments. Those supporting this view hold the potential losses far outweigh any possible gains in shifting policies under present conditions. Moreover, they submit, future developments both in the PRC and in Taiwan are extremely unclear, making any American move premature. They do not regard it as essential to rush into some type of "settlement" prior to Mao's death for the reasons outlined earlier. Rather, they favor emulating the Chinese on this occasion, exhibiting a patience that would defy Mao's definition of Americans as an impatient people, unable to sustain any policy over time.

The opponents of such a policy enlist the basic arguments that have already been outlined, namely, that postponement of a settlement can only make more painful the ultimate solution, cause a worsening of Sino-American relations, and threaten a swing of the pendulum toward Sino-Soviet rapprochement. Some individuals see Asia as China's logical sphere of influence, and believe that Taiwan will be annexed, irrespective of American desires and policies—even if it results in war.

There is a final alternative, namely, that of having the United States actively support an independent Taiwan, taking such political, economic, and military measures as are necessary to that end. Proponents assert that only in this fashion can the United States remain true to its principles, since it is abundantly clear that the great majority of people on Taiwan do not wish to be amalgamated into the People's Republic of China, and if there were any doubts on this score, a plebiscite could be held under UN or other auspices. It is also maintained that neither the United States nor Japan—nor for that matter, the USSR—are well served by projecting the PRC into the western Pacific via Taiwan. Mao himself, it is recalled, in the late 1930s, championed the right of the Taiwanese for independence, so "liberation" is not an historic Communist theme.

Opponents point to the fact that self-determination is a principle more honored in the breach than in the observance these days, and that larger issues are here at stake. Hence, a major nation like the United States must be primarily attuned to its relations with the key powers of the region. They further submit that in the final analysis, the American people would not be prepared to fight for the independence of Taiwan.

The present evidence would suggest that the United States will find the Taiwan issue very difficult to handle in such a fashion as to achieve all of its objectives while avoiding further damage to American prestige and integrity. Washington would like to normalize its relations with Peking so as to bring them into greater symmetry with American-Soviet relations. Thus, recent administrations have repeatedly asserted their commitment to further progress in the task of normalization "in accordance with the provisions of the Shanghai Communiqué." But the Shanghai Communiqué was deliberately ambiguous on the critical issue. While the United States acknowledged that all Chinese recognized that China was one, and that Taiwan was a part of China (a patent untruth since a large majority of the Taiwanese do *not* recognize any such thing), the United States did not assert that *it* took that position. Moreover, the American position has consistently been to insist that any solution to the Taiwan issue should be reached in a peaceful manner, whatever the final result.

Thus, the twin issues are those of sovereignty and the avoidance of force in reaching a solution. To suggest that the Japanese formula provides the answer, as some have done, is insufficient. The United States is not Japan, and the critical difference lies in the fact that the U.S. has had a security commitment to Taiwan, a commitment of major importance. Should ambiguity be used in sliding over this problem, it could easily create the conditions for a worsening, rather than an improvement of American relations with the PRC. No doubt, at some point in the future, negotiations will be undertaken with Peking to ascertain whether an acceptable formula can be discovered. From the American perspective, a minimum condition must be a peaceful solution, whatever the length of time involved, and in the interim, an American-Taiwan relation that permits the security of Taiwan to be guaranteed. Otherwise, severe damage will be done to American credibility, and the purposes of normalization itself will be undermined.

It should be noted that if the United States seems highly unreliable, both South Korea and Taiwan can be expected to consider the possibility of developing nuclear weapons. Indeed, there is ample evidence that both of these nations (particularly South Korea), along with various other small states, have already treated this as an option. Thus, in considering policy alternatives, the United States cannot avoid weighing the risks of nuclear proliferation if its credibility in Asia continues to decline.

In sum, Northeast Asia represents one of the truly critical regions for American foreign policy. If some broad equilibrium is to be maintained—and currently, there are no other promising routes to peace—ties with Japan must be strengthened, and the security of Korea and Taiwan must be underwritten pending some longer-range answers to these issues. At the same time, the American-Japanese relationship must not be regarded as an exclusive one; the United States must not succumb to an enclave policy. Nor should America cease in its efforts to obtain major power agreement on some of the critical issues of the region. Negotiations with both the USSR and the PRC should continue on ways of reducing tension and enabling peaceful coexistence to be effective here.

Asian Mainland

Already, American relations to the continental center of Asia has been raised in the foregoing discussion, but the subject deserves some additional attention. It has been commonly asserted that Washington cannot influence Sino-Soviet relations, and that to attempt to do so would be dangerous and quite possibly, counterproductive. This statement is only partly true at best. American actions—or inactions—have had and will have an influence on Sino-Soviet relations, but any conscious sustained effort to manipulate policies with this in mind might indeed boomerang. Caution must be the byword where intervention is concerned.

What are American interests with respect to Sino-Soviet relations? Clearly, the extremities of either war or renewed alliance would not be in the interests of the United States, nor of most other nations, Communist as well as non-Communist. Whether limited détente would have its advantages is debatable. It can be argued that a reduction of tension would enable greater progress not only upon arms controls, but also upon the overriding issues of food, population, and similar problems which now too frequently provoke polemics rather than constructive contributions, especially from the PRC. Or would such a détente merely lend itself to a unified Communist position adverse to the interests of the non-Communist community? It must be admitted that while the United States did not consciously create the Sino-Soviet cleavage, it has profited from it, and the burden of proof therefore rests with those who feel that some change is desirable.

Another issue is of equal importance. Should the United States seek a position of equidistance between the two major Communist states, or should it tilt toward one? One school of thought argues that in Asia at least, the United States should consistently tilt toward the PRC. Its thesis is that the Soviet Union is the only power that has the capacity to seriously damage America, and that since it is a global power like America, Washington should strive to exercise leverage against it in Asia by strengthening China, thereby counteracting Soviet capacities in Europe and the Middle East. There are numerous serious problems with this thesis, however. Firstly, such a policy, once perceived, would almost certainly lead to Soviet retaliation, and that retaliation could take many unpleasant forms. Secondly, in Asia at least, China may well be less compatible with American interests on certain issues than the Soviet Union, and as we have seen, that is, indeed, the case. Moreover, such a policy would seriously affect the policies of all Asian states, non-Communist and Communist alike, risking a serious disequilibrium in this vital region. Thus, American interests will be best served by neither a sustained uniform tilt nor mechanistic equidistance, but by selective, mutual tilts toward China and the Soviet Union, with each issue and problem considered on its individual merits.

Southeast Asia

Turning to Southeast Asia, it is not appropriate here to resurrect the issues relating to Vietnam in any detail. Today, everyone draws lessons from Vietnam, usually the lessons that serve to underwrite each individual's preestablished positions. Thus, all "lessons" should be subject to careful scrutiny and some skepticism, but several are worth noting. Firstly, the United States cannot fight a protracted limited war without enormous costs and the serious risk of defeat. The role of the media, the nature of American institutions, and a host of other factors, make this clear. Korea provided the first evidence, Vietnam the last. The implications of this fact will have to be taken seriously by American policy-makers, and in some respects, they reduce United States options in the peace-conflict continuum.

Secondly, defeat in war is enormously costly for a major power, contrary to earlier notions that "the United States was powerful enough to take defeat in its stride." Despite all efforts to minimize recent events on the part of some, the Vietnam debacle was regarded everywhere as a major American political-military defeat, and it raised the most profound questions about American credibility, in Europe as well as in Asia. Its repercussions in the United States, moreover, are still being felt, and the serious struggle for control of American foreign policy between the president and Congress has been productive of further doubts concerning American capacities abroad.

Thirdly, the United States continues to suffer from an inability to mesh its own tempo with that of other cultures, and hence, to work out correctly the appropriate combination of indigenous versus American components in an alliance, and the proper mix of economic, political, and military elements in the defense against aggression. American culture is grounded upon rapid, maximum commitment. "Get the job done, and then come home!" is a time-honored American maxim. Anything short of this is inefficient. In such situations as World War II—and the occupation of Japan—this approach proved effective. In more complex situations, such as Vietnam, it could not possibly succeed. As one astute Vietnamese put it, "You came up far too rapidly and on too massive a scale for us, and you went down the same way."

Other lessons are, in my opinion, more debatable including the thesis that Southeast Asia was a region of strictly secondary importance to the United States. One's position on this question depends upon the degree to which one sees this region linked with other parts of East Asia, and also a region in which the major powers of the Asian-Pacific area will inevitably find themselves involved. To date, the balance of evidence tilts toward both linkage and involvement.

Today, American policy alternatives for Southeast Asia would appear to be these: firstly, the United States can confine its presence primarily to political and economic interaction with those states interested, removing its military presence over time, and allowing major power competition resting upon military power to be conducted between the Soviet Union and the PRC, while at the same time giving moral encouragement to the development of indigenous regionalism. Alternatively, America can maintain a certain military presence in the region, based primarily upon Clark Field and Subic Bay in the Philippines, and aimed at encouraging the independent development of the Philippines and Indonesia particularly, but giving such sustenance as possible to the diplomacy of Thailand, Malaysia, and Singapore.

In all probability, some combination of the two possibilities will evolve. It is most unlikely that the United States will commit itself to the military defense of any nation in continental Southeast Asia, and the various states there are now seeking to accommodate themselves to that fact. At the same time, there will be no precipitous withdrawal of all American military power from the region, and military assistance to certain countries, among them, Indonesia, will continue. The premium will naturally be upon each state's ability to defend itself, both through its domestic socioeconomic and political policies and through its regional relations. Washington will render full moral and political support to such organizations as ASEAN, being quite prepared to see SEATO gradually dissolved. It will also stand ready to enter negotiations with the Soviet Union, PRC, and Japan when political or economic developments in the region warrant this. "Neutralization" or the emergence of a zone of peace carefully delineating the role of external forces would be wholly compatible with American interests.

No major regional or international agreements are likely to be reached quickly or easily, however. In the meantime, for obvious reasons—strategic as well as economic and political—the Philippines, Indonesia, and Singapore will be of particular interest to the United States. If a new equilibrium is to emerge in Southeast Asia, it will hinge heavily upon developments with respect to these countries. The probabilities are strong that American interaction with the newly created Communist states of Indochina will be minimal for the foreseeable future. Here, the United States should be content to observe developments, as various Communist factions and powers sort out their relationship.

South Asia

South Asia constitutes a region where American policies currently seem more clearly defined, more easily predicted. Despite the existence of some who wish it otherwise, this is a region of secondary importance to the United States. Its economic problems far outrun its potentialities for fruitful economic interaction. Its location does not give it a strategic importance to Washington even approaching that which it possesses for Moscow and Peking, and its politics provide linkages to the United States in decreasing degree.

Thus, an effort will be made to keep a low posture in this region, advancing friendly relations via cultural and economic exchanges wherever this is feasible, but making no effort to establish or reestablish close security ties, or any relations approaching those of alliance. Here, the United States will be content to pursue a relatively detached nonaligned role. An interest in the Indian Ocean has increased, evidenced by Diego Garcia, primarily because of its linkage to the Middle East and East Asia, and the concern over heightened Soviet naval activity throughout this region. It is very unlikely, however, that the United States would seek to develop a major naval presence in this region, the fears of Indians and certain Americans notwithstanding.

With respect to certain issues vital to South Asia such as food, population, and resources, the United States will exhibit an interest in participating in multilateral approaches. It will make a contribution, possibly a major one, but only if constructive participation by others, including the states most affected by the problem, is forthcoming. Apart from emergency humanitarian aid, the era of large-scale direct American economic assistance is over.

In conclusion, the United States—in the aftermath of its worst political-military defeat in this century—is in the process of reappraising its policies in Asia. On the broadest scale, its alternatives are three: strategic withdrawal, defining American interests primarily in regional, Western Hemisphere-Pacific terms; an enclave policy, geared to Japan in combination with West Europe; or selective internationalism, with East Asia, together with West Europe still considered important to American interests. The first alternative is neo-isolationism of the late twentieth century. It would ultimately have the most serious repercussions upon the negotiatory capacities of the United States, with former allies, with neutrals and with erstwhile opponents. Consequently, it could not be sustained, and might well lead to serious conflicts. The second alternative, as we have seen, is unrealistic, and at some point, would be rejected by the very parties involved, especially Japan. Thus, there is only one broad alternative, that of selective internationalism, and within that alternative, the United States must resolve many problems relating to the priorities and the timing of its policies.

Policy Options

In surveying the state of major power relations in Asia today and prospects for the future, the realist can find limited grounds for optimism. The most encouraging factor is a negative one, the increasingly prohibitive cost of war, particularly the type of war likely to be fought if major powers come to blows. One may hope that the realization of this sets the outer perimeters of major power confrontation, serving as the sanction that will prevent controversy from becoming conflict.

On the other hand, in the absence of effective regional or international institutions, or even firm understandings on vital issues, each important state is forced to operate in a world of few laws and little order. Consequently, the effort to define national interests and then defend those interests through balance-of-power policies represent the central thrusts of national foreign policies today, irrespective of ideological differences.

Meanwhile, the cleavages within the Communist bloc, the growing diversities also of the "advanced industrial world," and the emergence of a myriad of Third World states on the global stage have combined to change the nature of international politics in the late twentieth century. Exclusive alliances have given way to more flexible relationships. The power of the major states, and particularly that of the United States and the Soviet Union, is more awesome than ever, but with the complexity of the world having grown geometrically, that power can rarely be exercised in traditional manner. The superpowers, singly or together, are no longer in a position to serve in lieu of an international order—as was once the case. Even with allies, their relations have become complex and sometimes troublesome, subject to sudden, unexpected challenges. On the other hand, the violent rhetoric of various "radical" states and mini-states, together with their capacity to outvote others on occasion at the UN and in various international conferences, cannot mask the fact that on most issues, they are powerless to effect or enforce outcomes. Power and responsibility have become mightily confused—at many levels. Thus, internationalism, both in terms of organization and issues, drifts toward dangerous shoals, with polemics serving as a substitute for problem-solving, legitimacy and authority notable for their absence, and nationalism ascendant almost everywhere.

The hope is that the very seriousness of the issues confronting the world will force a process of cooperation, beginning with those most directly concerned, forwarded via intensive, continuous negotiations. These negotiations, already underway, take place at many levels and through many facilities: conferences, congresses, summits, and private gatherings. Through them, decisions may be reached which harden into binding covenants, procedures may be established which grow into institutions, and in an undramatic, often acrimonious fashion, a new world order—however incomplete, imperfect, and fragile—may emerge. This is the hope, but it would be a bold individual indeed prepared to guarantee the outcome.

Japan

In Japan, an agonizing reappraisal of foreign policies has been postponed or muted, largely because no major alternatives appear to be viable. Dissatisfaction and uncertainty have grown, however, and some issues cannot be avoided. Today, Japan is largely isolated even within its own region, as we have noted, and relations with both China and the Soviet Union constitute complex problems. Ideally, Japan would be best served at this juncture by a continuance of the special ties with the United States, while keeping relations with both Communist powers upwardly mobile and relatively equal. Recent developments, however, now make it clear how difficult it will be to achieve this policy.

Is there a threshold beyond which major changes in Japanese policies might be expected? Some combination involving the emergence of an intensely felt, sustained threat and a progressively declining American credibility could induce Gaullism. Dramatic internal changes in Japanese politics might lead to experimentation with "nonalignment," or even to a closer relation with another major power, presumably China. None of these possibilities, however, seems probable at this point. Rather, Japan is likely to move within the arena of present policies, augmenting its military capacities somewhat, increasing its independence, and continuing the effort to separate economics and politics to the maximum extent, while keeping its relations with the major powers as free of conflict as possible. It will treat trilateral relations with the United States and West Europe seriously, but not regard them as primary, putting more stock in its bilateral ties with America. Finally, it will show a strong interest in any international efforts toward resource management and the entire range of economic issues, being among all the major powers the most dependent upon an international environment conducive to open economic intercourse.

China

China seems almost at the opposite end of the political spectrum from Japan: underdeveloped, authoritarian, massive and essentially closed to the external world. China in general, and Chinese foreign policy in particular is marked by a series of contradictions at this juncture. Domestic considerations demand a high priority, given the precarious stage at which this new nation finds itself, and in one important part of itself, China looks inward. At the same time, a new nationalism is enroute in this society, one demanding external as well as internal recognition. As in the case of Meiji Japan, the slogan of the hour is "a rich country, a strong soldiery," and while the task of achieving this goal may be a lengthy one, China has already signalled in a variety of ways that it has special interests in Asia and further, that it intends to promote those interests. It also debates the degree to which its developmental goals necessitate an economic turning outward, and some substantial modification of self-reliance.

Whether China's interest in a sphere of influence or a buffer state system is "defensive" or "offensive" is a moot point. It is entirely possible that from different perspectives, attitudes and actions will be seen differently. Certainly, in contemplating its massive neighbor to the North, China tends to respond defensively. But on occasion, in incidents involving Korea, Vietnam, and India, when Chinese national interests were considered immediately involved, the action was "offensive" whatever the motivation. Basically, China manipulates state-to-state, people-to-people, and comrade-to-comrade relations in such a fashion as to parlay its still limited resources into a global presence and a regional power.

The immediate issues confronting Peking, however, are these: whether in this uncertain era to place the primary emphasis upon the long-term Soviet threat and hence maintain a firm stand against Russian "social imperialism," meanwhile inclining toward the United States as a counterweight; or, turn back toward a policy of accommodation with the Soviet Union, a limited détente that would reduce tension and also reduce reliance upon an uncertain America; or finally, mount a strategy based upon sustained attacks against both "superpowers," increased reliance upon a coalition of Third World states, and efforts to build an independent sphere of influence in Asia. There is some indication that in the post-Vietnam period, the PRC has inclined increasingly toward the last alternative, but without relinquishing its options on the first one.

It seems unlikely, in any event, that Peking will form a traditional type alliance with any other major power. Both historical and contemporary attitudes combine against any such move. Whatever the turn of events, moreover, relations with the Soviet Union will be the touchstone determining basic Chinese foreign policies. And even if limited détente is eventually realized, a development by no means certain, the elements of competition and conflict are likely to remain substantial in the Sino-Soviet relationship.

Conceivably, China could normalize its relations with India, the initiatives resting primarily with it. Intimacy, however, is scarcely possible. With Indonesia also, relations may be normalized over time, but a restoration of the Jakarta-Peking alliance would hinge upon great changes in the Indonesian domestic scene. With Japan, relations are likely to be much closer, but also highly complex, subject to the vagaries of internal Japanese politics and Peking's ability to draw the necessary lines between successful "influence" and counterproductive "interference."

Any survey of China's bilateral relations with the other major Asian states, as well as with the Soviet Union and the United States, suggests that China is not likely to dominate the whole of Asia, nor is this probable with respect to any single power. It is very possible, however, that in some regions—for example, Southeast Asia—the Chinese influence will grow to considerable proportions, exceeding that of other major states. The major variable probably relates not to will but to capacity—to the success or failure of China's ongoing drive for modernization.

India

India is another nation in which the critical variable appears to be the domestic one. In considerable measure, the great goal of Indian foreign policy has been achieved. Hegemony over South Asia is now a reality, with its promise and its problems for New Delhi. No nation of the subcontinent can seriously challenge India, but any political or economic breakdowns within these states may require or produce Indian intervention. Meanwhile, the goals of nation-building and economic development remain far from consummated, and India under Mrs. Gandhi has just moved into its most serious political crisis since independence. The repressive actions taken against a variety of political opponents, coupled with the efforts at economic amelioration signal at once the common dilemma facing emerging societies and the uncertain future that confronts the Indian polity.

Current domestic trends reinforce Indian foreign policy. They make the special ties with the Soviet Union more necessary and the development of alternatives to those ties less likely. Ideally, New Delhi would prefer a position of greater equidistance among the major powers, but it is unclear at this juncture whether Peking or Washington will cooperate. A dramatic political upheaval in India might bring to power leaders more appealing to one or another of these powers, and serve as a force for reorienting Indian foreign policy, but such a development does not seem in the offing. Thus, the Indian-Soviet alliance, despite some reservations and limits on both sides, will probably continue in force.

Even if India opts for nuclear weapons, this nation is unlikely to move from being a regional to becoming an international power of significance. The combined tasks of emergence as a nation and regional responsibility will surely tax the capacities of this society to the hilt. Although some additional attention may be directed toward the regions on India's immediate flanks, West and Southeast Asia, the priorities will be to the more immediate environs.

Indonesia

This is equally true of Indonesia where basic priorities were reordered more than a decade ago, in the aftermath of the abortive 1965 coup. Today, Jakarta is dedicated to placing its primary energies upon a developmental program, one that has thus far shown mixed results. Even if it were to choose a higher posture in the international arena, however, serious limits upon its capacities to operate effectively there would soon become apparent.

Southeast Asia is not now, nor will it soon be a compatible unit. A Communist tier of states presently marks its northern borders, and the degree of cooperation that can be expected from them in such organizations as ASEAN remains very unclear. The tendency of such states, however, is to use militantly nationalist as well as socialist themes in the effort to mobilize the citizenry, and in this case, considerable attention with respect to international relations is likely to be directed toward China and Russia. Thus, the prospects for an integrated approach to Southeast Asian problems does not seem promising.

Jakarta can be expected to continue its effots to strengthen ASEAN, nevertheless, transferring to it some of the functions performed by a now waning SEATO. Under extreme circumstances, if it felt its security directly threatened, Indonesia might be induced to intervene in neighboring societies. At least equally possible, however, is an aloofness from the troubles of the area, especially of the non-Malay regions. The most likely difficulties which Southeast Asia will face are those of an intrastate character, with regional, ethnic, or religious factors, not infrequently cast in an ideological setting, predominant. The temptation for external forces to manipulate dissidence is naturally strong, especially since national and ethnic-religious boundaries do not always coincide. Under these circumstances, the task of making peaceful coexistence something more than an empty slogan is quite possibly the most critical task facing the region.

Meanwhile, Jakarta's relations with the major powers is likely to remain similar to recent patterns. Grave doubts persist with respect to both the Soviet Union and China, the result of historical experiences and domestic vulnerabilities. At the same time, recent events have raised questions in Jakarta about American credibility, and relations with Japan reflect the problems of a rapid economic penetration. Hence nationalist themes, and those of greater self-reliance and equidistance have a new appeal, one broadly shared by other states of the region. These represent ideals, however, and in fact, the tilt toward the non-Communist powers is likely to continue, at least as long as the present leadership remains in power in Jakarta. Indonesia—like India—cannot afford to be without some major supporter, even though it will not play precisely the same regional role as New Delhi.

Soviet Union

The Soviet Union, as we have noted, is destined to become increasingly an Asian as well as a European power, and one with vital interests particularly in Northeast and South Asia, not to mention the continental center. These are regions that relate directly to the security as well as the economic and political interests of the USSR. But while Moscow will unquestionably manifest greater military power in Asia in the decade ahead, it will continue to operate in many Asian regions at a signal disadvantage. Unlike China, it has very limited cultural and ethnic linkages despite the incorporation of Central Asian peoples into the. Soviet Union. Russians remain foreign—very foreign—and that inhibits intimacy. Even the Communist movements of Asia have drifted out of range.

Partly for these reasons, the Soviet Union may incline toward the status quo. Few if any major changes that are likely would benefit it. Its hopes regarding China are more modest than those of a few decades ago, and whether even these can be achieved remains questionable. Meanwhile, it will continue to apply stick-and-carrot policies, containing China wherever possible, while offering accommodation. In Northeast Asia, as we have seen, the Russians could take the initiative, and significantly improve their relations with Japan, but their willingness to do so is doubtful. Soviet-American cooperation on the Korean problem could abet détente, but once again, Moscow's willingness to act in this fashion is doubtful. Up to date, the Soviet Union has been less than successful in its goals for Northeast Asia—a fact that may stimulate its Siberian developmental program. Will military power be substituted for political weakness?

In South Asia, on the contrary, the achievements are more conspicuous. Here, the Soviets have sponsored a winner, and watched with satisfaction the humiliation of Peking. But will the future be a projection of the past? From time to time, the Russians have been concerned about the scope and implications of their commitments to India, just as the Indians have had similar concerns. The alliance is likely to retain its validity, but it is nonetheless dependent upon both domestic and regional developments. Meanwhile, Moscow will probably seek an extension of its naval base system, so that the Middle East and Northeast Asia can be linked, making this a matter of concern both to the indigenous states of southern Asia and the United States.

Soviet interests in Southeast Asia are secondary, but any opportunity to further the containment of China will be utilized, and in this connection, the Soviet Union can be expected to participate in the Byzantine politics of Indochina, hoping to use Hanoi as its surrogate. Despite Peking's warnings, however, the Soviet Union has no real chance to exercise hegemony in this region. In the Pacific Ocean region, also, Russian power and interests will grow, but no frontal challenge is likely to be made to the United States.

Flushed with the success of the Helsinki Conference, the Russians can be expected to continue to push the idea of an Asian collective security agreement, the counterpart to its European plan, possibly under a different label. The fact that this policy is currently viewed with coolness by most Asian states will not deter the Soviets from keeping it alive, especially since persistence paid off in the West.

United States

Finally, there is the United States, still under the trauma of a major political-military defeat and a serious economic recession. For the American people, three basic alternatives present themselves, as we have seen: strategic withdrawal, an enclave policy, and selective internationalism. No full consensus regarding an

Asian policy is likely, but the probabilities are that the final option will be for the last of these alternatives, given the consequences of the others. Much will hinge, however, upon domestic trends in the United States itself. Here too, we have had a revolutionary situation, perhaps the most revolutionary of the modern world, and one far from completed.

In broad terms, the United States is likely to treat the Pacific and Northeast Asia as regions of primary importance, with certain continuing commitments in the Southeast Asian region to provide the necessary linkages. South Asia will be of secondary concern. In the Pacific, the United States will seek to protect and preserve its strategic dominance. The long-term arrangements now being worked out regarding Micronesia signal that fact. In Northeast Asia, the special ties with Japan will remain paramount, as will the efforts to build a stronger linkage among the advanced industrial states. America will shape its Korean policies with the issue of Japan in mind, but it will also seek some solution here that has the support of other major powers, a task likely to be difficult and long term. Similarly, there are no easy solutions to the Taiwan question, and once again, this will be a test of American patience and the United States capacity to live with unsettled issues.

In relations with China and the Soviet Union, the United States is best served by limited détente, and varied tilts depending upon the issue. If these relations are to be satisfactory, however, a continued American credibility and presence in Asia is essential. Moreover, reciprocity—not unilateral concessions—represents the only standard that can be applied if détente is to serve American national interests and to be supported by the American people. In this connection, the recent policies of both Communist states in Asia, but particularly China, are worrisome. For Peking, the cold war is still on, judging from Chinese rhetoric and actions at various international gatherings. Nor are Chinese positions on a number of specific issues such as Korea, Taiwan, and Southeast Asia encouraging.

In Southeast Asia, the United States faces a reordering of the mix that has gone into its policies, with the military quotient downgraded, and the economic, political and cultural elements raised. It is doubtful that America will withdraw from this region in any full sense, even militarily. Important distinctions will also be made as to policy mix, state by state. In Indochina, the lowest conceivable presence is likely for the foreseeable future, as events there are observed from the sidelines. An intermediate posture will probably be assumed in Thailand and Malaysia, with the combination of domestic and regional developments imping- ing upon these states again matters of great interest. Somewhat stronger commitments will be made to the Philippines, Indonesia, and possibly Singa- pore—thus representing a policy of building a continuum with graded postures and commitments, making flexibility the cardinal ingredient.

Only under the most extraordinary of circumstances could the United States be induced to make South Asia a region of primary concern and involvement. It is here that the principles of multilateralism will be tested, and that the successes and failures of conferences and congresses devoted to substantive issues of great import will have their greatest impact. Washington can be expected to participate in these undertakings but with a much greater insistence than in the past upon reciprocity and mutual responsibility. In these terms, as in some others, the quotient of American nationalism may well rise appreciably—in conformity with the much broader trend in that direction that now operates in the world.

The considerations just raised highlight the fact that we are moving into an era when issues that cut across national and regional lines will vie for international attention with problems of a state to state type. The major powers in particular cannot avoid serious involvement in the critical questions of resource procurement and allocation, maritime and space jurisdiction, and demographic and refugee concerns to mention only a few of the issues that will dominate the rest of this century. To handle these matters with a minimum of satisfaction, most states will need a new policy-making apparatus, new expertise, and above all, new attitudes. Old concepts of security as well as those relating to international economic political intercourse will probably undergo major transformation. Even under these conditions, however, the Asian-Pacific area will be of critical importance, since in its combination of area, population, resources and power configuration, it dwarfs all other areas of the world.

Multipolarism is a very unsatisfactory term in seeking to capture the essence of contemporary international relations, especially as they apply to Asia. It is the asymmetry of relations, produced by the extraordinarily diverse character of the states and semi-states here that lies at the heart of current difficulties. An international order, like other orders, depends for its existence upon a suitable degree of consensus, and this in turn hinges upon some commonness of values, goals, and institutions. We are just emerging from an era when the West imposed these upon the world, lending a semblance of unity. Now, in the cold, grey afterdawn of colonialism, that unity has been revealed as spurious or is in the process of breaking down, given the adaptations that are being fashioned to cope with the problems of late development. Can the pace of this development be quickened in such a fashion as to permit the rebuilding of a suitable degree of unity—or are we doomed to a tumultuous period of noncommunication? Will we be reduced to that most minimal of hopes, that the internal problems of all states, the major ones included, will preclude extensive interference in the affairs of others? Or can the major powers set some constructive framework for interaction, given the urgency of the issues confronting them and the rest of the world? In all of these respects, the Asian-Pacific area represents a most critical test.

Index

About the Authors

DONALD C. HELLMANN, Professor of Political Science and Asian Studies at the University of Washington, Seattle, is a specialist on Japanese politics and Asian international relations and has wide experience as a consultant on public policy with government and private research organizations.

MYRON WEINER, Professor and Chairman of Political Science at M.I.T., is an eminent scholar on the politics of South Asia who most recently completed a four-volume study of Indian elections.

JOHN LEWIS, Professor of Economics and International Affairs at Princeton University, is a widely published international authority on aid and economic development who served as Minister/Director of the United States A.I.D. Mission in New Delhi from 1964 to 1969.

ALEXANDER WOODSIDE, Professor of History at the University of British Columbia, is a leading scholar on China, Vietnam and Mainland Southeast Asia. His most recent book is *Community and Revolution in Modern Vietnam* (1976).

ROBERT J. PRANGER, Director of Foreign and Defense Policy Studies at the American Enterprise Institute, has published widely in the fields of political theory and international politics and was Deputy Assistant Secretary of Defense from 1969 to 1971.

ROBERT A. SCALAPINO, Professor of Political Science at the University of California at Berkeley, is an international authority on politics throughout Asia and a frequent consultant on American policy toward this region. The most recent of his many publications is *Asia and the Road Ahead* (1975).